EXPLORATIONS IN PSYCHOANALYSIS

Ralph R. Greenson

International Universities Press, Inc.
New York

Library of Congress Cataloging in Publication Data

Greenson, Ralph R.
  Explorations in psychoanalysis.

  Bibliography: p.
  Includes index.
  1. Psychoanalysis—Addresses, essays, lectures.
I. Title [DNLM: 1. Psychoanalysis—Collected
works. WM460.1 G815e]
RC509.G73   616.8'917   77-90230
ISBN 0-8236-1810-2

Manufactured in the United States of America

for Hildi

Contents

Preface

I HAVE CALLED THIS BOOK *Explorations in Psychoanalysis* and
have tried to remain faithful to its title. The papers assem-
bled here represent selections from my scientific writings
spanning a period of more than forty years.

Explorations in Psychoanalysis does more than explore areas
of my interest, or document the development of my ideas; it also
tells you something about me. My overriding concern has
been to improve my therapeutic results. Most psychotics and
certain borderline patients still baffle me and, for that reason, I
have had trouble establishing an effective working relationship
with them. Most of my papers, certainly those which I consider
to be my major ones, therefore, stem from the treatment of
neurotic patients who tended to have certain problems in
common. It was not entirely a fortuitous circumstance that these
patients were all somewhat depressed, impulsive, and creative.
Whatever their neuroses, they all posed difficult problems in
therapy. From the beginning, all my publications were tilted in
the direction of technique.

My first two papers were written in 1935-1936 during the
nine months I had studied with Wilhelm Stekel in his "active"
psychoanalytic school. They were submitted to the *Psychoanalytic Review*, then under the editorship of William Alanson
White, and were published in 1936-1937. I left Vienna with
Stekel's reassurance that I had been a very talented student. "You
remind me of myself," he often mused. As time went on, how-

ever, I was dissatisfied with my therapeutic results. Thus in 1938, after much hesitation, I approached Dr. Ernst Simmel, President of the Los Angeles Study Group, concerning training to become a Freudian psychoanalyst. He recommended that I see Dr. Otto Fenichel who had recently arrived from Czechoslovakia. Fenichel told me frankly that he had misgivings about analyzing a "Stekelian"; however, we started a trial analysis, which eventually turned into a four-year training analysis.

In the spring of 1942, I gave my graduation paper to the San Francisco Society. (The two study groups together, Los Angeles and San Francisco, had only enough training analysts to form one Society.) My paper, "On Genuine Epilepsy," was published in the *Psychoanalytic Quarterly* in 1944. So much for the beginning of my career and my writings.

None of these early papers is included in this volume, which contains thirty-two papers chosen from sixty of my later publications. I have on the whole left the papers as they were originally written, though in some instances I would write them differently today. I have, however, deleted unnecessary repetitions, added new notes, and made cross-references to related issues.

Originally it had been my intention to classify the papers by the areas they cover. It soon became apparent to me that such classifications would be artificial because a paper on an affective state would start with a clinical problem but ultimately contribute to our understanding of technical and theoretical issues. I have therefore kept these papers in chronological order. This gives me—and the reader—the opportunity to place them historically in their proper developmental sequence.

Since this book represents a selection of papers, some published here for the first time, I should spell out the criteria of selection and omission. The principal question I asked myself was whether a particular paper made a contribution to psychoanalysis, and whether my conclusions were based on data gained in the analytic treatment of patients. There are only a few exceptions to this rule. This volume contains three articles based on my work at the Gender Identity Clinic at U.C.L.A. School of

Medicine, headed by Dr. Robert Stoller. I was introduced to the Gender Identity Clinic by my son, Daniel Greenson, when he had a summer fellowship there between semesters in medical school. I participated in the weekly conferences at this Clinic for some five years, and saw kinds of cases I had never seen before in all my clinical experience. These patients were not psychotic, not borderline, not neurotic—but they had some qualities of all three. I have included these nonanalytic cases because I believe that, viewed from an analytic vantage point, they contribute to our understanding of sexuality.

A few words regarding the omissions are in order. I have not included any survey papers nor my extensive writings for nonanalysts. I have excluded papers and lectures in which I attempted to explain psychoanalysis to general professional audiences. I have also omitted—in some instances with real regret—my various comments on and discussions of the work of other analysts, and my reviews of psychoanalytic books. In one instance, however, I could not resist republishing my review of *The Writings of Anna Freud*, Volume IV. Anna Freud's writing style, her numerous fascinating contributions (which influenced my own work), as well as my own personal relationship with her made it imperative for me to include this paper.

Thus, the final selection, I believe, is faithful to the title —*Explorations in Psychoanalysis*. A cursory look at the titles of the papers indicates that almost half of them specifically explore problems in psychoanalytic technique. This book may—and should—be read in conjunction with my *The Technique and Practice of Psychoanalysis*, which I could not have written without the experience gained in treating many of the patients described in the early papers included here. On the other hand, many of the technical papers deal with issues that were not treated in my earlier book—for example, my way of interpreting dreams. In other instances, technical problems that were mentioned briefly there are taken much further in this volume— for example, errors in technique, and working through. For all those who have been waiting for Volume II of *The Technique*

and Practice of Psychoanalysis, I offer this selection as a substitute—for the time being.

"Exploration" means a search, a way of probing. I have
used *Explorations* in the title in the sense of what a traveler does
who seeks new vistas in a recently discovered land.

Acknowledgments

I WISH TO THANK THE EDITORS of the following journals and publishers for their kind permission to reprint my papers: *Journal of the American Psychoanalytic Association, International Journal of Psycho-Analysis, Psychoanalytic Quarterly, Bulletin of the Menninger Clinic, International Review of Psycho-Analysis, American Imago*, International Universities Press, Associated Universities Press, Jason Aronson, Inc., and Association for Applied Psychoanalysis, Inc.

Some of my colleagues were very helpful to me in formulating and clarifying concepts and in focusing clinical material. I would like to acknowledge here my indebtedness to them for their inspiration and staunch support for more than two decades. They were: the late Hanna Fenichel, Alfred Goldberg, Nathan Leites, the late Max Schur, and Milton Wexler.

Some seven years ago, several of my colleagues and I formed an informal study group which met irregularly about every two weeks during the academic year. We worked on clinical material with the aim of helping one another with difficult patients, thorny technical problems, and new papers before they were published. This group consisted of Gerald Aronson, Lewis Fielding, Beatriz Foster, Alfred Goldberg, Joshua Hoffs, Thomas Mintz, Hilda Rollman-Branch, Morton Shane, Heiman Van Dam, and Miriam Williams.

Thanks are also due to The Foundation for Research in Psychoanalysis, Beverly Hills, California, Lita A. Hazen, President, for having funded the research projects on *Failures in Psychoanalysis*, and *Transference: Freud and Klein*.

Participating in these research projects, we had expert help from California, New York, and London. I would like to express my gratitude to my fellow researchers who were, from California: Bernard Brandchaft, Rudolf Ekstein, Sidney Fine, Lawrence J. Friedman, Joshua Hoffs, Edwin Kleinman, Henry Lihn, Thomas Mintz, Seymour Pastron, Norman Reider, Robert Wallerstein, Milton Wexler (Co-Chairman of the *Failures in Psychoanalysis* project), and Ernest White; from New York: Francis D. Baudry, Phyllis Greenacre, Edith Jacobson, and David Rubinfine; from London: Paula Heimann, M. Masud R. Khan, Joseph J. Sandler, and the late D. W. Winnicott.

I also wish to thank Dr. Robert Stoller for giving me the opportunity to work in the Gender Identity Clinic at the U.C.L.A. School of Medicine.

Without the help of Lottie M. Newman, not just a fine editor but a friend and comrade-in-arms, this book would never have been completed. She encouraged me, corrected me, and agreed with me—all of which was necessary for this new volume. I also want to thank my secretary, Lily Wallace, for her untiring devotion to my secretarial needs and, above all, for her meticulousness. Finally, I must thank my wife, Hildi, and my children Andreas and Joan Greenson Aebi, and Daniel and Barbara McSwain Greenson, for listening to and reading different versions of these papers.

1

On Gambling

(1947)

I

G AMBLING IS A UNIVERSALLY POPULAR social institution. In
our culture it enjoys a marginal position as an acceptable
social activity. The shade of immorality varies in different
countries and states, and in the various classes within those local-
ities. The sociologists have described some aspects of gambling in
different cultures. For example, Myrdal (1944) has pointed out
that blacks in America find gambling a favorite recreation
because it offers the possibility of a quick monetary return for an
economically repressed people. In addition, gambling is a form
of entertainment which requires little paraphernalia and is particularly suited for those in monotonous occupations. Veblen
(1932) noted that the leisure class finds reckless gambling an enjoyable occasion for the need to demonstrate conspicuous waste.
Rosten (1941) has suggested that the prevalence of gambling in
the movie colony may be due to the unpredictable and sudden
changes of fortune in that industry which accentuate the importance of luck.

In our society—monetary rewards are morally justified only

Presented, in part, before the Los Angeles Psychoanalytic Study Group,
June 21, 1946. First published in *American Imago*, 4:61-77, 1947; also in *The
Yearbook of Psychoanalysis*, 4:110-123. New York: International Universities
Press, 1948.

as the result of work, thrift, and sacrifice. Easy money is considered ill gotten. This sheds some light on the immoral connotation of gambling. On the other hand, several authors have pointed out the close association between gambling and religion. It is striking that in a Gallup Poll of 1938 it was found that 28 percent of the adult American population have participated in church lotteries—a greater number than the 21 percent who have played cards for money. Gambling has also been described in primitive cultures where it is intimately tied up with religious rituals (Stocking, 1931).

Some great literary artists have contributed to our knowledge of the unconscious motivations in gamblers. Dostoevsky (1866) portrays the character of the gambler as a sadomasochistically ridden individual who is unable to break himself of this addiction. Conrad's (1915) gambler is a homosexual with murderous hatred for all women.

Freud's contribution (1928) to the problem of gambling is to be found in his penetrating study of Dostoevsky. On the basis of the artist's writings, his wife's diary, and communications from Dostoevsky's personal friends, Freud formulated some of the basic concepts of gambling. Dostoevsky's gambling was an irrational, instinctlike force. He played impulsively and could never stop until he had lost everything. This need to lose was a self-inflicted punishment. Only after Dostoevsky had thus rid himself of guilt feelings was he able to return to creative writing. Freud pointed out that gambling is a substitute and derivative of masturbation. The emphasis on the exciting activity of the hands is the link which connects gambling and masturbation. The irresistibility of the urge, the oft-repeated resolutions, the intoxicating quality of the pleasure, and the enormous guilt feelings are present in both gambling and masturbation. Furthermore, in both activities there are unconscious fantasies of being rescued by a mother figure.

The psychoanalytic literature based on clinical material concerning gambling is very sparse (Bergler, 1942-43; Simmel, 1920). It is the purpose of this paper to organize the available clinical material and to present some theoretical constructions concerning the essential psychodynamics of the gambler. My experience is limited to the analysis of five male patients who gambled. None of these patients, however, came for treatment with gambling as his main problem. In addition, I have had occasion to make observations on gambling in the U.S. Army from 1942 to 1946, primarily among officers, and in civilian life, primarily among physicians. Since these data are limited in scope, more research is necessary before definite conclusions can be drawn.

The decisive characteristic of gambling which differentiates it from other contests and speculations is the coexistence of a gamelike quality and the importance of chance in determining success or failure. A game is a make-believe, a pretense, not to be taken seriously and not like real life. Chance refers to the unpredictability of the results, to the elements of risk and luck. The more unpredictable a game is, the more it conforms to the definition of gambling. The more that skill is involved in a contest, the less it resembles gambling, and the more it resembles a sport or a business.

It is possible to classify superficially three different types of gamblers: (1) the normal person who gambles for diversion or distraction and who can stop gambling when he wants to; (2) the professional gambler who selects gambling as his means of earning a livelihood; (3) the neurotic gambler who gambles because he is driven by unconscious needs, and who is unable to stop gambling. These three types gamble for different conscious and unconscious reasons; nevertheless, some of the same motivations are found in all of them. The neurotic gambler caricatures the normal and professional gambler and the psychopathology is most vivid in him.

The following is a brief description of readily observable habits, customs, and patterns found in watching a gambling game. The first striking characteristic is the atmosphere of excitement. This is visible in the tremor and sweating of the players, and in their motor restlessness. It is audible in the noise and in the hushed silences. There is a rhythm of tension discharge, which is constantly repeated. At the beginning of play it is quiet, gradually there is a crescendo of excitement until a peak is reached, and finally there is a period of quiet. The excitement, the rhythm, the tension discharge, and the final quiet bear an obvious similarity to sexual excitement. This seems to be borne out by the fact that the rolling of the dice is referred to as "coming," a slang expression for orgasm. It is further confirmed in the fact that the tension the players experience is a pleasurable one and the game ends with the players usually feeling spent (Laforgue, 1930).

Another noteworthy observation is that in poker and in dice games usually only members of the same sex participate. When women take part, they behave in an asexual manner, use masculine mannerisms and language, and seem to take the same position vis-à-vis the gamblers that the tomboy takes with boys. In bridge, where there is more skill and less gambling, there is usually an even distribution of the sexes and the women behave in a more feminine manner. In roulette, which is entirely a game of chance, women are present, but psychosexual differences are barely recognizable; the women expect and receive no special courtesies or attention. There is no flirtation at the gambling table. The antifeminine atmosphere of the gambling room is manifest not only in the exclusion of the opposite sex, but in the antifeminine vocabulary of the players; for example, queens are often referred to as whores. (Women sense the antifeminine atmosphere of the gambling hall and are usually antagonistic to their husbands' gambling.)

The vocabulary of the gamblers is very distinctive; it is profane, but not sexual, and it is highly aggressive. The stakes are always called "the pot," the player refers to "making a big pot" or to "cleaning up." A lucky player is often referred to as one who has "fallen into a barrel of shit," and dice are called "craps." Winning is referred to as "making a killing," losing as "being cleaned out." A special maneuver in poker is designated "sand bagging." When a player has a sure-fire winning hand, he may refer to his position as having the other "by the balls." When one of the gamblers misses his turn, he is told that "his nose is bleeding."

Another characteristic of all gambling situations is the prevalence of superstitions and magical rituals. There are a great many colorful and varied practices which are used as attempts to bring good luck. The players change seats, walk around chairs, change decks of cards, have good luck charms on the table or on their person, rub their cards or dice on various parts of their bodies, look at their cards in a certain prescribed order, wager high stakes on poor cards because of "hunches" and bet little on good cards because certain cards are unlucky, etc. Many of them believe that concentration will influence the sequence of cards or the roll of the dice. The dice player shouts as he throws the dice, exclaiming "be good to me dicey," or "come on Ada," when he needs an eight. Some poker players admit that they pray as they wait for a card.

Other behavior patterns of a stereotyped nature are readily observed among all players. Some constantly count, pile, and sort their money or chips. Others have their money and the various colored chips carelessly scrambled before them. Expelling of gas by some of the players is accepted as part of the ritual of the poker game in some groups. Marked extremes in neatness and sloppiness of dress can be observed. Some players fondle their cards gently and others fling them on the table. Bluffing is a daring technique which some players frequently use, and which others always avoid. (It is one of the few occasions in our society when the act of deception is not merely permissible, but an enviable talent.)

There is an unusual amount of eating, drinking, and smoking around the gambling tables. Most gamblers eat, drink, and smoke more during the gambling than they do in any other comparative period of time.

Some of the phenomena described above are seen in all types of gambling and in all types of gamblers. All these activities are of a regressive nature; they are all derivatives of infantile partial instincts. The phallic and homosexual manifestations are apparent in the exclusion of women from a situation where sensual excitement is present. The vocabulary of the gambler abounds in anal, scatological, and overtly sadistic expressions. Anal-sadistic derivatives are also seen in the extremes of neatness and sloppiness of dress, in the sorting and piling of chips, and in the expelling of gas (Simmel, 1920). Oral drives are accentuated in the overeating, drinking and smoking. Even the thinking of the gambler has regressed to a more infantile level, as is manifest in the superstitious, magical, and ritualistic procedures. All these observations indicate very clearly that the gambling situation permits the discharge of pregenital impulses. Phallic, anal-sadistic, and oral strivings may be discharged in this setting with a minimum of guilt feelings, since this behavior is accepted by the group and the guilt is shared by the other players. The regressive nature of these activities is confirmed by the archaic thinking and acting of the players in their attempts to influence luck. Since all people have remnants of pregenital instincts within them, and since our society imposes obstacles in the satisfaction of these instincts, and since gambling offers such a diversified opportunity for satisfaction of the many partial instincts, it is understandable why almost everyone in our society can gamble.

II

Having described and attempted to isolate phenomena which are common to all gambling situations and to all people who gamble, I shall now seek to formulate the specific conflicts which are decisive for the formation of a gambling neurosis. Here I refer to those people who must gamble, who cannot stop gambling, and who allow gambling to tyrannize and destroy their lives. There seem to be two crucial elements which are essential to the etiology of a gambling neurosis: (1) the neurotic gambler feels lucky and hopes each time he will be rewarded, despite all intellectualization to the contrary (Fenichel, 1945, p. 372); (2) the neurotic gambler is impelled to test out Luck or Fate. The normal and professional gambler may have either of these qualities, but the intensity of these drives is lacking. Feeling lucky and the need to challenge Fate and Chance are interwoven, yet it is possible to trace the genesis of these emotions separately.

The neurotic gambler hopes he is lucky and at times believes it. Consciously or unconsciously he believes in his right to ask Fate for special privileges and protection. He hopes that Fate will give proof that he is favored over all the others and he will be permitted to win. Winning is the proof that he is lucky. It is pleasurable not only for the money (some gamblers play for little or no money), but it is a token of special privilege and power. The neurotic gambler seeks a sign from Fate that he is omnipotent. His longing for omnipotence is full of doubts and contradictions; yet it is this archaic ego feeling which makes gambling at all possible. He dares challenge the Gods to give him a sign that will confirm this shaky belief in his omnipotence; yet he would never risk this challenge if he did not, in part, believe it. The neurotic gambler mistakes his strong yearnings for omnipotence for the feeling that he is omnipotent.[1] The regressive character of this state of affairs is in keeping with the infantile features of the neurotic gambler's thinking and actions which have a strikingly animistic, superstitious, and magical quality. The neurotic gambler dares to gamble since he wants to convince himself that he is lucky, i.e., omnipotent, and needs constant reassurance from Fate to calm his grave doubts.

The longing for omnipotence and the belief in one's omnipotence stem from early infantile life. Ferenczi (1913) has presented the concept that all infants originally have a feeling of unlimited omnipotence. This is lost when hunger and pain destroy the infant's narcissism. The adults who assuage hunger and pain become the omnipotent ones. By introjection and identification, the infant tries to participate in the omnipotence of the adults. On this infantile level, hunger and need for love are undifferentiated, satisfaction and security are identical. In the infant, milk satisfies the hunger and brings about a reunion with the mother, which produces oceanic feelings and restores the lost omnipotence (Fenichel, 1945, p. 39). It is this feeling which the neurotic gambler unconsciously is attempting to recapture.

[1] Dostoevsky's gambler says: "I only know that I must win, that it is the only resource left to me. Well, that's why, perhaps, I fancy I am bound to win."

The neurotic gambler is a personality on the brink of a severe depression. He deludes himself into feeling lucky and attempts to win from Fate a sign of favor which will simultaneously gratify his urgent need for satisfaction and security (Rado, 1926). I shall return to the question of why this attempt fails, but first wish to examine the concept of Fate and Chance in this situation.

Who or what is Luck or Fate? Luck and Fate are equivalent to God and to father. It is the powerful, omnipotent, protecting figure that can kill, castrate, abandon, or love. The neurotic gambler's attitude toward his father figure varies with the specific gambler and changes within him under certain circumstances. The gambling situation may represent:

(1) A challenge or a testing out of this father figure.[2] If luck is good it means the father has accepted you and you may share in his omnipotence. If luck is bad, it means you have been rejected. Winning often results in transitory euphoria and losing in temporary depression, both inappropriate to the amount of money won or lost.

(2) The game may represent a battle with Fate. It is a sham battle for supremacy, an attempt to supplant the father as the omnipotent one.

(3) Gambling may be experienced as an act of extreme submissiveness in which the gambler places himself at the mercy of Fate. The gambler's attitude is: "Here I am, do with me what you will."

(4) Gambling may represent an attempt to bribe this powerful father figure: "Here is my money, now am I allowed to enjoy certain forbidden pleasures?"

(5) The game may symbolize an occasion to court or woo the father figure, according to the formula: "I have been a good boy and have done all my tasks, now will you reward me and let me win?"

Luck is also a mother figure to some gamblers—

---

[2] Dostoevsky's gambler says, "A strange sensation rose up in me, a sort of defiance of fate, a desire to challenge it, to put out my tongue at it."

Lady Luck. Here, the mother figure is less frightening, but nonetheless powerful. Lady Luck is fickle, she is not to be trusted. She may deceive you, but she may also reward you. The demands of the gambler may be accepted or rejected, and he may challenge, battle, beg, or woo. Bergler (1942-43) stressed aggressions against the mother as the most important unconscious motives in the gambler he studied.

In the patients I had occasion to analyze, the figure of luck was determined by the specific emotional conflicts which were in the foreground at the moment. The attitude of the gambler to this figure varied from battling to wooing, depending upon the drives involved in the patient's most pressing psychic conflicts. In any case, the image and attitude toward Luck was determined by the oedipus constellation of the specific gambler. For example, a patient during the course of his analysis reacted to Luck as a father figure he was battling, when he was reliving his hostility toward his father in his analysis. Later on Luck became "Lady Luck," whom he wooed, when conflicts concerning his mother became the central point of his analysis.

To recapitulate: the neurotic gambler has regressed to infantile longings for omnipotence. He dares expose himself to Fate, since he has mistaken his longings for omnipotence, for the feeling that he is omnipotent. He enters this arena fearfully and hopefully, and expects a token from a parent figure, Fate, which will prove that he is really the chosen one. Since strong longings for omnipotence and oceanic feelings are evidence of a failure of the ego to maintain a mature level, one would expect to find in the history of neurotic gamblers severe deprivation and/or overgratification in childhood. This is confirmed by the clinical findings. One of my patients had a mother who never said no; he never learned to tolerate any rejection no matter how mild. It was significant that he gambled only when he was away from home—away from mother—as an attempt to prove that "Lady Luck" (his phrase) was still with him. In another case, father and mother each had their favorite child, but the patient was not the favorite of either. Sent overseas to the C.B.I theatre, he became depressed and felt abandoned and resorted to gambling, in part as a fight against Fate, father, for abandoning him and as a symbolic plea to Lady Luck, mother—a begging for a sign of love.

These attempts to recapture the lost feeling of omnipotence are unsuccessful. The neurotic gambler is unable to stop gambling because he cannot bear the feeling of abandonment and depression when he loses; nor can he bear the excitement of winning. In both cases, unresolved tensions require that he continue the game. The feelings aroused by winning and losing are so interwoven with guilt feelings that full satisfaction is impossible and the frustrated wishes return again and again, seeking gratification. Our next task shall be to explore the sources of these guilt feelings involved in the neurosis of gambling.

For the neurotic gambler winning is equivalent to triumph. As Fenichel (1939b) pointed out, the feeling of triumph results from the removal of anxiety and inhibition by the winning of a trophy. Possession of the trophy brings with it "oceanic" feelings, because it represents reunion with the omnipotent one. The trophy is a superego derivative since it is a symbol of parental power. The superego is a precipitate of the oedipus complex which is internalized and serves as an authority over the ego. Since a trophy is also a representative of the authority once vested in the oedipal figures, it, too, threatens the ego in the same way that the superego threatens the ego where unresolved oedipal fantasies are at work. The winnings of the neurotic gambler resemble the trophy of the hunter and threaten the gambler in a similar way. "Easy come, easy go" and "hot money" typify the gambler's guilt-laden attitude toward his winnings.

The unconscious fantasies of the neurotic gambler are identical with the masturbation fantasies of the individual and are responsible in part for the guilt feelings in regard to gambling (Fenichel, 1945, p. 373). Masturbation and gambling both start out as play. A play begins as an attempt to discharge tension in a regulated dosage at a specific time. In masturbation and in gambling, the stirring up of unconscious oedipal fantasies destroys the playful character of the act (Freud, 1928). The ego is overwhelmed by anxiety and guilt, and what started out as play is no longer play or pleasurable, but becomes a threat to the mental equilibrium. The neurotic gambler is conscious of his guilt feelings, but is unaware of the content of these guilt feelings. The forbidden nature of the fantasies stirred up in gambling is responsible for the fact that these fantasies must be maintained in repression. In gambling only distorted derivatives of these fantasies are permitted access to consciousness in the form of Fate and Luck fantasies. Since gambling only allows distorted derivatives of forbidden impulses to break through into consciousness, and since this is always accompanied by guilt feelings, the neurotic gambler's possibilities for complete gratification are nullified by these circumstances.

The neurotic gambler's constant losing is due in part to his inability to accept the dictates of the mathematical laws of chance. Simmel, in a personal communication, suggested that losing money can symbolize an anal orgasm for the pregenitally oriented gambler. "To be cleaned out" is a typical gambler's expression for losing. The unconscious guilt feelings are more important in explaining the neurotic gambler's need to lose. Describing the unconscious need for punishment, Freud (1916, p. 318) stated that some people act out forbidden fantasies in a distorted way in order to be apprehended. The unconscious guilt feelings of the neurotic gambler are responsible for the unconscious need for punishment (Freud, 1928). This punishment, losing, bad as it is, is a lesser evil than the terrifying punishment of castration or total loss of love. The need to lose may also be an expression of masochistic strivings (Bergler, 1942-43). Losing, i.e., being beaten, is erotized, and becomes an appropriate vehicle for masochistic fantasies.

The superego is, I repeat, a residue of the oedipus complex. In the healthy individual, the superego has been desexualized. In the pregenitally fixated person, there is a resexualization of the superego. In keeping with the regression to sadomasochistic object relationships, there is also a sadomasochistic relationship between superego and ego. In manic-depressive states, euphoria and melancholia are manifestations of this special position of the superego (Freud, 1917a). In the euphoric state, super-ego and ego are united, and there is a minimum of tension between them. In melancholia, the superego takes great delight in cruelly tormenting the ego. Similar superego-ego relation-ships are found in drug addicts and in neurotic gamblers. A longitudinal survey of the clinical course in the addict and gam-bler reveals frequent, sharp fluctuations of affect with recurring states of elation and depression (Rado, 1933).

III

The discussion, thus far, has been concerned with analyzing what "feeling lucky" means, what Fate represents, and why the neurotic gambler is unable to stop gambling. All this would apply to the solitaire players, the roulette player, and those who play alone against Fate or Luck, rather than against other play-ers. Competing against other players, as in cards or dice, had different meanings in the patients I studied. The fellow players served various purposes in the unconscious fantasies of the neu-rotic gamblers. The relationship of the neurotic gambler to his fellow gamblers may be schematized along the following lines:

1. The fellow gamblers are grownups and grant participa-tion in the forbidden and exciting activities of adults.

2. The fellow gamblers are "he-men"; sex and women are "sissy stuff." This is very reminiscent of the gang spirit in adoles-cents.[3] In the army, among personnel of late adolescence age (18-21), gambling for high stakes was considered masculine.

3. The fellow gamblers are cohorts in homosexual activities. Gambling with other men was equivalent, in the unconscious, to comparing penises with other men; winning meant having the largest penis or being the most potent. Excitement together often

---

[3] It is interesting to note that gambling with others only starts after puberty. Prior to that, magical and animistic games are very common, but these are usually carried on alone. Gambling with others is a continuation of magical thinking and acting within the limits of an acceptable social institution. Luck replaces the secret oracles of the child.

represented masturbation together. In passive homosexual men who love the type of man they would like to have been, contact with strong men in a game had the significance of gaining additional manhood.[4] Unconscious homosexuality is demonstrated by the neurotic gambler in his sparse or Don Juan type of sexual life. Two of my patients had overt homosexual episodes and turned to gambling during periods of sexual abstinence. Another patient became a gambler only after developing premature ejaculation. His gambling was, on the one hand, a disguised homosexual substitute for heterosexual satisfaction and, on the other, it was an attempt to deny his impotence. The expression "lucky in cards, unlucky in love," is a striking testimonial to the fact that neurotics with unresolved homosexual and heterosexual conflicts find gambling an appropriate outlet for their frustrations.

4. The fellow gamblers may be reacted to as father or mother surrogates and therefore may also fulfill the same function as the figures in the unconscious Fate fantasies. The neurotic gambler may act out in his card game a challenging, wooing, battling, or submissive attitude in relation to the other players.

Many of the pregenital instinctual expressions are obvious to the onlooker at a gambling game, but in analysis one specific series of characteristics emerges with greater clarity. The waiting for fate to decide, the passive attitudes of the gambler as he waits for his cards, the inordinate dependence on this external image (Luck), all of these characteristics rooted in the oral-receptive phase of libidinal development were the most stubborn factors to overcome in the cases analyzed.

The habitual kibitzer should be mentioned as a special type of neurotic gambler. He is a gambler without the courage to gamble. My clinical experience with chronic kibitzers has sug-

---

[4] Bergler (1942-43) points out that the need to be overwhelmed by Fate is the result of passive homosexual wishes toward the father and is especially true of those with the compulsive need to lose at gambling. For one of my patients, losing at cards meant a fulfillment of his unconscious wish to be homosexually possessed by the father.

gested that they are similar to the type of homosexual who is fixated to an older brother and who longs to participate in his success, a type described by Freud (1922). The kibitzer is afraid to participate in the game, but identifies himself with one of the players he would like to emulate. He avoids the risk of losing, but he also never achieves the satisfaction of having exposed himself successfully to danger. These men often go through life attached to a strong, older brother figure and by identification with him enjoy and suffer in small doses the older brother's triumphs and sorrows.

Summary

Neurotic gambling is based on an unconscious attempt to regain the lost feeling of omnipotence by fighting and/or wooing Luck or Fate. The gambler dares to expose himself to this situation because he already has regressed to a stage where the desire for this archaic ego feeling is misinterpreted for the feeling itself. Luck and Fate are derived from mother and/or father images and gambling offers an opportunity for the revival of unconscious oedipal fantasies. In addition, gambling offers possibilities for satisfying latent and unconscious homosexual, anal-sadistic, oral-receptive drives, and for gratifying unconscious needs for punishment. Because of the diversity of opportunities and the social sanction, it is understandable why almost everyone in our society can gamble.[5] It is clear that neurotics with unresolved longings for omnipotence and oceanic feelings would be predisposed to fall ill with this disease.

Neurotic gambling belongs in the category of the impulse neuroses (Fenichel, 1945, p. 367). It resembles the addictions and the perversions, in that the impulse to gamble is experienced

[5] It would seem to be very worthwhile to study the relationship between economic and political frustrations and the tendency to gamble. More specifically, it would be interesting to have a sociological framework for studying the relationship between specific kinds of economic and political frustrations and the specific kinds of gambling in different societies.

not as ego-alien, but as ego-syntonic. Though the impulse is not overtly sexual as in the perversions, nor is there the euphoric intoxification as in the addictions, the gambler likes his gambling—he feels forced to like it. The impulse to gamble is felt in the same way as normal people feel their instincts. It serves the purpose of denying an infantile sense of danger (i.e., abandonment) and simultaneously gratifies thinly distorted sexual and aggressive impulses. It has an irresistible quality: the tension has to be satisfied by action, not thinking, and immediately, not by postponement. (The gambler acts according to the pleasure principle, and in gambling games the pleasure principle is as valid as the reality principle.) The imperative demand for simultaneous instinctual gratification and need to be loved indicates a regression to an early libidinal phase, when instinctual satisfaction and striving for security were not differentiated from each other. To the neurotic gambler, people are transformed into merely potential donors of narcissistic gratification, a characteristic of the orally oriented individual.

All these factors demonstrate the severely regressive character of the disease. This suggests that the gambling neurosis, like so many of the impulse neuroses, is an effort at defense against an impending severe depression (see also Greenson, 1967b).

The course of this illness is a very stormy one; these patients often require periods of institutionalization. The only adequate therapy is psychoanalysis. The prognosis is not favorable, since there are frequent lapses; moreover, the secondary complications of gambling, namely, legal and monetary difficulties, often interfere with the treatment. In general, the course and the results of treatment are similar to those of the addictions and the perversions.[6]

---

[6] If I were to write this paper today, I would put more stress on the pre-oedipal conflict with the mother.

2

The Psychology of Apathy

(1949)

I

APATHY MAY BE DEFINED phenomenologically as a state of affectlessness (Leites, 1947). It is a term frequently used in the description of various psychopathological states. Apathetic reactions have been noted in catatonic schizophrenics and in depressives. It has been observed as a psychological sequel to organic diseases of long duration, and it is known to occur in otherwise apparently healthy human beings as a concomitant of boredom. In all of the above-mentioned conditions apathy was only a secondary or unimportant manifestation. During the war, however, it was possible to observe apathy as the predominant feature in certain types of war neuroses.[1]

Read at the Annual Meeting of the American Psychoanalytic Association, Washington, D.C., May 16, 1948. First published in *Psychoanalytic Quarterly*, 18:290-302, 1949.

[1] I have described other dominant reactions in severe war neuroses in which several categories of reaction could be distinguished in these previously healthy soldiers (Greenson, 1945, p. 204):

WAR NEUROSES

TYPE	CLINICAL PICTURE	THERAPY	PROGNOSIS
I. Danger-Anxiety	Tremor, sweating, restlessness, jumpiness; insomnia, battle dreams, startle reaction, excitability	Reliving under sodium pentothal, with working through of recovered repressed memories	Very good. Probably best of all, especially if early treatment is given

17

The most striking characteristic of the apathetic patient is his visible lack of emotion and drive. At first glance he seems to be depressed; closer scrutiny, however, reveals lack of affect. He appears slowed down in his psychic and motor responses; he shows an emptiness of expression and a masklike facies. These patients are often found lying in their bunks with their eyes

WAR NEUROSES (Continued)

TYPE	CLINICAL PICTURE	THERAPY	PROGNOSIS
II. Passive-dependent		Mild cases—Sympathy and affection from all personnel plus psychotherapy	Poor—from military standpoint. Fair on discharge
a. Deprivation-Passive (the subject of this paper)	Apathy, submissiveness, resignation, lack of interest, inactivity, fatigue	Severe cases—Discharge to return to loved ones	
b. Helplessness—pseudo-belligerent	Aggressiveness, cockiness, immaturity, insecurity. Loud talking and bragging to companions, crying and admission of loneliness and longings to psychiatrist	Sodium pentothal, releasing feelings of helplessness and longing plus reassurance and interpretation of bluff defense against these suppressed feelings	Quite good
III. Guilt-Laden			
a. Guilt-Belligerent	*Conscious* guilt feelings, belligerence, agitation, temper outbursts, hatred of superiors and army in general. Justifiable self-reproach elicited	Sodium pentothal only to obtain recital of guilty secret. Sympathy but hard, tough attitude toward the symptoms, not toward the patient	Guarded. Depends on seriousness of guilt-provoking situation and patient's real culpability
b. Guilt-Anxiety	*Unconscious* guilt feelings. Same clinical picture as Danger-Anxiety type	Sodium pentothal to obtain repressed material, plus slow working through and reassurance. If anxiety changes to belligerence, treat as III a above	Quite good
c. Guilt-Depression	Tremor, sweating, restlessness *plus* hostility, *plus* depression. Guilt precipitated by loss of a buddy	All of above techniques, depending on what attitude is in foreground. Usually deal with guilt feelings first, permitting normal grief and mourning. Sodium pentothal to release ambivalence and suppressed sorrow. Deal with recent ambivalences only. Utilize revenge motive for new duty assignment	Midway between III a and III b

open, staring endlessly at the ceiling. They exhibit no startle reaction; they do not tremble, nor do they sweat profusely. In general, they spend a good deal of time in bed, sometimes with their eyes closed, apparently asleep, but they can be roused instantly. They are well behaved, complying with all the rules and regulations. They complain rarely and make no demands, all of which is in marked contrast to other psychiatric casualties of the war. In "bull sessions" they listen to the stories of the other men, but contribute none of their own. They drink little and are not interested in women. They are often admitted to the hospital ward with a diagnosis of schizophrenia.

It was difficult to obtain histories from these patients because they had no urge to communicate their sufferings and no awareness of their condition. Since they were passive and complained little, they were often neglected. Their response to narcosynthesis was also quite different from that shown by the other types of war neuroses. The anxious patient, the depressed patient, and the patient with the traumatic neurosis would respond to intravenous sodium pentothal by reliving their recent past experiences and by abreacting strong, even violent emotions. The apathetic patients displayed noticeably little feeling.

One patient, twenty-one years old, formerly a tail gunner on a B-17, was stationed for twenty-five months in the Southwest Pacific and was admitted to the psychiatric ward because he showed no reponse to four months of the convalescent program. He was quiet and cooperative and rarely spoke to the other patients. In the psychotherapeutic interview he sat hunched in his chair, his eyes focused on the floor. He answered all questions accurately, but spoke slowly and laconically. He was given 10 cc. of 2½ percent sodium pentothal and fell asleep without a word. When he was aroused, he started chanting in a low, quiet voice, "I wanna go home, I wanna go home, I wanna go home." He paused, took a deep breath, and continued, "I wanna go home, I wanna go home, I wanna go home." He was slowly given an additional 4 cc., and again he fell asleep. This time he was more difficult to rouse, but finally his eyes opened and again he began to chant: "I wanna go home, I wanna go home." This procedure was repeated on several occasions with the same results. He never betrayed any emotion. He would say the same words in the same way for almost an hour; then he would fall asleep. This is a good example of the way apathetic patients talk. The flat and monotonous tone, the slow tempo, and the repetition of simple words—all are typical.

In the service history of such cases, there was a striking similarity in the kind of duty and stress to which these men were exposed. All were found to have spent long periods often free of actual danger, but with poor food, in bad climates, under conditions of severe boredom and in great loneliness. Most striking were those who had spent three or more years as prisoners of war of the Japanese, or who had been stationed for years on isolated islands in the Pacific. More cases came from Ground Force personnel than from the Air Force; and from the Air Corps there were fewer among flying personnel. This can be explained on the basis of differences in physical living conditions, monotony of duty, and the amount of deference received.

These records seem to indicate that deprivation over a long period of time results in the development of apathy. Observations on the course of development of this clinical picture show that apathy is not an immediate response, but the end result of deprivation when it reaches traumatic proportions. Prisoners of war described initial reactions of belligerence, rebelliousness, and aggressiveness; however, when angry rebellion and aggression brought continual defeat and humiliation, these reactions would subside and apathy would gradually come into the foreground. Furthermore, it was noted that patients recovering from apathy went through a phase of marked hostility and irritability. This transition is readily demonstrable in a single narcosynthesis interview, but can be observed just as clearly over a longer period of time without this procedure.

Another patient was a twenty-five-year-old crew chief who had been stationed for some twenty-seven months in the deserts of North Africa. He was extremely quiet, passive, submissive, never complained, and because his condition did not improve he was given 12 cc. of 2½ percent sodium pentothal. He fell asleep and then spontaneously began to talk in a subdued and mournful manner:

> The first thing we did was to find cockroaches—and then worms floating around—it was a bad crossing. We went five thousand miles to get to England and the food was bad. Then Africa—bad—bad. We marched seventeen miles, forced march—guys were dropping out—laying in the mud, sleeping on the floor, and then it was cold, your legs were stiff and you couldn't move, and there was no food— and we marched some more—for weeks and weeks there was mud up to your knees, and the Germans were close, and they bombed us and strafed us, and it was bad. And the food was bad, and the boys got killed [he began to cry softly]. Rough—rough—oh it was rough; and the planes went out every hour, and half the boys didn't get back. It was bad. We lived underground. Dust, sand, and the Jerrys strafed us and bombed us, and we lost a lot of men. We lost them—good boys, too. There was not much to eat. We worked all the time from daylight to dark, from daylight to dark. We got to Tunis and it was bad. German bodies all around, stinking. It was so hot. The tools burned your hands—it was bad. We were sick, the desert was hot, there were mines and booby traps. We had to work and work and there was no food. We moved—it was bad. The boys were starvin'. And the pilots would come back from their missions and there was nothing wrong with their planes [sob]. We'd work on them and we got chewed out. Work, work, work, and no food—not a bit left. There was no one around for miles and miles—just beggars—dust—dirt. Day after day—food full of dirt—work day and night—day and night. The C.O. told the line chief to eat us out—day after day we did our best—from daylight to dark—we worked. We were soldiers—we did our duty, but they didn't care. They beat us into the ground, because the pilots were scared. There was nothing wrong with the planes [sobbing]. Day after day, officers—young officers picked on us. We would

fix something for ourselves to be comfortable and the officers would take it. We fixed lights, and what did they do?
Took our generator that we built. We'd get parts, and they
took it away. Our bulbs, from home—my folks sent them,
and the C.O. would say we had too many bulbs and they
took them away. All the while, all the while, we couldn't do
anything—he had the rank. Rules—rules, rules. The clothes
were uncomfortable. From daylight to dark, cold, wet,
sleet, rain—heat so hot, but they didn't care. They had it
tough, but we were machines, tear ya down, tear ya down,
there was nothing left. I am sick and tired. We tried to be
happy, but they tear ya down. You couldn't sleep, you
couldn't eat. We were on C rations for five months. Our
stomachs hurt. We didn't eat. We were starvin' and what
did the doc do—laugh in your face [sob]. I want to be free,
live like a white man. You don't know, nobody knows, nobody knows how it is. Please, no [sobbing], no—no—no
never go back, please—please. I got to be free, so I can be
half a man again—just half a man—they tore us down, beat
us to the ground, machines. I don't know, I'll go nuts if I
have to go back [writhing]. I can't help it. I wanted to be a
soldier, a good one, but they beat me down. Never anymore, never anymore. They beat us down. I don't know. I
don't even want to go back to my wife the way I am. What
they did to me. I want to go home to a white man's life, not
a slave, not beat you. They took your manhood—your spirit
away—everytime—for so long you can't enjoy.—You don't
understand, they battered me, they beat me down. I don't
trust mankind anymore. Doc, don't send me back!

The transition is characteristic: the soft crying and the
mournful laments; then the complaints, and finally the flashes of
anger. Deprivation is clearly equated with castration, "Beat ya
down, beat ya down," and "They take your manhood away."
Exposure to danger may become traumatic deprivation
among men subjected to the stress of severe combat. Initially,
they developed states of anxiety; if they remained in combat for

more than twenty-five days, the anxiety receded and was replaced by apathy. Tremor, sweating, and restlessness persisted, but unaccompanied by anxious affect. Under pentothal, despite the fact that they recounted the most violent combat experiences in great detail, they spoke quietly and sadly, without tremor, sweating, or panic. This type of reaction was seen predominantly in Ground Force personnel and has been designated "combat exhaustion" (Swank and Marchand, 1946).

If one examines more closely the clinical picture of these apathetic patients, significant changes in all aspects of the mental life are demonstrable. Their instinctual drives seemed severely diminished and restricted. There was a complete loss of interest in genitality and in women (P. Friedman, 1949). Masturbation and homosexuality occurred in the early months of captivity and then ceased. There was also a history of much scatological talk and anal references. When the full-blown picture of apathy developed, the only instinctual preoccupation concerned food and eating. This was doubtless due to the fact that these activities became the primary factor for the individual's survival. It is also plausible to assume that constant frustration of genital and heterosexual wishes furthered the regression.

The ego also showed signs of regression which can be seen in the infantile quality of the thinking processes. At first there was much preoccupation with wish-fulfillment fantasies, which were rich and colorful. Then there was a trend to religion, magic, and rituals. Here you found "fox hole" religion—"Nobody is an atheist in a fox hole." Then this ceased. The men who returned from the Japanese prison camps did not pray or observe religious rituals. Here, too, the constantly repeated disappointments and frustrations were too painful. It was better not to hope and not to pray; it would only lead to disappointment. There was an impoverishment of the thinking processes, predominantly visual imagery, and little motility. These men loved to read cook books and study advertisements of food (Schiele and Brozek, 1948). This may be explained as a further regression to the primitive state of ego development in which all perception is conceived as oral incorporation.

The status of the superego in these patients was not very clear. There were no overt signs of guilt feelings or self-reproach. The apathetic soldier obeyed meekly, never rebelled, made no struggle in the sphere of self-esteem. As in the case of infants, authority seemed to be vested in the external world and was no longer internalized (Simmel, 1944a; Rado, 1942).

The personality structure of the apathetic patient indicates two important changes: there is evidence of a regression to a passive, oral, narcissistic, libidinal level as well as a severe restriction of ego functioning.

II

In order to understand how deprivation causes apathy it is important to remember the basic needs for food and love in the human infant. In order to survive, food is necessary in the first few days of life. Love and its derivatives seem to be essential already in the first few months of life. Infants who are given the proper amount of physical care but who do not receive an adequate amount of mothering manifest the clinical picture of apathy (Ribble, 1944; Spitz, 1945). Early in the infant's history the mother's milk serves to gratify both the instinctual and the narcissistic needs (Fenichel, 1945). The helpless infant is utterly dependent on some adult for his physical and mental equilibrium. As the infant gains motility and muscular coordination, he also wins psychological freedom. The need to be loved, which was essential for the infant, diminishes with the development of the superego: self-esteem then provides much of the security formerly derived from being loved. To feel loved and cared for, to be needed and wanted, are nevertheless necessary for the maintenance of self-esteem throughout life.

The equations of food and love, and of deprivation and abandonment, become apparent when we study the apathetic patient. On Corregidor this couplet became popular:

We are the bastards from Bataan;
No mother, no father, no Uncle Sam.

Irregular mail meant to these men, "Our loved ones at home have forgotten us." Bad climate was interpreted as: "Even God has abandoned us."

Starvation seems to play a dual role in producing apathy. Physiologically the lack of adequate nourishment brings about a state of marasmus, the physical response to the depletion of the essential bodily needs. Psychologically, the lack of food is felt as the loss of love. This loss of love then diminishes the feeling of self-esteem which results in the feeling of having been abandoned. Rado (1927) has shown that the infant's hunger is the prototype for the feeling of emptiness of which melancholics so often complain. The sequence of events also has its counterpart in the behavior of infants. Their first response to hunger is the rich affective discharge of rage, which only after repeated disappointments or protracted frustration gives way to apathy. This type of reaction has been noted in masses of people as well as in individuals. Immediately after the war, visitors to England and Europe frequently emphasized the apparent apathy of the people. It was especially vivid among displaced persons and in concentration camps. One of the factors responsible for the failure of oppressed peoples to rebel against tyranny is the development of a state of apathy from repeated defeats and disappointments (Portia Bell Hume, n.d.).

III

Since apathy occurs in the catatonic schizophrenic, in the depressed patient, and in the bored individual, it would be instructive to compare the dynamics of apathy in these conditions with apathy in war neuroses.

In the catatonic stupor the regression to an oral, passive, receptive level is clear. Autoerotic gratification is obviously manifested in uncontrolled urination and defecation and the necessity for tube feedings. Furthermore, one also sees here the withdrawal of the ego from reality. The difference between the apathetic soldier and the catatonic patient is based upon the relative intactness of the ego in the former. The soldier regresses primarily because of external stress, and restricts perception without confusing internal and external reality. Although there are some signs of archaic ego functioning, the most striking feature in the soldier is the impoverishment of the ego. One can use Freud's analogy of an army in retreat and state that the apathetic soldier has retreated in good order to an early oral orientation, whereas the catatonic has been disastrously routed. In both, however, external perceptions are severely limited because they herald only pain or danger, and there is a retreat into a trancelike state.

The apathetic state also resembles the depressions in the subjective feeling of emptiness, the slowing up of motor and affect responses, and the oral orientation. Neurotically depressed persons suffer from the feeling of being unloved which is not in keeping with their real situation, and the depression is an attempt to force a disappointing love object to gratify the infantile narcissistic cravings. The apathetic patient no longer tries to wrest narcissistic supplies from objects in the external world. The apathetic soldier has renounced external object relationships.

In psychotic depressions, we find the same renunciation of external object relationships. Here introjection and ambivalence decisively color the dynamic picture. Freud (1917a), Abraham (1924), Rado (1927), and Fenichel (1945) have clearly described how the external objects toward whom the depressed patient was intensely ambivalent have been incorporated and a renunciation of objects in the external world occurs. The internalization of this conflict does not resolve it but only perpetuates it. Since the introjection took place on a sadistic basis, a bitter struggle now goes on internally between the superego and the ego, manifested by tormenting guilt feelings, self-reproach, and recrimination. In apathy this pathogenic introjection and the sadomasochistic conflicts between ego and superego do not appear and there is no evidence of internalization or ambivalence. The apathetic patient is able to avoid a psychotic depression because he is able to keep the deprivations and disappointments that the external world foisted upon him in the external world. Those who deprived him of food and love were objects he hated (Leites, 1947). He was not ambivalent; he only hated. This hatred was free of conflict. There was every justification for his hatred. When the apathetic patient regressively reached the predominating phase of oral incorporation, he could direct his aim toward food and eating, which were real factors in his survival. Finally, since there was a minimum of guilt in his predicament, conflicts between ego and superego were relatively unimportant.

Apathy may resemble more closely the primal depression described by Abraham (1924) which occurs in children before the oedipal wishes are successfully mastered. It is similar to what Fenichel (1945) calls a feeling of annihilation. This is described as occurring in children when a total lack of narcissistic gratification creates a sense of abandonment. It is intimately connected with oral frustration (Ribble, 1944; Spitz, 1945).

Boredom is also a state of apathy (Fenichel, 1934b). It is a mood of unpleasant indifference, of passive waiting, and a sense of loneliness. There is a disturbed awareness that time seems to stand still. There is a withdrawal of libido from the external world. Boredom, however, stems from a repression of instinctual aims, with the result that the external world is unable to offer any potentially satisfying stimuli. There is a restriction of perception for external and internal stimuli because the ego has to maintain the repression of forbidden sexual aims, and for the same reason is unable to face external stimuli which might remobilize these forbidden strivings.[2]

To summarize: the apathy of catatonia, depression, boredom, and war neurosis have in common a restriction of perception of and response to internal and external stimuli.

IV

It is characteristic of the ego to block perception when stimuli become traumatic. Fainting is the simplest example. Freud (1920) elaborated this theme in his theory of the stimulus bar-

[2] Boredom is more extensively discussed in chapter 4.

rier, as did Rado (1939) in a paper on the riddance principle.
Kardiner (1932) discussed the shrinking of the ego in epileptics in
a manner which conforms with these phenomena.[3] The
apathetic patient is partly unconscious; there exists a partial inhibition of consciousness, not as complete or intense as the loss of
consciousness in fainting or epilepsy, but more persistent. The
blocking of ego functions may be considered the cardinal manifestation of traumatic neuroses, and in this sense apathy belongs
in this category.

Apathy is a defense against painful perceptions and serves
the purpose of avoiding overwhelming feelings of annihilation.
It may be regarded as a milder form of this feeling of annihilation, in the same way that anxiety is a milder form of panic.
From this standpoint apathy can be regarded as a successful defense mechanism. Perhaps the relatively high number of survi-
vors with a childhood history of coming from broken homes or
orphan asylums suggests that early in life these men had been
able successfully to withstand severe deprivation.

Clinical histories obtained from men who returned from
three or more years of imprisonment in Japanese prison camps
confirm this hypothesis. Norman Brill (1946) stated that the men
who kept hoping, "Tomorrow, tomorrow we'll be liberated"—
these men died. It was the men who said, "No, it won't be tomorrow. Maybe later"—that survived. The men who ate their
meager portions of rice every day—who ate lizards, rats, and
worms, when they could find them—they survived. Those who
hoarded their food to have one, big meal—they died. The prisoners themselves could predict this. They knew the "rice happy"
ones were going to die. The rebellious prisoners quickly per-
ished. The men who gave up all hope and became depressed
died. As one of the patients himself expressed it when he was
questioned about how he managed to survive: "I just put my
mind in neutral."

Emanuel Windholz [4] has suggested that in apathy the over-

---

[3] See also Greenson (1944).
[4] Personal communication.

whelmed ego revives phylogenetically older mechanisms. The individual acts as though he were dead in order to avoid death. This phenomenon has been observed among lower animals and is known as the *Totstellreflex*. Living in this restricted, vegetative fashion was a means of conserving energy in order to maintain life (Simmel, 1944b).

V

The recovery of the apathetic patient is similar to that of the grief-stricken patient. The improvement is based on a mechanism which resembles, in reverse, the work of mourning in melancholia (Freud, 1917a). Grief is overcome in the grief-stricken patient by his resolving his attachment to the lost object piece by piece in various familiar situations, until the lost object is renounced in the external world and has been internalized. The apathetic patient renounces not an object but the whole world. He recovers by saying hello bit by bit to the world and to many objects he lost. During this process he relapses again and again into his state of not believing that he is no longer abandoned. For example, Americans freed from Japanese prisoner of war camps continued to eat voraciously many months after they had more than regained their lost weight. One officer had to repeat to himself every time he saw his wife, "Yes, it's true, it's really true. I'm back, this is real." When his wife left, he would become apathetic and only upon seeing her again would he become alert and responsive. Little by little, the apathetic patient gives up the constant image of disappointments and frustrations; lost objects are reinstated into the world and are once again charged with libidinal cathexis.

The only adequate treatment for these patients was to remove the basic etiological factor, namely, the deprivation. In the mild cases, warm, humane treatment and good food were enough. For the more severe cases, the army could not provide the love and care they needed. Sending these men home was the only hope for adequate treatment.

The prognosis for reestablishing the prewar mental equilibrium is favorable in the mild cases. Belligerence and hostility in the previously apathetic patient are hopeful signs.

On the basis of clinical observations I believe that apathy is a specific response to traumatic deprivation. In certain war neuroses apathy was found to be a defense against overwhelming feelings of annihilation. This defense was accomplished by restricting the ego's function of perception of and response to internal and external stimuli. Apathetic reactions also occur in the catatonic, the depressed, and the bored individual.

3

The Mother Tongue
and the Mother

(1950)

I

T HE ACQUISITION OF SPEECH marks a turning point in the psychological development of the human being. The use of words for purposes of communication signals the end of infancy and the beginning of childhood. Language is the organized system of verbal productions which has been established and perpetuated by the culture and which is now available to the individual. In this paper I attempt to investigate those factors which decisively influence the conscious and unconscious attitudes toward language and speech. The clinical material is based largely on the following case:

A thirty-five-year-old intelligent and attractive woman sought psychoanalytic treatment because of a sleep disturbance. Ever since the birth of her first child, she was unable to sleep in the same room with anyone and was terrified of resorting to sedatives. She feared the drug might not help her and that she might eventually become an addict. The patient was married to

Presented at the 16th International Psycho-Analytical Congress, Zürich, August 1949. First published in *International Journal of Psycho-Analysis*, 31:18-23, 1950.

a man much older than herself and had three children. She was Austrian by birth and had lived in Austria until the age of eighteen, when she came to America.

The first year of her analysis proceeded relatively smoothly and seemed to follow the course one would expect in a hysteric. The fear of *not* falling asleep was revealed to cover a still stronger fear of falling asleep in the presence of someone. Falling asleep meant losing control, and losing control meant becoming sexual. Sexuality had become repressed and was linked up with a strong oedipal attachment to the father associated with guilt feelings and enormous hostility to the mother.

A new development in the analysis occurred when the patient, under the impact of a strong, positive transference, started a relationship with a married man. This man was loved, worshiped and adored, while his wife was hated and envied. The obvious transference and oedipal nature of this affair was interpreted, but this brought no change in the relationship. At first, the affair seemed to represent an opportunity for forbidden sexual satisfaction, but this determinant proved to be secondary. Certain specific characteristics of the sexual behavior pointed to a more infantile origin of this conduct. The patient wanted intercourse every time and all the time she was with her lover. Orgasms were unimportant; what she wanted was to feel his penis within her because it made her feel full, rich, and warm. Without it she felt empty, poor, and cold. When she was away from him, she longed for him hungrily and was constantly tormented by jealousy fantasies. Gradually she became aware that this man was selfish, arrogant, and somewhat stupid, but this in no way influenced her longings to be with him. The only change in the patient's clinical picture at this time was that she was no longer afraid to sleep with someone in the room and was no longer afraid of becoming addicted. The reason for the latter is obvious—she had become addicted. Only now, instead of being addicted to sedatives, she was addicted to her lover. Fenichel (1949), Annie Reich (1940) and Frances Deri (n.d.) have described somewhat similar pictures in their work on the problem of extreme submissiveness in women.

The tenacity of the patient's addiction to the married man and the futility of all interpretations in a hitherto cooperative patient led to my conviction that the addiction served an important defensive purpose in addition to all the other meanings. This point of view was confirmed when new material came to the surface concerning some vague and fleeting memories of early childhood phobias. These phobias alluded to a fear of the night, a fear of water, and a fear of falling into a deep hole. The patient's resistances also changed at this point; whereas she had previously spoken easily and fluently and had had many vivid dreams, now there were hours with little to say and difficulty in remembering dreams. This was particularly manifest when an attempt was made to get the patient to talk about her mother. She would exclaim instantly and hotly that she hated her mother and that there had never been any warmth, affection, or tenderness between them. Previously when the patient had found it difficult to express herself in English, she had been quite ready to speak in German, but now she became reluctant to do so. One day she recounted a dream:

> I dreamed of a glass bowl and a baby girl was drowning in it. I wondered if the baby were dead. The baby had drops of water and honey on her face and I felt a great love for her.

Her associations concerned the fact that although she had talked about her fear of water, she was reluctant to think about it. She had the feeling she was the girl in the dream, and that was remarkable, because usually she dreamed of herself as a little boy. Honey was a cough remedy that her father used when he was ill with tuberculosis. Her father had died when she was six years old. The first interpretation made reference to the patient's childhood fears concerning the water in the chamber pots they used. These fears probably occurred at the time that she was worried about the question of being a boy or a girl. The patient responded to this that she now remembered having dreamed this dream in German. I suggested that she speak German, but she reacted initially with anxiety and said, "I am afraid. I don't want to talk German. I have the feeling that talking in German I shall have to remember something I wanted to forget."

In the first hour in which she spoke German the patient expressed her fear of having to say obscene words in that tongue. They were much easier to say, and were much "cleaner," in English. Then her thoughts turned to *Nachttopf.* "A chamber pot becomes alive if you say *Nachttopf.* It is ugly and disgusting and smells bad. In English a chamber pot is much cleaner. In German I am a scared, dirty child; in English I am a nervous, refined woman."

The course of the analysis changed at this point. The transference which had been of a positive, fatherly nature now took a negative turn, and the analyst became a disapproving, critical mother figure. Her husband, who had been sexually taboo because he was considered a father image, was now revealed to represent a nagging, fault-finding mother. The material which now came to the surface concerned anal activities, with many dreams and vague memories of dirty beds, spots on the mattress, sitting on the chamber pot, etc.

Then came a series of dreams full of great anxiety, of which the following is a sample:

> I have to cross a bridge and down below are crocodiles. One of them seems to be devouring a man. Then the crocodile turns into a man. This was unbearably frightening and I awoke, only to fall asleep again. Then I dreamed I was on a big bed and on it a man and woman were sleeping. I screamed and awakened the people in the dream.

Her associations to the dream evoked a memory of her dread of going to the dentist when she was about four. This reminded her of her first analytic hour and her great fear of opening her mouth. Then she recalled a fragment of a hitherto forgotten dream where her girlfriend was pregnant and spat a lump out of her mouth which was an embryo. The crocodiles in the dream looked like a penis. The interpretations revolved around the patient's oral-sadistic misinterpretation of the primal scene. In response to this the patient related how poverty-stricken they had been in her childhood and how she had loved to eat corn on the cob and asparagus. When she came to America she ate asparagus almost daily, because she could not believe that it was true that she could have it any time she wanted it.

This dream and others of a similar content gradually led to the remobilization of an old fantasy. This fantasy concerned the image of a preoedipal, devouring mother with a phallus.

This patient could never call her mother *Mutter*. There was something sensual in this word, and she was always ashamed to use it. Instead she would use some diminutive form like *Mutterl* or *Mutti*. She then recalled that even more difficult for her than the word *Mutter* was the word *Busen* (bosom). She became aware that quite early in life she found her mother an "unappetizing," loathsome creature.

Early in the analysis her sexual dreams concerned men with huge, hard, dry penises. Moist and soft meant dirty to her. Then there was an occasional dream of a man with a limp, soft penis, which was somehow pleasurable. During the German-speaking phase of her analysis she was fascinated by the idea of watching a penis ejaculate. Still later on there were dreams of naked women and homosexual dreams. At first these dreams were accompanied by anxiety or repugnance. Finally, there was a dream in which she watched a man and a woman having intercourse, but her entire attention was focused on the woman's nipples. The woman's breasts were huge and her nipples were lacquered. In this dream she was surprised to feel how sexually excited she was. The scene for this dream was a European hotel which had dirty toilets but was being remodeled. The focus of attention on the woman's breasts, the largeness of these breasts, and the fact that the nipples were lacquered all indicate the intense cathexis with which the breast was now charged. Her recent interest in the soft, limp penis and fascination with the ejaculating penis were forerunners of this piece of insight. It was now clear that one of the most important determinants of this patient's stubborn preoccupation with the penis was the fact that it served as a screen for her more deeply repressed longings for the breast. In the dream the European hotel with the dirty toilets being remodeled rather transparently indicates the patient's awareness of the changes which the therapy was accomplishing.

During this period there was much working through in German of what had already been covered in English, specifically the obscene words and images which heretofore had only been expressed in English. For example: to masturbate in English was to masturbate politely. The word *Onanie* meant to masturbate with fantasies, fantasies concerning her mother and father. In English one masturbates like a lady and one has no fantasies. The change in the imagery was accompanied by a change in the sexual satisfaction from masturbation. Before there was little sensation, little pleasure, and much dissatisfied tension. Now for the first time the patient could feel clitoral sensations and could have orgasms which were strong and would induce sleep. In German her lover did not exist as a vigorous force. He existed only in English. As her relationship to her mother began to dominate the picture, the importance of her lover began to dwindle. As she worked through her feelings toward the preoedipal, phallic mother, she lost all interest in this man and was able to renounce him completely.

For approximately three months all the analytic sessions were carried on in German. During this time most of her dreams were in German. Later on the language of the interviews varied, sometimes in English, sometimes German, with the patient choosing the language. Only when specific resistances against remembering or recapturing feelings about the mother occurred I suggested that the patient talk German. Toward the end of the analysis the patient spoke almost completely in English and there was no difference in her productions, no matter what the language spoken.

II

The clinical material presented thus far, incomplete and sketchy as it is, touches upon many different important theoretical and technical problems. I shall limit my comments to only a few of the many questions. (Some aspects of this case are discussed further in chapters 6, 9, and 21.)

To begin with, it might be fruitful to study the indications for the use of a second language in an analysis by comparing this maneuver with the use of obscene words or childhood expressions during the analysis. Ferenczi's (1911) classical paper on this subject illuminates many important considerations. He pointed out that obscene expressions are usually closely connected to oedipal fantasies, the sex life of the parents, questions about pregnancy and birth. There is a further close connection between obscene words, curses, and pregenital impulses. Freud (1905c) demonstrated that obscene words have the peculiar power of forcing the listener to imagine the thing referred to in a concrete, realistic way. This does not happen in using adult language or scientific expressions. The obscene words force the listener to a regressive, hallucinatory reexperience of memory pictures. Originally all words have a hallucinatory quality. In the beginning words are associated to wish-fulfilling, visual images. Only gradually does the child learn to distinguish these images from reality. With maturation and the increasing development of the ego, the child learns to distinguish between these images and thoughts. Eventually this process ends with the capacity for abstract thinking. This is not accomplished at one stroke, but continues back and forth throughout childhood. Children treat words as though they were objects, which is characteristic of the primary process. This also happens in the dreams of adults. Obscene words retain a closer tie to visual imagery and to muscle innervation than do ordinary words. For purposes of communication most words lose this hallucinatory component in order to facilitate their more economic use. The exception to this rule occurs when the images associated to words concern conflictual situations. These words then remain the living bearers of unresolved conflicts. Since the learning of language occurs primarily during the first years of life, it is understandable that those words associated to the most important emotional conflicts of the first years of life, namely, the pregenital conflicts, will be more likely to retain their visual, hallucinatory character. Obscene words are predominantly pregenital words.

In the case presented above, the language problem concerned not only the use of obscene words but also the use of the mother tongue. The structure of this difficulty, however, was identical with the structure of the problem to be found in the use of obscene words. The mother tongue was the pregenital tongue and the bearer of important unresolved conflicts.

The technical questions which come to the fore in considering the use of obscene words or infantile mannerisms of speech in analysis are primarily problems concerning dosage, timing, and resistance. In each situation the therapist must weigh the consequences of his using or refraining from using the obscene expression. Sometimes the obscenity helps break through a piece of resistance, as obtains when the patient needs to know that the analyst really is not shocked by pregenital strivings. On the other hand, the premature use of such expressions may frighten the patient or it may serve as a transference gratification or be felt as a provocation and seduction to exhibitionistic or scoptophilic acting out. The same indications and contraindications were applicable in the above-mentioned case in regard to the mother tongue as one ordinarily considers in patients regarding the use of obscenities.

The *new* language, in this case English, offered this patient an opportunity to build up a new defensive system against her past infantile life. Edith Buxbaum (1949) demonstrated this very point. In her paper she accented the superego qualities that the new language assumes. (Her clinical evidence, however, seemed to indicate that the foreign tongue helped to repress incestuous memories and feelings which would have been more accessible in the mother tongue.) The new language by successfully aiding the defenses against the old infantile impulses helps to create a new and somewhat better interstructural relationship. By this additional wave of repression, new values and new ego images are set up. Erikson's (1946) conception of ego identity is helpful in these considerations. A new language offers an opportunity for the establishment of a new self-portrait. This may supplant the old images, or new images may coexist along with the old, which might lead to a kind of "multiple" personality. These considerations, however, are beyond the scope of this paper.

The use of the mother tongue was a technique designed to help to break through the strong defenses which isolated the old structural constellation from the newer one. The German language was the vehicle which established contact between her newer, more conscious self and the old, isolated one. It made possible a working through of many insights which heretofore in the therapy had been experienced only in the newer ego identity.[1]

In this particular case the most interesting phenomenon was the relationship between the mother tongue and the mother. True, the new language helped to maintain in repression and isolation some oedipal and anal material. However, it was the recovery of the feelings and attitudes connected with the preoedipal mother which made possible the final resolution of this neurosis.

Previously there was an attachment to men, seemingly like an oedipal fixation. The addictlike quality of this attachment,

[1] This patient could not have been successfully analyzed, I believe, by someone who did not speak German. In my book, *The Technique and Practice of Psychoanalysis* (1967a), I present the difficulties of analyzing a black man. This patient used to speak to me in "Uncle Tom talk" until I had raised his fee to a "white man's fee" (p. 352f.). If there had been a black psychoanalyst available, the patient would have had a better analysis, I believe. Whenever it is determined that the new language is being used as a defense against the old self image, we have to think of changing analysts.

At other times, however, I find that being conversant with the patient's mother tongue is valuable but *not* decisive. A case in point is that of Professor X, who spoke of his childhood humiliations. I had used the Yiddish word *pischer* because he spoke Yiddish as a boy and to add impact to the childishness of his mortification (Greenson, 1967a, p. 385f.). A longer interpretation without the Yiddish word would also have worked, but not as quickly or as succinctly. Whenever stalemated situations occur regularly in psychoanalysis, one should consider the possibility that the patient and the analyst are not communicating on the same wavelength. For example, I would not refer a Brooklyn-bred girl who is now a Hollywood starlet to a prim, cultured, central European analyst. They would not speak the same language.

however, indicated that this was a screen for an oral relationship to men, and behind this, an oral relationship to the mother. The quality of the patient's longing was identical with Ruth Mack Brunswick's (1940) description of the preoedipal oral longings for the breast. These demands go back to a period when putting something in the mouth and swallowing bring about an oceanic feeling. This is not an object relationship but is an attempt to re-establish that archaic unity of breast and mouth (Lewin, 1946). At one point the patient stated, "I don't want to have the penis in my vagina. I only want to look at it. Then I can see it and remember it and I will have it in my mind forever after." (Incidentally, this also bears out the oral factor in scopto-philia.)

Perhaps the fantasy of the mother with a phallus represents on the one hand a longing for the union with the mother's breast as well as a recathexis of the mother's breast with penis qualities during the early castration conflicts of childhood. The phallic mother is the last stand of the preoedipal mother fixation. (The anatomical tongue of the mother may play a special role in this situation since it offers a concrete substitute for this concep-tion of a mother with a phallus. This patient's preoccupation with a soft, limp, moist penis and her fantasy of the hidden phal-lus of the mother hint in this direction.)

III

How generally valid is this relationship between mother and mother tongue? The very term *mother tongue* implies a close relationship between mother and speech. In Western civili-zation the first language is called the mother tongue (Schrecker, 1949). Margaret Mead[2] has stated that even in societies where the women speak a different language from the men, the mother's language is first taught to all the children by the mother and only later do the boys learn the father's language.

[2] Personal communication.

Most of our clinical knowledge about patients with speech disorders stresses primarily the anal-sadistic conflicts around the use of language. Fenichel (1945) emphasized in addition the oral and exhibitionistic conflicts. Glauber (1951) contends that the decisive factor for the development of the stutterer is a disturbed oral relationship of the mother toward her child. In general, it is well known that language which is felt as beautiful and poetic is perceived not as an anal product but as an oral offering. "Obscenities are shit, but poetry is milk and honey." This can be observed both in the clinic and in literature. Patients who like to hear the sounds of the analyst's voice are reexperiencing the drinking in of milk. It is quite typical to talk of words pouring forth, streaming out, or to speak of drinking in the sounds and words of others (Wormhoudt, 1949).

Sapir (1921), the anthropological philologist, has stressed that there is no strict organ of speech and that all the organs used for speech are only secondarily employed in this capacity, their primary functions being elsewhere. Children brought up without exposure to speech do not talk. Before making sounds becomes a means of communication it serves only as an auto-erotic discharge opportunity and cannot be considered language. The production of sounds becomes language only when it is used for communication. A crucial factor in the development of speech seems to be the auditory sphere. Isakower (1939) has demonstrated the importance of the auditory sphere in establishing permanent introjections. The parental figures are incorporated within the ego in the form of spoken commands and prohibitions. Language is the most important vehicle for this phenomenon. The relationship between words and objects is therefore closely connected with the functions of the superego. There is something like a moral quality in finding the "right" word.

In all ego developments which represent a transition from passivity to activity, identification is the significant mechanism (Brunswick, 1940). Thus it appears that the auditory incorporation of words is a critical factor in the maturation of the child. Speech is a means of retaining a connection with the mother as well as a means of becoming separated from her. The child who suckled at the mother's breast now replaces this by introjecting a new liquid of the mother—sounds. In addition, the child now has the opportunity to repeat actively this old passive gratification. Thus the child replaces passivity and mother attachment by activity and mother identification via the language. It can easily be imagined, therefore, that the earliest relationship between child and mother's breast will have a decisive influence on the relationship of the child to his or her mother tongue.[3]

Observations on learning a new language confirm some of these hypotheses. Stengel (1939) described some differences between children and adults learning a new language. The child uses simple and complete identification and echolalia is typical. The adult tries to learn the language rationally. Learning a new language involves introjecting new objects, and resistances to giving up the old objects may become an obstacle in this process. It is well known that there is a reluctance to give a new name to an old object. It is easier to take on new words and a new vocabulary than to take on a new accent and new intonation. Vocabulary and grammar can be learned rationally, but accent, tone, and rhythm have to be imitated, i.e., incorporated. It is this inner core of language, so intimately related to the earliest child-mother relationship, which is so difficult for adults to change. Probably, the facility in learning a new language is also determined by the outcome of the early relationship to the mother. The patient described above had a remarkable fluency in speaking English. She had an unusually large vocabulary, and spoke grammatically, with a mere trace of a foreign accent. She wanted to incorporate new objects and in her new language she found a suitable opportunity. It would be interesting to study cases where there is a stubborn persistence of the mother-tongue

---

[3] In this context see Anna Freud's and Sophie Dann's (1951) description of the development of a group of children who spent their first years in a concentration camp. They showed related problems in the development of object relations and language.

accent in the new language, in order to investigate whether un-resolved fixations to the mother are operative.

I have attempted to demonstrate the way in which a pa-tient's emotions and attitudes toward her mother tongue were specifically determined by her preoedipal, oral, mother fixation. Further, I believe that the early mechanisms of auditory incor-poration and identification necessary for learning to speak and learning a new language are decisively influenced by the outcome of the conflicts between mother, breast, and child.

4

On Boredom

(1953)

I

BOREDOM IS A PHENOMENON which is easier to describe than to define. The uniqueness of the feeling of being bored seems to depend upon the coexistence of the following components: a state of dissatisfaction and a disinclination to action; a state of longing and an inability to designate what is longed for; a sense of emptiness; a passive, expectant attitude with the hope that the external world will supply the satisfaction; a distorted sense of time in which time seems to stand still. (The German word for boredom is *Langeweile*— which, literally translated, means "long time.")

Boredom is seen to occur in healthy people as a transient state. In the neurotic, boredom usually does not play an important role since the patient is preoccupied with anxieties, depressions, frustrations, and obsessions. In the psychoses, boredom

Presented at the Annual Meeting of the American Psychoanalytic Association, Cincinnati, May 1951. First published in *Journal of the American Psychoanalytic Association*, 1:7-21, 1953.

proper is rarely described, but we do see similar reactions in apathy and in the depressions.

I propose to investigate, on the basis of clinical material, the various dynamic and structural factors responsible for the state of boredom. The most systematic and comprehensive analysis of this subject was made by Fenichel (1934b), who demonstrated that the bored person is in a state of dammed-up instinctual tension, but the objects and aims are repressed. He described two forms of boredom, one characterized by motor calmness, the other by motor restlessness; but he found the same essential pathology. He, and later Spitz (1937), depicted the peculiar role of monotony in producing both states of high excitement and boredom. In addition, Fenichel indicated the importance of orality and sketched briefly some connections between boredom, depersonalization, and depression. Other writers, namely, Ferenczi (1919a), Spitz (1937), Winterstein (1930), and Bergler (1945) have contributed to one or another aspect of the problem. In further exploring boredom, I shall place particular emphasis on the disturbances in the thinking processes, the vicissitudes of the oral impulses, and the defense mechanisms involved in this syndrome.

A twenty-nine-year-old, attractive married woman with four children entered analysis with the chief complaint that she was terribly bored. For the past five years, her main preoccupation was trying to fill up her empty life. Her husband, her children, her many acquaintances, her social activities, all bored her. She had tried various hobbies, took lessons of all sorts, had begun drinking, had become promiscuous—all to no avail. Her life remained empty. She could not get emotionally involved with anybody or anything and her only aim was to kill time, to push the hours away, hoping the intolerable boredom would somehow vanish. About a year before coming to treatment she had gone through an acute depression, but after a suicide attempt with sedatives the depression disappeared and the old feeling of boredom returned.

The relevant part of the patient's present situation can be summarized as follows: Her husband was a kindly man whom she had married ten years previously because he was wealthy and good to her. She was fond of him but had never loved him. In recent years she noted an increasing resentment toward her husband because of some of his characteristics which she considered "motherly." He was overly protective toward the children, extremely emotional with them, and completely inconsistent. The patient herself was fond of the children, but only in a rather distant way. She was unable to become really emotionally involved with them and felt much more like their sister than their mother. She had no idea of how to spend time with them, how to talk or how to play with them. She hired a nursemaid to care for them and rarely saw them.

The patient's recent sexual history revealed that she had been faithful to her husband for many years and had started having extramarital affairs only when her boredom became extreme. She enjoyed these affairs because of the intrigue; they were interesting and diverted her mind. Her sexual satisfaction was greater with her husband, however.

Since the onset of the boredom, the patient had taken to drinking quite heavily and consumed about ten to fifteen alcoholic drinks per day. She did not consider herself an alcoholic, since, in her social sphere, this quantity of drinking was usual. Her own reason for drinking was that it made her feel pleasantly quiet and it made the time pass quickly.

The significant past history of this patient disclosed that her father had deserted the family when the patient was two and a half years of age and she was abandoned by her mother at three. From that time on the patient lived with grandparents, aunts and uncles, being shifted about at irregular intervals. From time to time her mother would visit and spend time with her.

The patient's mother was a warmhearted, irresponsible, promiscuous, alcoholic woman. In the first years of life the patient yearned for this mother because she was so warm and giving in her ways in contrast to the cold, austere grandparents. Later on she turned against her, felt great conscious hatred toward her and was determined never to become the kind of woman her mother was. During the course of the analysis the fear of becoming like her mother was uncovered to be one of the dominant anxieties in the patient's life.

The patient's early sexual history is noteworthy because of the many traumas and because of the ease with which she was able to recall these experiences. From age two she could remember primal scenes; at age four she experienced cunnilingus with dogs; somewhat later there were doctor games, and before six clitoral masturbation. At twelve there was a resumption of masturbation, at fifteen the first heterosexual experience. She had an abortion at age sixteen, syphilis at seventeen, a homosexual affair at eighteen, and indulged in various perverse acts until nineteen, when she was married. Most of these activities were pursued because they were a means of establishing an interpersonal relationship. The patient felt she had little else to offer anyone and she was grateful for any emotional warmth shown her. The search for sexual satisfaction was an unimportant factor in this behavior.

II

The analysis began with the patient pouring forth a flood of memories with much painful affect. It was striking that these memories had not been repressed but were readily available. With the production of these memories and the affects connected with them, the boredom vanished; instead the patient became tearful and depressed. This, however, she felt as a relief from her usually torturesome boredom. Within two weeks after the recital of the many traumatic events, the boredom returned and it was now possible to study more minutely what this boredom represented. It quickly became clear that in the bored state the affects connected with the traumatic events were repressed. When she was bored it was possible to get her to describe a traumatic event, but this was done without any emotion. The initial welling up of strong affect was possible because of a strong early positive transference. The return of the boredom indicated the reestablishment of the old defenses, directed against affects primarily, not against memories.

During the bored state the patient would describe her feelings as follows: "I can't get with it. I'm nowhere. I'm gone. I feel empty. I am constantly hungry, but I don't know what for." During these periods she would drink excessively, usually awakening with an amnesia for the evening's events. At these times the patient would experience short-lived, acute obsessional ideas concerning the fear of becoming fat and she would go through periods of alternately starving herself to undo this and stuffing herself to celebrate her accomplishment. Wulff (1932) described a picture of food addiction with this manic-depressive undertone. She consumed a great deal of time looking at her image in the mirror, carefully scrutinizing her figure to determine any minute changes. She squandered hours in beauty parlors and at cosmetic counters and had frequent massages. In the evenings she would watch television for hours on end. It was at these times that she hungrily searched for a sexual affair because it would give her something to think about.

During this phase of the analysis it was characteristic for the patient to report in exact detail the trivia of her daily life. It was particularly striking that she was never silent and although she would describe activities and happenings, she never voluntarily talked of her emotions or thoughts. Her statement, "I can't get with it; I'm nowhere," represents her awareness of the fight against feelings, impulses, and fantasies. The struggle against the fantasies was a key point of her defenses. This patient would experience the most vivid night dreams, yet her associations went to the day remnants and then on to the minutiae of her everyday life. There was no link from the night dreams via associations to fantasies, thoughts, or memories. Yet she was apt to describe other people's fantasies very readily. She could imagine what her friends might be imagining. Her night dreams were so vivid that she ususally felt them to be real. Often her husband would relate that she spoke or acted out something in these dreams. The content of these dreams dealt primarily with some traumatic event of early childhood; but her defenses when awake rendered the recital of these dreams into a monotonous performance.

The absence of fantasies was most vividly demonstrated in

the patient's sexual life. In order to reach orgasm it was necessary for her husband to tell her stories of some sexual perversion which he had committed or imagined in the past. The epitome of this kind of behavior was using pornographic motion pictures projected on a screen in the bedroom prior to intercourse. Even in masturbation the patient would get bored because she had "nothing to think about." (In the past, however, she had been able to obtain autoerotic satisfaction by imagining cunnilingus being performed on her, usually by a dog or a woman.)

The impoverishment of the fantasy production also manifested itself in the patient's language. She spoke in a very simple slang and used a minimum of words. Her description of her bored state was typical. "I'm gone. I'm nothing. I'm nowhere." An evening's conversation with friends was dismissed with "Some friends dropped over for some routine dialogue." If she changed her coiffure, she would ask me, "How do you like my new *type*?" If I made an interpretation which was meaningful, the patient would simply say, "Bong!" If the interpretation seemed far-fetched, her response would be, "No bong." Her language contained a minimum of metaphor and verbal imagery. Metaphor is personal and individual and is determined by the speaker's specific past history (Sharpe, 1940). In this patient's language one sees her struggle against individuality, against her own past history. Further, the concreteness and the condensation character of her speech have the qualities typical for the primary process rather than the secondary process. The patient's responses to interpretations, "bong" and "no-bong," are typical examples of this. It seems that her ego could use the primary process and not only be overwhelmed by it. Freud (1905c) in his explanation of wit and Kris (1950) in his paper on preconscious mental processes describe related phenomena (see also Freud, 1915c; Goldstein, 1944).

The inhibition of the fantasy life of bored people has been stressed by Fenichel (1934b) and Winterstein (1930. The analysis revealed that fantasies (and even thinking and feeling) had to be fought against since they were a threat. Freud (1915c) described the unique position of fantasy among the mental phenomena, in that it possesses both preconscious and unconscious qualities. Kris (1950) stressed the point that in fantasy more libidinal and aggressive energy is discharged than in effective thinking, where neutralized energy is used. Fantasy is closer to the id and the primary process than reflective thinking. Thus fantasy is closely linked to both voluntary motility and involuntary discharge. In addition, since visual imagery was particularly exciting for this patient, as manifested in her sexual practices, it was imperative that fantasy be curtailed. It is pertinent to recall that the patient's night dreams were extremely vivid; most of the time they felt real to her. This can be construed to mean that as long as motility was blocked by sleep, it was possible for her to endure strong visual imagery. Furthermore, fantasy depends on and leads to memory. For this patient, to remember meant either to feel the traumatic abandonment of early childhood or the guilt feelings and anxieties derived from her later experiences. Thus the motive for the ego's inhibition of fantasy seems to be based on the fact that fantasy could lead either to dangerous actions or to painful remembrances. Throughout her analysis when states of boredom were lifted one could see the transition either to severe depressive reactions or to impulse-ridden behavior.

The method by which this inhibition was achieved is more difficult to formulate. The answer seems to lie in the shifts of cathexis required for the perception of preconscious thought. The censorship between systems Cs. and Pcs. prevents the necessary hypercathexis or the connection to verbal imagery, thus blocking the gateway to consciousness and to motility (Freud, 1900; Rapaport, 1950; Kris, 1950). In general, one sees in this patient a severe disturbance in the thinking processes of the ego. The contrast between the vividness of the dream imagery and the emotional impoverishment of the waking thoughts indicates the patient's struggle against perceiving her fantasies. It also indicates the losing struggle, in the sense that the dreams seemed more real. This would indicate the weakness of the ego's ability to defend itself from the affects attempting to break through into consciousness. Freud (1940) and later Lewin (1950) describe such phenomena in discussing psychotic states.

III

Despite the seeming absence of drives during the apathetic bored intervals it was possible to discern some remnants of libidinal strivings. The most prominent feeling in this patient was the sensation of emptiness, which she construed to mean hunger. She was afraid to eat, since eating would make her fat, and being fat would make her like her mother. She was also unable to accept being a mother, for this meant she would be *her* mother. As stated above, she did not feel like her children's mother, but rather like an older sister. The many-sidedness of this struggle was evident in her frequent failures at dieting, her marrying a "motherly" man, and in her preference for cunnilingus. To be fat meant to be well fed, contented; but it also meant to be like her mother, to be dirty, to have a vagina, and to be unlovable. To be thin was to be clean, to be a penis, and to be worthy of love. Yet thinness meant to be empty and to be constantly hungry. The few times in her life when she was relatively content were when she was pregnant, for then she was full, but not yet a mother. After delivery she was impelled to combat the awareness of being a mother.

The drinking was, at first, a defense against the impulse to eat. Later on it was a means of becoming unconscious, i.e., to have an orgasm. Drinking meant she was able to indulge in sexuality without having to remember her fantasies. Drinking also gave her a feeling of having something in her without feeling unpleasantly full. The patient claimed that when she drank she felt quiet. Finally, drinking also meant to be like her mother, and thus eventually was also intolerable.

The promiscuity which was prevalent before the analysis was basically a means of maintaining some semblance of interpersonal relationship. In her homosexual relationships, the patient usually sought strong, protective women, who would do things for her sexually. The promiscuity and the homosexuality had to be renounced when they became linked to the patient's conception of her mother.

The analysis revealed that the patient's primary libidinal orientation was focused on her oral strivings, which is in accord with Fenichel's findings. On the surface the libidinal aim was passive, i.e., the wish to be sucked. For the patient, this symbolized the greatest token of being loved; it was a means of simultaneously gratifying libidinal and narcissistic needs. It was an attempt to undo the traumatic deprivation of her early childhood. It was interesting that when cunnilingus was being performed upon her, she felt like the little one who was being cared for by the adult— man or woman was unimportant. But beneath this passive oral impulse there was an active oral striving to "melt" her mouth into the genitals of another woman (Fenichel, 1934b). At these times she would describe her aim as wanting to lose the awareness of the boundary between her mouth and the woman's genitals. This was the most deeply repressed and the most resistant unconscious impulse. This patient, despite her conscious hostility and contempt for her mother and her fear of becoming like her mother, unconsciously was searching for an oral reunion with her mother. She wanted to reestablish the infantile unity of mother and child via the mouth. The acute depression one year prior to the analysis was precipitated by a sudden, irrational jealousy of her husband's relationship with a woman very similar to her mother.

It was possible to observe how this patient in her struggles against these impulses had attempted to give up object relationships and had regressed to identifications in various forms. Then, when these identifications proved threatening, she attempted to renounce all actions reminiscent of her mother, became withdrawn and more narcissistically oriented. The looking in the mirror, her preoccupation with her body, the occasional choice of homosexual partners who resembled herself, all pointed in this direction. This narcissistic withdrawal, however, brought with it the feeling of not being here, of being gone, which also was painful, but which served the purpose of denying the existence of her body with the incorporated mother image. Her attempts to escape from the nothingness then led her back in the direction of unconsciously seeking a relationship to a woman, or a man, like her mother. Thus this patient vacillated between different kinds of object relationships with men or women who were mothers in some aspects of their relationship to her, but she could not maintain one where motherliness and sexuality were combined. When the awareness of the motherliness became too clear, she resorted to finding new sexual objects which led to promiscuity, only once again to be reminded of her mother. The vicissitudes of the patient's attempts to cope with her oral-incorporative urges toward her mother are reminiscent of the struggle between superego, ego, and introject in psychotic depressions (Freud, 1917a; Abraham, 1924; Fenichel, 1945; Lewin, 1950). A part of this patient's object relationships was aimed at finding a good introject in order to neutralize the bad introject which had already been incorporated.[1] This is similar to the question of good food versus bad food (Rado, 1933), which obsessed her during her struggles with eating.

Apparently, one of the ways this patient was able to avoid a psychotic depression was by discharging different oral-incorporative impulses in eating, fasting, drinking, homosexuality, cunnilingus, and pregnancy. However, she was not merely an impulse-ridden personality; her main complaint was boredom. Most of the time she did not feel driven. On the contrary, she complained of feeling empty and longed to fill up the emptiness. A further study of this feeling of emptiness and of the mechanisms responsible for it provides the key to the understanding of her boredom.

IV

The feeling of emptiness combined with a sense of longing and an absence of fantasies and thoughts which would lead to satisfaction is characteristic for boredom. In patients who suffer

[1] The nature of this patient's identifications is discussed further in chapter 6.

from apathy we also find a feeling of emptiness, but here there is no more longing and a far greater inhibition of the ego's thinking and perceptive functions (see chapter 2). In the depressions, too, there is a feeling of emptiness, but it is the world which is felt as empty; the self is sensed as heavy, weighted down, or low. Further, in depressions there is a rich, though morbid, fantasy life concerning specific objects or their derivatives.

The emptiness in boredom is in the first place due to the repression of the forbidden instinctual aims and objects along with the inhibition in imagination. However, there seem to be additional determinants for this empty feeling. Emptiness represents hunger. The patient ate, drank, looked at television or in the mirror when bored. Most bored persons resort to oral activities. The bored individual's feeling of emptiness is similar to the experience of the child waiting hungrily for the breast. The aim and object, sucking, breast, and mother, are repressed, however, and only the feeling of emptiness remains. It seems that we are dealing here with the substitution of a sensation for a fantasy. Instead of having imagery involving derivatives of her mother and her longing, the patient regressed to a more archaic thought form and perceived, instead, a sensation of emptiness. This is a manifestation of ego regression, a primitivization of ego functions, to use Kris's term (1950). This phenomenon brings fantasy closer to the id and the primary process. The emptiness is not merely a sensation, however, it is a psychic representation (Isaacs, 1948). This conception may be expressed as follows: the emptiness represents the hungry child with the image of "no-mother," "no-breast," "mother-will-not-come." (This may help to explain the agonizing slowness of the passage of time in these patients. The experience of time seems to be dependent upon delay of impulse discharge. Excessive discharge delay seems to slow down the passage of time, whereas quick impulse discharge makes time seem to pass quickly [Fenichel, 1934b; Rapaport, 1950].)

If we return to the problem of the feeling of emptiness, it seems plausible that the formulation of the hungry child with the image of "no-mother" may also represent an attempt to deny that the mother was incorporated within the patient. It may be that through the boredom the patient was saying: "It is not true that my mother is within me. I'm just a little baby waiting hungrily for some satisfaction." The denial of the introjection appears to be the decisive defense mechanism which made it possible for this patient to develop boredom and at the same time to ward off a severe depressive reaction.[2] The mechanism of denial is further illustrated by the fact that the bored person often claims to be in a state of lack of tension, and boredom has been described as a displeasureful lack of tension. The denial seems to becloud the fact that the patient is full of tension, but it is a special kind of tension—the tension of emptiness. "The bored person is full of emptiness." Another aspect of the denial can be seen in the readiness of bored persons to describe situations and people as boring rather than to acknowledge that the bored feeling is within. "It bores me," is more ego-syntonic than "I am bored." When one is bored even the most exciting events can be felt as boring. (At this point one might speculate upon the connection between boredom and elation, which also makes extensive use of denial mechanisms [Lewin, 1950].)

The feeling of emptiness is thus seen to be overdetermined. The mechanism of denial is an important factor in producing this sensation. In this way the ego has attempted to ward off the awareness of strong oral-libidinal and aggressive-incorporative impulses. This defense succeeds since it temporarily prevents the outbreak of a severe depression or self-destructive actions. This defense failed in this case of severe boredom, since the self-inflicted deprivation stirred up feelings from the traumatic deprivation of early childhood and therefore brought with it the feeling of being overwhelmingly bored, which was also intolerable.

[2] Edith Jacobson and Edward Bibring, in discussing this paper at the Annual Meeting, stressed the fact that boredom is an affective state which is the result of certain complicated defense mechanisms. I am indebted to both discussants and to David Rapaport for many suggestions which were helpful in the final formulations.

V

The crucial therapeutic factor in this case was the transference. The patient was able to develop a strong, positive transference which eventually led to a change in the character of the incorporated objects which were now reliable and permissive. Gradually she was then able to tolerate object relationships on a higher libidinal level.

An interesting aspect of this improvement was seen in the patient's reactions to the purchase of a new and beautiful home. The patient's attitude to possessions was noteworthy. If she bought something which she liked and considered beautiful, it was not merely her possession, but it was she. She would exhibit a beautiful vase to her friends with the phrase, "Look at me." She would exclaim when she saw a pretty dress she wanted, "This is me." She did not like her rented home because it represented a part of her she preferred to disavow. It was big, rambling, i.e., fat, sloppy, like mother. The new and beautiful home was sleek, pretty, and thin; for her, it meant, "The new me, the me I want to show." Whereas previously she had often felt homeless despite her luxurious setting, she now felt "at home" with the newly purchased home with which she could identify. It should be emphasized that the patient's utterances about her possessions were always said with tongue-in-cheek, as though part of her ego were well aware of her ego boundaries.

As the apathetic bored state disappeared and fantasies began to return, one could discern a different kind of boredom: agitated boredom. Some feeling of emptiness persisted, but with the perception of fantasies the patient began to do things. The actions undertaken, however, were not satisfying and there was an atmosphere of restlessness and dissatisfaction in these activities. Fenichel (1934b) and Spitz (1937) have described the fidgetiness in children who are in a high state of conflictual excitement about the parental night noises they hear. A similar condition can also be observed in the agitated boredom of the prepuberty child. In my patient it seemed that the agitated boredom was due partly to her dissatisfaction with the available activities. In the transitional phase the real aims and objects of her instinctual demands were not yet accessible to her. Nevertheless, since body sensations had begun to become capable of translation into visual imagery and thought, the gateway to motility was opened. In a sense, however, the images and thoughts were still deflected and distorted by the persisting censorship and therefore led to the "wrong" fantasies and hence to dissatisfying actions. Many people suffer from boredom of this type. They are characterized by a great need for "diversions and distractions." The very meaning of these terms confirms the persisting censorship between impulse and action. These people do not enjoy true satisfaction and therefore have to resort to frequent "distractions."

VI

On the basis of the foregoing formulations, it now seems possible to attempt to explain the occurrence of boredom in normal people. One might construct the following sequence of events: at the behest of the superego, certain instinctual aims and/or objects have to be repressed (Spitz, 1937; Windholz, n.d.). This step results in a feeling of tension. At this point, if the ego has to inhibit fantasies and thought derivatives of these impulses because they are also too threatening, we have as a consequence a feeling of emptiness. This is perceived as a deprivation, a self-administered deprivation. We thus have a combination of instinctual tension and a vague feeling of emptiness. The instinctual tension is without direction due to the inhibition of thoughts and fantasies. Tension and emptiness are felt as a kind of hunger—stimulus hunger. Since the individual does not know for what he is hungry, he now turns to the external world, with the hope that it will provide the missing aim and/or object. I believe it is this state of affairs which is characteristic for all boredom. (If fantasies or other derivatives of forbidden impulses would break through into consciousness, there would be no boredom; instead there would be either frustration, anxiety, depression, or obsession, as we see in other neuroses.)

Boredom can occur on any level of libidinal organization. However, the hypotheses set forth above, the clinical case described, and the general experience that boredom occurs more frequently in depressed patients indicate that people with strong oral fixations are particularly predisposed to boredom. The explanation for this lies in the role played by deprivation in the production of boredom as well as in the related states of depression and apathy. Depressed people feel deprived of love, either from an external or internal object, or both. In apathy, too, traumatic deprivation plays a decisive role—only here the external world is responsible. In boredom we find a self-administered deprivation: the loss of thoughts and fantasies which would lead to satisfaction. Depressed persons are full of fantasies in their struggle to regain the unloving object. Apathetic persons have given up the struggle and their fantasy life is restricted to factors concerned with the question of survival. In boredom there is a longing for the lost satisfactions similar to what one sees in the depressions along with the feeling of emptiness characteristic for apathy.

5

On Moods and Introjects

(1954)

THIS CONTRIBUTION DEALS WITH rather complicated affects—moods.[1] The essence of this paper is to be found in the saying, "I am not myself today," an expression quite typical for people who suffer from frequent fluctuations of mood.

A mood is a compound of different affects which give a specific character or coloring to one's emotional state (Glover, 1939b). It is usually a transitory phenomenon; its duration may be long or short, but it is usually measurable in hours or days. For the most part moods last longer than single affects and shorter than attitudes which are of more chronic duration. I shall describe the analytic findings in several patients with pathological disturbances of mood in an attempt to ascertain the dynamic structure of certain moods and to make some theoretical speculations concerning the origin of moods in general.

Presented as part of the Symposium on The Psychoanalytic Theory of Affects, Annual Meeting of the American Psychoanalytic Association, Atlantic City, May 1952. First published in *Bulletin of the Menninger Clinic*, 18:1-11, 1954.
[1] The other contributions to this panel were summarized by Rangell (1952c). See also Rapaport (1950) and Jacobson (1953a, 1953b).

I

A forty-year-old man came for psychoanalytic treatment
because of periodic, uncontrollable eruptions of aggressive, destructive behavior which threatened to ruin his marriage and his
business career. These episodes began in his latency and
continued throughout his life, occurring once or twice a year.
Until recent years, his impulsiveness consisted in stealing and
lying, then it came out in sexual promiscuity and reckless business ventures which were not only illegal but unnecessary and
unprofitable. The patient could not understand this behavior
since he considered himself happily married, sexually well-
adjusted, a contented and proud father, popular with his
friends, and financially secure.

The most outstanding finding in this patient's analysis was
that he was almost always in a good mood—cheerful, genial,
good-natured, and optimistic. He not only stated this; he acted
accordingly. Even the impulsive behavior had but a brief
sobering effect upon him. This chronic good mood proved to be
a stubborn defense and resistance in the analysis. The rigidity of
this affective state, coupled with the eruptions of aggression, was
indicative of its defensive nature (Fenichel, 1941a). One further
early sign suggested that the good mood was a protective device.
Occasionally, when I made an interpretation about his early
childhood, particularly about being unloved, tears would stream
down the patient's face. The tears and the mixture of sadness
and pleasure that accompanied them puzzled him. (Actually,
the feeling of being understood, i.e., loved, by a man was
responsible for this reaction.) The analytic hour became a pleasant, friendly chat, unless the defensive aspect of the mood was
systematically pointed out. Lewin (1950) has described a similar
resistance in analyzing states of elation.

Perhaps the most transparent example of the dynamic function of this mood can be seen in the analysis of the patient's
marital situation. It was noteworthy that he never reported any
disagreement with his wife, any annoyances, or any irritability.

He was conspicuously affectionate and loving to her. After listening for several months to this tale of marital bliss, I was somewhat surprised when the patient readily admitted when questioned that he was often unfaithful to her. He had insisted that his sexual life was completely satisfactory and that his wife was by far the best sexual partner he had ever had. He did not feel his infidelity to be a contradiction.

Careful questioning about the details of his home life brought to light many curious inconsistencies. He would describe incidents in a smiling, agreeable manner, when one would have expected feelings of anger, hostility, or sadness. For example, he would recount how he would arrive home at the end of a hard day's work to find his wife asleep, the children crying, the house a mess, and nothing in the house for dinner. He would cheerfully awaken his wife, bundle the children into their clothes, and trot off to get the groceries. (In the first years of the analysis, this material only came out accidentally. He never volunteered it.) His typical remarks after such incidents would be as follows: "It is *not* that my wife hates the children. . . . It is *not* that my wife is a poor housewife. . . ." He admitted that his wife often behaved in a manner that *might be* construed as inconsiderate, like forgetting to pick him up at the office or refusing to make his breakfast in the morning, but he believed that these actions had no real significance. It was true that she often refused to greet him and accepted his kiss passively and indifferently, but he knew that really she loved him dearly and was a fine, loving wife and mother. He knew it because there were times when she did take care of the house and children and did return his kiss. Those were the instances he reacted to and retained, although they were by no means the typical responses of his wife.

The patient apparently perceived the situations which one would have expected to cause him pain, but he negated them. This is in accord with Freud's finding (1925c) that the patient makes the perception, but acts as if the perception does not count. Actually, the patient not only negated his wife's unhappy behavior, he contradicted it. "She is a wonderful housekeeper, a wonderful wife, and a wonderful mother." This seems to be a combination of negation and denial.

This patient perceived the stimuli described above: they were not repressed; they were accessible to recall. However, he seemed to select only certain perceptions to react to. This selectivity of response to perceptions was also exhibited in regard to his children, friends, and business associates. He always managed to find some pleasant quality in them which he focused on and reacted to with a warm, benevolent attitude, disregarding the many qualities in them which would have stirred up anxiety, hostility, and discontent. This phenomenon is somewhat similar to the hunger for screen experiences which Fenichel (1945) mentions in discussing screen memories and denial.

We can reconstruct the following sequence of events: perception, negation and denial of painful perceptions, and focus shifted onto pleasurable or innocuous stimuli. The patient withdrew cathexis from the painful stimuli and hypercathected the pleasant or innocuous ones, which then served as a countercathexis. He split off the idea from the affect-charge, and the accompanying pleasurable affect.[2] The affect-charge from the original perception was blocked from consciousness and erupted in his outbursts. It is significant that the patient's affective state, his emotional tone, corresponded to those screen perceptions.

During the course of a long analysis, the working through of the defensive function of the patient's chronic good mood led eventually to the emergence of many painful affects as well as dangerous instinctual impulses. It became clear that behind the patient's good mood, there was an underlying sadness, remoteness, loneliness, and despair. This patient led an extremely narrow, empty life, emotionally. He smiled but never laughed; he never wept. There were no friends, "People dropped in." Evenings he read the newspaper and fell asleep on the couch. There was no communication or conversation with his wife. Weeks might go by before he realized that he had had no sexual desire. It seemed that by extensive use of the defenses of nega-

---

[2] Leo Rangell, in a personal communication.

tion, denial, and isolation, the patient was able to maintain an affective state which itself had a defensive function.

Lewin (1950) was the first to call such affective states screen affects. Fenichel (1941a) has described affects which are reaction formations against other affects. Landauer (1938) writes about the two opposing tendencies present in all affective states. The clinical material described above seems to put this patient in the same clinical category. Just as character traits can be used as a countercathexis against instinctual impulses, so can affects be used against other affects and/or impulses. The chronic good mood was a countercathexis against depression and aggression. It was made possible by negation and denial of perceptions and the use of screen perceptions. The negation and denial operated against single perceptions. In this way, cathexis was withdrawn from painful perceptions; pleasant perceptions were hypercathected and served as a countercathexis. The narrow, restricted life was a result of these mechanisms and in a larger sense made possible a withdrawal of cathexis from life situations which might threaten his equilibrium. The rigid good mood was the countercathexis, the screen affect, against the depression and aggression which lay underneath. Prior to the analysis, the eruption of sudden aggressive, destructive behavior was the only known sign of these underlying feelings and impulses. I believe that all of this demonstrates that the chronic good mood was a defensive emotional constellation composed of different affective tones which were made possible by the extensive use of the mechanisms of negation and denial. The good mood did on a large scale what the screen perceptions did to single perceptions.

II

Certain additional features in this patient's past history seem to have been of particular significance for the formation of his affective state. Further, many of these findings seem to be typical for patients who suffer from this kind of affective disorder. Just as the patient used screen perceptions in regard to his marital situation, he also employed various screen formations in regard to his past. Just as he could make perceptions about his wife which he discounted, he could do the same in reference to his mother and father. He maintained that his mother was a warm, loving, good-natured, devoted woman, despite the fact that in the next breath he could recite blithely that she forbade her children to wear their shoes in the living room, or she prohibited the family from smoking in the house. (Note the similarity in his relationship to his wife.) Similarly, he maintained that his father was a cruel, violent, stingy, irritable man, and a few sentences later he could state that his father gave him an expensive car for a graduation gift. Or, he could remember his father impulsively giving him his tie and belt when they met at a railroad station. In both instances, the memories which would seem to be in contradiction to his feelings did not produce any change in his feeling tone toward his mother or his father. He steadfastly tried to maintain the picture of the eternally loving mother and the constantly combative father. Most neurotics repress some aspects of their ambivalence to the parents; but they are consciously aware of some mixed feelings. It was remarkable in this patient how absolute the portraits of his parents were and how long they persisted in the analysis. He seemed unable to bear any conscious awareness of ambivalence (see chapter 2).

The analysis of this inability to bear any conscious ambivalence toward an object was instructive. It shed some light on the historical origin and early function of the mechanism of denial. The crux of the matter is the patient's way of trying to hold on to object relationships. The patient's relationship to his parents was the model for his later difficulties in relation to people and to reality.

From his earliest childhood, the patient claimed he could remember nothing but quarrels and animosity between his father and mother. He said that his mother repeatedly told him that she hated his father and that she made it clear that the father was sexually and physically repulsive to her, and that she had no sexual relations with him. The boy's pleasure in being so obviously preferred to the father was rudely shattered, however, when his mother gave birth on three later occasions. His mother had lied to him. He could not bear the disappointment and so he now did unconsciously what his mother had done consciously— denied her sexual relations with his father. In his fantasy, his mother never had sexual relations with his father and secretly yearned only for the patient. Further, the mother apparently wanted him to dislike his father and she felt betrayed when he showed any affection toward him. It became clear in the analysis that the boy did not want to be like his father because to be like father was to be unloved by mother. His whole life was dedicated to the proposition: "I am not like my father. Mother loves me." His good mood, his attitudes, were a proclamation: "I am the opposite of my father. I am my mother's favorite."

The young boy is caught in the following situation: his mother seduces him into sexual fantasies by involving the boy in her sexual loathing of his father. His mother increased his oedipal sexual feelings for her and his oedipal hostility toward the father. However, his mother had lied to him and was at best an unreliable person. He could maintain a positive relationship to her only by negating and denying many painful perceptions. An example of his method of doing this was in the way he remembered the parental quarrels. Both parents screamed in anger at each other, but he only reacted to his father's anger. He denied and displaced his reactions to his mother's temper by putting it all on his father. Conversely, although it was true that his father was often violent verbally and physically, he was at times a pathetic figure. The pathetic aspect of the father was denied and displaced onto the mother. Thus each parent became indelibly painted in black and white. The mother's *conscious* attempt to get the boy to hate the father and to love her, plus her lying which led to his use of the denial mechanism, seemed to be of decisive importance.

His object relationship to the mother was only a scantily disguised incestuous one. But its outstanding characteristic was its thinness, its narrowness, its very lack of substance. He clung to his mother, to his falsified picture of her, because he had no other objects which were more suitable.

His object relationship to his father was more difficult to pin down. On the surface the patient felt hatred and anxiety toward him. This feeling was constant, but without any real intensity or without any live affect. (Below the surface and deeply repressed, and/or denied, were strong positive longings—the patient wept when he felt "understood" by the analyst.) The patient's main attempt to cope with his father, however, was to evade him as an external object altogether and to resort to more regressive means of dealing with him.

III

The patient's struggle with the introjected father imago was, I believe, the single most important determinant of the patient's neurotic structure. He struggled against those impulses, attitudes, and behaviorisms which resembled his father in order to insure his mother's love. Latency, that period in which there occurs the consolidation of the incorporated parental images, was extremely difficult for him. He attempted to deny that he had within him the introjected father. In part he accomplished this by separating his life at home from his life at school. At home he was the opposite of his father, submissive, friendly, eager, good-natured; in school he could be mischievous, rebellious, truant, and extremely active in sports. He also attempted to achieve this denial of the internalized father by a typical family romance fantasy: he was not his father's son but the son of a prince (Freud, 1909a). Yet, beginning in latency, this attempt to deny the introjected father would fail and the patient would suddenly be overwhelmed by some impulsive, aggressive, sadistic impulses.

That these outbursts were not merely eruptions of instinctual tension, but were related specifically to the father, could be seen in the nature of the activities. The father was regularly dishonest in his business practices, which the patient knew. The boy occasionally would find himself stealing or cheating in school for no rational reason. The father was known to be sexually promiscuous with the personnel in his office; this is precisely the kind of sexual objects the patient chose. It is clinically interesting to note that in latency the patient developed a phobia that he had a tapeworm within him which kept him from growing tall. In college he took a course in parasitology and was fascinated by the adaptive skill of the parasite. He was so intrigued by this subject that he was tempted to become a parasitologist. All of this material indicates that there was an internal father imago, but the patient did not consider that part of the self.

I have seen this attempt to deny the existence of the introjected parent in two different patients. One was a woman who suffered from severe and chronic boredom and who constantly felt a terrible sense of emptiness (see chapter 4). It seemed to me that her feeling of emptiness was an attempt to deny that her hated and loved mother was within her. She consciously dreaded being like her mother. She, too, suffered from eruptions of impulsive actions—usually exactly like her mother's.

Another patient, a man, had a persistent mood of bravado about him which was often inappropriate. It was significant that his mother despised his father for being a coward. The patient in his bravado was denying that he was like his father, i.e., that his father was within him. The breaking down of this defense led to a temporary feeling of depersonalization. For several weeks the patient felt he *was* his father and, therefore, he himself was gone, lost.

In each of these cases, the patients maintained a conscious hatred of the parent of the same sex. In each case, this parent was a formidable figure, powerful and intimidating. The patients were apparently unable to cope with these figures as objects since both loving and openly hating such terrifying objects were too dangerous. The love impulses were repressed and were the most resistant impulses to bring into consciousness in the analysis. The hate was perceived, but denied access to motility or open affective expression. The intensity of the hatred was magnified because, in part, it served as a defense against love impulses. Further, part of the hatred was deflected from the other parent onto the single, same-sexed parent. These patients

all used introjection as a method of avoiding object relationships
to this parent, but here their problem was complicated. They
could introject, but not reveal any identification with the hated
parent since this would incur the loss of the other parent's love.
These patients struggled to remain unaware of the internalized
object within them. Their distorted moods were derivatives of
this struggle with the internalized object.

Freud (1915b) described the content of the purified plea-
sure-ego, which I believe is of value in understanding some of the
problems involved here. At this level of ego development, the
child considers all that is good to be inside himself and all that is
bad to be outside himself. Freud (1925c) later pointed out that
the first judgment of the child has to be thought of in oral terms:
Shall I swallow something or shall I spit it out? In other words,
the question of what is me or not me, in childhood terms, is essentially a question of is it inside me or outside me. It seems that
the patients described above have regressed, in regard to the
internal object, to this early level of ego functioning. This can be
formulated as follows: "Since I feel this object to be bad, I do not
consider it part of me—it is not me; it is outside of me." The
cheerful patient could discern no resemblance in himself to his
father; even the obvious impulsive actions he did not connect to
his father.

As one might expect with patients who use denial mechanisms so prevalently, all these patients had difficulty in their reality testing. The cheerful patient, it should be stressed, was of
high intelligence, and was in no strict sense psychotic, yet the
restrictions in his perceptions often led to inappropriate reactions
which made a strange impression. For example, he could find
himself enjoying and participating as an equal in the company of
people who were unintelligent, insensitive, and uninteresting,
without any feeling that he did not belong in this group. He
could relate himself just as easily to psychotics, where he had no
sense of strangeness or anxiety. His conception of himself, his ego
identity, was amorphous and unstable. He could consider himself a successful businessman, a happy-go-lucky kid, a responsible father, a severe neurotic, and a healthy, typical, American

male in rapid succession and without feeling puzzled by the inconsistencies. It was another characteristic of his trouble in reality testing that his ego could bear conscious contradictions without the need to integrate the conflicting opinions or disbeliefs. He could say that he never thought about his brother, for example, and five minutes later tell me many thoughts that he had had about his brother, and finally state that he was worried about his brother. If one pointed out the contradiction, he was puzzled, because he did not feel it as a contradiction.

His relationship to his body was similarly disturbed. This was particularly striking in regard to his penis and his sex life. At first he maintained that he enjoyed all of his sex life and was never able to distinguish any difference in the quality of his orgasms or in the sensitivity of his penis. It took years of analysis for him to realize that he was not aware of what was going on in his penis. He did not notice any difference in sensitivity when he used a condom and when he did not. He never had any difficulty with his erection or in controlling his ejaculations. Even after he became aware of his wife's mistreatment of him, for a long time his penis reacted as mechanically as before. It was a big step forward in his analysis when he was impotent attempting intercourse after a particularly miserable day with his wife. Once he took his child to have a tooth extracted. The dentist had to tell him to sit down when he noticed the patient was dripping wet, a green color, and trembling. The patient not only did not feel it—he thought he was calm. The bravado patient I mentioned briefly was often unable to distinguish when he had a cold or when he was beginning to feel depersonalized. The bored woman would state, "I am gone, nowhere, I can't get with it."

All of these examples indicate a deep disturbance in the reality-testing function of the ego. It seems to be an outcome of the patient's struggle with the internalized objects. Freud (1925c) formulated that reality testing is intimately dependent on internal objects and images: "what is real is also there *outside*" (p. 237). The first and immediate aim of the process of reality testing is to *rediscover* an object, that is, to find an object which once was present and responsible for the original internal image. The external object is sought for on the basis of the internalized image. (One's own body is an external object in relation to the ego's perceptual apparatus.) Rapaport (1942) considers judgment a higher representation of the functions of introjection and projection. Jacobson (1971) in her work on depression has described the complicated fate of introjected objects which in many ways seem to touch upon some of the problems that come up here. In the patients described above, I believe that the lack of stable internalized objects was responsible for the unstable relationship to reality (Milton Wexler, personal communication).

One can discern the following relevant events: these patients had introjected and identified with many aspects of the consciously hated parent. The lovable qualities could become an acceptable part of the self as long as the connection to the external parent was denied. The hated characteristics of the parent were also internalized, but these introjections were combated by denial or repression, in a vain struggle to keep these qualities from becoming recognized as part of the self. In the cheerful patient, the father was perceived only as a hateful external object; the lovable aspects were displaced or denied as an internal object. The hated father was denied as belonging to the self, despite the unmistakable evidence to the contrary. The patient considered himself a loving father, again made possible by his denying the various actions which would contradict this. Furthermore, his picture of himself as the loving father was severed completely from any connection to his own father. The picture of himself as the loving father was also based on his conception of his mother's ideal of the kind of man she could have loved.

It seemed that this patient tried to maintain his psychic equilibrium by withdrawing cathexis and hypercathecting only certain aspects of the internal objects and the external objects. Perhaps one can approach this problem by assuming that early introjections are usually fragments of an external object. Only with maturity do these fragmented internal objects become fused with one another, and only then does one have a more composite and fully rounded picture of the self.

The patient described above attempted to withdraw cathexis from the hated father within himself and attempted to deny that those pieces of behavior which pointed in this direction had any connection to his father. His chronic cheerfulness and good-naturedness proclaimed to the world and to himself that he was a good and loving father and constantly contradicted the hated father within him. It was only the eruptions of the aggressive, destructive behavior which indicated that he had within himself also the hated father. At times the withdrawal of cathexis from the hated internalized father imago failed, and it became hypercathected. This hypercathexis made for a transient identification with the hated father and brought with it the affects and actions of the hated father. There are many steps between the hypercathexis, the identification, and the affective state, but at this point I am unable to be more exact. However, it seems clear that the fate of the internalized objects is of crucial importance for the affective state and for the relationship to reality.[3]

The predominant use of the mechanisms of negation and denial, particularly in regard to the internalized objects, seems to be of special importance for disturbances of reality testing and disturbances of mood. This patient was uncertain and unstable about his conception of himself. He often did not know his own mood or how he felt. Similarly, his conception of who he was, was variable and amorphous. This confusing situation is often expressed by people in the words, "I am not myself today." This expression conveys the ego's awareness of a mood which is based on elements one would like to disavow from the self. I believe the expression, "I am not myself today," also points out the close connection between the questions "How are you?" and "Who are you?"

One can describe moods in terms of objects. They can be personified. The patient described above, for example, would not become angry, but would become his angry father. It seems to me that with moods, this is usually the case. Patients do not

[3] Further vicissitudes of introjection and identification are discussed in chapters 6, 11, and 19.

just become depressed, but they become the rejected little boy they once were in childhood. The anxious patient is not just a frightened adult, but is the scared little child of the past. Moods are not only derived from the internal representatives of external objects, but are often the representatives of one's own past state of mind; one's conception of oneself in the past.[4] All of these considerations lead me to conclude that there is a very close connection between alternations in the cathexis of internal objects and moods. One's outlook on the world and one's conception of oneself are determined by the status of the various internalized objects.

---

[4] Moods and affective states are discussed further in chapters 9, 10, and 13; their relationship to the self image is elaborated in chapter 9.

6

The Struggle Against Identification

(1954)

I

ORDINARILY IDENTIFICATION IS CONSIDERED to be a means of maintaining a close relationship to an object. In fact, Freud (1921) ventured the opinion that identification was perhaps the earliest expression of an emotional tie to another person. At a later date Freud (1923a) remarked that it may even be that this identification is the sole condition under which the id can give up its objects. This presentation is devoted to the psychoanalytic findings in a group of patients who struggled against identifying themselves with an important parental figure. This was not an incidental finding, but was indeed the major factor in understanding the dynamic structure of the clinical picture.

Before presenting the case material and the theoretical hypotheses, I believe it would be wise to clarify and define some of the concepts which are so frequently used interchangeably and inexactly in discussions on identification. The reader is referred

Presented at the Panel on "Problems of Identification" at the Midwinter Meeting of the American Psychoanalytic Association, New York, December 1952. First published in *Journal of the American Psychoanalytic Association*, 2:200-217, 1954.

to the writings of Freud (1921, 1923a), Glover (1939a), Fenichel (1926, 1945), Hartmann, Kris, and Loewenstein (1946), Jacobson (1953a), and Hendrick (1951), whose papers provide the source material for these formulations.

Incorporation is an oral instinctual activity which has as its aim the taking of an external part of the world into the mouth, swallowing it, and in this way making it part of the physical self. The aim of incorporation is satisfaction without regard to the object. In this sense it indicates neither hatred nor love (Fenichel, 1926). *Introjection* is that psychic phenomenon which is parallel to incorporation and is modeled after incorporation (Glover, 1939a). It is an attempt to take into the self objects in the external world in order to reexperience that pleasurable sense of satisfaction which was originally felt in the gratification of hunger. In the infant, introjection is used as a method of getting and retaining within the self pleasurable experiences which in reality depend for their renewal on objects in the external world. In the beginning introjection is primarily in the service of the instincts. Later on it can be used as well for a variety of defensive purposes. Some of the confusion in the use of the terms incorporation and introjection is due to the fact that introjection, which is a psychic energic action, often results in changes of the physical self.

Identification is a much more complicated process than incorporation and introjection. The mechanism of introjection is a necessary part in the process of identification. It is true that other mechanisms may be involved (Knight, 1940), but in all instances it is the introjection which is the most significant mechanism that leads to the identification (Glover, 1939a; Fenichel, 1945; Hendrick, 1951). If one compares introjection with identification, it can be seen that introjection is an instinctual aim toward an object, while identification is a process which may result after the instinctual aim of introjection has taken place. This can be demonstrated when introjections occur which do not lead to identification. In the depressions, for example, one can observe the introjection of the ambivalent object without transformations indicative of identification. Similarly, in hypochondriasis and paranoid states, one can ascertain the presence of internalized objects which do not necessarily lead to identifications. Identification with an object means that, as a result of introjection, a transformation of the self has occurred whereby the self has become similar to the external object. This is manifested by certain changes which have taken place in the self as a consequence of the introjection, so that one can observe behavior, attitudes, feelings, posture, etc., which are now identical to those characteristics belonging to the external object.

The transformations occurring as the result of identification influence more than the ego of the subject; the entire self is involved. The term self is used in this connection as distinct from the term ego. Jacobson (1953a) and Hartmann (1950) have indicated that it is important to clarify the distinction between the two. One should talk of the self in contradistinction to another object. We should limit the term ego to differentiate it from other substructures of the personality. The opposite of object cathexis is self cathexis and not ego cathexis. Self cathexis includes the id, ego, and superego. Narcissism is the libidinal cathexis not of the ego but of the entire self. In the ego we have both object representations and self representations (Jacobson, 1953a). The self representation is derived, on the one hand, from a direct awareness of our inner experiences and, on the other, from indirect perceptions of our bodily and mental reactions viewed as an object. The earliest self images come from our body sensations and body images. In the beginning the self image is fused and confused with object images and therefore is constantly changing. The self representations fluctuate greatly as to how much of a specific one and what aspect of it are accessible to consciousness. Our concept of ourselves or our awareness of ourselves is dependent on our conscious and preconscious feelings, thoughts, impulses, wishes, attitudes, and actions. Self perception is an ego function; self judgment is in part based on the ego's function of perception, but is predominantly influenced by the superego (Jacobson, 1953a). In identification, the entire self may be transformed.

Introjection and identification are unconscious processes,

although identification can sometimes be initiated by conscious imitation. While the actual process of identification is unconscious, there is a significant degree of variation in the awareness of identification having taken place. Sometimes there is a conscious awareness that one apparently has identified oneself with an external object. At times one is only preconsciously aware of an identification having taken place. Some identifications are ego-syntonic; others are ego-alien. Some have developed very early in life, and some arise only at later stages of life (Hendrick, 1951). There seem to be many different kinds of identification. One can differentiate between total and partial identifications. There are symptomatic identifications, as is seen in hysteria; transient identification, as in the play of children; multiple identifications, as is seen in melancholia (Abraham, 1924); rudimentary identifications, etc. There are early identifications which precede object relations and identifications which replace object relations. Behind the formation of the superego there lies hidden the direct and immediate identifications which take place earlier than any object cathexis (Freud, 1923a). Bisexuality, ambivalence, and regressive defusion of instincts seem to play an important role in the vicissitudes of identification (Freud, 1923a).

These general statements indicate the great scope of problems touched upon in considering the metapsychology of identification. This paper is limited to an analysis of four patients who struggled against identification. The patients to be described introjected and also identified with a hated parental figure. They tried to remain unaware of this identification.[1] Furthermore, their entire way of life was predominantly an attempt to contradict the fact that this fateful introjection and identification had taken place. They tried to deny any resemblance to the hated external object by adopting characteristics, actions, and behavior which were in direct opposition to these qualities in the hated parent. A significant additional factor in

[1] Other variants of this struggle against identification are discussed in chapter 19.

these cases was the coexistence of a great eagerness to identify with new objects; but this was always transitory, superficial, and unstable. This could be observed particularly clearly in the transference. These patients had the tendency to make quick identifications with the analyst in some trivial mannerism of his; on the other hand, they had great difficulty in identifying with the analyst in any of his more important attitudes or behavior. All of this indicates that there seems to be a variety of identifications which should be differentiated from one another. I hope that the following clinical material will clarify some of these problems.

II

CASE 1

A young woman came for psychoanalysis because of a complicated sleep phobia (see chapter 3). She was afraid to resort to sedatives because she feared that she might eventually become an addict. During the course of her analysis she developed an inhibition and aversion to speaking her mother tongue, German, a language she had spoken exclusively until she was eighteen years of age. This was in marked contrast to her remarkable fluency and vocabulary in English. In her analysis there were manifestations of what looked like a strong oedipal attachment to her father, which she acted out with a married man of her acquaintance. This love affair, with its extreme submissiveness to the man, had an oral, addictlike quality (Reich, 1940; Deri, n.d.). The inhibition in speaking her mother tongue, which was overcome in part by carrying on this portion of the analysis in German, revealed that behind the oedipal and oral strivings toward the man, there was a much more important oral, sexual and aggressive relationship to the mother. This patient could never call her mother *Mutter*. There was something sensual in this word and she was ashamed to use it. Even more difficult for her was the word *Busen* (breasts). She could not permit these words to pass her lips. It was significant that one of her favorite words for describing her mother was "unappetizing." This patient had a strong conscious hatred of her mother, whom for many years she avoided completely, as an external object. On another level, however, the analysis of her troubles with her mother tongue revealed strong, oral, sexual, passive and aggressive strivings toward her mother. Furthermore, her battle against this language was an indication of her struggle to deny that this mother imago was within her. It was striking that despite the conscious aversion to the mother, from time to time this patient acted out impulsively in a way which was identical with her mother's. She neglected her son, was aggressive toward him, and was sexually promiscuous in exactly the same way her mother had been (Rangell, 1952a). Although she was ashamed of this behavior, she was quite willing to explore this, until one attempted to demonstrate that she had identified herself with her mother. This was worked through when the transference situation changed and the analyst became for her a mother figure. This patient had a fear of falling asleep and a fear of falling into a chasm and had many dreams of breasts and being eaten by crocodiles. All of this, I believe, indicated the presence of strong fears and wishes to be devoured. Her struggle against the introjected mother and her struggle against the identification which was manifested only sporadically seems to me to have been a struggle against the oral libidinal and sadistic strivings which were involved in this identification. She fought against the old introjected object and primitive identification and instead sought after the new language which indicated her wish to introject new objects in order to make new identifications. She had an entirely different personality in English than she had in German. "In German, I am a scared, dirty child; in English, I am a nervous, refined woman." I believe such material indicates some of the different ways the patient struggled with the introjected object and the identification, and is the key to understanding the dynamic structure of this case. Freud (1923a) hints at similar material when he describes identifications which are incompatible with one another or which may lead to a disruption in cases of so-called multiple personality.

CASE 2

A young woman came to analysis because of chronic and severe boredom which at times reached such intensity that she attempted suicide (see Chapter 4). This patient considered as the
most torturesome aspect of the boredom a terrible empty feeling.
She would describe this feeling as follows: "I can't get with it.
I'm nowhere. I'm gone." Analysis of this empty feeling was very
complicated, but very rewarding. The emptiness was, in the first
place, a consequence of the inhibition of fantasies due to a
repression of forbidden instinctual aims and objects. Furthermore, the emptiness represented hunger. It was a substitution of
a sensation for a fantasy, a primitivization of an ego function
(Kris, 1950). Finally, and I believe most important in this case,
the feeling of emptiness was an attempt to deny that the mother
had been introjected. This patient consciously hated her mother,
who was a promiscuous, alcoholic, irresponsible woman; yet she
lived with an ominous feeling that she might turn out to be like
her mother, a state of affairs she dreaded. She alternated between moods of terrible boredom which she tried to handle by
going to beauty parlors, shopping, looking at television, examining herself minutely in the mirror, and similar activities. This alternated with periods of excessive drinking, sexual promiscuity,
and homosexual affairs, in which she deserted her husband and
her children, which was precisely the kind of behavior typical of
her mother. This patient was married to a man much older than
herself, whom she could not stand because he was so "motherly."
What looked like an oedipal situation turned out to be a
preoedipal relationship to the mother with a very strong homosexual component. This patient's boredom, which was her most
tormenting symptom, accomplished one purpose: she felt empty,
which meant she did not have the mother within her; she was
not like her mother. It was only when the boredom failed that
she then resorted to activities which indicated that the mother
had been introjected into the self. The main reason for the empty
feeling in this patient was her struggle against this very primitive
identification.

CASE 3

A middle-aged man came for analysis because he was given
to periodic, uncontrollable eruptions of aggressive, destructive,
sexual behavior, which threatened to ruin what he considered an
otherwise happy marriage and successful business career (see
chapter 5). Generally, this man was in a state of a chronic good
mood. His analysis was characterized by screen memories and
screen perceptions. The good mood was a screen affect which
was found to be a countercathexis against an underlying depressive, aggressive state, made possible by the extensive use of negation and denial of perceptions (Lewin, 1950). This patient had a
rather obvious and transparent incestuous relationship to his
mother, but its outstanding characteristic was its shallowness, its
thinness, its very lack of substance. His relationship to his father
was much more complex and important. On a conscious level he
hated his father and he spent his life trying to evade him as an
external object. He fantasied himself someone else's son. It
became clear that this relationship was more intricate when he
described his interest in parasitology and came forth with many
dreams which concerned the presence of a worm within him. It
then turned out that his hatred of the father was so strong in part
because he had displaced all positive feelings onto the mother.
Nevertheless, the eruptions of impulsive behavior indicated that
he had introjected and identified with his father because this behavior was identical with the very behavior he loathed in his
father. Behind the avoidance and hatred of his father, there was
found to be strong, passive oral fears and longings in regard to
his father. He tried to remain unaware of this internalized father
imago because he wanted to remain oblivious of the oral libidinal and sadistic impulses which he felt toward his father.

CASE 4

Some years ago I analyzed a young man who struggled particularly hard against recognizing his identification with his
father in certain characteristics, namely, those characteristics

which his mother despised in his father. When his father visited him for the first time since the patient's marriage, a curious sequence of events took place. One day the patient had a copious bowel movement, which reminded him of his father's. This set in motion a growing feeling that he had become like his father. For several weeks he found that he was performing all sorts of activities exactly the way his father did. Along with this feeling of being like his father, there was the very uncanny feeling that he himself was lost, was gone. The patient found that this depersonalization and this exaggerated awareness of being like his father were absent in only one activity—intercourse. Analysis revealed that actually it was precisely in intercourse that he had always identified himself with his father. He behaved in the sexual act toward his wife exactly as he remembered or fantasied that his father had behaved in the sexual act with his mother. He attempted to ward off the memory of the reconstruction of the primal scene by the combination of depersonalization on the one hand, and this "hyperidentification," on the other. The so-called hyperidentification with the father was manifested in rather trivial actions and hid the more important identification with the father in sexual matters. On a still deeper level, however, for this patient to be identified with his father meant to submit to his father in an oral, sexual and passive way. At this time the vagina meant for him the father's mouth. For the first time during the analysis he had potency difficulties and a fear of falling asleep. It became clear that the father's visit had remobilized a very primitive identification with the father which still retained strong oral, sexual, passive and aggressive instinctual components.

III

Let us summarize what all these different patients had in common. In all of them there was a definite, but shallow positive oedipus complex, behind which lay strong pregenital libidinal and aggressive, passive and active, strivings toward the parent of the same sex. The women patients were attempting to repress or deny aggressive and homosexual impulses to the mother, and the men were doing the same in relation to the father. In the history of each patient there was found to be open resentment and contempt between mother and father. These patients were aware only of conscious hatred toward the parent of the same sex. The parent of the opposite sex tended to be overly seductive and stirred up incestuous feelings. Later on these parents were idealized and eventually became part of the ego ideal. Perhaps another determinant in the struggle against the hated introject and identification can be understood as the struggle between the good introject versus the bad introject, an intrapsychic representation of the battle between the parents. Abraham (1924) mentions a similar hypothesis in discussing the introjection in the manic-depressive psychoses. It may well be that in these cases the presence of one good parental figure—or more precisely, the patient's ability to maintain one parent as a good figure—made it possible for these patients to avoid a more psychotic regression (Jacobson, 1954a).

In all of them the nature of the ambivalence was striking. They did not have the kind of ambivalence toward an object which one usually sees, for example, in the compulsive-obsessive. There was no fusion of love and hatred; rather one found that one parent was loved almost exclusively and the other hated on a conscious level. In most neurotics there is some conscious awareness of ambivalence toward an object, but in these patients there was practically none. At times one could see sudden vacillations of love and hatred, but these were sporadic and definitely separated from one another. This appears to be much more of an infantile reaction than ambivalence. It is "preambivalent," in accordance with Glover's (1939a) conception of ambivalence rather than Abraham's (1924). Freud (1923a) has the impression that ambivalence represents a state of incomplete fusion of the instinctual drives. Nevertheless, it is more mature than the distinct separations of love and hatred in the preambivalent child. Fusion of affects seems to represent a higher level of maturation than rapid alternations of opposite affects.

All these patients tried to evade the parent of the same sex rather than contend with him or her as an object in reality. They had a stereotyped picture of this parent which was not corrected by experiences of everyday life. It was interesting that these patients repeated this kind of relationship with people throughout their lives. They would maintain a picture of an individual based upon little evidence and would not change this portrait in accordance with later experience. All their object relationships were diluted by a great admixture of identification. They made quick, temporary identifications with many people and the moment they became friendly with anyone they became like that person. Anna Freud (1936) has described this phenomenon in adolescents. It was an interesting contradiction that, on the one hand, these patients struggled so hard against the old identifications and, on the other, were so hungry to find new objects for the purpose of forming new identifications. They were hungry for objects, but had to deny the real objects of their hunger, i.e., the parents of the same sex.[2] The new objects were not only screens against the old introjects but were also an attempt to neutralize the "bad" introjects with the new "good" introjects.[3] (Theoretical speculations led me to consider the possibility that in all the cases it was the mother who was the real object of the hunger. This would fit in with the predominance of the oral needs. Unfortunately the results of my clinical investigations did not reveal this to be true of the men patients described, despite the fact that I looked for this.)

All of these patients were prone to disturbances in mood and though they resembled the depressives, they were not primarily depressed persons. In these moods they reactivated old identifications, as, for example, the lady with the mother-tongue problem, who became obnoxious like her mother when she was elated, or a dirty Viennese child when she felt forlorn. The men patients did not just get angry, but became their angry father. All these patients had marked fluctuations in their conception of themselves and had disturbances in relation to their body image,

[2] Milton Wexler, personal communication.
[3] Hanna Fenichel, personal communication.

body sensations, and reality testing. They often did not know how they felt; often stated that they were not themselves, and were easily influenced by others to change their moods. They were also prone to episodes of impulsive acting out, which bore the definite stamp of the consciously hated parent. In all of these patients the mechanisms of negation and denial seemed to be the method of choice in dealing with painful stimuli. They all had sleeping disturbances and eating disturbances. They seemed to have little anal or urethral difficulties, and they all made a superficially good sexual adjustment.

From the standpoint of diagnostic classification, these patients seemed to belong somewhere between the transference neuroses and the narcissistic neuroses, a position akin to the addictions and perversions. They were not overtly psychotic despite evidence of disturbance in some of their basic ego functions, including some difficulties in reality testing. Ives Hendrick (1931) writes about a prepsychotic patient who demonstrated the mechanism of oral ejection and who had some similarities to the patients described here. His patient, however, gave evidence of a schizophrenic development rather than the depressive manifestations so prevalent in the patients I have described. These cases also resemble the "as if" personalities described by Helene Deutsch (1942). Her patients at first glance looked as if they were normal, warm-hearted people, but closer scrutiny indicated that they were almost totally lacking in genuine object relationships. They took on other people's affects by means of quick imitations. In reality her cases were empty, schizoid personalities. The patients I have described also tried to take on other people's affects and values, but they had their own pathological affects, values, and impulses to contend with. However, most important was the fact that the "as if" quality in the cases I have described was based on their attempt to lead a life *as if* they had identified only with the "good" parent, whereas in reality they had made important identifications with the "bad" parent as well. In addition, all of these patients felt that the identification with the hated parent was ominous and frightening.

IV

In order to answer the question of why these patients felt so threatened by the identification, it is necessary to review the differences between the introjections and identifications which occur at different times of life. Although there are still many obscure areas in understanding problems of identification, we do know more about identifications which occur as an attempt to resolve the oedipus complex than we do about the earlier forms. Freud (1923a) pointed out that the child, in attempting to cope with his oedipal strivings, tends to renounce much of his sexual and aggressive impulses toward the parents in favor of introjections. The outcome is the formation of a precipitate in the ego consisting of mother and father identifications in some way combined together. This new psychic agency, the superego, now makes possible that the self takes over attitudes, values, and behavior which would be in accord with the idealized picture of the parents now internalized. Usually the character of the superego is dominated by the more frustrating parent, i.e., the parent of the same sex. Not only are the prohibitions of the parents introjected, however, but also the rewarding and protective aspects. The love and the awe of the parental images lend to these introjects a magnificence which sets them apart from the ego in the form of ego ideals. The renunciation of the external object, however, is only partial, since the child, after he develops a superego, still maintains an important relationship to the parents. The identification, however, has made a delibidinized and de-aggressified relationship to the parent possible. In this instance, the introjection and the following identification enable the child to preserve and develop his object relationships. In patients I described, the identifications replaced the object relationships. It should be added that the introjection of the parental figures does not result in exact identifications, since the introjected parental figures are more severe than the external objects. This is even more striking in the earlier introjections and is a characteristic that stems from the young child's inability to bear frustration to which he reacts with great aggressiveness. It seems that in superego formation the introjection and identification made possible a mastery over the instinctual drives, so that the instinctual drives themselves have given rise to anti-instinctual forces. As primitive as superego function may be, it is nevertheless far more stable, organized, and integrated than earlier introjections and identifications.

If we now turn our attention to the forerunners of superego formation, we realize that introjections and identifications have taken place long before, but have a much more rudimentary, primitive, and disorganized form. Freud (1923a) stated that the earliest emotional expression toward an object in the prehistory of every person is the identification with the parent, which is not the consequence of or outcome of an object cathexis. It is a direct and immediate identification and takes place earlier than any object cathexis. I believe that these remarks refer to "primary" identification and its relationship to early perception. In the infant, stimulus discharge, perception, and motor reaction are almost inseparably interwoven. One perceives by changing one's body in accordance with the perceived object and then taking cognizance of this bodily change (Freud, 1925b; Fenichel, 1945). At this time of life, to put into the mouth and to imitate in order to perceive are one and the same and represent the very first relationship to objects. In this activity instinctual behavior and ego behavior are not differentiated (Fenichel, 1945).

Thus, incorporation and introjection are the first aims toward objects. The original purpose is to get close to an object, to take it in, in order to get satisfaction, to be reunited with it, and then later to control and master it. It is plausible to assume that introjection, the psychic counterpart of incorporation, will be called into play when the object is missing, and therefore cannot provide the milk, nipple, or breast. Clinical experience would seem to confirm that frustration and deprivation tend to increase the readiness to introjection (Jacobson, 1943). Freud, as quoted earlier, indicated that it seemed to him that the only condition under which the id will give up an external object is by introjection. Since the infant has so little capacity for postponing instinctual discharge, it is plausible that introjections which take place early in life occur under great oral libidinal and aggressive stress. "The more primitive the demands of instinct the more violent the frustration; the more violent the frustration the more sadistic is the infant's reaction; the more sadistic the reaction, the more does the child project this sadism on the parents, thereby converting them into 'bad' objects" (Glover, 1939a, p. 85). In the earliest phases it seems that the frustrating objects will turn into "bad" introjects. In earliest childhood the "good" introjects and the "bad" introjects are separated from one another. As the ego matures, there seems to be a tendency to fuse "good" and "bad" introjects into a composite introject. Instead of alternating between cathecting "good" introjects and getting rid of "bad" introjects—as the ego is able to retain objects, it seems to become able to retain the "bad" introject even while it hypercathects the "good" introject. I have the impression that with maturation of the ego there is a fusion of the "good" and "bad" introjects into a composite introject and a corresponding fused external object. I believe this is accomplished during that phase of libidinal development which corresponds to the anal-retentive phase. That phase is characterized by ambivalence. Ambivalence means the coexistence of hate and love toward the same object. I have the impression that along with the libidinal development, the ego demonstrates analogous development in its capacity to fuse "good" and "bad" internal object representations into a composite introject. Just as ambivalence is a more mature emotional relationship to objects as compared to the preambivalent alternation of love and hate, so is fusion of good and bad introjects a more advanced development as compared to the separate internalized objects which are either good or bad.[4] Glover (1939a) seems to describe the same phenomena when he discusses the origin and development of "ego nuclei." Ives Hendrick (1951) also seems to be describing the same point when he distinguishes between the partial ego functions based on partial identifications

[4] Milton Wexler, personal communication.

and the later and better organized functions which are derived from total ego identifications. Hartmann, Kris, and Loewenstein (1946) have suggested similar formulations.

In the early phases of the infant's development, as long as the ego and the id are not completely differentiated from one another, the situation seems to be that perception and primary identification, and the establishment of separate good and bad introjects according to frustration and satisfaction take place. At this time, introjection and identification cannot be separated from one another because perception implies a transformation of the self, at least partially, in accordance with the characteristics of the perceived object. In some adults one can still see phenomena which are traceable to this early phase of ego functioning. There are grown-up people who when you speak to them move their own lips as they mouth the words you are saying. As the ego matures, perception and introjection no longer automatically lead to identification or transformation of the self. In accordance with Jacobson's conceptions (1953a), this would indicate the clearer differentiation between self representations and object representations. As the infant matures and is better able to bear tensions and frustrations, his conception of himself and of his external objects as well as their internal representatives undergoes a change. His relationship to objects is no longer characterized by the "all-or-nothing" quality; and objects are no longer either good or bad but both good and bad. As the child can achieve an ambivalent object relationship to an external object, he seems able to retain a fixed and composite internal object representation as well as a differentiated and composite self representation. The later fate of the object representations, namely, the postambivalent object relationships, is beyond the scope of this paper.

V

Let us finally return to the question of why the patients described above dreaded permitting the imago of the internalized parent to gain access to perceptual consciousness or motility. The most obvious and superficial answer is that if they became like the hated parent of the same sex, they would be hated by the parent of the opposite sex. This answer, however, does not adequately describe the clinical picture; rather, the answer seems to lie in the primitive and regressive nature of this introjection and identification. It seems, on the one hand, that these patients sensed the archaic instinctual drives involved in their primitive identifications. They were terrified of identifying with the parents as though they dreaded being devoured by this parent. It seems as though they had intuitively felt the oral-sadistic nature of their early introjections. Furthermore, the denial of the hated introject had made a way of life and a conception of the self possible which would have to be abandoned once the defensive aspects were brought to light.[5] The man who became depersonalized when his father visited had been potent as long as he remained unaware of "borrowing" his father's potency. He was loath to give up this potency and slowly build up his own, genuine potency. Finally, and I believe most important, the regression to the fragmented introjection was felt as a loss of a cohesive self representation and therefore brought forth the possibility of the loss of sense of identity (Erikson, 1950). Freud's allusions (1923a) to the liberation of destructive energies which accompanies the regression involved in identification may offer some further answers to these problems.

On the basis of this clinical material and theoretical speculations, I believe it is permissible to assume that there is a hierarchy of introjections, both self and object representations starting with the earliest days of life and going on throughout life. The earlier introjections and identifications are characterized by strong oral-sadistic instinctual elements, whereas the later introjections and identifications stem from a different, less primitive order of instinctual energies. Early introjections tend to remain isolated, whereas later introjections tend to blend and fuse, therefore taking on a more composite character. I believe

[5] Hanna Fenichel, personal communication.

that in the cases described above, a regression took place in terms
of objects, so that external object relationships were extremely
shallow and internal objects became more important. These patients could not form object relations or identify permanently on
a higher level. These patients were predisposed to this regression
by the history of excessive deprivation, frustration, and satisfaction in early childhood, and the violent parental discord. When
disappointments in their later lives caused them to abandon
external objects, they regressed to more primitive, internal objects. The regression also influenced their aim toward objects,
and they became more orally oriented—they were hungry for
objects.[6] This was manifested in the many quick, transitory
object relationships which were so full of identification. At the
same time the remobilized orality cathected the more regressive
internalized objects.

All of the foregoing considerations seem to imply that a
deep regression has taken place. These patients appear to have
returned to a level where the ego is unable to maintain a separation between the introject and the self. These patients tend to
feel that they were being devoured by the introjected object, or
that they were the hated introject. These patients could not differentiate between resembling the parent or being the parent.
To them, resembling and being were the same. As a result of the
fragmentation or defusion of the internalized object and the self
representations, the ego has to combat the early identifications
because this primitive kind of identification brings with it the
feeling that the patient is being devoured or is losing his identity,
which in either case is intolerable.

---

[6] This point is taken further in chapter 9.

7

About the Sound "Mm . . ."

(1954)

T HE CLINICAL MATERIAL of this brief presentation is a fragment from the analysis of a male patient who suffered
from severe and unpredictable fluctuations of mood. During one of his brief and infrequent euphoric intervals, the patient
stated that he felt a constant pleasant humming sensation in his
lips. Although no audible sound came from him, he felt as
though he were making the sound "Mm . . . ." This particular
mood accompanied by the humming sensation and sound lasted
for several days and it was possible to uncover some of the determinants.

The humming sensation was a manifestation of a sense of
contentment and well-being. The good mood had been precipitated by an event in the patient's life which had made him feel
lucky or fortunate. (It was characteristic for this man to react
either with feelings of guilt or a transient hypomania when he
believed that circumstances or fate had smiled upon him.) The
sense of well-being was recognized to be a repetition of those few
occasions in his life when he believed himself to be his mother's
favorite and that she really loved only him. The euphoria also

---

Presented at the Midwinter Meeting of the American Psychoanalytic
Association, New York, December 4, 1953. First published in *Psychoanalytic
Quarterly*, 22:234-239, 1954.

represented a successful denial of quite the opposite feeling, of
being abandoned and deserted, which was the deeper and more
consistent mood of this particular patient (Lewin, 1950).

A dream fragment at this time concerning a piece of velvet
cloth led to associations about especially "delicious" and rich tactile temperature and taste sensations localized predominantly in
the hand and in the mouth. To this patient velvet was a sensuous
material; it was very "feely." He recalled his mother's stories that
he would fondle a particularly soft woolen blanket or some other
soft object when sucking on the breast or the bottle. Later on he
could not sleep unless this special woolen blanket were in the
crib with him. In his adult life the patient could not sleep unless
he embraced a pillow or touched the body of his wife in some
way. As one would expect, he also had rather complicated disturbances of sleep. The "Mm . . ." sensation produced a very
pleasurable feeling in his lips. It had a very definite and positive
erotic sensory component. The manifest dream and the latent
dream thoughts seem to indicate that the velvet material could
be understood as a dream screen in accordance with Lewin's
ideas (1946) on this subject.

All of this material seemed to point to the fact that the "Mm
. . ." sensation was derived from the memory or fantasy of the
pleasurable experience of being at the mother's breast. Shortly
after this piece of analytic work, I accidentally listened to a
singing radio commercial about a certain soup. The song which
advertised the virtues of this dish began with "Mm . . . Mm . . .
good." Almost at the same time, I noticed a billboard advertising
the deliciousness of a certain breakfast food. It pictured a young
boy delightedly smacking his lips and patting his abdomen. The
only words accompanying this sign were "Mm . . . Good." It
then occurred to me that in America and in other Western European societies the utterance "Mm . . ." as produced with a
humming or musical intonation indicates a pleasurable oral and
gastronomic experience. Literally "Mm . . ." means that the
perception which causes the sound would feel good in the mouth
and stomach. It should be noted that the humming "Mm . . ."
sound referred to here is quite different in its meaning from

"Mm . . ." sounds made in different intonations. It is also quite different from the "Hm . . ." sound which has another connotation. The musical quality of this "Mm . . ." sound is probably related to the fact that the contented mother hums cheerfully herself as she feeds her baby or rocks him to sleep. She hums by way of her identification with the baby's pleasurable satiation and thus echoes a sound she felt as a child. The "Mm . . ." indicates a sense of contentment and satisfaction rather than a more high-pitched joyous emotion.

Further reflection led me to the awareness that in most of the European languages with which I am familiar the word for mother begins with the letter "M" and in all of these languages the colloquial word for mother is Mama, or Ma in some form or other. A little research on the subject led to the finding that the "Mm . . ." sound is predominant in the words used for mother in a great number of languages: Greek, *meter*; Latin, *mater*; French, *mere*; German, *Mutter*; Spanish and Italian, *madre*; Albanian, *Ama*; Assyrian, *Ummu*; Hebrew, *Em*. Jesperson (1922) also noted that the prolonged sound of "m" was used by the child to express delight over something that tastes good and illustrates this with many examples from different tongues. (Incidentally, in some languages the word for breast is very similar to the word for mother.)

Lewis (1936, 1948), who systematically recorded the development of the speech of infants, states that the first utterances of the infant occur in discomfort and are expressed as vowels. Semi-consonants appear later, and at about two months the "Mm . . ." sound is made in discomfort and particularly in hunger. Observations of infants indicate that the hungry infant makes anticipatory sucking movements which if phonated nasally will produce the sound "m" or "n." The sound "n" is made like the sound "m" with the difference that the tongue is pressed up against the palate in the "n" sound and rests at the floor of the mouth with the "m" sound. The sounds occurring during comfort are less distinct. The "m" and "n" sounds which are made in states of discomfort at the age of two months are later produced only in states of comfort from the age of six months. It would seem that the infant's memories of having his hunger gratified and the expectation of the satisfaction accounts for this transition. The "Mm . . ." sound which is now uttered in a state of contentment indicates the expectation of oral gratification.

At this point it would be worthwhile to review briefly some of the general functions of the utterance of sounds.

1. The utterance of sounds is a discharge expressive of pleasure or pain; it accompanies instinctual activities and is an indicator of affects.

2. The utterance of sounds has an autoerotic component. There are physically pleasurable sensations produced as the result of making certain sounds. The expulsion or retention and forming of column of air which is made by each utterance involve activities of the diaphragm, lungs, larynx, palate, tongue, lips, teeth, and mouth. Any one of these organs may be the site of some autoerotic pleasure. Other sounds of the more explosive nature offer the possibility of satisfying the aggressive instincts. The auditory perception of sounds and the feeling of mastery that may accompany the production of sounds can also serve as a source of pleasure. The tension-discharge function and the autoerotic function of producing sounds can be readily observed in the babbling of infants, particularly of deaf children, who are as noisy as, if not noisier than, children with good hearing. Dorothy Burlingham and Anna Freud (1943) have reported that children brought up without mothers will babble as much if not more than other children, but their development of language lags far behind children who are brought up by parents. In chapter 3 I have discussed some aspects of the relationship between the mother tongue and the mother.

3. The utterance of sounds is a means of interpersonal communication in the form of language. This is the last function of speech to be developed and is dependent upon the successful development of object relations as well as the maintenance of the proper admixture of autoerotic and expressive functions of speech.

If one now returns to the clinical fragment presented above, one can discern that the "Mm . . ." sound was a pleasantly toned autoerotic expression. The fact that the sound "Mm . . ." is made with the lips closed and continuously so throughout the utterance seems to indicate that this is the only sound one can make and still keep something safely within the mouth. Apparently it is the sound produced with the nipple in the mouth or with the pleasant memory of expectation of its being in the mouth. The word Mama which consists of a repetition of this sound duplicates the pleasurable labial sensations that are associated with the act of nursing. Piaget (1923) and Spielrein (1922) have come to similar conclusions about the word Mama on the basis of their clinical material. All of these comments would seem to explain the universally joyful connotation of the sound "Mm . . ." and the ubiquity of the word Mama. (The word "me" may have a similar origin, but this is purely speculative.)[1]

As a postscript to this subject, I should like to make a brief reference to the American slang word "sucker." The patient described above also possessed the character trait of gullibility that is inherent in this term. It is noteworthy that he unconsciously liked being a sucker. When he was not "down in the mouth" with depression or euphoric with the "Mm . . ." sensation, he went about openmouthed, ready to accept without discrimination anything anyone had to offer. In this way he tried to perpetuate the fantasy that the world was full of bearers of narcissistic and instinctual supplies. To be a "sucker" meant to him to live as though the whole world was a huge breast; all one had to do was to hold one's mouth open and the milky goodness would pour in. Being a "sucker" was a pathological form of optimism. It was also another means of denying deprivation and rejection. When he was fortunate he was euphoric for having "proven" that he was God's favorite. If he was unfortunate he could always blame his failure on being a "sucker" and thus attempt to ward off the underlying depression. I believe the character type of the "sucker" will be found to have relevance to some of the elements sketched above in regard to the "Mm . . ." sound and the word Mama.

[1] For a further discussion of sounds, see chapter 12.

8

Forepleasure

Its Use for Defensive Purposes

(1955)

I N RECENT YEARS psychoanalytic literature has stressed ego psychology, the role of aggression, applications of psychoanalysis, and as a result there has been relatively little written
about sexuality. This presentation is an attempt to formulate
some frequent and typical dysfunctions in the realm of
forepleasure. The aberrations described here are by no means
rare or unusual but should be noted precisely because they are so
often seen in practice and so rarely described in the literature.

It is well known that the function of forepleasure is to build
up sexual tension in order to insure the fullest discharge in both
partners. The ultimate objective of forepleasure is mutual orgasm.[1]

In forepleasure activities, a person reveals his attitudes
toward his own pregenitality,[2] erogenous zones and aims. He has
the opportunity to discover the preferences, needs, fears, likes
and dislikes in himself and in his partner. Furthermore, the

Presented at the Annual Meeting of the American Psychoanalytic Association, Los Angeles, May 1953. First published in *Journal of the American
Psychoanalytic Association*, 3:244-254, 1955.

[1] In this regard, human beings differ from other animals because in the
lower animals the purpose of forepleasure is apparently to insure fertility
(Ford and Beach, 1951).

[2] Pregenitality as used here includes the phallic phase.

study of a patient's forepleasure behavior gives the analyst a chance to trace the fate of the infantile instinctual components and particularly their relationship to end pleasure, genitality and orgasm. However, the analyst sees in forepleasure not only the instinctual components but also the results of defensive processes and maneuvers in regard to those instinctual elements. Not only does one see the results, but one can actually observe a variety of defensive maneuvers in action. My clinical experience indicates that forepleasure offers one of the richest opportunities to observe the interaction between instinctual drives and defenses. It is true that patients often have very strong resistances against becoming aware of and communicating their forepleasure activities. When these resistances have been overcome and the patient is able to describe his actions in and reactions to forepleasure activities, one has direct access to a great variety of the instinctual drives and the ego's defensive maneuvers.

It would be well at this point to attempt to differentiate between normal and pathological forepleasure activities. Forepleasure is in essence a preparatory act, hence we can formulate empirically that all forepleasure leading to satisfactory end pleasure, i.e., mutual orgasm, may be considered normal. However, since there are end-pleasure disturbances apart from forepleasure disturbances, this is not a completely reliable criterion, for it is conceivable that normal forepleasure might not fulfill its purpose because of some disturbance in the end-pleasure experience.

Generally speaking, however, satisfying mutual orgasms in the sexual partners is usually a sign of successful forepleasure. An orgasm is hard to describe qualitatively and quantitatively, and the patient's version is often unreliable; therefore it is advisable to seek other criteria for determining whether the forepleasure experience seems to be within normal limits. It is well known that human beings indulge in a great variety of forepleasure behavior, the normality or abnormality of which cannot be described in terms of a single zone or aim or component impulse. Certain typical patterns, however, are easily recognizable as pathological.

1. Lingering at forepleasure activities to a point that orgasm occurs during forepleasure or immediately thereafter, minimizing the end pleasure, is an indication of pathology in forepleasure. In this situation one or another aspect of the foreplay has supplanted the executive function of the genitals. This often stems from a combination of pregenital fixation and regression to pregenitality due to the inability to handle castration anxiety or penis envy.

2. Total elimination of forepleasure activities also indicates pathology, usually as a result of inhibitions due to some combination of anxiety, guilt, or shame in regard to pregenitality.

3. Rigid and unchanging patterns of forepleasure activities are also indications of pathology in foreplay. This usually means that forepleasure not only serves instinctual needs but also has important defensive functions.

Forepleasure patterns in healthy human beings are variable and flexible, a characteristic which distinguishes the sexual drives from the more fixed patterns of the other instinctual drives.

The foregoing remarks are a general introduction to some clinical and theoretical findings which emphasize the use of forepleasure activities for defensive purposes.

Aberrations in the Relationship between Forepleasure and End Pleasure

Overemphasis on Forepleasure

Freud (1905b), in describing the dangers of forepleasure, gave as an example too much forepleasure and too little end pleasure. At one time he considered the mechanism of the perversions to be of such a nature; a lingering at one of the preparatory acts in the sexual process. The overemphasis on foreplay is to be seen in people who are pregenitally fixated and relatively impotent or frigid genitally. Kinsey's report (1948) seemed to demonstrate that a high percentage of American males engage in this kind of sexual activity with a preponderance of forepleasure activity and end pleasure of a very short duration. The analysis of people who demonstrate such patterns in their sexual behavior usually reveals that the overemphasis on forepleasure has the purpose of avoiding some specific anxiety related to the genital act. Their forepleasure, therefore, has a defensive purpose, as can be demonstrated in the following case.

A compulsive-obsessive young woman with a strong homosexual component always insisted that her sexual partner stimulate her clitoris manually until she had a small orgasm. Only after that was she able to continue with the rest of the sexual act, which ended in vaginal intercourse and produced another small orgasm. It became clear in the analysis that this forepleasure activity was not only a phallic pleasure, but also served many defensive purposes. This aspect of her sexual activity was a means of using her boyfriend to reassure her that masturbation was permitted. It also made possible the discharge of a certain quantity of sexual tension and warded off the danger of a big orgasm with its full discharge. She feared that in a big orgasm she might completely lose control of herself. Despite many interpretations in reference to these points, the patient was unable to give up this practice or to modify it in any way, until I suggested that she consciously try to avoid the preliminary clitoral orgasm. She reported in the next hour that she complied with this suggestion; had had some preliminary sexual play, and then proceeded with intercourse. As her excitement mounted during intercourse, she was seized with an irresistible impulse, and bit her lover severely on the shoulder, so badly that he required medical attention. This indicated that the phallic forepleasure activity served to ward off her intense hostility toward the man which was based on her penis envy. The small orgasm was a partial discharge to prevent loss of control in the full orgasm. For her, the clitoral stimulation meant: "I have a penis of my own and I can have an orgasm of my own. Only then am I able to participate in a sexual act with a man's penis without the danger of destroying it." This case also demonstrated that multiple orgasms during the sexual act are incomplete orgasms and an unconscious means of avoiding the full orgasm with its momentary loss of consciousness and control. It also suggests that prematurity of orgasm is a problem not only of men but of women as well.

OMISSION OR SEPARATION OF FOREPLEASURE FROM END PLEASURE

There are many people who avoid forepleasure, because for them sexual relations are a serious matter or a matter of health or a matter of marital duty. One patient put it very aptly when he would respond to his wife's flirtatiousness with: "Do you mean business?" He meant by this, do you mean intercourse? Intercourse was business, as distinguished from sexual play. For such patients forepleasure is essentially play, and therefore does not rightfully belong in the category of the more serious sexual activities. To these people forepleasure may mean masturbation or pregenitality, which in either case is immoral. One female patient avoided clitoral stimulation in order to maintain in repression her infantile masturbation memories. Only after the infantile amnesia was broken through could she permit and enjoy clitoral stimulation during forepleasure. Occasionally one comes across patients who use a different person for forepleasure and for end pleasure. A male patient once put it very succinctly when he stated that he had intercourse with his wife and "extra"-course with his girlfriends. "Extra"-course was dirty, bad, and immoral, and therefore not a fit practice for his loving wife. Adolescent personalities often separate forepleasure and end pleasure in this way.

Aberrations in Regard to the Role of the Sexual Partner

USE OF THE SEXUAL PARTNER FOR REASSURANCE

There are many persons who use foreplay to obtain reassurance from the sexual partner in regard to one or another aspect of sexuality, particularly the pregenital aspects. In this way they strive to avoid feelings of anxiety, guilt, shame, or loss of love. Sometimes this succeeds, leading to relatively good orgastic po-

tency. Often it fails, leading to loss of erection, premature ejaculation, lack of orgasm, or weak orgasm. There are men, for example, who need to have the female partner fondle their penis
and insert it eventually into the vagina. This is done not merely
for deriving pleasure from tactile sensations, but as a symbolic
permission to have penis sensations, to have an erection, and to
indulge in intercourse. In some men the insertion of the penis by
the female means, "I am not committing rape," or "The sexual
act is not my responsibility." Similar reactions in regard to clitoris stimulation are to be seen in women. I have frequently seen
this pattern in women and men who require oral stimulation of
their genitals by the sexual partner. Again, these actions are performed not only because of the pleasurable sexual sensations, but
because they fulfill an important narcissistic need based on the
formula, "Love me, love my genitals." Particularly in women it
seems that the genital kiss of the man is needed proof that the
genital is not dirty, is not repulsive, and that she is lovable. In
men the request for fellatio often is aimed at getting reassurance
in regard to their castration anxiety. The mouth of the partner is
more familiar and less frightening than the vagina. After having
passed through this test, the man now has the courage to insert
the penis vaginally. It is often a rehearsal for men who have the
unconscious idea of the vagina dentata. Another frequent forepleasure pattern with a defensive purpose is getting the partner
to use obscenities. Ferenczi (1911) has pointed out the overdetermined meaning of obscenities. For these people obscenity implies a permission to be sensual and also as a denial of the fact
that this might be an incestuous object, according to the formula
that the mother would not use such dirty words.

DISTURBANCES IN EMPATHY

In order to insure mutual satisfaction, a high degree of
empathy is necessary in foreplay. There are many persons who
are unable to empathize with their sexual partners and therefore
are particularly clumsy in foreplay or avoid it altogether. These
disturbances, however, go beyond the realm of this paper which

is limited to the use of forepleasure activities for defensive purposes. One does see a variety of aberrations in forepleasure where normal empathy for the sexual partner is achieved at the price of giving up one's own personal sexuality. These patients not only gratify their homosexual components in this way but also ward off and avoid their own sexuality at the same time.

The most flagrant examples of this kind are to be seen in those people, men, for example, who perform some sexual activity for the female and have their orgasm, not on the basis of their own sexual stimulation but at the time when they imagine their sexual partner is having an orgasm. Men who have orgasms performing cunnilingus have identified themselves with the women and are, in this sense, indulging in a homosexual act. This is equally true of women who reach orgasm before performing fellatio. I have seen a similar situation in a hysterical woman who had an orgasm at the moment the penis penetrated the vagina. This was based on the patient's tendency toward identification with the aggressor (Anna Freud, 1936). In men such heightened empathy, in the last analysis, can be traced to their fear of castration, and in women to unresolved penis envy. They assume the identification with the opposite sex in order to avoid anxiety or disappointment in their own sexual role. There are similar cases resembling the exaggerated altruistic individuals whom Anna Freud (1936) described. They seem to get their vicarious satisfaction from an object they once envied and resented and with whom they now have identified.

People who so readily identify with their partner in sexual activities typically also manifest disturbances in reality testing, especially in regard to their conception of the self. Analysis reveals that this stems from a disturbance in the integration of their internalized objects.

Forepleasure Activities as a Means of Enacting Fantasies

This category of aberrations is an extremely large one and contains elements of the groups described above. It is very striking how frequently one finds that rigid patterns of forepleasure activity are really the enactment of a fantasy. These fantasies serve not only instinctual drives, but simultaneously serve a very important defensive function. It is this combination of instinctual satisfaction and protection which makes for rigidity.

A henpecked, compliant, passive male patient had the following routine in his sexual play with his wife. First of all, he would stimulate her nipples until they became erect. Then he would press both her breasts together so that they would form one large column. Then he would stimulate her clitoris manually until he felt it was erect. After that he would press her labia together in such a way that they would make a bulge. After this he would apply his mouth to her vulva and suck on the clitoris for a while, and then proceed to have intercourse. He would fall asleep immediately thereafter, only to awaken a few hours later, finding himself in the bathroom, washing his mouth, brushing his teeth, and scrubbing his penis. He had no conscious awareness of wanting to do this, but found himself doing so. Analysis of this behavior was complicated, but very rewarding. The first phase of the forepleasure activities was the enactment of a fantasy of making many penises on his wife. In this fantasy his wife was a big woman and he was a good little boy who came *not* to hurt her sexually or to take anything away from her sexually, but, on the contrary, to give her something, a penis. In this way he was unconsciously trying to appease his wife's hostile, castrative attitudes, of which he was aware in other connections but not in the sexual situation. He knew his wife envied and resented the man's role in society, and in foreplay he was prophylactically counteracting her castrative penis envy. Furthermore, in this activity he was symbolically denying his wife's penislessness in order to assuage his castration anxiety. In addition, this behavior was a means of enacting the role of a good provider. This was important to him, because his wife constantly reproached him for not giving her enough money, clothes, luxuries, etc. The cunnilingus was a reaction formation and a denial of his underlying loathing of his wife's genitals. In this way he was unconsciously proclaiming to his wife, "It is not true that you are slovenly, unkempt, and unlovable." He undid this denial by washing two hours later when he was in a half sleep. This loathing, however, which the reaction formation and denial covered, was itself a reaction formation against the still deeper anally determined love of the vagina. The cunnilingus was also an opportunity to act out a nursing child-mother relationship.

I believe one can see here the enactment and acting out of several fantasies. "I am a good boy who does not hurt a woman sexually. This woman is not without a penis; in fact I bring her many penises. She is clean, and I shall prove that she is not dirty by applying my mouth to her genitals. A woman does have a little penis which she gives me to suckle on." By means of this behavior the patient was able to allay his underlying fear, hatred, and loathing of his wife and her genitals, and could enjoy some amount of sexual satisfaction.[3]

Similar behavior can be observed in women who during foreplay prefer to have the penis protrude between their legs, as an attempt to deny their penis envy and counteract their hostility. Women often enjoy lying on top of the male during intercourse, not only because it affords a better stimulation of the clitoris, but also because it affords them an opportunity to fantasy that they have a penis in order temporarily to deny their feeling of having been castrated. In this connection it should be mentioned that many people enjoy watching the penis enter into the vagina because it gives them the illusion that the penis belongs to both of them. It also is a reenactment of watching the primal scene.

A very frequent forepleasure activity is the telling of sexual stories. These stories are usually primal scene stories or stories of infantile sexuality. Their defensive function, however, lies in the fact that it is a distraction from the sexual activities at hand; by conjuring up the images of the story, one becomes an onlooker

---

[3] Anna Freud (1936) has described denial by means of fantasy and acts in the games of little children. The structure of this behavior, I believe, is very similar to that described here.

and not a participant in the sexual act. It is a denial that one is actually performing the sexual act.

Another interesting enactment of a fantasy was observed in a man patient who had the fantasy of being a woman's penis. Fenichel (1949) described a similar situation in women in a paper entitled "The Symbolic Equation: Girl=Phallus." His article refers to women who have a fantasy of being a man's penis. In the patient I wish to describe one of the outstanding features was a strong female castration complex, i.e., this male patient was dominated by the idea that he had already been castrated, and as a result he had a great need to ingratiate himself with everybody. In his sexual life with women he was overly empathic and pathologically altruistic. He devoted almost the entire sexual foreplay to anticipating every wish and whim of his female partner, with little regard for his own instinctual impulses. Part of the forepleasure was based upon the formula of giving girls penises as described above. The most striking activity, however, was one in which the patient would lie upon the woman in such a way that his neck rested upon her pubic arch, with the rest of his body stretched out taut between her widespread legs. This behavior was based on the unconscious fantasy "I am a woman's penis." On the one hand, this fantasy was a means of appeasing the woman's penis envy and hostility; on the other hand, it was a means of re-creating the fantasy of the powerful mother with a penis. In general, he used foreplay as a means of enacting fantasies which would deny the penislessness of women.

As one would expect, people who make such frequent use of the mechanism of denial in their forepleasure activities also use denial mechanisms in other aspects of their lives. As a consequence, these patients suffer from certain disturbances in ego functioning and in reality testing. These people are often confused in regard to the conception of their ego identity; they are uncertain as to who they are (see chapter 5).

Many people enact, in forepleasure activities, a past experience which was originally of a frightening nature. For example, a man who was shocked at the sight of a photograph in a medical book of a woman in a gynecological position regularly used to make his wife repeat this particular position during foreplay. Similarly, a woman who had a traumatic experience as a child of being raped by an older boy would ask her husband to tell her stories of rape during foreplay. It is true that in part these experiences were pleasurable; nevertheless, the reenactment of these traumatic events also served the purpose of making sure that one was now master of these situations and no longer afraid of them.

There are many other fairly common forepleasure activities which have a defensive purpose, but it would lead beyond the scope of this paper to attempt to enumerate them here. One should mention the many masochistic actions which are a means of paying in advance for some later forbidden pleasures, often of a sadistic nature. By permitting oneself to suffer pain, one has purchased the right later to enjoy sexuality. Touching is often used in foreplay as a means of testing out with the hand before entrusting the genitals to the sexual partner. Exhibitionistic and voyeuristic practices are used to deny that one or one's partner is castrated.

Summary and Conclusion

I have tried to demonstrate that, although forepleasure is primarily devoted to the various pregenital instinctual components, zones and aims, it is also frequently used for important defensive purposes. Forepleasure offers an excellent opportunity to study the direct results of the mechanisms of defense and also many of the ego's more complex defensive measures in action. It is particularly striking how frequently people use forepleasure activities to enact and act out a fantasy which has the purpose of denying or counteracting some frightening aspect of sexuality. Indulging in fantasies seems to have the overall purpose of distracting the individual from the sexual act in which he is engaged. There seems to be an antagonistic relationship between the amount of fantasy in forepleasure and the object relationship. The greater the amount of fantasy, the less the object and the self are cathected in forepleasure. All of these considerations seem to point to the fact that forepleasure is often not just pleasure but also a serious matter.

9

On Screen Defenses, Screen Hunger, and Screen Identity

(1958)

IN THE EARLY YEARS of psychoanalysis, patients coming for treatment were suffering from symptom neuroses, a relatively clean-cut and well-defined group of pathological formations. The clinical picture changed as society changed and after World War I, patients seeking therapy were found to be suffering from character disorders, an ill-defined, heterogeneous form of neurosis. Since I resumed practice after World War II, it seems to me that once again there is a change in the prevailing clinical picture of patients coming for psychoanalytic treatment. They are still preponderantly character disorders, but now the pathology seems to be centered around a defective formation of the self image, an identity disorder. The struggle to establish

Presented at the Annual Meeting of the American Psychoanalytic Association, Chicago, April 1956, under the title "Characters in Search of a Screen." First published in *Journal of the American Psychoanalytic Association*, 6:242-262, 1958.

one's self image or self representation has been elucidated in the psychoanalytic literature in the writings of Erikson (1950), Jacobson (1954a, 1954b), and Hartmann (1950). Erikson goes so far as to state that the study of identity today is as strategic as the study of sexuality in Freud's day. There is no doubt that disorders of the self image are being described more frequently today (Hanna Fenichel, n.d.; McDowell, n.d.). In part this certainly is due to our particular interest in studying the vicissitudes of ego development.

Ever since the character disorders dominated the clinical scene, psychoanalysts have focused their attention on the ego functions. The ego's methods and motives in coping with the dangerous instinctual demands and painful reality are the decisive factors in character formation. Among the most important means available to the ego in this struggle are the defenses. The problem of defense is complicated because as yet we have no systematic classification either in regard to chronology or to complexity (Anna Freud, 1936). Freud (1926a) suggested, however, that it might be helpful to relate particular forms of defense to specific clinical disorders. This presentation is an attempt to demonstrate how certain defenses, called screen defenses, decisively influence the personality formation in a distinct and discernible group of patients. These patients seem to be driven by a hunger for "screen experiences." The result of the screen defenses and screen hunger seems to be the formation of a screen identity. These terms will be clarified by the clinical material.

In 1916 Freud very briefly sketched his clinical findings in three types of neurotic characters: the "exceptions," "those wrecked by success," and "criminals from a sense of guilt." In later years other psychoanalysts have enlarged our collection of clinical portraits, among them Abraham (1925), H. Deutsch (1942), Fenichel (1939c) and A. Reich (1954). In this essay I shall attempt to portray the significant characteristics and formative factors compiled from the psychoanalyses of seven patients studied in the last eleven years. This is not an attempt to establish a new diagnostic category but to describe a specific clinical syndrome and a particular type of defense.

Screen Patients

The screen patients make a rather distinct clinical impression. Although their initial complaints may vary from phobic reactions to depressions, they share significant personality traits. They appear ready and eager to make contact and to communicate. They are very conscious of their skill or awkwardness with words and language. They seem warm and giving in pouring forth their life history, despite anxiety or shame, since they keenly need to feel understood. Although they are quite successful in their work, they belittle their accomplishments and have little faith in their genuine merits. They are talented, with a flair for the creative aspects in their field; but their productivity is sporadic and unreliable. They are unduly concerned with their social standing and long to be accepted, popular, and entertaining. Situations involving exhibitionism and scoptophilia are either excessively exciting or frightening or both. Though prone to severe mood swings, they usually display a chronic optimism. They become easily enthusiastic and sentimental. They are impressionable, suggestible, with a tendency toward credulousness, bordering on gullibility. They tend to exaggerate to the point of lying and may have a touch of the swindler about them. They are sensitive, perceptive, and empathic—qualities they use for ingratiation. All of this is readily discernible in the initial interviews.

There are certain characteristic features which distinguish the general course of analysis in the screen patient. They take to the method of free association easily and there is little silence. Their productions are rich in fantasy and there is a copious dream life. These patients often have a surprising access to some areas of their unconscious. They are psychologically minded and often spontaneously come upon important insights, yet they have great difficulty in integrating these new insights effectively. Although their analysis is of long duration in years, the analytic hour moves quickly. It is typical for these patients to develop a strong positive transference from the very beginning of the analysis. Despite their general emotional lability, this positive

transference remains relatively fixed. Although this serves a predominantly useful function in the first years of analysis, it eventually becomes the most important stumbling block to the successful final resolution of their neurotic conflicts. These patients
tend to protect the analyst from their aggressive impulses and
displace these impulses onto scapegoats, particularly onto other
analysts. This tendency to separate what ought to be fused can
be seen in other aspects of their lives as well. These patients often
display a markedly different set of character traits at work and
at home, with their family or with strangers. Similarly, the
entire analysis may be isolated from the rest of their lives or
important segments of their lives may remain outside of the
analysis for years at a time. These patients make extensive use of
the mechanisms of negation and denial. They are prone to neurotic actions and tend to act out instead of remember. They frequently maintain the fantasy of being the analyst's favorite
patient and cling to this despite persistent interpretations. All of
this colors the clinical picture and complicates the therapeutic
task.

The analytic material of these patients reveals constellations
which might be conventionally classified as a combination of
hysteria and depression. As the analysis progresses, the depressive elements predominate over the hysterical features. Actually,
the situation becomes even more complicated because the depressive component in these patients turns out to be a mixture of
neurotic depression and impulse disorder. These patients are essentially impulsive depressives with a hysterical superstructure.

Screen Memories and Other
Screen Formations

Before going on to a more detailed description of the clinical
findings, I would like to survey briefly our present knowledge of
screens in order to indicate how we may broaden our conception
of screen functions. Freud's writings on screen memories (1899,
1901) are the starting point and the models for the later formula-

tions. He began by noting that many people remembered, consciously and with great clarity, experiences from early childhood that were either obviously trivial or obviously falsified. Freud explained this phenomenon as a compromise solution in a conflict between the wish to remember and the wish to forget. The innocuous or falsified screen memory is retained in consciousness because it is associatively connected to an important and more painful memory which has been repressed. Freud stressed another aspect of screen memories, namely, that they are visual memories and one sees oneself in the memory. Later Freud (1914a) suggested that screen memories are related to childhood amnesia in the same way as the manifest dream is related to the latent dream thoughts.

Sachs (1923) and particularly Fenichel (1927, 1939a, 1946) emphasized the economic function of screen memories. The screen memory affords some derivative discharge for the repressed memory, thus insuring the success of the repression. This parallels the state of affairs in symptom formation in general: distorted instinctual derivatives are permitted access to consciousness and motility, thereby facilitating the ego's task of repressing the underlying impulses. Glover (1939a) demonstrated that even traumatic memories may serve a screening function for a more severe trauma. Fenichel's (1928) concept of the "command to remember" and Freud's (1914b) views on *déjà vu* and *déjà raconté* are related phenomena in structure and function.

The following example may illustrate the dynamic and economic functions of the screen memory: a young man, early in his analysis, described the pleasant memory, going back to age six, of tasting his first Coca Cola. He recalled it as a strange bitter-sweet taste. For a long time the retention of this innocuous experience in his memory was unexplained. Several years later, it was revealed that he was given his first Coca Cola because he was upset by an unpleasant experience earlier that day. On that day he had for the first time seen dead bodies, a man and a boy who had drowned. This was his first "taste" of death. Some time later, an additional memory of that day broke through into consciousness. On the walk going for the Coca Cola he became aware of his mother's flirting with a strange man. This was one of his first bitter-sweet "tastes" of his mother's infidelity. Thus the memory of the first Coca Cola was a relatively pleasant screen for two painful and disturbing memories. Such screen memories are very frequent findings in the analysis of the screen patients.

The next major advance in our understanding of the function of screen memories was accomplished by Fenichel (1939a), who, following the ideas of Anna Freud (1936), regarded the screen memory as an attempt to deny and contradict a painful reality. Just as fantasies and games do not merely negate painful situations but contradict them and proclaim the opposite, so the screen memory often does not merely conceal the original experience but falsifies it in a pleasurable direction. The screen memory may be considered a compromise in the struggle between the ego's wish to contend with painful reality and the wish to avoid it. The result is that only part of the reality is remembered; the painful aspects have been hidden and camouflaged, often to the point of distorting the reality. The frequent childhood memory of "seeing" a female with a penis is a typical example of such a deformation of reality (see Greenacre, 1949; Waelder, 1951).

Whereas originally the concept of screens was limited to memories, in recent years other phenomena have been described which seem to parallel screen memories in structure and function. Fenichel (1939a) and later Greenacre (1949) described screen perceptions. In traumatic situations patients would select and react to only certain relatively painless perceptions and would use these to conceal more terrifying perceptions. Lewin (1950) introduced the term "screen affect" in describing how pleasant affects may be used to ward off painful affects. And I tried to indicate how certain moods may be screens against more painful moods (see chapter 5). Fenichel (1927, 1928, 1939a, 1939c, 1945, 1946) broadened the usage of the term "screens" by employing the phrases "screen experiences," "screen formations," and "screen activities." Reider (1953a) recently formulated some ideas about screening functions which would include screen symptoms and screen character structure.

I believe we can extend the concept of screen formation or screen maneuver into the realm of identification. I have previously (chapter 6) tried to demonstrate how certain identifications had the function of denying and contradicting other more painful identifications. I tried to show how certain patients struggled to remain unaware of "bad" identifications by eagerly forming object relations and new identifications with "good" objects in order to reinforce the denying function of some earlier "good" identifications. Ferenczi (1909) in a paper on "Introjection and Transference" described suggestible and transference-hungry people who also manifested this identification hunger. I believe that one may term identifications which serve this dynamic and economic purpose "screen identifications."

Just as one can describe screen formations in regard to memories, affects, moods, and identifications, I believe one can do the same in regard to the self image.[1] As an example of such a problem, I refer to the young woman (described in chapter 3) who developed a great aversion to speaking her mother tongue. She described her predicament as follows: "In German, I am a scared, dirty child; in English, I am a nervous, refined woman." As long as she spoke English, her picture of herself was the English-speaking, refined lady. The moment she spoke German, her self image changed, and she became a scared and dirty child. The English identity was a screen against the German identity. It served the purpose of maintaining in repression the painful German self image as well as offering an opportunity to exhibit a more pleasing aspect of the self.

All the phenomena described above, as diverse as they may appear on the surface, have a similar form and function. Psychic phenomena of a given class are used to contradict or deny phenomena of the same class, i.e., a memory versus a memory, an affect versus an affect, a perception versus a perception, etc. I shall therefore use the term "screen" to refer to all such psychic

[1] The term "self-image" is used in this paper in the same sense as Erikson uses the term "ego identity" and Jacobson and Hartmann use the term "self representation." I prefer the term self image because it seems to me the simplest and clearest designation.

events. This is to differentiate screen activities from other defensive maneuvers, as, for example, a thought used to ward off a feeling or an attitude maintained in opposition to an impulse. (This definition was derived from a discussion with Nathan Leites.)

In ordinary language the word screen may mean to conceal, to filter, or to camouflage. In the psychoanalytic sense, I believe we use the term screen for describing activities of concealment, defensive maneuvers for the purpose of avoiding pain. One method of avoiding pain by utilizing screens is to filter, or strain, or sift out the painful and only permit the innocuous or harmless to gain access to consciousness. Another method is to use the screen for camouflage, or for distortion, so that the painful is coated over by a pleasurable misrepresentation. One might differentiate between filter screens and falsified screens. The innocuous memories of childhood and the bizarre memories would be examples of each (Simmel, 1925; Kennedy, 1950). All people make use of one or another screen formation in the course of their lives, but the screen characters I am describing make extensive use of these maneuvers in a vain attempt to maintain their psychic equilibrium. They belong to that group of neurotics who need to employ denial mechanisms and maneuvers exclusively in order to support their failing ability to repress. The screen formation attempts to patch over what repression has failed to handle (Waelder, 1951). These patients make predominant use of the falsified screen experience rather than the filter screen. Their screen activities do more than negate the painful; they contradict by proclaiming the pleasurable even at the price of disturbing reality testing. The falsified screen is to the filter screen as contradiction is to denial, as reaction formatin is to repression.

The Function of Screen Activities

Screen activities are not only defensive operations but also simultaneously offer important opportunity for gratification

(Waelder, 1930). In 1927, Fenichel introduced the concept of screen hunger. He referred to the imperative, urgent, and repetitive quality in the behavior of certain patients. In my experience, the screen patients seem to be driven by an insatiable hunger for new experiences and new objects. They cannot be alone or unoccupied and prefer miserable company to aloneness and quiet. This hunger is overdetermined and has varied manifestations. Obviously, the perpetual hunger is an indication of instinctual frustrations in regard to a need-satisfying object. This dissatisfaction is true for all neurotics. What is typical for screen patients is that the frustrations goad them on to find new objects and new experiences. The "new" always seems to awaken new hopes. They cannot take no for an answer. They dare not, since the "no," if accepted, would remobilize their underlying depression. The new objects and new experiences not only offer instinctual and narcissistic gratifications in the present but deny misery and insecurity. The new objects and the new experiences, however, do not eradicate the old depression and anxiety but serve as a screen. These patients do not try to overcome the ill effects of the past; they try to deny the past. The screen maneuvers and the screen hunger give a distinctive stamp to their personality. The imperative, urgent, and repetitive quality of the behavior is due to the fact that the screen activity attempts simultaneously to satisfy libidinal, narcissistic, and defensive needs.

In all patients in whom acting out is an outstanding feature of the neurosis, we find the same irresistibility of behavior. The pervert indulges in overtly sexual activities of an infantile, pregenital nature in order to deny his castration anxiety. The impulse neurotic attempts the same by sexualizing some symbolic representation of pregenital activity. The screen-hungry patient acts out in a very general way, utilizing for this purpose a great variety of everyday experiences, including a façade of genital activity to deny his or her pregenitality. To further clarify the differences between the screen character and other types of neurotic characters, I should like to describe certain outstanding features of the clinical picture.

Ego Functions in Screen Characters

If we examine the ego functions of the screen character patient, we find that he or she is essentially and ordinarily well oriented to reality, of good intelligence, highly accomplished, and socially successful. He may be eccentric but not weird, withdrawn but not inaccessible. He may manifest some ego dysfunctions, but they are transient and limited in scope. Usually they concern insufficiency in his integrative and synthesizing ego functions. The creative and artistic patients could readily regress to the primary process for intuitive sensing of the unconscious without really understanding its meaning (Kris, 1950). Disturbances of body perception could also be observed, particularly in regard to body image. Sudden and intense change of mood seemed to bring about the temporary disruption of these ego functions.

The memory disorder in these patients has several striking features (H. Fenichel, n.d.). There are usually large areas of amnesia, not only for early childhood, but also for recent events. One also sees a great deal of falsification of memories. One patient stated that for the first three years in his seven-year-old son's life he awakened almost every night to feed and change him. He later reported that when he told this to his wife, she stated simply that he had done this twice in three years. He reported this laughingly and shrugged it off. Another feature of the memory disturbance is the clinical finding that almost all the important people of their past lives are remembered as essentially one-sided black or white figures. Only in dreams or in neurotic actions does one gain a glimpse at the more complex structure of these object relations. Rapaport (1942) has pointed out that in patients described as multiple personalities whole sets of memories and affects are not available to consciousness and become available only in trance states and dreams. Finally, the struggle against remembering can be seen in these patients by the frequency of their acting out and their tendency to relive instead of to remember.

These patients have a rather disturbed relationship to time, another point which Hanna Fenichel (n.d.) has stressed. Past and present are very near to each other, and they tend to blur remembering with reliving. When they recount a past event, they tend to relive it without recognizing even afterward the passage of time that has taken place since the actual experience occurred. Their closeness to their past gives them a youthful quality and their self picture is many years younger than their chronological age. Though they dread old age, death is unreal to them; and they tend to believe in their immortality. They want their plight to change, but they hope that the world will do the changing. They come to analysis in order to change their past, to falsify their past, rather than to change the ill effects of the past. They search for experiences that will serve as memories which will distort the past. They are memory collectors. This curious relationship to the past also disturbs their capacity for anticipation. They cling to the hope of a better past and mistake this for a better future.

It is characteristic of these patients to feel that they are the lucky ones, the favored ones. In this way they bear a resemblance to Freud's "exceptions" (1916). They secretly believe this not only in regard to their family and friends, but also that they are God's favorite and that they are pursued by good fortune. I have already mentioned that in the transference situation they tend to believe that they are the analyst's favorite patient and they expect some special relationship to him during and certainly after the termination of treatment. Along with this feeling of being the lucky one, one occasionally sees evidence of feelings of omnipotence and expansiveness. This occurs in moments of triumph or in rage. When angry, these people tend to feel invulnerable and unbeatable. They also have a megalomanic attitude when they feel guilty and belabor themselves with monumental self-punishment with which no one may interfere. They are prone to use the words "never" and "always," frequently and dogmatically. Apparently these people confuse the *wish* to be the favorite with the feeling that they *are* the favorite (Annie Reich, 1953, 1954).

This confusion about feeling lucky is but one manifestation of these patients' difficulty in maintaining a consistent and integrated self image. Although there is still much unclarity in discerning the different phases of development in the establishment of a self image, we can recognize certain disorders in terms of a disorder in the self image. Edith Jacobson (1954a, 1954b) in particular has stressed how vicissitudes of the introjects may play a decisive role in the formation of the self image. Erikson (1950) has emphasized the sense of integrity, continuity, and sameness necessary for the formation of the self image. I can only report on the clinical finding that the screen patients all manifested striking incongruities in their self images.

These patients seemed to have multiple identities which gave an unstable and often contradictory picture of their personality. The patient with the mother-tongue problem is a case in point. She could vacillate between feeling like a dirty, scared child or the refined, nervous lady, depending on the state of her self-esteem. A lowering of her self-esteem not only made her feel guilty or ashamed but radically altered her self image. A writer patient, who was experiencing difficulty in his work, felt not that he was writing poorly but that he had *never* been able to write at all. These people not only change jobs, they frequently change careers. These patients try to use one self image as a screen against another, more painful self image. When these attempts are not completely successful, we see how these patients behave in a way which we may describe as "out of character" for that particular person. Alcohol often precipitates some unpleasant surprises. In analysis, episodes of acting out or the sudden fluctuation of a mood will bring to light these shifts of the self image.

Although these patients have multiple self images, the self image is not fragmented as it is in psychotics. Each self image is a relatively well-organized unit. Yet these people lack the whole, composite, fused self image we observe in mature people. Clinical signs of this identity disorder can be seen in the fact that five out of the seven patients I have studied changed their names in an attempt to change their identity. One female patient had a boy's nickname. Several underwent plastic surgery. In each of them these maneuvers were analyzed and revealed as attempts to maintain a certain image of the self and to deny simultaneously another picture of the self. The result was limited, isolated, but acceptable self image.

Essentially, these disturbances in ego functions give these people great difficulty in their sense of perspective. I believe Piaget's (1937a, 1937b) ideas on this subject to be particularly relevant. These patients have difficulty in locating themselves among other objects in space and in time. They are unable to renounce their need for "immediate experience" and therefore are not capable of recognizing the limitations of the moment in relation to the past and future. In order to acquire a sense of perspective, the child has to renounce his immediate experiences in favor of more permanent coordinated experiences in memory. Ordinarily this occurs in children at about the age of six. Apparently the successful resolution of the oedipus complex and the establishment of a permanent superego are essential to this process.

Object Relations of Screen Characters

The screen characters demonstrate certain typical idiosyncracies in their object relations. Already in the first interviews one is struck by their eagerness to make contact and to communicate. Their readiness to relate quickly and intensely to people not only indicates their hunger for objects but also hints at the transference nature of their object relations. While it is true that there is some admixture of transference in every later object relationship, it is extremely prominent in these patients. One patient, a man, over a forty-year period had three different close friends, each of them with the same first name. In his case, each of the friends was revealed to be a relatively undistorted later edition of the idealized father. In addition to the transference features in their object relations, one usually finds important elements of identification. When they like somebody, they take over certain character traits of that person. This adolescentlike quality is also to be seen in their frequent infatuations with men and women alike (Anna Freud, 1936; Annie Reich,

1953). To like someone and to be like someone are very closely related in these people. In part, this is an attempt to get close to the object, and in part it is a method for getting to know the object so well that one can anticipate the needs and wishes and thereby ingratiate oneself. They are such profuse givers in order to get love.

These patients are not ambivalent in the ordinary sense of the word; namely, there is no coexistence, no simultaneity, of love and hatred toward the object. Their feelings of love and hatred to the same object alternate. There are definitely discernible periods of love and separate periods of hatred. When they hate, there is no vestige of remembrance of the previous love; and when they love, there is only a dim memory of any previous hatred. These patients use a more primitive method in dealing with their ambivalence than does the compulsive-obsessive (Glover, 1939a). The object they love is different from the object they hate. They resemble a little child who loves the good mother and hates the bad mother; and these are quite separate people for the child. These patients apparently do not have the capacity to fuse the loved and hated object into a single object.

The oedipal situation is a complicated one in these patients. Either a positive or a negative oedipus complex is present in the foreground, tenaciously covering the complementary aspect which is deeper in the unconscious. Analysis, however, has revealed that the most significant relationship is the negative oedipus complex which has a strong oral and homosexual cast. This oral component is derived from the early, pregenital mother relationship. In part, they use their orality as a defense against their oedipal situation, a point stressed by Bergler (1949) and L. J. Friedman (1953). Because of the partial regression and fixation to the oral level, the later significant object relations contain varying mixtures of oedipal, oral, and homosexual strivings. One woman married a man twenty-five years her senior who was very motherly. Several patients married outside their religion in order to make sure they were not marrying a relative. They needed this island of denial since in many other ways the spouse had unmistakable features resembling the parental figure. In other interpersonal relations besides the marriage, one could observe how these people tend to "oedipalize." Friends and enemies turned out to be parents, siblings, etc.

Another characteristic of their personal relations is their tendency to perceive and to react to only a part of an object. Their wives, friends, and enemies are not perceived as whole, composite human beings. By means of selective perceptions they can deny certain aspects of these people and hypercathect other aspects. Their ability to maintain a preambivalent emotional attitude is due to the partial object relationship. Those aspects of the object which are not consciously perceived are unconsciously perceived and break through in dreams and in moods when the patient is "not himself."

The outstanding characteristic of the object relationships of these patients is their hunger for objects. In part, this has been discussed as a manifestation of their oral-libidinal and narcissistic needs. However, there are other purposes which objects fulfill for the screen-hungry people. They need objects as witnesses to testify to the fact that the patient's aggression has not damaged the object; they use witnesses to give permission for instinctual activity. Furthermore, the object offers them an opportunity to master belatedly their anxiety in regard to objects. The screen-hungry patients libidinize their anxiety; and for this purpose, too, they need objects (Fenichel, 1934c). Their object relationships are essentially gratifying, but the tendency to transference reactions, identifications, "oedipalization," and splitting of objects makes for only partial and transitory satisfactions, restlessness, and discontent.

Libido Orientation of Screen Characters

The libidinal orientation of these patients is also impressively uniform. Essentially they are fixated to both the oral and phallic libidinal zones and aims. Their orality is manifested in their hunger for experiences and objects. They love food and eating. The quickness of their attempts to communicate and their tendency to feel lonely and abandoned if they do not feel close also indicate orality. Their preoccupation with verbal communication deserves special scrutiny. To them, the mouth is a bisexual organ. In part, it is a receptive-getting organ. The tongue, however, is also important for them. It is not merely a phallic, exhibitionistic, penetrating organ; it is also a breast that pours forth a stream of language as a means of pleasing and wooing the object. In the men and women patients, the tongue is both masculine and feminine; it is a combination of penis and breast (Deri, personal communication; see also chapter 3). These patients are hungry, not greedy. They give in order to get, but they are not able to hoard the narcissistic supplies that they need. They also give as a reparation for past, unconscious, hostile feelings.

The importance of scoptophilia and exhibitionism in these patients is derived mainly from the oral significance of the eye. For them, the eye is an incorporating, devouring organ. Looking gives them an opportunity to share, to participate, to become close, and above all to identify with an object (Fenichel, 1935).

Their bowel habits are also interesting. They are not fixated to the anal sphere, as are the anal characters. They are not constipated, nor do they usually suffer from diarrhea. They have quick bowel movements. They can postpone their bowel movements for long periods of time without the fecal mass ever becoming hard or compact. They are not retentive as the compulsive-obsessive, but expulsive. They are unable to consolidate the fecal mass, as the compulsive is able to do. There is a striking parallel in their inability to fuse their external objects and the way they handle their internal objects and the bowel movement. Apparently in their bowel training they had been willing to give up their bowel pleasures for the love of the parent.

Their sexual life is relatively satisfying in that these people are sensitive, empathic, have frequent intercourse with great emphasis on the forepleasure. However, its main function is to give the feeling of closeness and belonging. They seek intercourse when there is marital discord. It is not primarily the orgasm which is sought but the satisfying sense of fusion. Their forepleasure is full of fantasies which are reenacted (see chapter 8). As one patient put it in describing his vacillating potency: "My sexuality depends on who I am at the time of intercourse, who I am doing it with, and what I imagine I am doing. At times, I am a little boy having intercourse with a big lady. At other times, I am a big, cruel man doing nasty things to a little girl. Sometimes I am a doctor examining a patient. Occasionally, I am who I am, doing what I am doing, namely, a man having intercourse with his wife." The men patients usually have good erectile potency and the women have some pleasurable orgasmlike response. In both, the sexual act is sought after as a means of reassurance and love. In the man, the penis is an organ for establishing contact and for giving pleasure rather than an erotic organ for genital satisfaction. In the women, the important organ is the vagina and not the clitoris. The sought-for sensation is to feel the fullness of the penis within the vagina; the orgasm is only secondary. The clitoris is used for masturbation and remains outside the interpersonal sexual act. Often the clitoris is anesthetic, whereas the vagina is not. In both, the sexual act is an attempt to achieve a unity, a oneness, rather than orgasm. They often weep at the point of orgasm, for, to them, it is the moment of aloneness.

In general, the libidinal development seems to indicate fixations at the oral and phallic levels. The hysterical, impulsive-depressive clinical material would speak for this. It seems that these patients experienced important gratifications at the oral level and then went on to the anal level where they experienced primarily frustrations. In some patients this seems to have led to a pathological progression, a premature phallic phase. Others seem to have regressed to the oral phase but belatedly went on to a relatively strong phallic and oedipal period (Marmor, 1953). The etiological factor will be discussed later.

The Superego in Screen Characters

The superego in these patients also exhibits some noteworthy characteristics. First of all, there is the tendency to ex-

ternalize, to reproject, and isolate the superego functions. Instead of feeling "ought" and "should," they regress to the attitude, "you made me." They prefer to feel obligated to others in
the hope of manipulating the external object instead of perceiving feelings of guilt.

Their superego is corruptible because it is composed of
heterogeneous introjects. The parents of these patients openly
disagreed as to what was right and wrong, good and bad, valuable and trivial. They could play one aspect of the superego
against the other by merely externalizing one introject and
thus avoid the internal conflict. Unfortunately these maneuvers fail, and these patients feel guilty, either consciously or unconsciously. The guilt feelings are often inappropriately lacking
at a given time, only to occur unexpectedly and intensely. When
these patients feel guilty, they tend to react as depressives do
with a self-reproach that is obviously inappropriate and violent.
It is not the consistent, nagging, self-reproach of the chronically
sadistic superego of the compulsive-obsessive. When guilt feelings are not conscious, one can observe a tendency to accident
proneness, a sudden spurt of recklessness—often during a period
of acting out.

The Etiology of Screen Characters

Why did these patients develop this particular mode of
handling their conflicts? Why did they not merely become
phobic and attempt to avoid all derivatives of their neurotic conflicts? Or, why did they not become manic-depressives and in-
ternalize their struggle with objects? I believe that the answer to
this question lies in the historical fact that all these patients had
important gratifying experiences at crucial times of their lives. It
was apparent that all of these patients suffered from traumatic
deprivations and frustrations. This would have made for ordinary neurotic developments, but it is the gratifications which occurred at critical times that, I believe, were responsible for the
specific development of the screen-hungry character.

In each of these patients there were important gratifications on the oral level, on the oedipal level, and in adolescence, which made for fixations at these levels. According to my clinical experience, frustrations and deprivations make for regression; gratifications make for fixations. In the patients described, in the oral phase, although their mothers were unreliable givers, there was a period when they were the only or favored child and received a predominance of gratification. In the oedipal phase, each of these patients was unusually gratified, as well as deprived, by one or both of the parents. In each case, there was open and violent marital discord between the parents. In each of them, each parent at different times indicated that he or she preferred the child to the marriage partner. It is true that these gratifications were unreliable, but they did occur and there was always the hope that they would be repeated.

These patients, during the turbulence of adolescence, also experienced important satisfactions. The female patients were unusually attractive women. The young woman with the mother-tongue problem was at age fourteen taken from her poverty-stricken home into luxurious surroundings by a wealthy benefactor. Another woman patient was loved by the most popular male in their school. The men patients in their adolescence were unusually successful in athletics or in scholarship or in the courting of the belle of the town, etc. In all of these patients, I believe the gratifications during the oral, phallic, and adolescent phases made for fixations at these levels. These gratifications were not only instinctual gratifications, but narcissistic ones as well. They simultaneously served to deny and ward off both anxiety and guilt. The parent who previously was a frightening object and who then became the loving object not only gratified the libidinal needs of the child but also reassured him or her against anxiety and guilt. It is the combination of gratification and security which made for this type of fixation.

The disturbed marital life of the parents was an important factor in the development of these patients. Not only did these parents dislike each other, but they had contempt for each other and for each other's values. The open devaluation of the parents made for a heterogeneous and unstable superego development

(Jacobson, 1954a). The parents lied to each other and to the child. I believe that parents who lie create children who deny. If parents distort reality consciously, this gives the child an impetus to distort reality unconsciously.

In my opinion, these historical facts explain at least in part the choice of the neurotic disorder in these patients. Their hunger and optimism come from their history of unreliable but nevertheless real gratifications. They cling to object relations and to their instinctual drives because they expect eventually to be gratified by the unreliable object. Their uncertainty and the memory of disappointments are handled by their screen experiences which deny their past failures. Their superego is as corruptible as the parents. They feel lucky to avoid feeling depressed (see chapter 13 for a detailed case history).

The Screen-Hungry Personality

Finally, I should like to compare the screen-hungry personality with other clinical types described in the literature. These patients resemble the "exceptions" described by Freud (1916). However, his patients *demanded* the right to step beyond the ordinary bounds because they suffered some harm in early childhood for which they felt guiltless. My patients *expected* extraordinary gratifications since they adopted the role of the favorite by denying their childhood deprivations.

These patients resemble the counterphobic people Fenichel (1934c, 1939c, 1946) described in his papers on the counterphobic attitude and on stage acting. The screen-hungry characters use counterphobic methods in attempting to deny their anxiety.

Helene Deutsch's (1942) "as if" characters also bear some resemblance to my patients. Her patients were empty, schizoid personalities, ready to take on anyone's characteristics since they felt they had no character of their own. Her patients were much sicker than the ones I have described. My patients had an identity they wanted to preserve and proclaim, and another identity they were attempting to deny.

The patients Annie Reich (1953, 1954) described also bear a strong similarity to the screen-hungry characters. In my patients, too, I was able to ascertain that they often chose objects on a narcissistic basis. The marital partner was frequently some infantile idealized past conception of the self. My patients also manifested pathology in the realm of their feelings of omnipotence. Whereas Annie Reich's patients seemed to have episodes of megalomanic activity, my patients seemed to develop certain chronic grandiose attitudes. However, by and large, I feel we are both describing similar patients.

The screen-hungry characters differ from ordinary neurotics in the way they handle their dangerous impulses and their object relations. The ordinary neurotic represses the dangerous drives, which then undergo partial regression. When these drives break through in the symptom formation, they are felt as ego-alien. The ordinary neurotic develops anxieties and inhibitions in regard to gratifying his instincts. In his object relations, too, he is usually inhibited and withdrawn in order to avoid the stimuli that might stir up his repressed instinctual drives. The ordinary neurotic is usually more phobic, whereas the screen-hungry patient is counterphobic. By giving up certain ego functions, by the use of screen devices in the service of denial, they manage to retain some capacity for instinctual gratification, relatively speaking. Whereas the ordinary patient comes to analysis because he does not like who he is, these patients come to analysis to find out who they really are.

Are these borderline cases? The ego dysfunctions, the prominent orality, and the use of denial would speak for this. However, the classification of "borderline case" is so general as to be of little value. It seems advantageous to classify them more specifically as neurotic character disorders with a mixture of hysterical and impulsive-depressive features. Or perhaps one should stress the identity disorder and make this the diagnostic label. They might be classified as one of the neurotic identity disorders—screen identity.[2]

[2] In recent years such disturbances would be called "narcissistic personality disorders" (Kohut, 1971).

The social background of the screen-hungry patients seems to indicate that this disorder is prevalent in first-generation Americans, members of minority groups, musicians, actors, writers, and psychiatrists.

These patients need a long and classical psychoanalysis. Though the temporary ego dysfunctions may require some transient modification, it is rarely necessary. These patients need a reliable, predictable, and incorruptible analyst. The turning point in the treatment is their ability to experience their aggressive feelings in regard to the previously idealized analyst. The treatment duration is long, but it is interesting and rewarding.

Although I believe we can explain identity disorders on the basis of the family history and the personal experiences, perhaps Erikson (1950) is right in stressing the fact that identity disorders are a product of American culture. In an uncertain world, one searches for salvation in a variety of ways. Among them, in a country like America where we have so many choices and so many pressures, we often search for a new identity instead of a fuller and richer identity.

10

Phobia, Anxiety, and Depression

(1959)

T HE FIRST OBJECTIVE of this presentation is to reexamine and reevaluate the conventional psychoanalytic attitude which holds that phobias are a manifestation of hysteria. In order to do this, it is necessary first to review our present-day views about anxiety, since the forerunner of the phobia is the anxiety attack. Phobic symptom formation, its specific qualities, characteristics, and functions are then described, in order to determine whether phobias can be tied to any diagnostic category. The final section of this paper concerns some speculations arising from a comparison of the anxious and the depressed patient.

A phobia is a special variety of neurotic fear. The anxiety in the phobias is bound and fixed to certain specific conditions. By avoiding the anxiety-provoking situations, the phobic patient attempts to avoid the severe anxiety attack which preceded and led

Presented in part at the Panel on Phobias and Their Vicissitudes, Annual Meeting of the American Psychoanalytic Association, April 1957, San Francisco, California. First published in *Journal of the American Psychoanalytic Association*, 7:663-674, 1959.

to the formation of the phobia. A phobia is a defense against anxiety. One form of anxiety is used defensively against another. Apparently, anxiety which is linked and tied to certain circumstances and conditions is more controllable and therefore less frightening than free-floating anxiety.

Phobias may arise suddenly or gradually, may fluctuate considerably in intensity, or remain relatively rigid and chronic. They may occur singly, although that is rare and usually a morbid indication. Ordinarily, there are constellations of phobias: major ones and minor ones, early ones and later editions or derivatives, often arranged defensively around some primary and central phobia. There are phobic attitudes when phobic reactions influence character formation, and one can speak of phobic character types—restricted, inhibited personalities with latent phobias. Phobias may be limited to relatively innocuous areas of life, or they may encroach upon life's most vital goals. Patients who seek psychoanalytic treatment for phobias generally have multiple phobias, severe enough to interfere with important functions of life. There is a tendency to decompensation, or spreading of the phobia formations and increased anxiety attacks.

Anxiety and Trauma

In the history of the phobic patient, the phobia was immediately preceded either by an acute attack of anxiety or by spells of free-floating anxiety (Freud, 1926a). The phobia proves to be a defense against the anxiety attack as well as a derivative of it.

The anxiety attack which leads to phobia formation is a traumatic event. It is this fact of being traumatic that impels the ego to such extensive defensive maneuvers as seen in phobia formation. Trauma refers to any psychic event which overwhelms the ego against its will. In a traumatic situation the ego is flooded, robbed of its functions. It cannot bind or master the stimuli impinging upon it. The traumatic event is experienced passively by the ego. Emergency vegetative discharges occur involuntarily. It is a state of psychic helplessness. The core of phobia formation is this experience of anxiety of traumatic proportions.

Traumatic states are determined by two sets of factors: the condition of the ego, and the quantity of the stimuli imposed upon it (Fenichel, 1945). If the ego is depleted in the amount of energies it has available for coping with a new influx of stimuli, it can react to a relatively innocuous situation as though it were a trauma. It can be overwhelmed and rendered helpless. In neurotics, in whom the ego is struggling with maintaining its equilibrium against the many unresolved unconscious conflicts, we usually find the occurrence of such relative trauma. The result is a traumatic neurosis with subsequent symptom formation. In healthy people, an overwhelming influx of stimuli can also lead to a traumatic state, but if this experience does not become linked up with unconscious neurotic conflicts, it leads merely to a self-limited traumatic neurosis.

At this point, it is necessary to review briefly the present state of our knowledge about anxiety. Freud's newer formulations in *Inhibitions, Symptoms and Anxiety* (1926a) and the *New Introductory Lectures* (1933) are the cornerstone of our current theory. Two papers by Max Schur (1953, 1958) contain some important additions and modifications. Rangell (1955) has provided a detailed review of the subject. Here I can only present a highly condensed version of the theory of anxiety, limiting myself to what seems pertinent to the discussion of phobias.

The traumatic anxiety reaction which precedes and leads to phobic formation is itself a precipitate and repetition of primal, infantile, traumatic experiences (Freud, 1926a, 1933). The first traumatic experience is presumed to occur at birth. The loss of the sustaining object and the consequent physiological repercussions occurring during this procedure provide a magnitude of stimuli which produces a traumatic reaction. It is a moot point whether we can consider this traumatic experience an anxiety reaction, since for anxiety we need an ego, and it is questionable whether at birth there is sufficient ego functioning present for an anxiety reaction. Perhaps there are inborn channels and structures already present, as Rapaport (1953) suggests. At any rate, the traumatic experience of birth serves as a model and forerunner for primal anxiety which arises as soon as ego functioning develops (Greenacre, 1941; Spitz, 1950). Later events of infancy and childhood also have a traumatic effect: loss of love objects, loss of body parts, particularly castration anxiety, and social anxiety. Every later traumatic anxiety reaction is linked genetically to the old traumatic situations of childhood.

Before ego development is well established, all anxiety reactions are traumatic reactions. As maturation occurs, the ego learns to cope with this traumatic anxiety. As perception, attention, memory, and thinking develop, the ego learns to anticipate the trauma. We have the awareness of *potential* trauma, i.e., the concept of danger. Danger refers to the situation which may precipitate the traumatic anxiety. It is a displacement from the internal feeling of helplessness to the external situation which occasions it.

With maturation, the reaction to anticipated danger becomes more remote from the reaction to traumatic situations. The transition is gradual and is subject to regressive reactivation. Eventually, anxiety becomes desomatized, limited, and purposeful (Schur, 1953, 1958).

The transition from primal traumatic anxiety to more mature anxiety has been amplified by Freud (1926a) with the concept of signal anxiety. The ego produces and uses a small amount of anxiety actively to warn of impending trauma. The danger now has shifted from the internal, economic, traumatic situation to the external circumstances that mobilize it; i.e., in the child, the loss of the mother will bring anxiety before the helplessness is felt. There is some disagreement with parts of this formulation. Schur (1953) believes that the ego does not produce anxiety. It re-creates the memory of danger and passively experiences the anxiety. This experience of anxiety induces the defenses. The ego produces memories of danger, not anxiety. Brenner (1953) believes that two different ego functions are involved. One perceives danger, and the other gives the warning signal.

A person may regress in two ways in danger situations: (1) in his evaluation of the danger: from adult insecurity to infantile helplessness; (2) in his response to the danger: from thought of danger to a full resomatization reaction (Schur, 1953, 1958).

Anxiety is a reaction to danger, but it may become a danger in itself. The warning signal function may fail, and the anxiety signal may set off panic or a traumatic anxiety reaction (Fenichel, 1945). This is the typical situation in the phobic patient.

Phobic Symptom Formation

All the psychic structures participate in the formation of a neurotic symptom. A symptom is a compromise formation in which the id, the superego or its forerunners, and the ego all attempt to gain their ends. The id demands some form of instinctual gratification, the superego demands moral rectitude, and the ego tries to mediate between these two agencies as well as to fulfill its synthetic function and maintain its contact with the external world. Neurotic symptoms stem from unresolved unconscious conflicts between the forces of the id on the one side, opposing the ego on the other, with the superego on one or both sides of the struggle (Fenichel, 1945). What is characteristic for the phobias is that the neurotic symptom is anxiety and that this anxiety is fixed and bound to specific conditions.

As stated earlier, the history reveals that prior to the development of the phobia, there was an attack of traumatic anxiety. This anxiety spell can be traced to two different factors, one general, and one specific. The general factor deals with the economic findings regarding the ego state and the quantity of stimuli. The phobic patient, prior to his anxiety attack, was in a state of dammed-up instinctual tension due to his many unresolved conflicts; he was in a state of anxiety readiness. The specific factors deal with the special events which triggered the outbreak of traumatic anxiety. In this state of dammed-up instinctual tension, in the state of anxiety readiness, an event occurs which upsets the neurotic equilibrium. An event stirs up specific, pathogenic id strivings, intensifies the crucial neurotic conflict, and weakens the ego's defensive capacity. For example, a young woman patient, unhappily married and struggling with impulses of infidelity, was visited by her beloved father, who stayed in her home. During this interval she went to a beauty parlor where a male operator seemed lovingly to caress her hair, an activity performed by her father during childhood. She responded by having her first (consciously remembered) traumatic anxiety attack, which included fainting, nausea, heart palpitation, sweating, and motor weakness. She then developed a fear of going to beauty parlors, which spread to a fear of leaving home. Here we can see the ego depletion and the id stimulation very clearly. After the traumatic panic reaction, an attempt was made to avoid the danger situation which occasioned it. We have a shift of the danger from the economic situation of ego helplessness to the external danger which triggered it.[1]

When this happens, the anxiety motivates the ego to combat the id strivings which were responsible for the untenable position. Repression is reinforced by regression. New anxieties now arise—pregenital anxieties. The ego tries to limit the anxiety by fixing it, binding it to a variety of external situations. The danger is displaced from an internal source to an external one. But every phobic symptom is linked to the pathogenic impulses and the traumatic experience, and thus every phobic symptom has to be fought. It is striking how hard it is to determine from a phobic patient what he is really afraid of. He attempts to conceal the real content of his fears, and therefore his description of his anxiety is very nebulous (Freud, 1926a, 1933). The symptoms are displacements from the original conflicts and the traumatic anxiety state, which itself is linked to the terrifying helplessness of the primary infantile anxiety reactions.

The specific phobic symptoms are determined by the nature of the drives warded off and by the historical setting of the particular patient. Phobic situations usually represent unconsious instinctual temptations, sexual or aggressive or both.

---

[1] This patient is described in greater detail in Greenson (1967a, p. 19ff.).

Instinctual aims, impulses, or body sensations may be displaced and projected in the phobic situation. Fears of being bitten, damaged, penetrated, contaminated; fears of rhythmic noises, pulsations, closed places, etc., are examples of this. Furthermore, the phobic situation may simultaneously represent punishment for instinctual wishes. Fears of disease, injury, death are obvious examples. Lewin (1952) has described phobic symptoms as parallel in structure to dreams, and Arlow (1953) has compared the dynamics of masturbation to phobic symptoms.

In the final analysis, the anxiety in the phobia is displaced and derived from the terror of the psychic helplessness of the traumatic anxiety attack, which was induced by the mobilization of the pathogenic conflict. The anxiety is shifted from this helplessness onto situations which symbolically represent instincts or punishment or both. The anxiety is changed from the fear of helplessness and anxieties which create this, like castration anxiety, to different anxieties regarding other parts of the body and other frightening ego states. The aim of the phobia is to create new and less frightening dangers and to avoid them by a variety of distance-making procedures. Displacements and projections are the defense mechanisms of choice.

These maneuvers usually fail (in patients seeking therapy) and clinically one sees persons with many phobias which do not succeed in binding or limiting the anxiety. The phobic formations keep expanding, and nevertheless there are attacks of panic anxiety.

In treatment, as one succeeds in uncovering the meaning of a particular phobia, one frequently sees the return of anxiety attacks and free-floating anxiety. Then one sees new phobias transiently formed during treatment or old phobias, hitherto unknown, returning. In successful treatment one eventually arrives at a revival of the original primal anxiety states of childhood and infancy. The protection of the transference neurosis makes it possible for the patient to relive this panic during treatment and now successfully to cope with it. In this phase, one can see how in the acute anxiety state, the loss of ego functions against one's will—the loss of memory, perception, motility, the loss of the sense of identity and body integrity—is the most terrifying experience for the phobic patient. At different times, a phobic patient of mine toward the end of her treatment, in the reliving of her infantile anxieties, experienced the loss of the meaning of words, of memory, of identity, and of motor functions.

Phobias as a Diagnostic Category

Freud (1926a) very definitely believed that phobias belong in the category of anxiety hysteria. He found that the dominant fear was castration anxiety and that the oedipal struggles were in the center of the clinical picture. He used the Little Hans case to demonstrate this thesis (1909b). In recent years, other writers have described phobias in other types of clinical pictures. Phobias have been described in obsessional neuroses and in obsessional characters by Glover (1939a) and Rangell (1952b). Glover also observed phobias in paranoid patients. Ruth Mack Brunswick's later work (1928) with the Wolf Man stressed the pregenital elements. Lewin (1952) in particular emphasized the oral features in phobias.

My own clinical experience, gathered during the last nineteen years, is based on the analysis of four cases in whom the main symptoms were phobias. Two patients were analyzed for two to three years and then had to be interrupted due to World War II. My information about them is therefore incomplete. The other two patients were treated rather exhaustively, one for five, and one for six years. All four patients demonstrated hysterical features, but no single patient was essentially a hysteric. The oedipal conflicts were heavily cast with pregenital, oral, anal, and urethral impulses. All four patients were essentially pregenitally oriented. One patient was a rather typical compulsive-obsessive with more than a little paranoid coloring. The other three cases would be difficult to classify in any conventional way, except to describe them as mixed pregenital neuroses.

Three out of four had paranoid features, but only in one was this marked. In two, there were hypochondriacal features. In one, there was an important depressive element. Again, all I can say about three out of the four cases is that they were essentially mixed pregenital neurotics, with oral, anal, hypochondriacal, and paranoid trends. Their outstanding clinical characteristic was that they were anxiety-ridden and had struggled either against overt anxiety or a variety of phobias all of their lives. (I have seen *transient* phobias in patients from every known diagnostic category, above all, in children.)

All of these considerations would seem to indicate that phobias are more loosely connected to any diagnostic category than has been heretofore acknowledged. There seem to be hysterical phobias, obsessional phobias, and paranoid phobias, as well as mixed pregenital phobias. These findings parallel those described as valid for conversion phenomena by Rangell (1959). (Incidentally, if we take away conversion phenomena and phobias from the realm of hysteria, what is left of the concept of hysteria? Schur, in a personal communication, suggests the necessity of revising our entire conception of hysteria.)

A few words seem to be in order regarding the establishment of a diagnosis. In arriving at a nosological evaluation of a patient, what criteria do we employ? Ever since Abraham's (1924) detailed work on the stages of libido organization and its connection to object relationships, we use these two factors. Anna Freud's (1936) systematic description of defense mechanisms and our greater knowledge of ego functions have added this element to our diagnostic considerations. We know that to some extent all patients have features from various levels of development, and we seek to establish what is predominant, essential, and typical, in terms of the libidinal phase, the object relations, and the mechanisms of defense. Perhaps we ought to add a consideration of the predominant anxiety as an aid in our diagnostic evaluation.

Every level of development has its specific and characteristic fears. On the phallic level, castration anxiety predominates. Fear of loss of sphincter control and loss of body contents is typical for the anal phase. The fear of being devoured, the fear of loss of body integrity, the loss of ego functions, and the loss of identity seem to be the specific fears of the oral phase. Thus a knowledge of what kind of anxieties dominate the life of a patient may be a valuable indicator of the diagnosis. It is to be stressed that it is the quality of the anxiety and not the intensity which is of prime significance for the diagnosis. One ought to be able to differentiate between neurotic and psychotic anxieties (Milton Wexler, personal communication). There is a distinct qualitative difference in anxiety when one is dealing with a patient suffering from a fear of castration as compared to one suffering from a fear of losing his identity.

Speculations

After all these considerations, I asked myself: how do these phobic patients compare to my other patients? The phobic patients seem to resemble the compulsive-obsessives and the schizoid patients and are remarkably different from the group of neurotic depressives. In fact, I believe I can divide my practice into two large groups: the anxiety-ridden patients and the depressives. (In this discussion, I shall omit the mixed group.) The phobic patients are avoiders, distance-makers, projectors; the depressives are always seeking to get close, even to incorporate objects. The anxious patient avoids objects except for a special few; the depressives relate even too quickly to objects, except for a specific few. The anxious patient will sacrifice object relations for security; the depressive needs objects for his security. The anxious patient is prone to react with hostility to objects; the depressive is essentially libidinal although sadomasochistic. The anxious patient develops phobias and inhibitions; the depressive is counterphobic and acts out. It seems to me that inhibition is to anxiety as acting out is to depression. The anxious patient fears the state of helplessness and is a pessimist; the depressive fears hopelessness and is an optimist. Anxiety concerns anticipated and future dangers, whereas depression essentially concerns experiences which have already happened in the past. One can add to this list of differences, but I believe my point is clear. Anxiety and depression are two basic ego reactions which seem to be diametrically opposed to each other. Edward Bibring (1953) has stressed this point, although we are not in agreement on some of the above formulations.

I am reminded of Freud's unanswered question in the addendum to *Inhibition, Symptom and Anxiety* where he asks: why does separation from an object cause anxiety on one occasion and grief on another? I should like to suggest a tentative answer. When a child cries in sadness, he knows what he is sad about; he recalls the memory of the lost object; he has an internal object representation and he longs for its external representation. When a child loses an external object and becomes frightened, he seems to approach a state of helplessness. He seems to have lost not only an external object but also an internal one, and thereby is in danger of losing his ego functions. Freud (1933) once said that the ego is a precipitate of abandoned object cathexis, i.e., identifications. Thus it would seem that a loss of object cathexis can lead to a loss of ego functions. (These and the formulations which follow both resemble and differ from those expressed by Melanie Klein and her followers [1952].)

Depression and grief are painful states of longing for something or somebody the ego knows, remembers, at least unconsciously. The something exists, but is lost or not available for the ego. Depression, above all, is a state of deprivation, a loss of love—from an external or internal object. The introjective mechanisms so prevalent in the depressions are attempts to reinstitute the lost object in order to avoid the terrible emptiness and hopelessness of psychotic apathy.

Panic anxiety is a state of psychic helplessness. In this state there seems to be a loss of internal object cathexis as well as the loss of cathexis of the external object. As this happens, there seems to occur a loss of ego functions. When signal anxiety regresses to panic or traumatic anxiety, we seem to have a regression to objectlessness. Clinically, this seems to be due to a stirring up of primitive hostility which apparently leads to a temporary destruction or decathexis of the internal objects. I would like to illustrate this by some clinical material from one of my phobic patients. For years, this patient reacted with panic whenever I went on vacation. She would state that she did not miss me, because when I had gone, I was destroyed for her. She could not remember me; I was dead. True, she could recollect certain isolated fragments about me—the color of my hair, my moustache, my clothes; but these were facts or ideas and did not form a picture or a memory of a human being (loss of synthetic ego function?). While I was gone, she "knew" I would not return; in fact, she doubted whether I had really ever existed. She felt emotionally numb and "sleepwalked" away the days in quiet desperation. She felt dead, and she and the world seemed unreal (depersonalization?). After I had succeeded in uncovering the primitive hostility which lay underneath her strong erotic and dependent transference and after she was able to express this and cope with this, a change slowly occurred. Now when I left for vacation, she missed me, she remembered me, she was depressed and miserable; but at least she was alive.

It seems to me that primal anxiety and primal depression are two basic ego states which represent different stages of development.

Primal anxiety is the earlier state, and primal depression a later one. In primal anxiety, the loss of the external object precipitates a loss of cathexis of the internal object and results thereby in a loss of ego functioning. In primal depression, the loss of the external object does not destroy the internal object and ego functioning, but recuperative mechanisms now occur.

Perhaps all neuroses can be traced back either to primal anxiety or to primal depression. If this proves to be correct, then one should be able to establish a hierarchy of anxieties beginning with the primitive and malignant fears of being devoured, loss of body integrity or sense of identity, and reaching the relatively benign fears of castration. One should be able to construct a similar scale of depressive reactions. The primal depressions would refer to the state of feeling utterly abandoned, with the accompanying feelings of desolation and self-hatred. This reaction would be quite different in quality from the sadness which results from the state of feeling rejected in the oedipal situation. My clinical impression is that paranoid, schizophrenic, obsessional, and phobic reactions are all derived from primal anxiety. The manic-depressive, alcoholic, gambler, and neurotic depressive stem from primal depression.

These speculations are still in a preliminary stage of development and are therefore incomplete and impressionistic. If these ideas prove fruitful in the continuing exploration of problems of anxiety and depression, they shall be developed further.[2]

[2] I believe these speculations have been carried much further by the works of Edith Jacobson (1964) and Margaret Mahler and her co-workers (1968, 1975).

11

Empathy and Its Vicissitudes

(1960)

MOST EXPERIENCED PSYCHOANALYSTS will agree that in order to do effective psychotherapy a knowledge of psychoanalytic theory and the intellectual understanding of a patient are not sufficient. In order to help, one has to know a patient differently—emotionally. One cannot truly grasp subtle and complicated feelings of people except by this "emotional knowing." It is "emotional knowing," the experiencing of another's feelings, that is meant by the term empathy. It is a very special method of perceiving. Particularly for therapy, the capacity for empathy is an essential prerequisite. Although I believe these points are well known, it is striking how little psychoanalytic literature exists on the subject of empathy. Freud (1912b, 1921), Ferenczi (1928), Glover (1955), Sharpe (1930), and Fenichel (1941b) comment only briefly on this topic. There seems to be a tendency among analysts either to take empathy for granted or to underestimate it. There also seems to be some antagonism between theory and empathy.[1] The systematic theo-

Paper read at the 21st Congress of the International Psycho-Analytical Association, Copenhagen, July 1959. First published in *International Journal of Psycho-Analysis*, 41:418-424, 1960. Also as: Zum Problem der Empathie. *Psyche*, 15:142-54, 1960. L'empathie et ses phases diverses. *Revue Française de Psychanalyse*, 25:802-814, 1961.
[1] An exception to this statement is Schafer's paper (1959).

reticians have neglected this field and the empathic clinicians write little theory and then unsystematically (Reik, 1936, 1948). Finally, one frequently hears the phrase that empathy cannot be taught or learned; one either has it or one hasn't. Perhaps all these elements play some role in the relative obscurity of this important chapter.

I shall first attempt a preliminary definition of empathy as we use the term in psychoanalysis. To empathize means to share, to experience the feelings of another person. This sharing of feeling is temporary. One partakes of the quality and not the degree of the feelings, the kind and not the quantity. It is primarily a preconscious phenomenon. The main motive of empathy is to achieve an understanding of the patient.

Empathy is to be differentiated from sympathy since it does not contain the element of condolence, agreement, or pity essential for sympathy. There are other vicarious experiences besides empathy, where one participates in the joys and sorrows of another person, for example, in the theater, but in these the aim is quite different. Imitation and mimicry also bear some resemblance to empathy, but they are conscious phenomena and limited to the external behavioral characteristics of a person. Finally, empathy needs to be differentiated from identification, although there seems to be a close relationship between them. Identification is essentially an unconscious and permanent phenomenon, whereas empathy is preconscious and temporary. The aim of identification is to overcome anxiety, guilt, or object loss, while empathy is used for understanding (Olden, 1958). The relationship between empathy and identification will become clearer later on.

Pathology of Empathy

My attention was drawn to problems of empathy by studying the errors in dosage, timing, and tact of interpretation which I had opportunity to observe in my own work and during supervisory work with psychoanalytic students. The crucial question in estimating dosage and timing can be formulated as follows: How much insight can this patient's ego bear at this time? How can I present this insight so as to be sufficiently meaningful and yet not traumatic to the patient? Essentially one has to be able to assess the patient's ego capacities at the given moment, and then one has to imagine the effect of the interpretation upon the patient's ego structure. It is true that lack of clinical experience may occasionally be responsible for errors in dosage, timing, and tact. However, in my opinion, disturbances of empathy are usually the decisive factor. I have seen beginners who already had considerable skill in this regard; and I have seen analysts with long clinical experience make repeated errors. I believe one can distinguish two different types of disturbance in the capacity for empathy.

INHIBITIONS OF EMPATHY

There are some students who have repeated difficulty in recognizing the affects and motives, particularly the subtle affects and unconscious motives, of their patients. (This is true not only of students, but I shall use the term student to refer to those with difficulties, since most of my *quotable* clinical observations have come from students.) I have found this difficulty to exist in intelligent, astute, and otherwise perceptive people. It is quite typical for such students to be extremely silent and passive in their work with their patients. They seem bent upon collecting more and more data, waiting for additional evidence, before confronting the patient. They remain oblivious despite the clarity of the patient's material. For example, a student related to me how a young woman patient recounted, for the first time in her analysis, how she succumbed to the temptation to masturbate. Then the patient fell silent. The student went on to describe her behavior on the couch in such a way that I could visualize the patient's feeling of embarrassment and shame; yet the student had no idea about what was going on. He waited silently, looking for more material and further clues, trying to remember her previous dreams, etc. The patient talked trivia the

rest of that hour and for several hours thereafter, yet the student
who was bright and conversant with psychoanalytic theory was
completely in the dark. He had failed to recognize that the patient had *confessed* something to him in the previous hour and
therefore overlooked the obvious connection between the masturbation and the ensuing silence. He missed her shame reaction because at that particular time and on that subject, he was
unable to feel along with the patient, to empathize with her.

I have observed students give very painful interpretations to
patients early in the analysis and then be surprised when the patient seemed traumatized. They could answer correctly in a seminar if one were to ask, "How will the patient react if one gives
too deep an interpretation?" Clinically, however, they fell into
this error because they were unable to feel along with the patient. They did not anticipate via empathy what repercussions
the painful insight would have.

Such inhibitions in the capacity to empathize with the patient may be transient or chronic, generalized or localized. They
may occur in students during a particular phase of their own
analysis and be a result of some temporary neurotic disturbance
within them. The transient and localized inhibitions of empathy
have a good prognosis, whereas the chronic and generalized inhibitions have a poor prognosis. The latter type is frequently
found in those who have a chronically precarious mental equilibrium or who deeply mistrust their feelings, impulses, and their
unconscious. These people have proved to be rigid, severe compulsive-obsessives, or else schizoid personalities struggling to
maintain their hold on reality.

Loss of Control of Empathy

In doing supervisory work and also in a retrospective examination of my own work, I have often come upon another type of
disorder in the capacity to empathize. In such situations the
therapist begins by being able to empathize with his patient, but
this empathy does *not* lead to understanding and then to the
proper confrontation of the patient. Some other reaction inter-

venes and the understanding is either blocked or is misused, or only takes place after a detour. Let me give an example.

A student was analyzing a difficult patient and in the course of an analytic session detected that the patient was hinting to him about some sexually provocative behavior she had indulged in, in regard to her child. The patient did not explicitly relate this, nor did she completely evade it; she hinted about it, testing the student's reaction. The student readily picked up this rather subtle behavior because he was in good empathic contact with the patient. The patient suddenly changed her mode of talking and directly asked the student whether it was harmful to a child when a mother expressed sexual feelings toward her son. The student, instead of dealing with the meaning of this question, impulsively answered the patient. He assured her that a parent's sexual feelings toward a child were natural and even good for a child. When the student reported this clinical experience to me, I noticed that he was ill at ease and upset. When I questioned the correctness of his procedure, he readily admitted that he was puzzled by his own behavior and could not understand why he had done this. I did not attempt to explain his error, but only indicated that this might be brought up in his own analysis. A week later he voluntarily told me that he now understood his actions. Apparently he had acted out with his patient the role he wished his own analyst would take with him, namely, to absolve him of his guilt for sexual impulses and feelings he had toward his own child. In this instance, empathy led not to understanding but to a countertransference reaction.

There are many other examples which come to mind as illustrations of the loss of control of empathy. Perhaps the most typical situations are those in which the young analyst picks up the sexual or hostile undercurrent of feelings in his patient via empathy and then permits himself to react to the patient, which then interferes with his capacity for objectivity and understanding. Or the student detects some subtle resistance in the patient, but sympathetically identifies with the resistance instead of demonstrating it to the patient.

It should be mentioned that one often sees combinations of both types of disturbances in the capacity to empathize.

Preliminary Formulations

On the basis of the clinical material sketched and indicated above, I believe we can now attempt some preliminary formulations about the function of the capacity to empathize.

1. Since empathy means to share, to participate partially and temporarily, it means that the therapist must become involved in the emotional experiences of the patient. This implies a split and a shift in the ego functioning of the analyst. In this process, it is necessary for the analyst to oscillate from observer to participant and back to observer (Sterba, 1929). Actually, the role of observer is shorthand for designating the different functions of analyzing, i.e., observing, remembering, judging, thinking, etc.

2. The inhibited empathizer is afraid to get involved with the patient. He is unconsciously unwilling to leave the isolation of the position of the uninvolved observer. He is able to think, remember, observe, but he is afraid to feel the affects, impulses, or sensations of the patient, and he therefore misses all the subtle, nonverbal communications and their meanings.

3. The uncontrolled empathizers do participate in the emotional experiences of their patients, but tend to become too intensely involved and therefore cannot readily become uninvolved. They make the transition from observer to participant, but run into difficulties regaining the position of observer or analyzer. They tend to identify or act out or have strong instinctual reactions, all of which interfere with their ability to observe and analyze.

4. The aim of empathy in psychoanalysis is to understand the patient. When the patient becomes an object mobilizing strong sexual feelings, or aggression, or guilt, or anxiety, the patient has probably become a transference figure for the therapist. The therapists in group 1 are afraid of their countertrans-

ference and inhibit their reactions. The "uncontrolled" therapists give in to and act upon their countertransference reactions instead of using them for the analytic work (Ekstein and Wallerstein, 1956).

5. The wish to understand is a derivative of oral introjective aims, skin erotism, anal mastery, sexual curiousity, and scoptophilic impulses and drives (Fenichel, 1945). Under ideal conditions the ability to understand is a neutralized, autonomous ego function (Hartmann, 1939). In the examples given above, the wish to understand has been reinvaded by its genetic predecessors. The inhibited behavior in the one group and the uncontrolled behavior in the other would indicate that a reinstinctualization has occurred. Understanding by empathy has become an instinctual temptation which is either a danger to be avoided or a pleasure to be enjoyed. In either case the capacity for empathy will be disturbed.

6. It seems that it is essential for the development of the optimum capacity for empathy that the therapist be able to become both detached and involved—the observer and the participant, objective and subjective—in regard to his or her patient. Above all, the therapist must be able to permit transitions and oscillations between these two sets of positions. Freud (1912b) described the suspended, even-hovering attention and listening which is necessary and preferrable for the analyst. This implies the partaking of both detached and involved positions and oscillations between them. Only from the evenly suspended position can one readily shift from observer to participant and back. Ordinarily this occurs automatically and preconsciously, but these shifts can be consciously initiated and interrupted. Ferenczi (1928), Sharpe (1930), Reik (1948), and Fliess (1953a) also have described the need to oscillate between observation and introspection.

Psychology of Empathy

All of the foregoing is mainly a description of some of the more obvious findings in disorders of empathy and I would now like to probe a little deeper into the phenomenon of empathy—in the therapist. I should like to use a clinical example to illustrate some of the points I want to make, but it is not easy to find an appropriate one. I shall have to use myself as the example because in my experience I have only been able to study empathy in a very fragmentary way in others since the pursuit of this subject led contrary to my therapeutic task with my patients. No matter what example I may choose, there is some amount of distortion because essentially the process of empathy is an automatic process and one only observes it in retrospect. Furthermore, in order to clarify the various events one has to magnify the intervals and separate steps in an occurrence in which much seems to happen very rapidly and perhaps simultaneously. Finally, the best examples of empathy and the clearest occur where there is some difficulty in the empathy. In using the approach I have chosen, two questions immediately come to the fore: (1) Is this state of affairs true for all analysts? (2) Is this state of affairs valid for empathy in general or only for empathy in psychoanalytic work?

The clinical example I have chosen is a relatively simple and innocuous situation. I had been treating a woman for several years and usually with good empathic understanding. In one hour she recounted the events of a weekend and focused in particular on a Saturday night party. Suddenly she began to cry. I was puzzled. I was not with it—the crying left me cold—I couldn't understand it. I realized that I had been partially distracted by something she had said. At the party she mentioned a certain analyst and I had gotten sidetracked, wondering why he was present. Quickly reviewing the events she had recounted, I found no clues. I then shifted from listening from the "outside" to participant listening. I went to the party as if I were the patient. Now something clicked—an "aha" experience. A fleeting event told to me as the outsider had eluded me; now in my empathy this event illuminated the crying. At the party a woman had graciously served the patient with a generous portion of food. To me, as the observer, this event was meaningless. But to me, as the experiencer, this woman instantly stirred up the picture of the patient's good-hearted and big-breasted nursemaid. The "aha" I experienced was my sudden recognition of this previously anonymous figure. Now I shifted back to the position of the observer and analyzer. Yes, the longing for the old nursemaid had come up in the last hour. In the meantime the patient herself had begun to talk of the nursemaid. My empathic discovery seemed to be valid. (When the analyst's association precedes and coincides with the patient's, it confirms that the analyst is on the right track.)

THE SEQUENCE OF EVENTS

1. Listening, observing, thinking about the patient's material were insufficient. There was the recognition of not being in good emotional, nonverbal contact—feeling "out of it." She cried and I was puzzled.

2. I shifted—from listening and observing from the outside to listening and feeling from the inside. I permitted part of myself to become the patient.

3. As I had worked with this patient day by day, I had slowly built up within me a working model of the patient. This consisted of her physical appearance, her affects, her life experiences, her modes of behavior, her attitudes, defenses, values, fantasies. This working model was a counterpart or replica of the patient that I had built up and added to from my new observations and understanding. It is this working model which I now shifted into the foreground of my listening. I listened through this model.

More precisely: I listened to the patient's words and transformed her words into pictures and feelings from *her* memories and *her* experiences and in accordance with her ways. To put it another way: the events, words, and actions the patient described were now permitted to permeate the working model. The model reacted with feelings, ideas, memories, associations, etc. In the above example, the working model of the patient produced the significant association to the nursemaid.

4. By shifting the working model of the patient into the

foreground, the rest of me was relatively deemphasized and isolated. Only those personal experiences and reactions of mine similar to the patient's remained near the model or might be used to fill out the working model. All that is peculiarly or uniquely me was shifted into the background.

5. If the empathy is successful, I will feel in emotional contact with the patient and the patient's communications will be likely to stir up some kind of an "aha" experience. I use the term "aha" experience to epitomize that involuntary and pleasant sensation of suddenly grasping and understanding something hitherto obscure. (Sometimes in listening to patients one also has "oi weh" or "ach" experiences.)

6. The "aha" experience indicates that an association in the working model has alerted my analyzing ego, which had been relatively distant to the proceedings. This analyzing ego now comes to the fore and attempts to ascertain the meaning of the goings-on in the model.

7. The analyzing ego now determines the desirability of making some communication to the patient by testing out the proposed intervention on the working model. Again there is a shift from observer to participant. The reactions within the working model will determine the dosage, timing, and tact.

Usually all of this happens automatically, preconsciously and quickly. The steps do not go in a straight sequence, but there are oscillations and variations and simultaneous occurrences.

Some Qualifying Additions

1. The working model of the patient within me is not merely a replica of the patient. If that were so, the model would have the same resistances as the patient and would not supply me with clues. The model has similar resistances and defenses in quality but less in degree. It is close enough so as not to distort, but different enough to be of help.

Clinical Note: For proper empathy it is necessary to forget and re-repress *almost* like the patient does. Reading and memorizing notes about the patient interfere with empathy. Data gathered from external sources also create the same kind of obstacle.

2. The working model is not identical to the patient in that the model also contains our expectations and anticipations of the patient's potentials (Erikson, 1956). We listen to the way the patient reacts with the inner awareness of alternative reactions the patient might have had—often an "oi" experience. These potentials of the patient influence the interpretations and change during the course of psychoanalysis.

3. The working model also contains insights and interpretations which have not yet been given but are close to the patient's consciousness. Our theoretical knowledge and past clinical experiences are also lightly sketched into the model.

4. Thus the working model consists of:
   (a) All I know of the patient: experiences, modes of behavior, memories. fantasies, resistances, defenses, dreams, associations, etc. All this is the skeleton and basic structure.
   (b) I diminish the quantity of resistance.
   (c) I add my conception of his potentials.
   (d) I add my theoretical knowledge and clinical experience.
   (e) I add all my experiences with similar kinds of people and situations—real or fantasied.

All of these additions fill out the model and give it a three-dimensional form. My unique experiences are isolated—for emergency use only. It is important to differentiate what is the patient, what is the model, what is me.

5. Empathy is to some extent a two-way relationship.[2] One's capacity for empathy can be influenced by the other person's resistance or readiness for empathic understanding. There are patients who consciously and unconsciously want to remain ununderstood; they dread being understood. For them, to be

[2] Douglas D. Bond, personal communication.

understood may mean to be destroyed, devoured, unmasked. The analyst's attempts at empathy leave the analyst frustrated and the patient untouched. In one such case I found myself refusing to try to empathize; I was annoyed. When I recognized this, it occurred to me that perhaps the patient preconsciously wanted this. She wanted to remain ununderstood—mainly to hide a secret so terrible, she thought its revelation would cause me to throw her out. My interpretation led to confirmatory materials.

Patients eager for empathic understanding increase the empathy in the therapist. Also, patients pick up the analyst's lack of empathy. I have seen this kind of reaction between speakers and listeners, actor and audience, artists and audience.[3] This is also to be seen in candidates being supervised or in presenting cases: the fear to be understood, i.e., revealed, may cause difficulty in empathizing.

6. There are special problems of empathy in supervisory work, since here it is necessary to empathize with the candidate as well as with his patient. Actually, in doing psychoanalytic work, one not only empathizes with the patient, but one needs to do so with the other significant persons in the patient's life; only in this way can one form some perspective and be able to evaluate the patient's behavior.

7. One begins to empathize with the patient as soon as one goes to open the door, even before seeing him. This might explain the special preoccupied look of the analyst which many patients notice. The patient may believe the analyst is preoccupied with other patients, whereas actually he is partly preoccupied with the working model of the present patient. The analyst is looking then at both the patient and the working model. This might also explain the special startle reaction which happens to analysts when they find the wrong patient in the waiting room. It is more than the astonishment at the unexpected; there is something disorienting about it, due I believe to the cathexis of the internal working model.

---

[3] Charles Tidd, personal communication.

Some Metapsychological Considerations

1. Empathy, as we use it in analytic work, requires the capacity for controlled and reversible regressions in ego functions. The primitivization and progression of the ego in the building of the working model bears a marked resemblance to the creative experience of the artist as formulated by Kris (1950).

2. The conception of a working model of the patient implies a special kind of internal object representative. It is an internal representation which is not merged with the self and yet is not alien to the self.[4] By cathecting the working model as a supplement to the external patient, one approaches the identificatory processes. Empathy may be a forerunner, an early, tentative form of identification.[5]

The capacity to empathize seems to be dependent on one's ability to modulate the cathexis of one's self image. The temporary decathexis of one's self image which is necessary for empathy will be readily undertaken only by those who are secure in their sense of identity. Analysts with too restricted an identity or with amorphous or multiple identities will probably be inhibited or unreliable emphathizers (Erikson, 1956).

3. Empathy begins in the nonverbal, skin, touching, intonational relationship of mother and child (Olden, 1953).[6] The mother shares the child's experiences by feel or touch, and at a distance by visual and auditory signs. The child learns to recognize and share the mother's feelings by primitive perceptions where perception and mimicry are very close to each other (Fenichel, 1945). Less verbal mothers are more prone to empathize, as are loving mothers.

4. One might express these clinical ideas in terms of ego psychology, i.e., neutralization and conflict-free, autonomous ego functions (Hartmann, 1939, 1950).

---

[4] Alfred Goldberg, personal communication.
[5] Hanna Fenichel, Alfred Goldberg, Rudolf Ekstein, personal communications.
[6] Anny Katan, personal communication.

Some Remaining Questions

1. Is the hypothesis on the formation of the internal working model the only means of explaining empathy? Fliess's ideas (1953a) about transient identifications pursue another line of thought.

2. Empathy and intuition are related. Both are special methods of gaining quick and deep understanding. One empathizes to reach feelings; one uses intuition to get ideas. Empathy is to affects and impulses what intuition is to thinking. Empathy often leads to intuition. The "aha" reaction is intuited. One arrives at the feelings and pictures via empathy but intuition sets off the signal in the analytic ego that one has hit it. Intuition picks up the clues that empathy gathers. Empathy is essentially a function of the experiencing ego, whereas intuition comes from the analyzing ego. Yet there are antitheses between the two. Empathic people are not always intuitive and intuitive people are often unreliable empathizers. Intuitive people may use intuition to avoid empathy, i.e., involvement. It is less emotionally demanding. Intuition may warn you *not* to empathize.

Both intuition and empathy give one a talent for psychotherapy; the best therapists seem to have both. Empathy is the more basic requirement; intuition is an extra bonus.

3. Is empathy teachable? One can remove inhibition and misuse of empathy—the disorder may be cured—but the *capacity* for empathy cannot be taught. If it is available, one can be taught how to use it properly.

4. Since the empathy originates in the early mother-child nonverbal communications, it has a definite feminine cast.[7] For men to be empathic they must have come to peace with their motherly component.

5. Empathy and depression. One empathizes to reestablish contact—with an elusive object. One resorts to empathy when more sophisticated means of contact have failed and when one

[7] Anny Katan, personal communication.

wants to regain contact with a lost object. To not understand is a form of losing or rejecting an object. One makes a model—and internal object—an introject of sorts. This is in accordance with Freud's view (1917a) on the process of grief and mourning in regard to the lost love object. This formulation is also similar to Rapaport's ideas (1951) on hallucinatory wish fulfillment by cathecting memory traces of lost need-satisfying objects.

For the empathizer, the ununderstood patient is a kind of lost, need-fulfilling love object. Empathy, then, is an attempt at restitution for the loss of contact and communication. In line with these considerations I have the impression that people with a tendency to depression make the best empathizers.[8]

[8] Other aspects of the analyst's empathy are discussed in chapters 17 and 31. See also Greenson (1967a).

12

On the Silence and Sounds
of the Analytic Hour

(1961)

I

THIS CONTRIBUTION TO THE PANEL on the silent patient is essentially a clinical one. I should like to begin by stressing the importance of differentiating between two large categories of silence: silence as a resistance, and silence as a communication. The most frequent silence met with in psychoanalytic practice is the silence of resistance (Freud, 1913). This silence means that the patient is either consciously or unconsciously unwilling to verbalize. Since the patients in our psychoanalytic practice are attempting to communicate to us in accordance with the basic rule, i.e., attempting to put all their thoughts into words, if they become silent, it means that they are opposing the procedure of psychoanalysis. It is then our task to overcome this obstacle by attempting to find the motives for this resistance. Here, we are often aided in our task by the fact that the patient communicates *despite* his resistance (Levy, 1958).

Contribution to the Panel on The Silent Patient, held at the Midwinter Meeting of the American Psychoanalytic Association, New York, December 6, 1958. First published in *Journal of the American Psychoanalytic Association*, 9:79-84, 1961.

The patient may betray either the motive or even the content of his resistance by his posture, his movements, or his facial expression (Zeligs, 1957).

For example: a patient who had been talking now falls silent. Her face which had been turned so that it was visible to the analyst now is averted. Her hands which had been lying calmly and openly at her side become fidgety. She plays with her ring and then covers her breasts with her arms. Her legs are now tightly crossed at the ankles. Her eyes are downcast; her lips twitch nervously; her face is flushed. She squirms uncomfortably on the analytic couch. It appears that the patient is embarrassed. Her silence had proclaimed to us that she did not wish to communicate, yet despite this resistance her demeanor revealed the reason for her resistance. She did not want to communicate because something embarrassing had come to mind. In this kind of situation the silence is a consequence of a resistance. The patient wants to hide something. The embarrassment, however, reveals to us that she is hiding because she is embarrassed. Thus the embarrassment provides us with the important first clue to the unraveling of this resistance.

Silence, however, not only may indicate a resistance to a certain content but may itself be the content which the patient is trying to convey. For example, patients may fall silent during an analytic hour when they are unconsciously repeating some historical event in which silence was an important element. Primal scenes and primal auditions often make their first appearance in the analytic hour as a restless, agitated, wide-eyed silence. The patient is repeating in the presence of the analyst the silent excitement and anxiety of the primal experiences.

Silence may indicate an identification with a silent object. This happens frequently in the analysis of candidates, who in this way identify with their silent analyst. This should be kept in mind when the silent patient seems to be not only comfortably silent, but confidently and poisedly silent. Furthermore, silence can represent an identification with an inanimate object, a sleeping object, or a dead object. This reaction, however, I have seen only in extremely disturbed and regressed patients.

In general, it is important for our understanding of the different meanings of silence to recognize that silence in an analytic hour may be a reenactment of a historical event in the patient's life in which somebody's silence was of particular significance.

II

Between silence and speech lies the important but neglected realm of sounds. Great emotions are wordless but not soundless. Panic, rage, grief, and ecstasy are expressed not in speech but in sounds. So, too, is the orgasm. An involuntary cry, gasp, moan, or laugh usually accompanies these intense emotional states. Despite the differences of the affect, these exclamatory sounds are difficult to differentiate from one another. This may be due to the fact that in all these emotional states there is the common feeling of being overwhelmed. This sensation of being overwhelmed produces the involuntary cry, which is on the one hand a discharge phenomenon and on the other may represent a primitive appeal for help. Apparently, in such extreme emotional situations, the complicated ego function of verbalization is lost and only the more primitive function of noise production is retained.

Emotional states of lesser intensity may also be accompanied by sounds. In such instances a certain sound may be quite distinctive for a particular mood. The sound can become the auditory representation of the mood—an affect equivalent. For example, the sound "Mm . . ." when produced with a humming or musical intonation indicates a pleasurable oral or gastronomic experience (see chapter 7). The particular feeling of contentment seems to be universally expressed by this "Mm . . ." sound. This linkage between the sound "Mm . . ." and the contented oral experience apparently transcends the boundaries of language (Piaget, 1923). The word for mother in many different languages begins with the sound "Mm . . ." (Jesperson, 1922). This may be derived from the universal experience of the infant nursing at the breast. The sound "Mm . . ." is the only sound that one can make with the lips continuously closed, i.e., with the nipple safely in the mouth.

Perhaps a careful study of other moods may reveal that they too are linked to specific sounds. It is noteworthy that in the development of speech in the infant, the first sounds uttered by the infant are uttered in pain and are vowels. Only later on does the infant produce sounds in comfort and they are consonants (Lewis, 1936). These observations may be of help in understanding the sounds emanating from the speechless patient. So often the nonverbal patient may be expressing himself preverbally in sounds.

III

Another clinical observation may be of value in our attempt to understand the meaning of the patient's silence. I refer to the fact that some patients in their silence lie there with their eyes open and some with their eyes closed. I have often found that this difference in the behavior of the eyes may be a helpful hint about the underlying feelings in the resistance. I realize that any generalization about such a vast group of patients cannot be altogether reliable. Nevertheless, in my clinical experience, silence with open or closed eyes indicates something about the meaning of the silence. Silence with open eyes is more likely to be derived from hatred and rejection, whereas silence with closed eyes is usually derived from love and acceptance. If one reflects a moment about these occurrences in everyday life, I believe that actions expressing love, tenderness, and closeness are usually performed with the eyes at least partially closed. The state of bliss is always expressed with the eyes closed. In part this may be an attempt to heighten the pleasurable perceptions, to savor the feelings, or to maintain an illusion. Above all, it indicates a trust of the other object.[1] On the other hand, one keeps one's eyes

---

[1] Some patients close their eyes in order to shut out external stimuli.

open to be alert, wary, to test and check reality, to be prepared. No matter what else open eyes may represent, it is vigilance and therefore can indicate mistrust toward another object. One closes one's eyes when one approaches a love object, and one keeps them widely open when one approaches an enemy. Lovers close their eyes when they embrace, fighters keep them open even when they clinch. Eyes clamped tightly shut have still another meaning. This usually indicates either an attempted preparation for a blow which is about to fall from without and toward which one is helpless, or it may mean an attempt to keep locked within some terrible feeling in order to protect the analyst.

IV

Silence is a very frequent reaction to an interpretation. The silence may indicate either the correctness or incorrectness of the intervention. The correct interpretation may leave the patient breathless with a sense of surprise, with the "aha" feeling of sudden recognition. Some patients need some "silent time" to mull over, to contend with, to digest the new insight. This will be followed by confirmatory material if the interpretation is correct.

It is a much more frequent occurrence, however, to find that patients will react with silence to an incorrect interpretation. In this situation, silence generally indicates the disappointment in not being understood. Usually such silences in response to interpretations are transient.

Prolonged silence after an interpretation always means that the interpretation has been incorrect. The patient's silence is a reaction to being misunderstood, but more specifically, he feels being misunderstood as an act of hostility by the analyst. This seems more likely to occur when interpretations are given which are correct in content but wrong in timing and dosage. The patient is vulnerable to the interpretation because of the correct content but reacts traumatically and violently to the tactlessness of the analyst. The prolonged silence of the patient then is a kind of flooding of the analyst with silence as a defense and as a retaliation. This sequence of events is very similar to the behavior of certain animals who flood an enemy with some obnoxious substance in defense and as a retaliation.

Some years ago in treating a young, paranoid, phobic woman, I interpreted, just prior to a weekend interval, some of her homosexual strivings for the first time. The patient responded by going into a state of almost complete silence for approximately ten days. It took several months for the patient to recover sufficiently so that I was able to fully understand her reactions to my poorly timed interpretation. She felt that what I had said had been correct, but I was not correct as a therapist who brought her some helpful insight. Rather, I was correct as a cruel, relentless, pursuing enemy who caught her and poured over her some deadly information. At first she was panic-stricken and then furious. She covered herself with silence to protect herself; to be dead so I would leave her alone; yet she was too dependent not to come to her hour. She exuded silence to keep me away, to get rid of me, to destroy me, but also to protect me from her more venomous angry feelings.

Our patients react not only to our interpretations but also to our silences. We are all aware how often our patients react to our silence by transference reactions. It should be remembered, however, that sometimes the patients correctly perceive the emotional quality of our silence. This seems to be particularly true in very ill and regressed patients.

As an example I would like to mention the supervision of a candidate who was treating psychoanalytically a severely depressed compulsive-obsessive patient, who for a variety of reasons often became silent. Sometimes after she had been silent and her analyst had been silent, she would remark that she felt that he was sitting there angrily and impatiently because she was silent. The candidate usually did not respond verbally to such remarks and continued to wait for her to produce some "material." I could discern from the way the candidate reported such hours that the patient was right and he was annoyed with her because she frustrated him by not giving him "material" for his supervisory session. The candidate readily acknowledged this state of affairs when I mentioned this, but wondered how the patient was able to perceive this. I told him that it seemed to me some patients had the capacity to detect differences in our silences, perhaps due to certain minute differences in our breathing, bodily movements, posture, and from this they intuitively detected our emotional state. In our discussion of this situation, I told him that it was not necessary to fill up the supervisory hour with a great deal of the patient's material. I also suggested that he try an experiment the next time his patient became silent; he should try to wait silently but pleasantly just to see whether the patient would detect this difference. In the next supervisory hour the candidate reported how to his surprise the patient said after some minutes of her silence, "I have the feeling your silence is different today. You seem to be smiling."[2]

---

[2] See Greenson (1967a) for a much more extensive discussion of the meaning and technical handling of silence. See also chapter 17.

13

On Enthusiasm

(1962)

ENTHUSIASM IS A HAPPY and joyous state of mind. It is a condition of high spirits—a special form of elation. Enthusiasm has some of the buoyancy of euphoria and the activity of mania, and it is obviously different from the blissful and peaceful elations. It is my aim to differentiate enthusiasm from other varieties of elation and to distinguish several types of enthusiasm. Then I shall attempt to formulate some of the metapsychological elements which make for the phenomenon of enthusiasm.

Enthusiasm is a passionate state of mind. It is exciting, active, and noisy—not quiet or passive like bliss. In this regard it resembles the hypomanias, only the activities are more realistic and adaptive. The more incongruous or bizarre the activities, the more likely that we are dealing with pathological enthusiasm or a hypomanic state.

There is an air of extravagance and expansiveness about enthusiasm—a readiness to use superlatives. The enthusiastic person feels not merely good or even very good, but great—in

Presented as the Plenary Lecture at the Fall Meeting of the American Psychoanalytic Association in New York, December 11, 1960. First published in *Journal of the American Psychoanalytic Association*, 10:3-21, 1962.

fact, "the greatest!" There is a sense of exuberance, richness, an abundance of good fortune; yet with it all, there is some awareness that one is exaggerating; but it is enjoyable, and one is reluctant to give it up.

Enthusiasm has the quality of an infatuation, and indeed it is always present when there is infatuation. However, enthusiasm can occur without romance and without sex, and in regard to inanimate objects. But enthusiasm, too, contains a feeling of being captivated, an awareness of folly, a loss of one's reason. It is characteristic for both enthusiasm and infatuation to occur suddenly.

A person filled with enthusiasm is generous, and has an urge to share his richness with others. To be enthused means to feel full of goodness, as contrasted to feeling full of badness in the melancholias, and feeling full of emptiness as in boredom (see chapter 4). The wish to share with others is urgent, even compelling. One cannot remain enthusiastic alone. As in laughter, one needs cohorts, accomplices. They have to be converted to enthusiasm or else the enthusiasm is endangered.

For all its noisy busyness, enthusiasm is fragile and capricious. It can be punctured like a balloon. There is something inflated about enthusiasm which makes it so vulnerable. The lack of response from a "wet blanket" can easily smother its flame, and a bigger enthusiasm can shrivel it up. Normal enthusiasm is a temporary state of mind. When it is prolonged, it is likely to be neurotic or a hypomania. One can become repeatedly enthusiastic about the same thing, but the state of enthusiasm is a temporary one.

By and large, enthusiasm is contagious. It is easy to find cohorts. There seems to be a readiness in others to participate vicariously in enthusiasm, like with laughter. When that happens, there is the feeling of joining and being a member of a group—a feeling of belonging. But in those who do not share in the enthusiasm, one can frequently observe a response of enthusiasm envy. People who coldly watch another's enthusiasm often have a feeling of being left out, cheated—of not belonging. The enthusiastic human being has an air of possessing something valuable, and those without it or without the opportunity to participate in it feel like "have-nots." People who are prone to evoke enthusiasm often become leaders, and it is indeed one of the most valuable characteristics in determining leadership potential.

Enthusiasm transforms the total personality; it is a mood, and not an emotion. The entire self and object world is changed (Jacobson, 1957a). One finds qualitative alterations in feeling tone, behavior, thinking, attitudes, values, and expectations.

For all its fanciful quality, in normal enthusiasm there is always an awareness of reality, and perhaps a kind of tongue-in-cheek attitude, for the enthusiastic person is well oriented. Furthermore, enthusiasm lends itself frequently to adaptive, constructive, and even creative actions. Although it contains some element of play, enthusiasm can also be used for serious work.

This much is the more or less manifest picture of enthusiasm. I now propose to explore more carefully and deeply some of the structural, dynamic, economic, and genetic findings. Furthermore, I shall attempt to differentiate between the normal, mature and the pathological varieties of enthusiasm. The pioneer work in this field of affects and moods has already been done by Freud (1917a, 1921), Abraham (1924), Lewin (1950), and Jacobson (1953a, 1957a). Rado (1927, 1933), H. Deutsch (1933), E. Bibring (1953), and many others have also made valuable contributions (M. Klein, 1921-45; Fenichel, 1945; see also chapter 5). This presentation is derived from their findings, and is an attempt to extend them.

Typical Examples of Infantile Enthusiasm

1. A woman buys a hat and becomes enthused. She has bought many hats, many of which she liked, but this particular hat brings enthusiasm. Why? She says, "It does something for me, it's not just a hat." It does something? What does that mean? She doesn't merely look prettier in that hat. It changed her.

Analysis revealed that it changed her self image. The hat altered her picture of herself. Just prior to buying the hat, her analysis was concerned with her feelings of inferiority due to her exaggerated awareness of being penisless and therefore unattractive. The new hat changed this; it lent her some penis quality; it contradicted her feelings of inferiority. She was enthused and rushed to her friends to share in and confirm her good fortune.

    2. An adolescent girl is unexpectedly given a gift of a beautiful European sportscar. She is enthusiastic. Her old car pleased her, but she was never enthused. But this car was "for me." The other car was middle-aged and married-looking. This car was sleek and shiny and graceful. She gave it a name—a girl's name —and a European name, to suit its personality. She drove differently, masterfully. She lost weight and became sleek and shiny and accented the European features of her appearance. She became colorful instead of her usual retiring self. It was like an infatuation. She fell in love with the car and, as adolescents do, identified with it. Her self image changed. She had found a new and a better identity. She was a "new person."

    What can we learn from these examples? Apparently the hat and the car made some qualitative change in the self image and in the object world of these people. The possession took on some highly valuable quality—it became idealized. The object seemed to possess precisely those qualities which represented a wish fulfillment in the individuals described. The possession turned out to be a projection of the ego ideal onto the object. The possession then represented an idealized aspect of the self. By possessing such an idealized object, a change occurs in the self image. As one of my patients put it succinctly when she waxed enthusiastic over the purchase of a new house: "It is not just mine; it *is* me."

    Apparently possessing such an idealized object brings with it a feeling of being joined with it, a feeling of incorporating it, identifying with it, and making it part of the self. The slang expression used currently in reference to an object evoking enthusiasm is: "I eat it up." This puts it very well. When you feel you have eaten it, it is part of you, then you can become enthused.

This feeling of being joined to some idealized object resembles the fusion of ego and superego which Freud (1917a, 1921), Lewin (1950), and Jacobson (1953a) describe as typical for states of elation; but there is an important difference. In enthusiasm, the feeling of being joined to or joining is to an external object; it is temporary, and it is partial. In pathological states like the hypomanias, the fusion is with an internal object. In enthusiasm, external objects are needed in order to perpetuate the state, whereas the manias are relatively independent of external objects. Carnivals and holidays evoke enthusiasm. One needs the confirmation and approbation of others in order to maintain one's enthusiasm. The sense of fusion is temporary and limited, and extremely vulnerable to the influences of the external world and reality—yet enthusiasm seems to share with the hypomanias this feeling of being joined to some idealized object.

How typical is this for enthusiasm? The word enthusiasm is derived from the Greek word *entheos*, meaning to be inspired by God, or to be possessed by God or some superhuman power. The German word *Begeisterung* has the same meaning. The enthused human being feels as though he had breathed in, inspired, something divine and wondrous. And like inspiration, enthusiasm leads to a creation—a creation of a modified self image, which is richer and grander (Kris, 1952). Now one has to share it or prove it; hence the running to friends and cohorts. In normal enthusiasm, there is little exaggeration and what there is, one is aware of. In mature enthusiasm, the objects which evoke it are more in accordance with one's conscious ideals; in infantile enthusiasm, the objects are derived from childhood values. In any case, enthusiasm denotes a temporary leave of absence from reality and the superego (Kris, 1952). The changes which occur in the state of enthusiasm are a result of wish fulfillments and represent a triumph of the pleasure principle. The objects or situations which produce enthusiasm are "dreamy." American slang seems to confirm some of Lewin's ideas about sleep, the dream, and elation. Enthusiasm is a kind of dream state, enacted while awake.

Normal and Pathological Enthusiasm

But the pleasure gain which occurs in enthusiasm is not only derived from the union with an idealized object. Part of the joy comes from having successfully denied and contradicted something painful. The new hat denies the penisless state; it contradicts it by proclaiming the possession of something penis-like. The new hat performs on a phallic level what the new car does on an adolescent level for the nineteen-year-old girl. A new and shiny identity denies and contradicts the previous drab identity.

Various methods of denial obviously play a great role in the production of elated states, as many authors have found (H. Deutsch, 1933; A. Freud, 1936; Lewin, 1950; Jacobson, 1957a, 1957b; see also chapter 9). In enthusiasm, too, denial may be necessary in order to achieve the idealization of the enthusiasm-producing object. One may need a selectivity of perception in order to hypercathect the good qualities and decathect the bad, so that the idealization can take place. The more one has to resort to denial to achieve idealization, the more pathological is the enthusiasm. Normal enthusiasm is inducted by worthy objects, which do not have to be distorted. For example, one can become enthused by listening to a great artistic performance. One does not have to deny the existence of a few wrong notes in order to be normally enthusiastic. If one does, then we are no longer dealing with normal enthusiasm, but with enthusiasm needed for some neurotic purpose. Normal enthusiasm is a bonus, not a need. It is true, however, that normal enthusiasm is a welcome change from the ordinary deprivations and disappointments of everyday civilized life. But it is evoked by worthy objects and situations; it is temporary and helps one to face reality after the detour of enthusiasm. Neurotic enthusiasm, on the other hand, is evoked by objects or situations which are inappropriate, and is prolonged to ward off some other painful, underlying state, as the following clinical material illustrates.

A thirty-five-year-old male patient of mine whose usual mood was dour and mistrustful had the following experience during his third year of analysis. In an hour, he felt my tone of voice to be critical. He reacted to this by whimpering, becoming petulant and tearful. In this hour I handled the situation by admitting that it was possible my tone might have been critical, but it did not seem to justify his childish reaction. His reaction must have come from something else. He mulled this over and then recalled, at first vaguely, and then more clearly, some hitherto hidden memories of childhood, in which he had this whimpering reaction to his father. The patient left the hour in good spirits. Two hours later he phoned, something he had never done before in his analysis. He was enthusiastic; a rare mood for him. He could not work, he was impelled to call me, to tell me this was the greatest analytic hour he had ever had, and he had had several years of previous analysis, and I was the best analyst he had ever had. My technique was superb, I had handled him magnificently, he was so grateful that I had taken him as a patient, and on and on. . . . I said nothing. Eventually, his ardor was spent and he closed by saying, "I want to thank you for everything, and I'll see you on Thursday." I replied: "All right, but your next hour is Wednesday." Silence on the other end of the phone.

The next hour, Wednesday, he reported grimly that my remark had killed his good mood. Then he bitterly complained of my sarcasm, my irritability, how disappointed he really was in me as an analyst, and how I really was like his father, and on and on.

In the course of the next several hours, I learned something about this patient's neurotic enthusiasm. During that hour of the childish whimpering, as I began to talk, before he actually grasped the meaning of my remarks, he was afraid I was going to punish him. When he realized my tone and my words were not punitive, but compassionate, he felt relieved and grateful. He then eagerly sought to confirm my hypothesis that his reaction did indeed come from his past. He found some real memories which proved this, but gave them to me as a gift, to repay me for my gift to him. The hour ended with his feeling he was not a whimpering child caught in some infantile act; on the contrary, he was a hardworking patient. My intervention which evoked this whole sequence of events was selected and magnified into becoming a wonderful interpretation and then this was so generalized that I became a superb analyst. He participated in my greatness and was transformed into the lucky fellow who was fortunate in being able to join me in this intimate and wonderful relationship. Once we were joined in this way, he became enthusiastic. The entire experience hinged on his use of my intervention to ward off his underlying anger and disappointment. He confirmed my interpretation and avoided his hostility by escaping into his past reactions to his father. His enthusiasm was the result of this successful denial plus the feeling of union with me. It was a screen mood, to hide as a reaction formation, another, opposing mood (chapter 9). The enthusiasm became a resistance, a temporary obstacle in the analytic work, as Lewin (1950) has pointed out in regard to the elations.

This patient called me to share in his good mood; but, more important, also to confirm and perpetuate his good mood. He sensed it was false and shaky and he needed me to maintain the artificial good feeling. His remark, "I'll see you on Thursday," indicated the breaking through of his hidden anger and disappointment.

How does this situation compare to normal enthusiasm? Let us take the experience of listening to a great artistic performance. One goes with some positive expectation, but there are misgivings; the music is strange, there are a few wrong notes, but then the great artistry of the performer becomes strikingly apparent and one is enthused. It seems that here too one has to overcome something opposite to become enthused. The big difference is that one does not have to deny this or repress it in normal enthusiasm. One can admit one's previous misgivings or the lack of perfection and still be enthused.

The more pathological the enthusiasm, the more it is created by and used for denial. Such enthusiasm requires cohorts and accomplices who will help maintain the denial, not just witnesses and sharers. It is a denial à deux—a happy phrase suggested by Hanna Fenichel (personal communication).

There is a wide range of enthusiasm going from the normal through the neurotic to the hypomanic elations. In all there is the feeling of being joined to something wonderful. In enthusiasm, normal and neurotic, one feels one is fused to an external object and this is partial and temporary. One is aware of being in a special state of mind. These enthusiasms are correctible and influenceable by external reality factors. Hypomanic enthusiasm is tied up with an internal fusion, between ego and superego, and is not easily amended by reality. Normal enthusiasm requires little denial, only the overcoming of some slight discontent or misgiving. Pathological enthusiasm requires a good deal of denial in a variety of ways.

Sources of Enthusiasm

Experiences which produce enthusiasm are those which simultaneously evoke the pleasurable feeling of possessing or being united with a wondrous object and also denying an underlying deprivation. As I have already indicated, certain possessions can do this. Enthusiasm can be elicited in relation to possession of objects on any and all phases of psychosexual development. There seem to be oral, anal, phallic, and adolescent enthusiasms. The hat and the car were examples of enthusiasm on a phallic and adolescent level. Financial gain, the acquiring of a big pile of money, can give rise to an anal enthusiasm. The pleasurable eating experiences of a gourmet are obviously oral enthusiasms.

Achievements and successes of certain kinds can also produce enthusiasm. Creative work, coming upon a new idea, making discoveries, are very apt to evoke enthusiasm. Children, sweethearts, and pets are particularly suitable as enthusiasm producers. Participating as an audience in certain events can do the same. The sports fan reacts to his team as the music lover does to his favorite artists. The observer feels joined to the performer and participates in his triumphs. The beauty of nature can also stimulate a reaction of enthusiasm, although this quickly becomes a more peaceful and blissful kind of elation. One gives oneself up to the beauty of nature rather than making it part of oneself. At any rate, in all the above instances, the feeling of being united and joined to a wonderful object, the temporary and partial sense of identification, makes it possible to deny the discontents of everyday life and one is enthused.

Economic Considerations

Enthusiasm is a state of great activity. An enthused person seems suddenly to have acquired a great abundance of energy and the world seems pliable and accessible. There is a plethora of enterprise, talk, gregariousness, and imagination. A question that now arises is, where does this new quantity of energy come from. Freud (1921), Jacobson (1957a), and others have noted the striking economic changes which occur in all joyous states. It is as though an abundance of psychic energy, which had been ordinarily consumed elsewhere, had now become free and available.

It has been hypothesized that the fusion of ego and superego in manic states is responsible for the liberation of this energy. The union with an idealized object does away with all tensions between ego and superego; the superego temporarily gives up its functions. Thus, the id is free from pressure and is permitted greater discharge.

There is another reason for the surplus of energy. The process operating in enthusiasm is similar to what we see in laughter. The joke makes the ego's defenses unnecessary, and so does enthusiasm. The energy which has been used for defense can now be utilized for enthusiasm. All the dangers from the id, superego, and the external world are denied, making other defenses unnecessary. It is a triumph of the pleasure principle, and the ego has the world as its oyster.

The activities which are indulged in, in enthusiasm, are often creative and worthwhile. Enthusiasm can serve an adaptive ego function; in fact, one may perform not only well, but extraordinarily well. The enthusiastic teacher is an apt example. The enthusiastic person feels as though he has borrowed strength from the object of his enthusiasm—he has been inspired. Actually, he has borrowed strength from himself. The increase in capability comes from his sense of fusion with the idealized object which he has created from unconscious sources within himself. It resembles the kind of feats of strength one can see in hypnosis (M. Wexler, personal communication). The activities of the enthusiastic person are different from the activities of the hypomanic; there one sees more agitation and less accomplishment.

The energy which is freed seems to be essentially instinctual and libidinal and not neutralized. Enthusiasm is a passionate state of mind. The activities which are pursued with enthusiasm are loved in some form or other. It is my clinical impression that enthusiasm frees and channelizes great quantities of energy, but the quality of the work which is accomplished lacks the evenness and steadiness that one sees when neutralized energies are utilized. It seems to me that here one is dealing with a deneutralization in the service of the ego (W. Stewart, personal communication). The instinctualized energies, however, seem to be predominantly libidinal. When enthusiasm acquires an important aggressive coloring, we are usually dealing with fanaticism and not enthusiasm.

The activity of enthusiasm distinguishes it from the blissful, serene, and ecstatic states of elation. First, the enthusiast has to do something to maintain his pleasurable state of mind. The ecstatic person has achieved it. Second, the enthusiast has actively incorporated and taken into himself something wondrous, whereas in blissful ecstasy, there is the feeling of having given oneself up to something bigger. The reactions to the beauty of nature seem to belong to this second category. There seems to be a different kind of identification in enthusiasm and in bliss (Lewin, 1950). Blissful ecstasy has an element of passive surrender, while enthusiasm is actively struggling. More will be said about this later.

Structural Considerations

Enthusiasm brings with it, as do moods in general, a partial regression in the state of mind (Jacobson, 1953a). We can see it in the ego functioning with the tendency toward distortions in thinking, the denials, the generalizing, exaggerations, and flighty judgments. The superego manifests its regression by renouncing its critical functions, by the fusion, the externalization, and the idealization. In the object relationships we see transference reactions, object hunger, and identifications predominantly. From the standpoint of the id, the pregenital strivings seem to be in the foreground. And the activities seem to be performed with libidinal energies, deneutralized energies.

However, it is to be stressed that although all these regressions can be seen in enthusiasm, they are temporary and selective. They can be brought to a halt immediately, even though reluctantly; and despite the regressive features, much creative work and achievements can be accomplished. Work performed in enthusiasm is a true example of regression in the service of the ego (Kris, 1952). This is in contrast to the more permanent and all-inclusive regressions which we see in the hypomanias.

The Vicissitudes of Enthusiasm

It is striking how differently people react when one describes someone as being enthusiastic and when one calls someone an enthusiast. Enthusiasm is not only reputable, but enviable; whereas the enthusiast is in disrepute. Apparently, when enthusiastic reactions become a character trait, a habitual, chronic response, although they do afford pleasure to the bearer and the audience, they also devaluate.

The enthusiast is a caricature of normal enthusiasm. First of all, he is not as selective and the occasions which evoke enthusiasm are less worthy. The enthusiast is felt to be gullible, credulous, and somewhat of a charlatan for he seduces you in his enthusiastic responses more than occurs in normal enthusiasm

(Hoffer, 1955). Although his enthusiasm about a particular item is temporary, he is so frequently enthused. He has the zeal of a true believer, only he is fickle. He is like the fanatic, only less venomous (Hoffer, 1955). He resembles the Don Juans of achievement whom Fenichel (1945) describes, a relatively successful acting-out character, who restlessly goes from one triumph to another without ever achieving contentment. Diagnostically, the enthusiast belongs to the group of oral character disorders with a chronic optimistic attitude (A. Katan, 1934). The hunger for new objects and new experiences which Abraham (1924) described in the manias is also characteristic for them, but the enthusiasts still retain their reality testing. Each single instance of enthusiasm is influenceable and changeable, but it is the constant search for new experiences which will evoke enthusiasm and this factor gives them their driven character. In the enthusiast the emotional intensity serves an important defensive as well as expressive function, a point which has been made by several authors (Siegman, 1954; Weiss, 1959; see also chapter 9). I believe they are characters in search of a screen; furthermore, Rado's (1933) ideas about drug addiction seem to be quite relevant in understanding some of the problems in the enthusiast.

I would like to describe some of the clinical findings in an enthusiast I analyzed some years ago in order to bring up some special points for discussion. The patient, fifty-five years old, was an extremely successful man who came for treatment because of a sleep disturbance and a fear of becoming addicted to sleeping pills. He had reached the top of several professions and at the time of his analysis had reached the pinnacle of success in his third field. His propensity for enthusiasm was a vital factor in his success in each endeavor. He enjoyed his successes, but restlessly sought new worlds to conquer. He claimed to have had a happy marriage for thirty years, despite the fact that he was constantly involved in different extramarital love affairs from the beginning of his marriage. The affairs were not merely sexual adventures, but were intense, romantic involvements where he fancied himself in love and loved, and he was exuber-

ant and enthused. When these infatuations ended, and the patient ended them when "the magic" went out of them, the
women remained his staunch admirers. His work was such that
he could hide his absences from home behind the cloak of his
profession. When he did spend time with his wife, he was easily
able to be kind and considerate and she felt herself fortunate to
have such an attentive husband whose only weakness was his
passion for his work. He was warm and devoted to his children
whenever he did spend time with them and they adored him. In
his social groups, and there were many, since he was never
able to be happily alone, he was beloved. In those sophisticated and jaded gatherings, he was the life of the party, where
much liveliness was needed to cover the agitated boredom
that prevailed. Every new venture, professional, sexual, or
social, he undertook with optimism, responded with enthusiasm;
and this was contagious.

The insomnia which brought him for treatment was of a
particular kind. He could readily fall asleep, but could only stay
asleep for a few hours. Once awake he became restless and
agitated. He felt impelled to get out of bed and eat or drink or
talk to someone. If he fell asleep again, it was a bad sleep full of
disturbing dreams. This was in contrast to the first sleep which
was a good sleep and full of pleasant dreams or no dreams (blank
dreams?). A "good" orgasm or a pill or a meal produced the good
sleep. A partial orgasm, alcohol, or fatigue produced the bad
sleep. He enjoyed naps. He slept well when he knew he only had
a limited time for sleep. He slept poorly after being the life of the
party. Physical pain helped him to sleep well. This pattern of
sleep disturbance had existed all his adult life. He began taking
sleeping pills some ten years before treatment and although he
increased the amounts, and it deepened his sleep, it did not
appreciably lengthen his sleep. Further, he began to like the
hangover sensation of the pills the next day. He felt pleasantly
dreamy, somewhat gay. He described it as a feeling of something
good having happened to him, a piece of good fortune, but he
could not remember it. He felt as though he had eaten something
delicious and the aftertaste lingered on the next morning in the

pleasurable hangover. After the bad sleep, he awoke with a bad taste in his mouth and was irritable.

Analysis revealed that "good sleep" was possible only if he felt pleasantly full, satisfied, virtuous, and not alone. The prospect of sleeping for eight hours made him feel lonely. As I said before, he could always nap, because then he could "see" the beginning and ending of the stretch of time he was to sleep. He felt as though the two hours of the nap were boundaries and he could touch them, whereas to sleep for eight hours was to be all alone and in a big bed with no boundaries to touch. He tried never to sleep alone and hugged the pillow if there was no person available. His marital situation deteriorated with his success, for then his wife acquired twin beds, and eventually a separate bedroom. He usually slept about four hours with pills, as though this were the greatest interval he could endure without being fed. This oral quality in his sleep activities was also pronounced in his sexual behavior.

In the course of the analysis, it became clear that this patient had an almost fetishistic attraction to the female breast. He always looked first at the breasts of every woman he met. If the breasts seemed voluptuous, he was interested. He had to be able to fantasy that the breasts were full, engorged, not withered or empty or even partly full. He needed to believe that the breast was on the verge of overflowing. Second, the woman had to appear cold and disdainful in some aspect of her behavior. What he loved above all was the delicious sense of surprise when a cold-appearing woman gave him, and him alone, her overflowing breast. An important feature of his relationships was that the woman experience the same kind and quality of enthusiasm that he did. As soon as he detected some loss of enthusiasm in her, he was through. He could enjoy the affair only as long as it was completely mutual.

His sexual activities were revealed to be oral sucking activities, no matter what parts of the body or whatever actions were pursued. There was a great deal of cunnilingus and fellatio, which he perceived as giving and getting of a breast. He and the partner would alternate in the active and passive roles and both

would have to take place. Intercourse proper was felt as a giving
of his penis-breast into a vagina-mouth. In intercourse he did not
take, he felt as though he were giving. He had his orgasm when
he imagined his partner did, on the basis of an identification
with her. In all sexual activities there was a big one and a little
one, a mother and a child, and he loved to play both roles. He
was the sucking child and the loving giver of the breast. More
than that, he fantasied in his sexual activities that he created
breasts. By exciting a woman, he imagined he gave her breasts
full of milk. When he was excited, the woman made his little
penis-breast into a big milk-containing penis-breast. He was
offended if his semen was not considered delectable. All
secretory products of his women were a delicacy to him. He
particularly enjoyed all those positions which obscured who was
doing what to whom. He strove to achieve a feeling of oneness, a
union. The quality and quantity of his orgasm depended on how
well he achieved this sense of fusion.

Apparently, at first his partners enjoyed the patient's sexual
virtuosity and seemed to respond in kind. Once they indicated
that they had lost any of their enthusiasm, he became disen-
chanted, the spell was over, and he departed. Obviously, he
needed to feel that he, and he alone, was completely satisfying.
He could not tolerate any semblance of a rival or any lessening of
the mutuality, the oneness.

The history of this patient reveals some of the sources of this
behavior. For a long time he maintained he was his mother's
favorite and he had many screen memories to "prove" it. He was
the product of an unhappy marriage and both parents openly
acknowledged this. He was the younger of two boys and
avowedly the favorite. But his entire behavior had a reactive
quality. Already in the initial interviews this was demonstrated.
When he was animated, his face seemed youthful and cheerful,
but when he paused, he looked even older than his years and
sad. During these pauses, he frequently sighed. This was particularly true during his analytic hours. Sighing, even in an
animated person, indicates a heaviness of heart, an inner
sadness.

But to return to the patient's history. He claimed to be the favorite, and he spent his whole life as though he were confirming this. However, a person who feels truly loved and favored does not have to continue to prove it. A person secure in his position is confident, trusting, and at peace, not exuberant, overly ambitious, and restless. He had a memory of early childhood where his mother is bathing him and saying with pride, "My, what a big penis you have." This is obviously a screen memory because he spent his life getting women to confirm this. If he had truly believed it, he would not have had to become promiscuous.

Behind the happy facade of screens, three important events came to light. He was breast-fed for a long time, which abruptly stopped when his mother became pregnant. She later miscarried. When he was six or seven years old, his mother had an affair, which almost precipitated a divorce. When he was 14 years old, his mother had another affair, and at this time the patient ran away from home, never to return except for occasional triumphant visits when he was much older. I believe it is this history of overgratification followed by unexpected and severe deprivations which makes for such an acting-out, oral, screen character (see chapter 9).

I would like to return to a consideration of the role of the breast in this man's chronic enthusiasm. I have described some of his overt behavior and fantasies which indicate his need to feel that he was being given the overflowing breast by a loving woman. I can add that his dreams were full of symbolism referrable to his mother's body and breasts. He dreamed of all kinds of fruits, persimmons, avocados, grapefruit, which clearly referred to sizes, shapes, textures, and tastes of breasts. There were many references to odors as well as temperature in his associations. In his nightmares, he was drowning or suffocating, or being smothered by substances which were warm, soft, moist, and had an odor. To be enveloped by such a substance could be immensely pleasurable or frightening. It seemed to depend on the aggression, or lack of it, in his superego, whether he could enjoy this envelopment or whether it terrified him in his dreams.

He considered himself lucky and "born with a breast in his

mouth." This feeling threatened to leave him, however, and he had to search for experiences which would re-create the sensation of the overflowing breast within him; then he would become enthused. Once he achieved it, he had enough to share with the world, but if it left him, he was depressed and agitated. Rado (1933) and Lewin (1950) have described similar findings in drug addiction and elation.

The patient could attain this feeling from the sexual activity described above, from his professional successes, or from an admiring audience. They all evoked the feeling "I've got it." Archimedes must have been enthusiastic when he shouted "Eureka—I have found it" (L. Peller, personal communication). The feeling of triumph also seems to be related to enthusiasm, although in triumph, the emphasis is on victory over adversity rather than possession. (The feeling "I've got it" is also expressed as an attitude in poise [Rangell, 1954].) To return to the patient, he did so much in his enthusiasm not merely to discharge the excitement, but to evoke it anew, to deny the underlying depression. The feeling of possessing the overflowing breast, or of remembering it, which was the trigger for producing his enthusiasm, had to be constantly sought for in the external world, because the memory of it in his past was a myth, i.e., some truth and much distortion.

Summary and Conclusion

The original model for this joyous feeling of enthusiasm appears to be derived from experiences at the mother's breast in nursing. Ecstasy seems to portray the giving up of one's self to this bigger entity, the mother, after one has gained complete satisfaction at the breast (Lewin, 1950). This seems to be true of all the blissful elations, which entail a passive submissive surrender to something bigger. One allows oneself to become incorporated; in Lewin's terms, one allows oneself to be devoured and to sleep. Enthusiasm, on the other hand, seems to be modeled after some other pleasurable aspect of the nursing situation. It appears plausible to reconstruct the following situation: a child has been hungry and is now given the breast willingly and warmly. The child sucks eagerly. He or she is able to remember the anticipated pleasure of satiation. However, he is also able to remember the previous deprivation, the feeling of hunger. When the child recalls the memory of the hunger while he is still nursing, he begins to nurse with enthusiasm as long as the breast is available and is given warmly. He is still not completely satisfied while he is enthused, but he is aware of being on his way to satisfaction. The mutual enjoyment of the nursing mother is a necessary component since it makes for the necessary amount of security which enthusiasm requires (A. Goldberg, personal communication). It is this combination of events which seems to be characteristic for enthusiasm.

If we scrutinize normal enthusiasm at a later date, we can find similar components. It is prefaced by some deprivation, no matter how mild; then some idealized object appears which offers the possibility for satisfaction. Possession of this object or mutuality in the object then brings about the feeling of enthusiasm. The enthusiastic person is not completely satisfied, but he has tasted some satisfaction, expects more, and the memory of past deprivation is temporarily overcome by the feeling of enthusiasm. He then feeds others who feed him back in their mutual relationship. It is this feature which makes the enthusiast so dependent and the enthusiasm so vulnerable. The combination of partial satisfaction with the hope of more and the dim memory of past deprivation makes the enthusiast seek enthusiastic cohorts and accomplices.

The patient described above repetitively searched for enthusiasm-evoking objects. The infatuations, the being the life of the party, the nature of his sexuality, the short-lived good sleep, the screen of being the favorite, and the dim memory of his past unhappiness—all seem to fit in with this formulation. In enthusiasm, the union which is sought for is really a reunion, an attempt to return to an older, unconscious, fuller satisfaction. People who lack all enthusiasm have abandoned hope of ever gaining even this partial and temporary gratification.

14

On Homosexuality and Gender Identity

(1964)

THIS CONTRIBUTION IS based on the proposition that a study of gender identity will offer valuable insights into some of the special problems concerning the fate of the homosexuality in various types of patients. *Gender Identity* refers to one's sense of being a member of a particular sex; it is expressed clinically in the awareness of being a man or a male in distinction to being a woman or a female. (The term was formulated in collaboration with Stoller [1964a], who deals with another aspect of this subject.) The starting point of this paper is the clinical finding that for most psychiatric patients in our society the appearance of homosexuality in their treatment stirs up a peculiar kind of dread (Freud, 1937a, 1940). It is my contention that for these patients the awareness of homosexuality poses

Contribution to the Symposium on Homosexuality, held at the International Psycho-Analytic Congress, Stockholm, July-August 1963. First published in *International Journal of Psycho-Analysis*, 45:217-219, 1964. Also as: Homosexualité et identité sexuelle. *Revue Française de Psychanalyse*, 29:343-348, 1965.

a threat to their gender identity. This seems to be true of neurotics, paranoid patients, and even some types of homosexuals, each of whom handle the problem differently. The only patients who seem to have no anxiety about their gender identity are the bisexuals and the typical overt homosexuals. I shall try to explain these differences.

The most obvious material comes from a curious finding in both male and female neurotics whenever homosexuality first enters the clinical picture. These patients react with a sense of dread and as a rule behave as though I had said: "You *are* a homosexual." Sometimes they actually misquote me as having said so; sometimes they express this statement as their own conclusion. At other times this is not verbally stated but can be reconstructed from their material. The notion "I am a homosexual" is perceived as an oppressive, earthshaking revelation and leads to a sense of impending panic. If we pursue the analysis of the idea "I am a homosexual," the patient will describe the feeling of losing a component of his self, a cornerstone he had taken for granted, something central to his sense of "Who am I," his identity in terms of gender. One of my patients put it very succinctly when he said: "I feel as though you are going to say to me: 'I have news for you; you are neither a man nor a woman, you are a freak.'"

It is striking that the neurotic adult reacts as though the gender of his sexual object determines his own gender. He does not respond as do most overt homosexuals, who seem to proclaim: I am a man even though I have sexual relations with men or play the role of a woman.

At this point I want to present an unusual clinical example which will highlight some of these points and lead us even deeper into the problem.[1]

---

[1] This material was observed in a research project on Gender Identity, at the University of California School of Medicine at Los Angeles. Dr. R. Stoller and Daniel Greenson provided many of the clinical data and N. Leites contributed some of the formulations. But it should be noted that the patients were not in analysis, and the material obtained was from a series of face-to-face interviews, psychological tests, social casework.

Clinical Example

A woman of feminine appearance in her late thirties presented herself in our research project, having been sent to us by the Department of Gynecology because a fistula developed between her rectum and an artificial vagina. Her story can be condensed as follows: The patient was born a boy and until puberty felt like a boy. Anatomically he had been a completely normal male. Then at age 19 he became sexually and romantically attracted to a man. This aroused such great anxiety that he could not yield to the instinctual temptation. Instead he was determined to find out whether he was a man or not—and volunteered in the Paratroopers. He successfully endured the invasions of Sicily and Italy, was wounded in action, and received many decorations. All in all he completed four years of combat duty as a thoroughly competent paratrooper in World War II. After the war, the patient realized he had proved nothing—he had felt lonely, and an outsider among the men. However, the prospect of sexual relations with a man was still abhorrent and frightening to him. This would be homosexuality, and the patient felt that this was both impossibly repulsive and also some vague kind of overwhelming threat. At this point he became possessed by the idea that he was "really" a woman. He then learned of operations being performed in one of the Scandinavian countries which would make for a surgical change in gender. He went to Scandinavia and he had his penis, testes, and scrotum removed. After he returned to the United States, he changed his name to a woman's name, dressed as a woman, regularly took estrogen injections, and in this state was able to embark on sexual relationships with men.

After the patient began a serious love affair with a man, he changed his gender on his birth certificate, married, adopted a baby girl, and then had the first of two operations for the purpose of building an artificial vagina in the perineal space. This was mainly for her husband's pleasure since the patient's sexuality was limited to cuddling and other aspects of skin erotism. When the patient appeared at our research clinic, she looked remarkably feminine, the sparse facial hair barely visible under her makeup. She had been legally married some five years, had an adopted baby of four years, was in the process of adopting a second child, wore women's clothes apparently naturally, talked and moved as a typical woman. We could not find any clear-cut signs of psychosis, borderline state, or conspicuously severe neurosis in our investigations.

The "transsexual" paratrooper had a dread of homosexuality similar to that of neurotic adults. His attitude toward his sexual object was also comparable in that it became decisive for his gender identity. He seems to have reacted according to the formula: If I love a man, then I must be a woman. Instead of repressing these ideas, he surgically "suppressed" them; he changed his anatomical gender. For this man there was something more precious than genital organs, and even his gender. He had to achieve that dissimilarity between gender of sex object and his own gender as it exists in heterosexuals. To do so he had to alter his body in order to support his belief concerning his gender. In a way the clinical picture can be understood as a circumscribed, well-organized, delusional system which was successful insofar as it made it possible for the patient to lead an apparently happy life as a woman (A. Goldberg, M. Wexler, N. Leites).

How different all this is from the situation in the usual overt homosexual. For the pervert, neither the gender of the sexual object nor the enactment of fantasies of being of a different sex influences his gender identity. He knows he is a man, even though he may play different roles. It seems that for him his anatomy is the determining factor. The same is true for bisexuals.

In order to begin to understand these different outcomes, it is necessary to formulate some ideas about the development of identity and in particular the development of gender identity in the child.

At first the infant cannot distinguish between self and external world. As perception and thinking develop, this step is made; the child can differentiate between me and not-me. This we may call the beginning of the core identity. But this has no sexual or gender connotation until the child becomes aware of the differences between the sexes. This seems to be brought about by three factors: (1) awareness of one's anatomical physiological structures; this would include sexual sensations and awareness of objects with different genitals; (2) the parental and social figures which label the child in accordance with his sexual structures and others in accordance with theirs; (3) a biological force which seems to be present from birth and which can be decisive in pushing a child in the direction of a particular gender. (Stoller's paper [1964a] illustrates this hypothesis.) At any rate, the awareness of the existence of two sexes comes about. Thus, "me-ness" becomes connected with gender—I am a boy; I am a girl. Gender has become attached to the core identity: I, John—"this person with this body, this penis, different from girls, I am a boy, etc." In the late phallic phase the gender identity becomes attached to and includes the impulse and fantasy: "I, John, a boy, like to do sexual things to those 'different' creatures, to girls."

I am distinguishing three different phases:

1. I am me, John.
2. I am me, John, a boy.
3. I am me, John, a boy, which means that I like to do sexual things with girls.

This is just a bare and primitive outline of what I imagine takes place in the development of gender identity.

It would seem that in each phase of development different elements are essential for the preservation of one's identity. Later pathological formations seem to indicate this. For example, the neurotic adult seems to need some awareness of sexual attraction to a person of the opposite sex in order to maintain his gender identity. He will attempt to ward off his hostility or loathing which might make him impotent and less masculine, but nevertheless he still feels he is a man. However, sexual excitement toward a man would throw him in a panic, his gender identity would be in jeopardy. This seems to be true of so-called normal people in our society.

This need to maintain a diversity of gender between love object and self (as a condition of maintaining one's own gender) seems to be true of the paranoid patient as well. He seems to project his homosexuality onto some other object, in order to deny that the homosexual impulses are his own. These patients seem to have reached phase 3 and, in attempting to maintain the diversity of gender between self and object, sacrifice a part of the self which is perceived as external voices, hallucinations, etc. Frank homosexual activity in paranoids is, I believe, extremely rare. Furthermore, confused and disoriented as such psychotic patients may be, they usually remain true to their gender identity. Even in their delusions, men may believe themselves to be Napoleon, or Caesar, or Hitler, but rarely, if ever, Cleopatra. Schreber felt he would be cured *if* he were transformed into a woman; but he never felt he achieved this and in the acute stage of his illness he was plagued by projections of his homosexuality (Freud, 1911a). The transsexual paratrooper seemed to accomplish what Schreber hoped for and failed. He did transform himself into a woman and he did seem to obtain some form of "cure."

The only adults who seem to be able to dispense with this diversity in gender between self and the love object are the homosexual perverts. I imagine some of them remain fixated to phase 2, and thus their sense of gender identity is independent of the sex of the love object. These would be the truly bisexual people who can enjoy sex with both genders. They rarely if ever come for treatment. The homosexual most often described in the psychoanalytic literature is usually strictly homosexual. He too is bound to a unit consisting of gender of object and gender identity, but differently. I would speculate that such persons did reach phase 3, but were severely traumatized at this level (Gillespie, 1956; Socarides, 1963; and Wiedeman, 1962). As a consequence they became phobic about the heterosexual object and became antiheterosexual. Then they regressed to the level of phase 2, but could not become bisexual because of their phobia about heterosexuality. This results in a rigid homosexuality. This is the type of homosexual we see most frequently in psychoanalytic practice.

I am well aware that all these speculations leave many questions unanswered which I hope future investigations will clarify. In the *Three Essays*, Freud (1905b) demonstrated the relative separateness of the triad: instinctual zone, sexual activity, and sexual object. The present contribution adds another element for consideration in sexual activity. Not only do we ask what part of the body is doing what to whom, but who am I who is doing this.

15

The Working Alliance and the Transference Neurosis

(1965)

T HE CLINICAL MATERIAL on which this presentation is based is derived from patients who developed unexpected difficulties in the course of psychoanalytic therapy. Some of these patients had undergone one or more analyses with other analysts; others were patients of mine who returned for further analysis. In this group there were patients who were unable to get beyond the preliminary phases of analysis. Even after several years of analysis they were not really "in analysis." Others seemed interminable; there was a marked discrepancy between the copiousness of insight and the paucity of change. The clinical syndromes these cases manifested were heterogeneous in diagnostic category, ego functions, or dynamics of personality. The key to understanding the essential pathology as well as the therapeutic stalemate was in the failure of the patient to develop a reliable working relation with the analyst. In each case the patient

Presented before the Los Angeles Psychoanalytic Society, May 1963, and the Cleveland Psychoanalytic Society, May 1964. First published in *Psychoanalytic Quarterly*, 34:155-181, 1965. Also as: Das Arbeitsbündnis und die Übertragungsneurose. *Psyche*, 20:81-103, 1966. It also appeared as chapter 3.5 in my book on psychoanalytic technique where many aspects of the concept introduced here are elaborated further. See also Greenson (1977a).

was either unable to establish or maintain a durable working alliance with the analyst and the analyst neglected this fact, pursuing instead the analysis of other transference phenomena. This error in technique was observable in psychoanalysts with a wide range of clinical experience and I recognized the same shortcoming in myself when I resumed analysis with patients previously treated.

In working with these seemingly unanalyzable or interminable patients I became impressed by the importance of separating the patient's reactions to the analyst into two distinct categories: the transference neurosis and the working alliance. Actually this classification is neither complete nor precise. However, this differentiation helps make it possible to give equal attention to two essentially different transference reactions.

My clinical experiences in regard to the working alliance were enhanced and clarified by Elizabeth Zetzel (1956b) in "Current Concepts of Transference." In that essay she introduced the term "therapeutic alliance" and indicated how important she considered it by demonstrating that one could differentiate between the classical psychoanalysts and the British school by whether they handled or ignored this aspect of the transference. Leo Stone (1961) gave further insight and fresh impetus in my attempts to clarify and formulate the problem of the working alliance and its relation to other transference phenomena.

The concept of a working alliance is an old one in both psychiatric and psychoanalytic literature. It has been described under a variety of labels but, except for Zetzel and Stone, it either has been considered of secondary importance or has not been clearly separated from other transference reactions. It is my contention that the working alliance is as essential for psychoanalytic therapy as the transference neurosis. For successful psychoanalytic treatment a patient must be able to develop a full-blown transference neurosis and also to establish and maintain a reliable working alliance. The working alliance deserves to be recognized as a full and equal partner in the patient-therapist relationship.

Definition of Terms

I start with as concise a definition of classical psychoanalytic technique: "Psycho-analysis is that method of treatment of emotional disorders in which the relationship between the patient and the therapist is so structured that it facilitates the maximal development of a transference neurosis. The analyst's interpretations are the decisive and ultimate instruments, used in an atmosphere of compassionate neutrality which enables the patient, communicating via free association, to recapitulate his infantile neurosis. The analyst's goal is to provide insight to the patient so that he may himself resolve his neurotic conflicts—thus effecting permanent changes in his ego, id, and superego, and thereby extending the power and the sovereignty of his ego" (Greenson, 1958b, p. 201).[1]

Transference is the experiencing of feelings, drives, attitudes, fantasies, and defenses toward a person in the present which are inappropriate to that person and are a repetition, a displacement of reactions originating in regard to significant persons of early childhood (Freud, 1905a, 1909c, 1916-1917). I emphasize that for a reaction to be considered transference it must have two characteristics: it must be a repetition of the past and it must be inappropriate to the present.

During analysis several transference phenomena can be distinguished. In the early phases we usually see sporadic, transient reactions, aptly called "floating" transference reactions by Glover (1955). Freud (1914a, 1916-17) described more enduring transference phenomena which develop when the transference situation is properly handled. Then all the patient's neurotic symptoms are replaced by a neurosis in the transference relation of which he can be cured by therapeutic work. "It is a new edition of the old disease." I would modify this concept and say that the transference neurosis is in effect when the analyst and the analysis become the central concern in the patient's life. The

---

[1] For surveys of the essentials of psychoanalytic technique, see Greenson (1959, 1974a).

transference neurosis includes more than the infantile neurosis; the patient also relives the later editions and variations of his original neurosis. The "floating" transference phenomena ordinarily do not belong to the transference neurosis. However, for simplification, the phrase, transference neurosis, here refers to the more regressive and inappropriate transference reactions.

The term "working alliance" is used in preference to diverse terms others have employed for designating the relatively nonneurotic, rational rapport which the patient has with his analyst. It is this reasonable and purposeful part of the feelings the patient has for the analyst that makes for the working alliance. This label, working alliance, was selected because it emphasizes its outstanding function: it centers on the patient's ability to work in the analytic situation. Terms like the "therapeutic alliance" (Zetzel, 1956b), the "rational transference" (Fenichel, 1941b), and the "mature transference" (Stone, 1961) refer to similar concepts. The designation, working alliance, however, has the advantage of stressing the vital elements: the patient's capacity to work purposefully in the treatment situation. It can be seen at its clearest when a patient, in the throes of an intense transference neurosis, can yet maintain an effective working relationship with the analyst.

The reliable core of the working alliance is formed by the patient's motivation to overcome his illness, his conscious and rational willingness to cooperate, and his ability to follow the instructions and insights of his analyst. The actual alliance is formed essentially between the patient's reasonable ego and the analyst's analyzing ego (Sterba, 1934). The medium that makes this possible is the patient's partial identification with the analyst's approach as he attempts to understand the patient's behavior.

The working alliance comes to the fore in the analytic situation in the same way as the patient's reasonable ego: the observing, analyzing ego is split off from his experiencing ego (Sterba, 1929). The analyst's interventions separate the working attitudes from the neurotic transference phenomena just as his interventions split off the reasonable ego from the irrational one.

These two sets of phenomena are parallel and express analogous psychic events from different points of reference. Patients who cannot split off a reasonable, observing ego will not be able to maintain a working relation and vice versa.

This differentiation between transference neurosis and working alliance, however, is not absolute since the working alliance may contain elements of the infantile neurosis which eventually will require analysis. For example, the patient may work well temporarily in order to gain the analyst's love, and this ultimately will lead to strong resistances; or the overvaluation of the analyst's character and ability may also serve the working alliance well in the beginning of the analysis, only to become a source of strong resistance later. Not only can the transference neurosis invade the working alliance, but the working alliance itself can be misused defensively to ward off the more regressive transference phenomena. Despite these inter-mixtures, the separation of the patient's reactions to the analyst into these two groupings, transference neurosis and working alliance, seems to have clinical and technical value (see chapter 23 and Greenson, 1967a, 3.6).

Survey of the Literature

Freud (1912a) spoke of the friendly and affectionate aspects of the transference which are admissible to consciousness and which are "the vehicle of success in psychoanalysis" (p. 105). Of rapport he wrote: "It remains the first aim of the treatment to attach him [the patient] to it and to the person of the doctor. To ensure this, nothing need be done but to give him time. If one exhibits a serious interest in him, carefully clears away the re-sistances that crop up at the beginning and avoids making cer-tain mistakes, he will of himself form such an attachment. . . . It is certainly possible to forfeit this first success if from the start one takes up any standpoint other than one of sympathetic un-derstanding" (1913, pp. 139-140).

Sterba (1929) wrote about the patient's identification with the analyst which leads to the patient's concern with the work they have to accomplish in common—but he gave this aspect of the transference no special designation. Fenichel (1941b, p. 27) described the "rational transference" as an aim-inhibited positive transference which is necessary for analysis. Elizabeth Zetzel's emphasis on the importance of the "therapeutic alliance" was discussed above. Loewald's paper (1960) on the therapeutic action of psychoanalysis is a penetrating and sensitive study of the different kinds of relations the patient develops toward the analyst during psychoanalysis. Some of his ideas are directly concerned with what I call the working alliance. Leo Stone (1961) devotes himself to the complexities in the relation between analyst and patient. He refers to the "mature transference" which he believed to be: (a) in opposition to the "primordial transference" reactions and (b) essential for a successful analysis (p. 106).

The Symposium on Curative Factors in Psychoanalysis presented before the International Psycho-Analytical Association (1962) contained many references to the special transference reactions that make for a therapeutic alliance and also some discussion of the analyst's contribution to the "good" analytic situation. Gitelson (1962) spoke of the rapport on which we depend in the beginning of analysis and which eventuates in transference. He stressed the necessity for the analyst to present himself as a good object and as an auxiliary ego. Myerson (1962), Nacht (1962), Segal (1962), Kuiper (1962), Garma (1962), King (1962), and Heimann (1962) took issue with him on one or another aspect of his approach. In some measure the disagreement seems to be due to failure to distinguish clearly between the working alliance and the more regressive transference phenomena.

This brief and incomplete survey reveals that many analysts, including Freud, recognized that in psychoanalytic treatment another kind of relation to the analyst is necessary besides the more regressive transference reactions.

Development of the Working Alliance

ABERRATIONS

The first clinical examples show how the course of development of the working alliance deviated markedly from that of the usual psychoanalytic patient. The reason for proceeding this way stems from the fact that in the classical analytic patient the working alliance develops almost imperceptibly, relatively silently, and seemingly independently of any special activity on the part of the analyst. The irregular cases highlight different processes and procedures which take place almost invisibly in the usual analytic patient.

Case 1

Some years ago an analyst from another city referred an intelligent middle-aged man who had had more than six years of previous analysis. Certain general conditions had improved, but his original analyst believed the patient needed additional analysis because he was still unable to marry and was very lonely. From the beginning of the therapy I was struck by the fact that he was absolutely passive about recognizing and working with his resistances. It turned out that he expected them to be pointed out continuously, as his previous analyst had done. It also impressed me that the moment I made some intervention, he had an immediate response, although often incomprehensible. I discovered that he thought it his duty to reply immediately to every intervention since he believed it would be a sign of resistance, and therefore bad, to keep silent for a moment or so to mull over what had been said. Apparently his previous analyst had never recognized his fear of being silent as a resistance. In free association the patient searched actively for things to talk about and, if more than one idea occurred to him, he chose what seemed to be the item he thought I was looking for without mentioning the multiple choices. When I requested informa-

tion, he often answered by free association so that the result was bizarre. For example, when I asked him what his
middle name was he answered: "Raskolnikov," the first name
that occurred to him. When I recovered my composure and
questioned this, he defended himself by saying that he thought
he was supposed to free associate. I soon gained the impression
that this man had never really established a working relation
with his first analyst. He did not know what he was supposed
to do in the analytic situation. He had been lying down in front
of an analyst for many years, meekly submitting to what he
imagined the previous analyst had demanded—constant and
instant free association. Patient and analyst had been indulging
in a caricature of psychoanalysis. True, the patient had developed some regressive transference reactions, some of which had
been interpreted, but the lack of a consistent working alliance
left the whole procedure amorphous, confused, and ineffectual.

Although I realized that the magnitude of the patient's
problems could not be due solely or even mainly to the first
analyst's technical shortcomings, I thought the patient ought to
be given a fair opportunity to see whether he could work in an
analytic situation. Besides, this clarification would also expose
the patient's pathology more vividly. Therefore, in the first
months of our work together, I carefully explained, whenever it
seemed appropriate, the different tasks that psychoanalytic
therapy requires of the patient. He reacted to this information as
though it were all new to him and seemed eager to try to work in
the way I described. However, it soon became clear that he
could not just say what came to his mind, he felt compelled to
find out what I was looking for. He could not keep silent and
think about what I said; he was afraid of the blank spaces, they
signified some awful danger. If he were silent he might think; if
he thought he might disagree with me, and to disagree was tantamount to killing me. His striking passivity and compliance
were revealed as a form of ingratiation, covering up inner emptiness, an insatiable infantile hunger, and a terrible rage. In a
period of six months it became clear that this man was a schizoid
"as if" character who could not bear the deprivation of classical

psychoanalysis (H. Deutsch, 1942). I therefore helped him obtain supportive psychotherapy with a woman therapist.

Case 2

A woman I had previously analyzed for some four years resumed analysis after an interval of six years. We both knew when she had interrupted treatment that there was a great deal of unfinished analysis, but we agreed that an interval without analysis might clarify the unusual obscurities and difficulties we encountered in trying to achieve a better resolution of her highly ambivalent, complaining, clinging, sadomasochistic transference. I had suggested that she go to another analyst since, in general, I have found a change in analysts to be more productive than a return to the old one. It usually offers new insights into the old transference reactions and adds new transference possibilities. However, for external reasons this was not feasible and I undertook the resumption of her analysis, although with some reservations.

In her first hours on the couch I was struck by the strange way the patient worked in the analysis. Then I quickly recalled that this had often happened in the past; it appeared more striking now since I was no longer accustomed to it; it seemed almost bizarre. After a certain moment in the hour the patient would speak almost incessantly; there would be disconnected sentences, part of a recital of a recent event, an occasional obscene phrase with no mention of its strangeness or that it was an obsessive thought, and then back to the recital of a past event. The patient seemed to be completely oblivious of her odd way of speaking and never spontaneously mentioned it. When I confronted her with this, she at first seemed unknowing and then felt attacked.

I realized that in the previous analysis there had been many such hours or parts of hours when the patient was very anxious and tried to ward off her awareness of anxiety as well as analysis of it. I recalled that we had uncovered some of the meanings and historical determinants of such behavior. For example, her mother had been a chatterer, had talked to the child as a grownup before she could understand. Her incomprehensible talking to me was an identification with her mother and an acting out in the analytic situation. Furthermore, the mother had used a stream of talk to express both anxiety and hostility to her husband, an essentially quiet man. The patient took over this pattern from her mother and reenacted it in the analytic hour whenever she was anxious and hostile and when she was torn between hurting me and holding onto me.

We came to understand that this mode of behavior also denoted a regression in ego functions from secondary process toward primary process, a kind of "sleep-talking" with me, a reenactment of sleeping with the parents. This peculiar way of talking had recurred many times during the first analysis; and although various determinants had been analyzed, it still persisted to some degree up to the interruption of that analysis. Whenever I tried to confront the patient with a misuse of one of the analytic procedures, we would be side-tracked by her reactions to my confrontation or by new material that came up. She might recall some past event which seemed relevant or, in the next hours, dreams or new memories would appear and we never really returned to the subject of why she was unable to do some of the psychoanalytic work. In her second analysis, I would not be put off. Whenever the merest trace of the same disconnected manner of talking appeared, or whenever it seemed relevant, I confronted her with the problem and kept her to this subject until she at least acknowledged what was under discussion. The patient attempted to use all her old methods of defense against confrontations of her resistances. I listened only for a short time to her protestations and evasions and repeatedly pointed out their resistive function. I did not work with any new material until convinced the patient was in a good working alliance with me.

Slowly the patient began to face her misuse of the basic rule. She herself became aware of how she at times consciously, at others preconsciously, and at still other times unconsciously blurred the real purpose of free association. It became clear that when the patient felt anxious in her relation to me, she would let herself slip into this regressive "sleep-talking" manner of speech.

It was a kind of "spiteful obedience"—spiteful insofar as she knew it was an evasion of true free association. It was obedience inasmuch as she submitted to this regressive or, one might say, incontinent way of talking. This arose whenever she felt a certain kind of hostility toward me. She felt this as an urge to pour out a stream of poison upon me that led her to feel I would be destroyed and lost to her and she would feel alone and frightened. Then she would quickly dive into sleep-talking as though saying: "I am a little child who is partly asleep and is not responsible for what is coming out of me. Don't leave me; let me sleep on you; it is just harmless urine that is coming out of me." (Other determinants not relevant to the central topic will not be discussed.)

It was fascinating to see how differently this analysis proceeded from the previous one. I do not mean to imply that this patient's tendency to misuse her ability to regress in ego functioning completely disappeared. However, my vigorous pursuit of the analysis of the defective working alliance, my constant attention to the maintenance of a good working relation, my refusal to be misled into analyzing other aspects of her transference neurosis had their effects. The second analysis had a completely different flavor and atmosphere. In the first analysis I had an interesting and whimsical patient who was frustrating because I was so often lost by her capricious wanderings. In the second, though still a whimsical patient, she also was an ally who not only helped me when I was lost but pointed out that I was being led astray even before I realized it.

Case 3

A young man, Mr. Z., entered analysis with me after he had spent two and one half years with an analyst in another city. The analysis had left him almost completely untouched. He had obtained certain insights, but had the distinct impression that his former analyst really disapproved of infantile sexuality, even though the young man realized that analysts were not supposed to be contemptuous of it. In the preliminary interviews the patient told me that he had the greatest difficulty in talking about

masturbation and previously often consciously withheld this information. He had informed the former analyst about the
existence of many conscious secrets, but nevertheless stubbornly
refused to divulge them. He had never wholeheartedly given
himself up to free association and reported many hours of long
silence. However, the patient's manner of relating his history to
me and my general clinical impression led me to believe that he
was analyzable despite the fact that he had not been able to form
a working alliance with his first analyst.

I undertook the analysis and learned a great deal about this
patient's negative reactions to his previous analyst, some of
which stemmed from his way of conducting that analysis. For
example, in one of the first hours on the couch the patient took
out a cigarette and lit it. I asked him what he was feeling when
he decided to light the cigarette. He answered petulantly that he
knew he was not supposed to smoke in his previous analysis and
now he supposed that I too would forbid it. I told him that I
wanted to know what feelings, ideas, and sensations were going
on in him at the moment that he decided to light the cigarette.
He then revealed that he had become somewhat frightened in
the hour and to hide this anxiety from me he decided to light the
cigarette. I replied that it was preferable for such feelings and
ideas to be expressed in words instead of actions because then I
would understand more precisely what was going on in him. He
realized then that I was not forbidding him to smoke, but only
pointing out that it was more helpful to the process of being analyzed if he expressed himself in words and feelings. He
contrasted this with his first analyst who told him before he went
to the couch that it was customary not to smoke during sessions.
There was no explanation for this and the patient felt that his
first analyst was being arbitrary.

In a later hour Mr. Z. asked me whether I was married. I
countered by asking him what he imagined about that. He
hesitantly revealed that he was torn between two sets of
fantasies, one that I was a bachelor who loved his work and lived
only for his patients; the other that I was a happily married man
with many children. He went on spontaneously to tell me that he

hoped I was happily married because then I would be in a better position to help him with his sexual problems. Then he corrected himself and said it was painful to think of me as having sexual relations with my wife because that was embarrassing and none of his business. I then pointed out to him how, by not answering his question and by asking him instead to tell his fantasies about the answer, he revealed the cause of his curiosity. I told him I would not answer questions when I felt that more was to be gained by keeping silent and letting him associate to his own question. At this point the patient became somewhat tearful and, after a short pause, told me that in the beginning of his previous analysis he had asked many questions. His former analyst never answered, nor did he explain why he was silent. He felt his analyst's silence was a degradation and humiliation and now realized that his own later silences were a retaliation for this imagined injustice. Somewhat later he saw that he had identified himself with his first analyst's supposed contempt. He, the patient, felt disdain for his analyst's prudishness and at the same time was full of severe self-reproach for his own sexual practices which he then projected onto the analyst.

It was instructive to me to see how an identification with the previous analyst based on fear and hostility led to a distortion of the working relationship instead of an effective working alliance. The whole atmosphere of the first analysis was contaminated by hostile, mistrustful, retaliative feelings and attitudes. This turned out to be a repetition of the patient's behavior toward his father, a point the first analyst had recognized and interpreted. The analysis of this transference resistance, however, was ineffectual, partly because the first analyst worked in such a way as to justify constantly the patient's infantile neurotic behavior and so furthered the invasion of the working alliance by the transference neurosis.

I worked with this patient for approximately four years and almost from the beginning a relatively effective working alliance was established. However, my manner of conducting analysis, which seemed to him to indicate some genuine human concern for his welfare and respect for his position as a patient, also mobilized important transference resistances in a later phase of the analysis. In the third year I began to realize that, despite what appeared to be a good working alliance and a strong transference neurosis, there were many areas of the patient's outside life that did not seem to change commensurately with the analytic work. Eventually I discovered that the patient had developed a subtle but specific inhibition in doing analytic work outside the analytic hour. If he became upset outside, he would ask himself what upset him. Usually he succeeded in recalling the situation in question. Sometimes he even recalled the meaning of that event that he had learned from me at some previous time, but this insight would be relatively meaningless to him; it felt foreign, artificial, and remembered by rote. It was not his insight; it was mine, and therefore had no living significance for him. Hence, he was relatively blank about the meaning of the upsetting events.

Apparently, although he seemed to have established a working alliance with me in the analytic situation, this did not continue outside. Analysis revealed that the patient did not allow himself to assume any attitude, approach, or point of view that was like mine outside the analytic hour. He felt that to permit himself to do so would be tantamount to admitting that I had entered into him. This was intolerable because he felt this to be a homosexual assault, a repetition of several childhood and adolescent traumas. Slowly we uncovered how the patient had sexualized and aggressivized the process of introjection.

This new insight was the starting point for the patient to learn to discriminate among the different varieties of "taking in." Gradually he was able to reestablish a nonhomosexual identification with me in adapting an analytic point of view. Thus a working relation that had been invaded by the transference neurosis was once again relatively free of infantile neurotic features. The previous insights that had remained ineffectual eventually led to significant and lasting changes.[2]

_____

[2] This case is described further in chapters 16 and 20, as is the relationship between the working alliance and the process of working through.

Those patients who cling tenaciously to the working alliance because they are terrified of the regressive features of the transference neurosis should be briefly mentioned. They develop a reasonable relation to the analyst and do not allow themselves to feel anything irrational, be it sexual, aggressive, or both. Prolonged reasonableness in an analysis is a pseudoreasonableness for a variety of unconscious neurotic motives.

Case 4

For about two years a young social scientist who had an intellectual knowledge of psychoanalysis maintained a positive and reasonable attitude toward me, his analyst. If his dreams indicated hostility or homosexuality, he acknowledged this but claimed that he knew he was supposed to feel such things toward his analyst but he "really" did not. If he came late or forgot to pay his bill, he again admitted that it might seem that he did not want to come or pay his bill but "actually" it was not so. He had violent anger reactions to other psychiatrists he knew, but insisted they deserved it and I was different. He became infatuated with another male analyst for a period of time and "guessed" he must remind him of me, but this was said playfully. All of my attempts to get the patient to recognize his persistent reasonableness as a means of avoiding or belittling his deeper feelings and impulses failed. Even my attempts to trace the historical origins of this mode of behavior were unproductive. He had adopted the role of "odd ball," clown, harmless nonconformist in his high school years and was repeating this in the analysis. Since I could not get the patient to work further or consistently on this problem, I finally told him that we had to face the fact that we were getting nowhere and we ought to consider some alternative besides continuing psychoanalysis with me. The patient was silent for a few moments and said "frankly" he was disappointed. He sighed and then went on to make a free-associationlike remark. I stopped him and asked him what in the world he was doing. He replied that he "guessed" I sounded somewhat annoyed. I assured him it was no guess. Then slowly he looked at me and asked if he might sit up. I nodded and he did. He was quite shaken, sober, pale, and in obvious distress. After some moments of silence, he said that maybe he would be able to work better if he could look at me. He had to be sure I was not laughing at him, or angry, or getting sexually excited. I asked him about the last point. He told me that he often fantasied that perhaps I was being sexually excited by what he said but hid it from him. This he had never brought up before, it was just a "fleeting idea." But this fleeting idea led quickly to many memories of his father repeatedly and unnecessarily taking his temperature rectally. He proceeded to a host of homosexual and sadomasochistic fantasies. The persistent reasonableness was a defense against these as well as a playful attempt to tease me into acting out with him. My behavior, in the hour described above, was not well controlled, but it led to awareness that the patient's working alliance was being used to ward off the transference neurosis.

The working alliance had become the façade for the transference neurosis. It was his neurotic character structure hiding as well as expressing his underlying neurosis. Only when the patient's acting out was interrupted and he realized he was about to lose the transference object did his rigidly reasonable behavior become ego-alien and accessible to therapy. He needed several weeks of being able to look at me, to test out whether my reactions could be trusted. Then he became able to distinguish between genuine reasonableness and the teasing, spiteful reasonableness of his character neurosis and the analysis began to move.

The Classical Analytic Patient

The term classical in this connection refers to a heterogeneous group of patients who are analyzable by the classical psychoanalytic technique without major modifications. They suffer from some form of transference neurosis, a symptom of character neurosis, without any appreciable defect in ego functions. In such patients the working transference develops almost imperceptibly, relatively silently, and seemingly independently of any special activity or intervention on the part of the analyst. Usually signs of the working alliance appear in about the third to sixth month of analysis. Most frequently the first indications of this development are: the patient becomes silent and then, instead of waiting for the analyst to intervene, he himself ventures the opinion that he seems to be avoiding something. Or he interrupts a rather desultory report of some event and comments that he must be running away from something. If the analyst remains silent, the patient spontaneously asks himself what it can be that is making him so evasive and he will let his thoughts drift into free associations.

It is obvious that the patient has made a partial and temporary identification with me and now is working with himself in the same manner as I have been working on his resistances. If I review the situation, I usually find that prior to this development the patient has experienced some sporadic sexual or hostile transference reaction which has temporarily caused a strong resistance. I patiently and tactfully demonstrate this resistance, then clarify how it operated, what its purpose was, and eventually interpret and reconstruct its probable historical source. Only after effective transference-resistance analysis is the patient able to develop a partial working alliance. However, it is necessary to go back to the beginning of the analysis to get a detailed view of its development.

There is great variety in the manner in which a patient enters into the preliminary interviews. In part this is determined by his past history in regard to psychoanalysts, physicians, and authority figures and strangers, as well as his reactions to such conditions as being sick or needing and asking for help (Gill et al., 1954). Furthermore, his knowledge or lack of it about procedures of psychoanalysis and the reputation of the psychoanalyst also influence his initial responses. Thus the patient comes to the initial interview with a preformed relationship to me, partly transference and partly based on reality, depending on how much he fills in the unknowns inappropriately out of his own past.

The preliminary interviews heavily color the patient's reactions to the analyst. This is determined mainly by the patient's feelings about exposing himself as well as his responses to my method of approach and my personality. Here too I believe we see a mixture of transference and realistic reactions. Exposure of one's self is apt to stir up reverberations of past denudings in front of parents, doctors, or others and is therefore likely to produce transference reactions. My technique of conducting the interviews will do the same the more it seems strange, painful, or incomprehensible to the patient. Only those methods of approach that seem understandable to him may lead to realistic reactions. My "analyst" personality as it is manifested in the first interviews may also stir up both transference and realistic reactions. It is my impression that those qualities that seem strange, threatening, or nonprofessional evoke strong transference reactions along with anxiety. Traits the patient believes indicate a therapeutic intent, compassion, and expertness may produce realistic responses as well as positive transference reactions. The clinical material from the third case indicates how the manner, attitude, and technique of the analyst in the beginning of both analyses decisively colored the analytic situation.

By the time I have decided that psychoanalysis is the treatment of choice, I shall have gained the impression that the patient in question seems to have the potential for forming a working alliance with me along with his transference neurosis. My discussion with the patient of why I believe psychoanalysis is the best method of therapy for him, the explanations of the frequency of visits, duration, fee, and similar matters, and the patient's own appraisal of his capacity to meet these requirements will be of additional value in revealing the patient's ability to form a working alliance.

The first few months of analysis with the patient lying on the couch attempting to free associate can best be epitomized as a combination of testing and confessing. The patient tests his ability to free associate and to expose his guilt and anxiety-producing experiences. Simultaneously he is probing his analyst's reactions to these productions (Freud, 1915a; Greenacre, 1954). There is a good deal of history telling and reporting of everyday events. My interventions are aimed at pointing out and exploring fairly obvious resistances and inappropriate affects. When the material is quite clear, I try to make connections between past and present behavior patterns. As a consequence, the patient usually begins to feel that perhaps I understand him. Then he dares to regress, to let himself experience some transient aspect of his neurosis in the transference in regard to my person. When I succeed in analyzing this effectively, then I have at least temporarily succeeded in establishing a reasonable ego and a working alliance alongside of the experiencing ego and the transference neurosis. Once the patient has experienced this oscillation between transference neurosis and working alliance in regard to one area, he becomes more willing to risk future regressions in that same area of the transference neurosis. Once the patient has experienced this oscillation between transference neurosis and working alliance in regard to one area, he becomes more willing to risk future regressions in that same area of the transference neurosis. However, every new aspect of the transference neurosis may bring about an impairment of the working alliance and temporary loss of it.

Origins of the Working Alliance

CONTRIBUTIONS OF THE PATIENT

For a working alliance to take place, the patient must have the capacity to form object relations since all transference reactions are a special variety of them. People who are essentially narcissistic will not be able to achieve consistent transferences. Furthermore, the working alliance is a relatively rational, desexualized, and deaggressivized transference phenomenon. Patients must have been able to form such sublimated, aim-inhibited relations in their outside life. In the course of analysis the patient is expected to be able to regress to the more primitive and irrational transference reactions that are under the influence of the primary process. To achieve a working alliance, however, the patient must be able to reestablish the secondary process, to split off a relatively reasonable object relationship to the analyst from the more regressive transference reactions. Individuals who suffer from a severe lack or impairment in ego functions may well be able to experience regressive transference reactions but will have difficulty in maintaining a working alliance. On the other hand, those who dare not give up their reality testing even temporarily and partially, and those who must cling to a fixed form of object relationship are also poor subjects for psychoanalysis. This is confirmed by the clinical findings that psychotics, borderline cases, impulse-ridden characters, and young children usually require modifications in the classical psychoanalytic technique (Garma, 1962; Gill, 1954; Glover, 1955). Freud had this in mind when he distinguished transference neuroses, which are readily analyzable, from narcissistic neuroses, which are not.

The patient's susceptibility to transference reactions stems from his state of instinctual dissatisfaction and his resultant need for opportunities for discharge. This creates a hunger for objects and a proneness for transference reactions in general (Ferenczi, 1909). Satisfied or apathetic people have fewer transference reactions. The awareness of neurotic suffering also compels the patient to establish a relationship to the analyst. On a conscious and rational level the therapist offers realistic hope of alleviating the neurotic misery. However, the patient's helplessness in regard to his suffering mobilizes early longings for an omnipotent parent. The working alliance has both a rational and irrational component. The above indicates that the analyzable patient must have the need for transference reactions, and have the ego strength or that particular form of ego resilience that enables him to interrupt his regression in order to reinstate the reasonable and purposeful working alliance (see Loewald, 1960). The patient's ego functions play an important part in the implementation of the working alliance in addition to a role in object relations. In order to do the analytic work the patient must be able to communicate in a variety of ways, in words, with feelings, and yet restrain his actions. He must be able to express himself in words, intelligibly with order and logic, give information when indicated, and also be able to regress partially and do some amount of free association. He must be able to listen to the analyst, comprehend, reflect, mull over, and introspect. To some degree he also must remember, observe himself, fantasy, and report. This is only a partial list of ego functions that play a role in the patient's capacity to establish and maintain a working alliance; we also expect the patient simultaneously to develop a transference neurosis. Thus his contribution to the working alliance depends on two antithetical properties: his capacity to maintain contact with the reality of the analytic situation and also his willingness to risk regressing into his fantasy world. It is the oscillation between these two positions that is essential for analytic work.

CONTRIBUTIONS OF THE ANALYTIC SITUATION

Greenacre (1954), Macalpine (1950), and Spitz (1956a) have pointed out how different elements of the analytic setting and procedures promote regression and the transference neurosis. Some of these same elements also aid in forming the working alliance. The high frequency of visits and long duration of the treatment not only encourage regression but also indicate the long-range objectives and the importance of detailed, intimate communication. The couch and the silence give opportunity for introspection and reflection as well as production of fantasy. The fact that the patient is troubled, unknowing, and being looked after by someone relatively untroubled and expert stirs up the wish to learn to emulate. Above all, the analyst's constant emphasis on attempting to gain understanding of all that goes on in the patient, the fact that nothing is too small, obscure, ugly, or beautiful to escape the analyst's search for comprehension—all this tends to evoke in the patient the wish to know, to find answers, to find causes. This does not deny that the analyst's probings stir up resistances: it merely asserts that it also stirs up the patient's curiosity and his search for causality.

Freud (1913) stated that in order to establish rapport one

needs time and an attitude of sympathetic understanding. Sterba (1934) stressed the identificatory processes. The fact that the analyst continuously observes and interprets reality to the patient leads the patient to identify partially with this aspect of the analyst. The invitation to this identification comes from the analyst. From the beginning of treatment, the analyst comments about the work they have to accomplish together. The use of such terms as "let us look at this," or "we can see," promotes this. Loewald (1960) stressed how the analyst's concern for the patient's potentials stimulates growth and new developments.

Fenichel (1941b) believed it is the analytic atmosphere that is the most important factor in persuading the patient to accept on trial something formerly rejected. Stone (1961) emphasized the analyst's willingness to offer the patient certain legitimate, controlled gratifications. I would add that the constant scrutiny of how the patient and the analyst seem to be working together, the mutual concern with the working alliance, in itself serves to enhance it.

CONTRIBUTIONS OF THE ANALYST

It is interesting to observe how some analysts take theoretical positions apparently in accord with their manifest personality and others subscribe to theories that seem to contradict their character traits. Some use technique to project, others to protect, their personality. This finding is not meant as a criticism of either group, since happy and unhappy unions can be observed in both. Some rigid analysts advocate strictest adherence to the "rules of abstinence" and I have seen the same type of analyst attempt to practice the most crass, manipulative, gratifying "corrective emotional experience" psychotherapy. Many apparently carefree and easygoing analysts practice a strict "rule of abstinence" type of therapy, while some of this same character type provoke their patients to act out or indulge them in some kind of mutual gratification therapy. Some analysts practice analysis that suits their personality; some use their patients to discharge repressed desires. Be that as it may, these considerations are relevant to the problems inherent in the establishment of the working alliance. Here, however, only a brief outline of the problems can be attempted. The basic issue is: what characteristics of personality and what theoretical orientation in the analyst will insure the development of a working alliance as well as the development of a full-blown transference neurosis?

I have already briefly indicated how certain aspects of the analytic situation facilitate production of a transference neurosis. This can be condensed to the following: we induce the patient to regress and to develop a transference neurosis by providing a situation that consists of a mixture of deprivation, a sleeplike condition, and constancy. Patients develop a transference neurosis with a variety of different analysts as long as the analytic situation provides a goodly amount of deprivation administered in a predictable manner over a suitable length of time. For a good therapeutic result, however, one must also achieve a good working relationship.

What attitudes of the analyst are most likely to produce a good working alliance? My third case indicates how the patient identified himself with his previous analyst on the basis of identification with the aggressor, on a hostile basis. This identification did not produce a therapeutic alliance; it produced a combination of spite and defiance, and interfered with the psychoanalytic work. The reason for this was that the personality of the first analyst seemed cold and aloof, traits which resembled the patient's father, and the patient was not able to differentiate his first analyst from his regressive transference feelings. How differently he reacted to me in the beginning. He was clearly able to differentiate me from his parent and therefore he was able to make a temporary and partial identification with me, and thus to do the analytic work.

The most important contribution of the psychoanalyst to a good working relationship comes from his daily work with the patient. His consistent and unwavering pursuit of insight in dealing with any and all of the patient's material and behavior is the crucial factor. Other inconsistencies may cause the patient pain, but they do not interfere significantly with the establish-

ment of a working alliance. Yet there are analysts who work
consistently and analytically and still seem to have difficulty in
inducing their patients to develop a working alliance. I believe
this may be due to the kind of atmosphere they create. In part,
the disturbance may be the result of too literal acceptance of two
suggestions made by Freud (1912b, 1915a, 1919): the concept of
the analyst as a mirror and the rule of abstinence. These two
rules have led many analysts to adopt an austere, aloof, and even
authoritarian attitude toward their patients. I believe this to be
a misunderstanding of Freud's intention; at best, an attitude incompatible with the formation of an effective working alliance.

The reference to the mirror and the rule of abstinence were
suggested to help the analyst safeguard the transference from
contamination, a point Greenacre (1954) has amplified. The
mirror refers to the notion that the analyst should be "opaque" to
the patient, nonintrusive in terms of imposing his values and
standards upon the patient. It does not mean that the analyst
shall be inanimate, cold, and unresponsive. The rule of abstinence refers to the importance of not gratifying the patient's infantile and neurotic wishes. It does not mean that all the
patient's wishes are to be frustrated. Sometimes one may have to
gratify a neurotic wish temporarily. Even the frustration of the
neurotic wishes has to be carried on in such a way as not to demean or traumatize the patient.

While it is true that Freud stressed the deprivational aspects
of the analytic situation, I believe he did so because at that time
(1912-19) the danger was that analysts would permit themselves
to overreact and to act out with their patients. Incidentally, if
one reads Freud's case histories, one does not get the impression
that the analytic atmosphere of his analyses was one of coldness
or austerity. For example, in the original record of the case of the
Rat-Man, Freud (1909c) appended a note, dated December 28,
to the published paper, "He was hungry and was fed." Then on
January 2, "Besides this he apparently only had trivialities to
report and I was able to say a great deal to him today."

It is obvious that if we want the patient to develop a relatively realistic and reasonable working alliance, we have to work

in a manner that is both realistic and reasonable despite the fact that the procedures and processes of psychoanalysis are strange, unique, and even artificial. Smugness, ritualism, timidity, authoritarianism, aloofness, and indulgence have no place in the analytic situation.

The patient will be influenced not only by the content of our work but by how we work, the attitude, the manner, the mood, and the atmosphere in which we work. He will react to and identify himself particularly with those aspects that need not necessarily be conscious to us. Glover (1955) stressed that the analyst needs to be natural and straightforward, decrying the pretense, for example, that all arrangements about time and fee are made exclusively for the patient's benefit. Fenichel (1941b) emphasized that above all the analyst should be human and was appalled that so many of his patients were surprised by his naturalness and freedom. Sterba (1929), stressing the "let us look, we shall see" approach, hints at his way of working. Stone (1961) goes even further in emphasizing legitimate gratifications and the therapeutic attitude and intention of the psychoanalyst that are necessary for the patient.

All analysts recognize the need for deprivations in psychoanalysis; they would also agree in principle on the analyst's need to be human. The problem arises, however, in determining what is meant by humanness in the analytic situation and how does one reconcile this with the principle of deprivation. Essentially the humanness of the analyst is expressed in his compassion, concern, and therapeutic intent toward his patient. It matters to him how the patient fares, he is not just an observer or a research worker. He is a physician and a therapist, and his aim is to help the patient get well. He keeps his eye on the long-range goal, sacrificing temporary and quick results for later and lasting changes. Humanness is also expressed in the attitude that the patient is to be respected as an individual. We cannot repeatedly demean a patient by imposing rules and regulations upon him without explanation and then expect him to work with us as an adult. For a working alliance it is imperative that the analyst show consistent concern for the rights of the patient throughout the analysis. Though I let my patient see that I am involved with him or her and concerned, my reactions have to be nonintrusive. I try not to take sides in any of his conflicts except that I am working against his resistances, his damaging neurotic behavior, and his self-destructiveness. Basically, however, humanness consists of understanding and insight conveyed in an atmosphere of serious work, straightforwardness, compassion, and restraint (Greenson, 1958b).

The above outline is my personal point of view on how to resolve the conflict between the maintenance of distance and the closeness necessary for analytic work and is not offered as a prescription for all analysts. However, despite great variation in analyst's personalities, these two antithetical elements must be taken into account and handled if good analytic results are to be obtained. The transference neurosis and the working alliance are parallel antithetical forces in transference phenomena; each is of equal importance.

Summary

Some analyses are impeded or totally thwarted by failure of patient and analyst to form a working alliance. Clinical examples of such failure are examined, showing how they were corrected. Formation of the working alliance, its characteristics, and its relation to transference are discussed. It is contended that the working alliance is equally as important as the transference neurosis. (For further elaboration see chapters 22, 25, and 26.)

16

The Problem of
Working Through

(1965)

A LTHOUGH WORKING THROUGH is one of the basic elements of psychoanalytic technique, there are few contributions to this subject. In part this seems to be due to some confusion about the meaning of the term. In addition, working through is the result of so many procedures performed simultaneously by the analyst and the patient that it is very difficult to describe systematically. Ordinarily one can best demonstrate it in a continuous case presentation. Finally, working through deals with processes which are not ordinarily articulated between analyst and patient; some aspects of working through proceed automatically and do not become an overt issue.

The purpose of this essay is to clarify the meaning of the concept of working through by singling out those elements which seem to be essential components of this complex process.

First published in *Drives, Affects, Behavior, Volume 2: Essays in Honor of Marie Bonaparte*, edited by Max Schur. New York: International Universities Press, 1965, pp. 277-314.

Survey of the Literature

Freud introduced the concept of working through in 1914, after he had finished the first analysis of the Wolf-Man. His treatment had become stalemated after more than three years of therapy. To quote Freud: "He listened, understood and remained unapproachable" (p. 11). Then, since the patient's attachment to Freud had become strong enough, Freud set a date for termination and, surprisingly, the analysis made rapid progress (Freud, 1918b). Although there is no discussion of the problem of working through in this later paper, it seems likely that the prolonged lack of change in this patient prompted Freud to a consideration of this subject, which he published under the title of "Remembering, Repeating, and Working Through" (1914a). It seems to me that whenever Freud wrote on working through, he always used as his clinical examples the relatively intractable patients and not the cases which responded well to psychoanalytic therapy. This may be partly responsible for Freud's search for, and emphasis on, the so-called "special resistances" which make working through necessary.

In the 1914 paper, Freud advanced the concept of the "compulsion to repeat" in explaining the patient's tendency to repeat the past in actions instead of remembering. Later on, however, the repetition compulsion was considered to be a manifestation of the death instinct (1920, p. 36).

In the *Introductory Lectures* (1916-17) Freud considered the "adhesiveness of the libido," i.e., the tenacity with which the libido holds to particular channels and particular objects, to be "an independent factor, varying from individual to individual, whose determinants are quite unknown to us" (p. 348).

In 1917 Freud introduced the concept of the "work of mourning." Freud did not directly connect this concept with that of working through, although later authors did (Fenichel and Kris). In discussing the work of mourning Freud said: "Reality-testing has shown that the loved object no longer exists, and it proceeds to demand that all libido shall be withdrawn from its attachments to that object." This demand can arouse such intense opposition that people never willingly abandon a libidinal position, "that a turning away from reality takes place . . . . Normally, respect for reality gains the day. Nevertheless its orders cannot be obeyed at once. They are carried out . . . at great expense of time and cathectic energy, and in the meantime the existence of the lost object is psychically prolonged. . . . [However,] when the work of mourning is completed the ego becomes free and uninhibited again" (1917a, pp. 244-245). These quotations seem to indicate that during psychoanalytic treatment old objects are relinquished only by the establishment of new object ties in the transference, and even then only after a period of time.

Subsequently Freud (1926a) again took up problems concerning working through:

> There can be no doubt . . . about the existence of this resistance [ego resistance] on the part of the ego. But we . . . find that even after the ego has decided to relinquish its resistances it still has difficulty in undoing the repressions; and we have called the period of strenuous effort which follows . . . the phase of 'working-through'. . . . It must be that after the ego-resistance has been removed the power of the compulsion to repeat—the attraction exerted by the unconscious prototypes upon the repressed instinctual process—has still to be overcome. There is nothing to be said against describing this factor as the *resistance of the unconscious* [pp. 159-160]. [Later on Freud called this variety *resistance of the id.*]

In "Analysis Terminable and Interminable" (1937a) Freud again returned to the problem of working through.

> If we advance a step further . . . we come upon resistances of another kind, which we can no longer localize and which seem to depend on fundamental conditions in the mental apparatus . . . the whole field of enquiry is still bewilderingly strange and insufficiently explored. We come across people, for instance, to whom we should be inclined to attribute a special 'adhesiveness of the libido.' The processes

which the treatment sets in motion in them are so much
slower than in other people because, apparently, they cannot . . . detach libidinal cathexes from one object and displace them on to another, although we can discover no
special reason for this cathectic loyalty. . . .

In another group of cases we are surprised by an attitude in our patients which can only be put down to a
depletion of the plasticity, the capacity for change and further development. . . . When the work of analysis has
opened up new paths for an instinctual impulse, we almost
invariably observe that the impulse does not enter upon
them without marked hesitation. We have called this behaviour, perhaps not quite correctly, 'resistance from the
id.' But with the patients I here have in mind, all the mental
processes, relationships and distributions of force are unchangeable, fixed and rigid. . . . Here we are dealing with
the ultimate things which psychological research can learn
about: the behaviour of the two primal instincts, their distribution, mingling and defusion—things which we cannot
think of as being confined to a single province of the mental
apparatus, the id, the ego or the super-ego. No stronger impression arises from the resistances during the work of
analysis than of there being a force which is defending itself
by every possible means against recovery and which is absolutely resolved to hold on to illness and suffering. One
portion of this force has been recognized by us, undoubtedly
with justice, as the sense of guilt and need for punishment,
and has been localized by us in the ego's relation to the
superego. But this is only the portion of it which is, as it
were, psychically bound by the super-ego and thus becomes recognizable; other quotas of the same force,
whether bound or free, may be at work in other, unspeci-
fied places. . . . These phenomena are unmistakable indications of the presence of a power in mental life which we
call the instinct of aggression or of destruction according to
its aims, and which we trace back to the original death instinct of living matter [p. 241ff.].

I believe the foregoing represents the crux of Freud's thinking about working through, namely, working through is necessary in order to overcome the resistances of the id, the psychic inertia, the adhesiveness of the libido, and the repetition compulsion derived from the death instinct. Freud said little about the technical problems. It is noteworthy that in one place (1914a) he stressed the work of the patient, and in another the work in common:

> This working through of the resistances may in practice turn out to be an arduous task for the *subject* of the analysis and a trial of the patience for the analyst.... The doctor has nothing else to do than to wait and let things take their course, a course which cannot be avoided nor always hastened.... One must allow the patient time to become more conversant with [the] resistance ... to *work through* it, to overcome it, by continuing, in defiance of it, the analytic work according to the fundamental rule of analysis. Only when the resistance is at its height can the analyst, *working in common with his patient*, discover the repressed instinctual impulses which are feeding the resistance [p. 155; my italics].

After this review of Freud's ideas, I must limit myself to a few words about the writings of others on the subject of working through.

Fenichel (1941b) considered working through a protracted process of resistance analysis aiming at the inclusion of the warded-off components in the total personality. After we analyze a resistance, the old resistance may return when the ego-id balance is disturbed. We may see repetitions or variants of old instinct-defense patterns in different contexts, since no single interpretation can include all danger situations. In facing the repressed, the ego has to rediscover something which has been wordless, condensed, and implicit. The ego has to recognize and abolish the isolation of the warded-off components from the total personality. We cannot work directly upon the id, only upon the ego. The repetition of the analytic work in working through seduces the patient to think differently, to try a new solution. Working through is like the work of mourning: the old representations are present in many memories and wishes and the detachment has to take place separately in each complex.

Essentially, Fenichel considered working through a repetition, extension, and deepening of the analysis of the resistances. He did not believe that a special type of resistance made working through necessary, nor did he find that any special technique was necessary for working through.

Lewin (1950) saw a parallel in the work of mourning and working through, namely, an attempt to correct faulty reality testing.

Greenacre (1956) seemed to be in basic agreement with Fenichel's point of view: she also emphasized the need to overcome resistances repetitively and progressively. Greenacre, however, stressed the special need for working through when there has been a combination of traumatic experience in childhood and "organizing" experiences in latency. Unless these traumatic events are thoroughly worked through, therapeutic improvement will not be maintained and the patient will relapse.

Kris (1956a) was mainly concerned with the problem of the effectiveness of insight and tried to establish criteria for ego functioning necessary for insight. He described several "circular processes" which are set in motion during analysis. Insight leads to some therapeutic benefit and therapeutic benefit leads to further insight. Insight leads to dynamic changes, which lead to more insight. In turn, insights change the ego and these changes make more insights possible. In another paper (1956b) Kris emphasized the special position of reconstruction and memory. He believed that all interpretive work must ultimately lead to reconstruction. A reconstructive interpretation facilitates memory. In this way, we help the ego in its synthetic function which serves as an aid to recall. Insight is in the center of a circular process, of which memory, the ego's integrative function, and the self image are also a part. Correct reconstructive interpretation may initiate this process. Kris as well as Fenichel felt that working through was like the work of mourning; the neurotic patterns may be treated like cherished possessions or love objects and it requires a great deal of psychological work to give them up.

Novey (1962) raised several cogent points. He linked the affective experience and learning theory, which had been neglected by psychoanalytic theory.

Stewart (1963) believes that working through refers to the time and energy required of the patient to change his habitual pattern of instinctual discharge, the resistances of the id. He stressed the work of the patient in this process. Stewart maintained that working through differs from mourning because in mourning the task is to come to terms with the loss of a love object, while in working through the objective is to alter the modes and aims of the instinctual drives. A special feature of Stewart's paper is the careful study of Freud's writings on this subject.

Working Definition

In attempting to arrive at a preliminary definition of working through, I have tried to consider the contributions of those who have written significantly on this subject. From this point of view as well as from my own clinical experience, it seems possible to formulate a definition of working through which centers around insight and change. We do not regard the analytic work as working through before the patient has insight; we do so only after some insight has been achieved. It is the goal of working through to make insight effective, i.e., to make significant and lasting changes in the patient. By making insight the pivotal issue we can distinguish between those resistances which prevent insight and those resistances which prevent insight from leading to change. The analytic work on the first set of resistances is the analytic work proper; it has no special designation. The analysis of those resistances which keep insight from leading to change is the work of working through. The analyst and the patient each contributes to this work. This may consist essentially of repetition and elaboration of the same procedures as performed in ordinary analytic work. In certain cases special problems may develop which may prevent insight from becoming effective and which may require special interventions.

These formulations may explain why in some patients the working through proceeds almost silently and never becomes a prominent issue in the analysis. Waiting, giving the patient ample opportunity to become familiar with the different qualities and quantities of his resistances, and repeated interpretations of the many determinants are sufficient. In other cases special hindrances may arise. It is possible for the patient to achieve insight, but then new or special factors might prevent the understanding from leading to any significant changes. For a more detailed view of these two different possibilities, I propose to illustrate the working through as it occurs in a fairly representative case and then in a patient in whom it became a special problem.

To summarize: Working through is the analysis of those resistances and other factors which prevent insight from leading to significant and lasting changes in the patient.

A Clinical Example of Working Through: Typical Case

I shall present material from a patient who was analyzed for four and a half years and who seems to illustrate a fairly typical and uncomplicated example of working through. A young married woman, Mrs. K., came for treatment because she was suffering from frequent episodes of depression and boredom and a peculiar state she described as "not being with it"—a mixture of apathy, boredom, and estrangement. She also complained of having rare and meager orgasms with her husband and of recently being plagued by obsessive ideas about having a sexual affair with a black or Arab. Prior to her relationship to her husband she had never been able to attain orgasm with anyone.

I shall describe only certain aspects of the case history and shall focus mainly on the progress of the analysis. The patient was twenty-seven years of age, attractive and intelligent. I was impressed by her determination to do something for herself, her straightforwardness and lack of sophistication. She had been married for two years to a man a good deal older whom she had set out to marry and finally had after having waited for five years until he had been able to divorce his first wife. She knew that he was a father figure for her in many ways, not only because he was considerably older, but because he was paternal toward her in many of his attitudes, protecting, educating, and indulging her. Her past history, which she related very early, indicated some of the reasons for her choice. Her parents' marriage had been very unhappy and her father had lived with the family only sporadically. He deserted them completely when the patient was two and a half years old. Her mother was a warm-hearted but impulsive and unreliable woman who adored her daughter but often neglected her child whenever she pursued a man in her constant attempts to get another husband. None of the mother's several marriages lasted very long. When the patient was ten years old, the mother married for a fourth time and this marriage seemed to offer some hope of happiness. For this stepfather the patient had strong feelings of love and she was shocked and depressed when he too abandoned the family after some three years. She had a three-year younger brother who was constantly belittled and criticized by the mother, so that the patient developed a rather protective attitude toward him. The family life was turbulent and unsettled; they moved from place to place, because of their poverty and the mother's moods, whims, and boyfriends. There was much changing of schools and no regular or consistent home life. Despite this the patient managed well in school and socially, developing a knack for coping with new situations. At age fifteen the poor financial situation and her mother's prodding motivated the patient to leave home. Since she appeared older than her years and was attractive, she was able to obtain a job in a fashionable department store as a clothing model, a job which she maintained very

successfully until at the age of twenty she met the man who
became her husband. She married him at twenty-five, and
began her analysis at twenty-seven. Although this marriage was
something which seemed to represent the fulfillment of all her
wishes, the many years of frustrated waiting had taken their toll,
so that by the time she married she was already disillusioned.
Spells of depression and boredom already had appeared before
and became worse after the marriage.

The patient began her analysis determined to uncover all
her painful experiences because she was very eager to get well.
She was particularly frightened by her recent obsessive-compulsive idea to have an affair with a black. In the first analytic
hours she confessed her biggest secret: masturbation. She felt
terribly ashamed because she believed this revelation would
make her appear loathsome and repulsive to the analyst. She had
no memory of masturbation prior to the age of twenty-one.
Already in the first hours she associated and equated her masturbatory activities with all sorts of shameful infantile toilet experiences. Talking about masturbation was like being seen or heard
on the toilet, like being found incontinent, or being examined
anally or vaginally. All this meant she would be revealed as
dirty, wet, and smelly, and therefore objectionable and loathsome. To associate freely was like being asked to lose control of
herself. She could relinquish control as little in the analytic hour
as in sexual relations. She was constipated on and off throughout
her life, just as in the analytic hour, where she felt she could not
produce. Above all, she was unable to go while she was being
seen. She could have a small clitoral orgasm in masturbation
because then she was alone. One of the most painful situations
for her was the prospect of being seen while she herself was
unaware of this. She was constantly preoccupied with the
fantasy that the analyst would suddenly become disgusted with
her and break off the treatment, which paralleled what she had
imagined her father had done. Her early transference feelings
were essentially those of an unworthy little girl who longed for
and worshiped an idealized father figure. To please him one had
to be clean, controlled, continent, and cultured. This picture

was in contrast to that of her mother, whom she considered impulsive, uncontrolled, and dirty. Her conscious dread of being like her mother was overdetermined and served multiple functions (Waelder, 1930). On the most superficial level this fear meant that then she too would never be able to hold on to a husband or an analyst. At this time a vivid childhood memory came up which was of great importance for understanding her two most important fears. The patient recalled seeing her mother lying in bed deeply asleep, with her naked body exposed, and the patient recalled feeling that her mother's body was ugly and repulsive. Associated to this highly charged memory were ideas that she had rotten insides which she had inherited from her mother.

During this period of analysis the patient manifested her resistances in a variety of ways. She would talk without feelings, in polite and sterile language, or postpone telling me about masturbation, or wait to tell me some painful material until after she had told me something positive, etc. These forms of resistance were repeatedly demonstrated to the patient; the fantasies behind her shame and fear of rejection were clarified and amplified, and attempts were made to get to the childhood events which were the origin of these reactions. The patient then felt ashamed of having resistances and tried to cover up and hide them until she slowly became aware that the analysis of her resistances was an important part of her treatment and not a shortcoming.

During this period, the patient discovered that she was already two months pregnant. At first she reacted to the pregnancy as another manifestation of her "bad insides" and had fantasies of some malignant or deformed growth within her. She experienced her pregnancy as derived from the bad husband, the hateful, frustrating father; moreover, becoming a mother meant becoming like *her* bad mother. The interpretation of her hostile oral impulses toward her husband and mother and their internal representation by the pregnancy helped to alleviate these feelings. She then had the fantasy that I was the father of the baby and it then became a good baby. At this time, after approximately six months of analysis, the patient joined me in another way: in forming a "working alliance"[1] with me, she began to detect and try to understand her resistances.

A new phase of the analysis began. The patient realized that she was holding back her feelings toward me and was determined to let them develop so that we could learn from them. She now became aware of a variety of strong sexual feelings and curiosity about me. Whereas previously her masturbation occurred without fantasies or with blank fantasies, now there was an abundance of masochistic humiliation fantasies, with a great deal of active and passive oral sucking and biting. Whereas previously she was terrified of being watched in any sexual activity, she now became aware that being watched added to her excitement. The obsessive idea of having an affair with a black or Arab symbolized for her sadistic, primitive, and dirty sexuality, which she now realized could also be exciting. Via her oedipal transference feelings the patient was able to recall memories of overhearing sexual relations between her mother and stepfather. At first these memories made her cringe in shame and fear and she resented and despised her mother and stepfather. But as her current sexual responses began to change, she realized that her original childhood reactions may well have been different from the screen memories she originally reported. She could recall and talk about the details of her "first" masturbation experience at age twenty-one. This occurred after she had fallen asleep while taking a sunbath. She awoke sexually excited and went into her bedroom to masturbate. Later she was surprised that she knew exactly what to do, although she had no memory of any previous masturbation. She now was able to use certain obscene words in the analytic hour and occasionally could also admit having an urge to urinate or to move her bowels during the hour. Her sexual activity with her husband, although it now occurred less frequently, became more satisfactory. She was frequently able to have clitoral orgasms from clitoral stimulation during intercourse and from cunnilingus. A baby daughter was born to her

[1] See chapter 15.

about the end of the first year of her analysis. The delivery was uncomplicated; she was delighted with the pretty and healthy baby and was eager to nurse her.

In the second year of her analysis the patient became aware that when she was alone she would talk to me instead of talking to herself. She realized that even when she was away from the analytic hour she felt a certain closeness to the analyst. The analyst had become the most important person in her life and her analysis constantly absorbed her attention. I had once again become predominantly the idealized father who would remain constant and faithful to her and would teach her everything, including sex, although not in a sensual way. She was able to be much more open in talking to her husband about her sexual desires. As a consequence her sexual relations continued to improve, although she became more aware that her marriage was not a satisfactory one. There was a change in her masturbation in that she was able to masturbate lying in bed on top of the bedclothes instead of hiding herself underneath and lying on her abdomen. Under the protection of the strong positive transference to me and the improved sexual relations to her husband, the patient was now able to recall her great love for and dependency on her mother prior to the marriage to the attractive stepfather. She had loved her mother dearly and had admired her beauty and warmth. A new neurotic symptom came to light; the patient would awaken from sleep with the awareness of having rubbed the roof of her mouth until it became sore. Whereas previously she had remembered her mother as dirty, she now recalled that her mother was particularly fastidious about her mouth and her vagina; she brushed her teeth after each meal and douched several times daily. The picture of the naked mother exposed in sleep now became somewhat attractive. Then homosexual dreams occurred in which the patient was making sexual overtures toward her daughter with her mouth. The interpretation led to reconstructions about the patient's early sensual feelings toward her own mother. The analytic work on this subject temporarily seemed to make it possible for the patient to have a vaginal orgasm for the first time in masturbation and shortly thereafter in intercourse with her husband. However, the homosexual material came up only sporadically and then disappeared. Her husband became seriously ill and this seemed to undermine her sense of security and interfered with their sexual life. The awareness of homosexual impulses now meant she *might be* a homosexual and this was terrifying to the patient. Her husband's sickness apparently made her too frightened to attempt any further work on this subject at this time. There was no obvious evidence of penis envy until now, only a series of screen memories. She recalled her mother laughing at her brother for having too small a penis, and the patient recalled being very upset and defending her brother. For the patient her beauty was a penis and she could feel no envy toward men in this regard. She could recall a period of envying glamorous women; they represented women with a penis and were in contrast to her picture of herself as a dirty girl.

In the third year of analysis, the patient was able to experience and describe a new kind of vaginal sensation in masturbation associated with the slang word "twot." This was a particularly shameful word which the patient's mother had used when the mother was drunk and out of control. For the patient it was associated to squat, shit, and fuck—toilet sounds and sounds of parental intercourse. What had been repulsive was now very exciting. During this type of masturbation she could become wet vaginally which she had previously inhibited. This led to hitherto repressed childhood memories of loving to get suppositories. Although she essentially still maintained the idealized and oedipalized picture of me, at times there were flashes of anger and resentment toward me.

Her husband's illness was incurable and he lay on the verge of death for many months. Despite many temptations the patient remained constant and faithful to him and performed her wifely duties very considerately. Her husband died and she went through a relatively normal period of grief and mourning. Shortly thereafter the patient fell in love with a different kind of man. He was of her age group, artistic, and not particularly masculine. The patient now had many overtly homosexual dreams about her daughter and later about other women. In these dreams the sexual actions were either sucking or phallic intrusive activities with a little girl or a lady who had a little penis. The patient's early childhood memories of her mother's nude body returned in greater detail. She could see the blue veins on the breasts and the reddish-brown nipples and the purplish color of the vulva. It became clear that what had seemed to be essentially a repulsive picture was also fascinating and exciting to the little child. Jokingly she said in one hour, her mother's genitals looked like raw hamburger (which she temporarily forgot she had told me she loved). At this time she became aware of urges and impulses to be close to someone; in fact, to get inside of someone. Intercourse was not enough. She wanted to get inside or to take someone inside her. She had fantasies of changing and being influenced by me through the process of osmosis. My supposed good character traits would seep into her just by our proximity. The sunbath which led to the first masturbation was felt as a kind of being warmed by a loving father who was also motherly. She now recalled memories of how beautiful her mother had been when she was a child and of a particular dress made of velvet which had a wonderful texture. This texture led to the interpretation and reconstruction of her love for her mother's body, particularly her mother's skin. The patient now could begin to imagine how beautiful and voluptuous her mother had been while she lay asleep in the nude. Toward the end of the third year the patient went away for a short vacation with her new sweetheart and reported ecstatically upon her return that she was able to have deep vaginal orgasms from intercourse. In addition, she was able to move her bowels without shame or embarrassment and she was not constipated. Her own body seemed to change; whereas she had thought of herself as thin and scrawny, she now felt voluptuous and attractive. She decided to go to school to continue her education. Whereas previously she had dreaded every Friday and could not wait for the Monday hour, she now found that she looked forward to Friday and to my vacations. Whereas previously I had been an awesome person for her and she was on probation, she now felt relaxed with me and believed I was truly interested in her.

In the fourth year of analysis the frank homosexual dreams occurred more frequently and were less distorted. The patient became conscious of oral homosexual impulses toward her daughter and was able to feel with conviction that she must have had similar impulses toward her mother, which were reciprocated. It was not clear how much of this had been experienced as fantasies or as reality. It seemed plausible to reconstruct that when her mother was drunk, which happened often, and they slept together in the nude, which was their custom, there was a goodly amount of bodily contact in a state of diminished consciousness. This must have been intensely pleasurable and traumatically exciting. At any rate, the patient was able to accept this reconstruction and to work with it. Simultaneously, although her sexual relations remained satisfactory for the most part, there now developed outbursts of primitive rage against the penis of the man. Whereas previously she had thought she loved the extremely large penis, she now resented it and considered it brutal, demanding, greedy, heartless. These feelings came out not only toward her sweetheart but also toward me. I was now lumped together with "the goddamned men with their stiff cocks who are just looking for any old hole." She realized that causing a man to ejaculate was a victory—a symbolic castration which she enjoyed. To have a penis in her vagina was an opportunity to choke it, strangle it, or devour it. She had daydreams of masturbating with a cucumber and eating it with triumph and gusto.

The patient reevaluated her old love for supermasculine men like the blacks and became aware that she ran to them because she was afraid of her homosexuality and her destructive impulses. Now she preferred men who had a certain admixture of feminine qualities. She could then enjoy a heterosexuality which also had some qualities of homosexuality. The men with feminine qualities permitted her to fantasy that she was that man and now she did to that man what she had hoped her attractive childhood mother with a penis would have done to her. At this time in her analysis she went through a phase of aversion to all men and would masturbate with a toy. This was based on the formula: Who needs you goddamned men; I have my own penis. She dreamed of wild animals who tore the insides out of people and ripped off their limbs. The hitherto hidden penis envy had erupted and brought deep oral-sadistic wishes to the fore. She had difficulty with intercourse and often could not be aroused. She devoted herself to her schoolwork and to her daughter, and men became temporarily despised and unimportant. Despite the strong negative transference, she continued to work exceedingly well in the analysis. She went through periods of anxiety and depression, but her determination to become free and independent, some of which she had already tasted, led her on. Moreover, despite her temporary hostility to men, she was not worried; she knew she would be able to find her way back to a satisfactory sexual relationship. The patient began to consider finishing her analysis. She herself was amazed that she could ever have reached such a point because she remembered how dependent she had felt upon the analyst and how she had worshiped him. She seemed quite secure in her ability to regain her grown-up state at the end of the analytic hours, no matter how regressive the material of the hour might have been. We agreed upon a tentative termination date for her analysis some eight months later. (The loss of the father at age two and a half and the unreliable mother seemed to call for a long termination phase.)

Although the patient had never graduated from high school, by dint of satisfying work in correspondence and extension courses she received in the fifth year of her analysis a certificate to enter a local college. She was sad at the prospect of finishing her analysis, but she was no longer depressed or bored or "not with it." She succeeded in completing the toilet training of her daughter without major difficulties. The little problems which did arise she readily understood and was able to correct. Although she was no longer in love, she was able to have vaginal orgasms on occasion. She was able to accept the fact that under certain circumstances she was not able to respond sexually to her boyfriend. Previously this had upset her and made her anxious; now she understood that there were fluctuations in her capacity to become excited. Not to have an orgasm no longer implied that she was homosexual. The obsessive idea about a sexual affair with a black had long disappeared. The patient was able to acknowledge some love for her mother and to see her good qualities as well as obvious weaknesses. Furthermore, she recognized that some of her own qualities resembled her mother's, but she no longer experienced this as a threat to her independent identity. She realized that she still had some misgivings about her ability to cope with her mother, but she believed that in time this too would be overcome. The patient was eager to have a period of time of living on her own, without the analysis, although this made her sad and there were still some problems to be worked out. The analysis was interrupted as planned after four and a half years of work.[2]

This presentation is a selective extract of a long case history covering approximately 1,000 hours of analysis. I have tried to present the material which seemed most characteristic for each important phase of the analysis. I did not trust my memory alone but examined my notes which covered some 700 analytic sessions. I paid special attention to those aspects which would demonstrate the preliminary phase of the analysis and then the working through of the most important resistances. One of the additional reasons for emphasizing the sexual material and the struggle with the mother in this case is my intention to contrast the course of the analytic work with that of another patient, in regard to similar material. However, I shall first review the different elements of the clinical material which I believe make up what we call working through.

The Work of Working Through

In this patient, most of the resistances in the beginning of the analysis were caused by shame and guilt reactions in regard to the sexual material which came up in her associations. Mas-

[2] Similar clinical material and dynamics may be found in chapters 4 and 6.

turbation was so humiliating because it was linked with being seen or heard on the toilet, which meant to be found loathsome. Free association meant losing control, which was equated with letting herself become dirty, wet, and smelly. She spoke hesitantly in polite, sterile language just as she was timid, clean, and constipated in her outside life. As she was made aware of her resistances, having them became an indication of defectiveness; she developed resistances to having resistances and tried to hide them. From the very beginning, I consistently attempted to show the patient *how*, *why*, and *what* she was resisting. Some of the feelings, fantasies, and impulses behind the resistances were exposed; some of the historical events which were the origin of the resistances were uncovered; and their function and meaning were interpreted.

After some six months of analyzing these resistances, a significant change became apparent in the patient's attitude. Whereas she previously had tried to cover up her resistances and to deny their existence, now she herself would become aware of some evasiveness in her free association and would ask herself: "How, why, and what am I resisting?" The patient had identified with me in regard to my attitude toward resistances; she had developed a working alliance with me (chapter 15), indicating that a coalition had been joined between the analyst's observing and analyzing functions and the patient's observing and reasonable ego. This does not imply that the patient will have fewer or less severe resistances; it refers only to the patient's willingness to work more actively on them. The reasonable ego is now more in the foreground.

The establishment of a reliable working alliance is a necessary precondition for the beginning of any consistent working through. The analysis of resistances which I have described up until this point is the analytic work proper. It continued from the beginning to the end of analysis, whenever the patient was unable or unwilling to contend with painful material. The working through began with this patient only after six months of analysis, and then only on certain subjects. In a sense, a working alliance had to be achieved for every new painful topic.

I now turn to the working through which, according to my definition, is the psychological work upon those resistances and other factors which keep an insight from being effective. This work occurred almost tacitly, in the sense that the processes and procedures never became a special subject for discussion. Many of the activities were performed simultaneously by the patient and the analyst and many of the procedures may be described from different points of view, which make it hard to systematize them. Nevertheless, it seems possible to single out certain measures which seem to be essential to the work of working through.

REPETITION

In order for an insight to be effective it is necessary for it to be repeated many times; single interpretations do not produce lasting changes. In part this is due to the fact that unconscious phenomena are condensed; translating them fully into conscious content is complicated and enormously time-consuming. The patient usually does not dare at first to respond fully to an interpretation. Repetition is necessary in order to overcome the patient's tendency to ward off painful affects, impulses, and fantasies. Finally, the reiteration of an insight gives the patient a further opportunity for mastery of anxiety and a chance to try out new modes of response. All these facts explain why working through takes a long time. The old was painful and yet familiar and safe; in this way it resembled an old love object. Repetition offers opportunities to part with the old, and to become acquainted with the new.

For example, throughout the first two years of the analysis it was necessary to repeat to the patient the interpretation that she had "toiletized" all sexual matters as well as the analytic situation. Cleanliness seemed to be the greatest virtue and losing control the greatest vice. She behaved as if good parents would abandon children and even grownups who did so. This is what she believed her father had done to her and her mother, and she dreaded that I might do it too. In the past she attempted to cope with this by becoming clean, controlled, constipated, and frigid. She turned against her mother who represented the regressive instinctual temptations the patient was determined to avoid; her mother was disgusting and frightening to her. Free associations worried her because they meant exposure and letting go, incontinence and involuntary destructiveness.

Although the patient confirmed the correctness of these insights from the very beginning, it took a great deal of time for her to be able to become aware of all the different affects, impulses, and fantasies that were condensed in her shame and guilt about her masturbation-toilet activities. Despite a good working alliance it took almost a year for her to dare to use obscenities in the hour, to talk more freely about masturbation, and to experiment a bit in intercourse with her husband. A marked change in her sexual behavior occurred in the early part of the third year when she recalled during masturbation the word "twot," an obscene word her mother had used when drunk. Her daring to remember this indicated her ability to contend with a hitherto unexplored set of positive feelings toward her mother and a desire for dirtiness and losing control. The two years of work that preceded this change were necessary and were not due to any failure in the work of the patient or analyst. She needed two years of testing and checking before she dared give up her old defensive attitudes and behavior.

ELABORATION

This term refers to a variety of procedures and processes for refining, amplifying, and completing an interpretation. These activities are necessary because all symptomatic psychic behavior is overdetermined and serves multiple functions (Breuer and Freud, 1893-95; Waelder, 1930). The psychoanalytic elaboration of an interpretation is an attempt to trace the different genetic sources of a piece of behavior. Furthermore, we also try to expose the different purposes a given psychic phenomenon can serve under different conditions. I shall now present some of the main, frequently overlapping steps which were followed in the elaboration of interpretations in the patient described above.

Uncovering the Multiple Determinants of Resistance

The Transference. Working through requires that the entire genesis of a piece of behavior be traced and exposed. By far the most important source of information is the transference. The patient's different transference resistances during the analysis revealed important information about the significant figures in her past and also indicated the different aspects of her ambivalence. The transference has to be traced to the past, the present, and through all the intermediary time intervals. Thus, the patient was ashamed to reveal herself to me at first because I was the adored, idealized father who despised all primitive sensuality. Later on her resistances stemmed from her feeling that I was sexually attractive but an unattainable oedipal figure for her; she felt rejected and frustrated. She experienced such feelings with her stepfather at the age of eleven and toward her husband at the beginning of her courtship. During this phase of analysis there was a change in her masturbation fantasies which now became full of masochistic and exhibitionistic elements and which contained some allusion to the analyst.

This sensual picture of the analyst alternated with one of him as an intellectual and artist more interested in the spiritual things in life. Later this developed into an image of a man with effeminate qualities. At this point the analyst was partly the little brother with the small penis and also the mother. The patient tended to be playfully contemptuous in the hour and often spoke in a teasing fashion. For a long time I was a kind of motherly father who guided and protected her from sadistic men and homosexual women. At this time her shame was no longer evoked by masturbation and toilet activities but had shifted onto her fear of homosexuality. Once she was able to have a vaginal orgasm with an artistic, effeminate man, her dread of homosexuality also diminished. Now she could vent her hatred of men and their penises and simultaneously she could give up her dependency on me.

This brief outline indicates how many different people from her past were involved in her shame reactions, which were all experienced in the transference situation. To work through her shame in regard to me it was necessary repeatedly to ask the patient the question: "Who am I today before whom you are ashamed?" The same kind of work was necessary with each of her different transference resistances.

Historical Events. Another aspect of elaboration is to explore *all* the historical events in regard to the particular behavior under analysis. Again I shall limit this to a brief survey of the history of the patient's inordinate shame. The mother was strict about toilet matters, although lax about other aspects of "clean and dirty." The father's desertion of the family when the patient was two and a half years old fixed the connection between being loved and being toilet trained. The birth of a baby brother some six months later was felt as a punishment for sensual and hostile fantasies. The absence of a father became something shameful and to be hidden. The mother, however, was quite exhibitionistic and constantly asked the girl to sing and dance before friends and relatives and stressed the girl's looks and clothes. Early in the patient's life the mother was beautiful and attractive in her fancy clothes or as she lay naked; later the mother was considered dirty and shameful because of her frequent sexual involvements with men. Mother's obsessive preoccupation with teeth brushing and douching confirmed the patient's idea that the insides of a woman's body are dirty. This was borne out in the patient's mind by the mother's losing of so many "fathers," another proof that men despised "instinctual" women.

These are just a few of the many historical events which lay behind the patient's shame reactions in the analytic situation. The uncovering of a single historical event is only the beginning of an interpretation. To work it through, we have to try to uncover all the important experiences which were formative in regard to a certain piece of the patient's behavior.

The Relativity of Resistances. No behavior serves the purposes of resistance or instinctual drives alone. A given piece of behavior may be used to ward off some instinctual activity and may also serve instinctual gratification under other circumstances, or some instinctual activity can be used as a defense against some more dangerous instinctual impulses (Fenichel, 1941b). One affect may serve as a screen to ward off another, or a painful affect can be libidinized. Each defense-instinctual drive unit may have relevance to a different period of life. A clinical fragment from the same patient will demonstrate the relativity of her resistances.

The patient's preoccupation with shame indicated on the one hand her dread of being seen in a sexual position. This fixation, however, also hinted at the opposite, her scoptophilia. Her readiness to imagine everyone was looking at her indicated that behind the fear of being seen was a longing to expose herself as long as she could hide certain parts of her body. (She did become a successful fashion model.) She feared being seen passively, but enjoyed exhibiting if she was active and in control. Yet, her first consciously remembered masturbation occurred from the excitement of sunbathing. She could not have an orgasm in intercourse at first because she was afraid of being seen out of control. Later on she preferred sexual relations with the lights on and near a mirror. At first she dreaded revealing infantile sexual fantasies and activities in the analysis. Later she developed a bravado for confessing primitive sexual fantasies which she used at first to taunt me, and finally as a means of degrading all men. At first the patient dreaded all things dirty, only to discover that she could revel in it once she felt it was permissible. The same was true for losing control sexually, anally, and in regard to her aggressiveness.

The patient loathed female bodies, especially her mother's and particularly the skin, breasts, and genitals. She loved men, but could not react sexually to the penis. Her promiscuity was an attempt to prove she was heterosexual and loved men and simultaneously to deny her homosexuality and her love for her mother. As sexual relations with men could be used more for pleasure rather than for defense, she could enjoy sexuality more and as a result she became more certain of her heterosexuality.

Once she could permit herself to enjoy her vagina and the sensation of losing control in an orgasm, she dared let her hidden hostility to men come up. Then she could hate the previously idealized men and indulge in overt homosexual dreams and fantasies. The screen memory of the loathsome naked body of her mother revealed behind it the voluptuous and appetizing body of the adored mother.

Another significant finding is that many different instinctual aims may call forth similar resistances. Reducing them to a common formula has an economic importance for the patient and helps clarify the search for the historical factors. For this patient, masturbation, bowel movement, and orgasm all stirred up the same resistances; they all meant incontinence and rejection.

RECONSTRUCTION

Historical Reconstructions

Another procedure of particular importance for the work of working through is reconstruction. I am using the term here in the way Kris (1956b) did: genetic interpretations which try to establish a historical context between various separated segments of the patient's material. It is usually the result of attempting to integrate isolated insights. In a sense all interpretations ultimately lead to reconstructions (Freud, 1937b). Of particular importance is the finding that reconstructions seem to facilitate recall. Establishing a historical context seems to stimulate the ego's synthetic function, thus increasing the ability to recall (Nunberg, 1932). The recovery of a memory becomes a part of a circular process, many of which occur in working through (Kris, 1956a, 1956b). Let me illustrate this with some of the patient's clinical material.

One of the patient's symptoms was the obsessive idea of having intercourse with a black or an Arab. In addition to the interpretation that this represented a superman clothed in anal-sadistic terms, this dark-skinned man was the direct opposite of a fair-skinned lady. Another symptom was her feeling of "not

being with it" and emptiness, which indicated that she did not
have a good contact with her "insides" and also some difficulty
in relating her inside world to the outside world. It also hinted
at some disturbance of consciousness. The feeling of having
rotten insides, which she blamed on her mother, also pointed to
her struggle against the introjection of the mother (chapter 6).
The first remembered masturbation occurring after sleeping in
the warm sun seemed to denote some oral, introjective quality to
her sexuality.

The patient's transference to me was essentially positive and
oedipal. However, the tenacity with which the positive transference persisted for some three years indicated that it must also
have been serving an important defensive purpose. This was
parallel to her tenacious loathing of her mother and the persistent memory of the naked mother as revolting and disgusting.

The first change occurred when the patient was able to
recall that her mother, remembered as sloppy and messy, was in
fact fastidious about her bodily cleanliness. The patient then
revealed another symptom, her tendency to rub the roof of her
mouth with her tongue while she slept. The patient's care of her
two-year-old daughter evoked frank oral sucking homosexual
fantasies in regard to the latter. She then recalled the word
"twot," used by her mother when drunk, and now an *exciting*
word for the patient in her masturbation. This led to her recall
of auditory primal scene experiences which had been exciting to
the little girl. She was now able to become excited vaginally and
have a wet vagina as she imagined her mother had had. As a
result she regularly had vaginal orgasms with her lover and
could also face her homosexual impulses.

A key factor in all these changes was the series of reconstructive interpretations of the memory of her drunk, naked
mother which began to take on many facets. At first it was recalled as an isolated instance at around age five, but it seemed
more plausible to reconstruct it as a recurrent event from age
two and a half onward, after her father had left. The picture of
the mother as loathsome and repugnant was interpreted to be a
screen warding off the awareness that mother's fair skin and

youthful breasts must have been attractive to the little child. A memory of a beautiful velvet dress of the mother's which evoked a voluptuous feeling in the patient in later years was reconstructed as a screen memory for the sensual attractiveness of her young mother's body. The patient's joking remark that her mother's exposed vulva was revolting, that it looked like a raw hamburger, took on an unexpected meaning when I pointed out her love for steak tartare. We reconstructed that the drunk, frustrated, and lonely mother used to fall into bed with her lonely little daughter and there must have been a good deal of pleasurable sensual body contact between them in a state of diminished consciousness. This would explain the patient's excessive dread of homosexuality, the feeling of "not being with it," the emptiness, the sexual obsession about blacks, the masturbation in the sun while asleep, and the relatively intractable positive transference.

These reconstructions proved to be a very effective bridge for the recovery of new memories which led to new insights. The patient was able to recall many more memories of loving her mother, worshiping her, even of having a phobia of returning to the house while the mother was away at work, etc. At the same time these insights permitted the patient to become aware of her hitherto warded-off deep-seated rage and hostility to men. For the first time she dared to face and express her fury, envy, and loathing of me and my penis. As a consequence she was able to become relatively independent of me and men and her object relationships lost their clinging quality.

Reconstructions of the Self Image, the Identity

The reconstruction of the self image, which is holding sway in the patient during a given piece of behavior, is especially helpful if one can point out how a past state of the self is still in operation in the present. For example, I could show to the patient that she behaved in bed with her husband as though she was a little girl who had no right or desire to enjoy sexuality, who had to deny that she became sexually excited. Another example of identity reconstruction would be my asking her:

"Who am I before whom you are so ashamed?" or "Who are you today who is so full of shame?"

In the beginning of the analysis the patient behaved in regard to me as though she were a waif who was tolerated only because of the analyst's generosity. She felt that she was on probation and every hour dreaded the possibility of being told she would have to leave. This waiflike identity came from the early years after her father had deserted the family. As long as she felt the waif toward me, her main concern was to gain a secure place with me, a good foster home. This interfered with her ability to work analytically. I had to remind her that the reality was different; she was not a waif, in analysis on suffrance, but a grown-up woman with whom I had chosen to work. It took some six months for the patient to begin to assume a more adult identity, but the waif often returned in times of stress.

The Work of the Patient

Until now I have stressed the procedures that are performed essentially by the analyst. I now want to focus on what the patient has to contribute to the working through. A necessary *precondition* for working through is that the patient permit himself to regress and develop a transference neurosis. However, working through can begin only when the patient can simultaneously develop a working alliance with the analyst. Only then is the patient able to work along with the analyst when he makes his confrontations, clarifications, and interpretations. This means that the patient can participate both actively and passively in trying to comprehend and associate to the analyst's interventions. He will test the validity of the analyst's interpretations and report his reactions and associations. The partial identification with the analyst will make him alert to the importance of recognizing and analyzing resistances. Furthermore, the working alliance will enable him to dare regress to more infantile transference reactions with which he will then try to work in the analysis.

In the patient described above this became abundantly

clear from the sixth month of her analysis onward. She could get herself to talk more openly about her sex life with her husband; she brought in new masturbation fantasies and changes in her masturbatory behavior; she recognized how she tended to evade certain painful issues and mentioned these even if she could not get herself to change. She talked to herself and persuaded herself to try new ways of reacting; she risked allowing new feelings toward the analyst to arise and to bring them into the analytic hour.

Finally, in working through the patient must be willing to try to assimilate and integrate the insights gained from the analysis and to do some of the analytic work outside of the hour. This involves rather complicated processes but may transpire relatively silently. For example, I did not ask the patient to change her self image during intercourse with her husband; I only pointed out how inappropriate her self image was. It was she who dared to assume a new attitude in this situation. When I made a reconstruction, e.g., about the homosexuality with the mother, I did not tell her how to imagine it in order for it to become a living experience; she relived my reconstruction and made it seem real. Introspection, mulling over, the testing out of new reactions and new behavior, adopting an analytical attitude are all part of what is necessary for the assimilation and integration of new insights. However, for the most part all of this went on silently in this patient and in those cases which are making favorable progress.

If one reviews the various procedures and sequences of events which I have described, one can see how an insight may lead to a reconstruction, which can lead to a memory, which then leads to changes in the patient's past history and a change in the patient's self image. This change in the self image serves as a new vantage point and makes possible further new insights which lead to new reconstructions and memories, etc. I believe a variety of such circular processes constantly occur throughout the process of working through (Kris, 1956a, 1956b).

These seem to be the essential processes which occur in the work of working through. Fenichel (1941b), Greenacre (1956), and Kris (1956a, 1956b) would concur, I believe, in this description, namely, that repetition, elaboration, and reconstruction are the core of working through. I shall now turn to the clinical material of another patient in whom the process of working through presented a special problem. The special pathology of this case highlights some of the processes which go on relatively silently in other cases.

Special Problems of Working Through

The outstanding feature in this patient was that he did not show any significant change after six years of ostensibly competent psychoanalytic therapy (see chapter 15, case 3). Yet there was initially no obvious pathology to explain this stalemate. I shall present this case as an example of the intractable patients Freud seemed to have in mind in his discussions of working through. This case may also substantiate some of Greenacre's ideas (1956) about the special effects of traumatic experiences. The opportunity to compare and contrast the working through in two different patients may illuminate some of the obscure areas.

A thirty-year-old man came to me after having recently completed two years of analysis with a competent analyst. He stated that he was never able to overcome certain of his resistances and therefore made little progress. He blamed primarily himself and only indirectly his analyst. His greatest difficulty was his inability to talk about masturbation. Despite all the interpretations given by his former analyst he remained unable to communicate about this subject in any meaningful way. The patient told me, furthermore, that early in adolescence the same analyst had treated him because of shyness and inability to form social relationships with boys or girls. This phase of analysis had lasted for approximately one and a half years and had been of little benefit. However, between the first and second analyses the patient had been able to graduate from college and also satisfactorily perform his military duty. Although he was still shy, he had been able to form some transient friendships with men and to have sporadic sexual and romantic involvements with women. His main reason for seeking analysis again was his awareness that all his relationships remained relatively superficial. He felt essentially lonely and was unable to establish a deeper involvement.

The young man appeared to be an intelligent, emotionally responsive, earnest individual of attractive appearance. He knew a good deal about some of the meanings of his problems and did not overly intellectualize. He appeared to establish good contact with me and also seemed to be in good contact with his own feelings. There was nothing bizarre, inappropriate, or empty about his affects that would lead one to think diagnostically of anything beyond a neurosis. I undertook the analysis, therefore, quite hopefully.

The patient was the only child of an unhappy marriage. His parents divorced when he was about two years old, at which time his mother took a trip around the world for about six months. During that interval the patient lived with his wealthy grandparents who left him in the care of a nurse and a chauffeur. After his mother returned, he lived with her alone in an apartment for about one year, when the mother remarried. The stepfather was a warmhearted but ineffectual man who was completely under the domination of his wife. The patient's mother was a highly emotional, demonstrative woman who was very attached to her own father. She behaved more like the favorite, spoiled daughter of the grandfather than as a wife or a mother. She was charming and entertaining, but irresponsible and essentially narcissistic. When the patient was five, she gave birth to another son and again left the family for a six-month journey. The mother belittled her husband and ignored their child. What little attention she gave to her own family she gave to my patient. The patient visited his real father on weekends, but this relationship was never very satisfying because his father was somewhat austere while his stepfather was warmhearted and affectionate.

The patient worked very hard in his analysis; was extremely

conscientious in trying free association, in recognizing his resistances, and in attempting to understand the meaning and implications of my interpretations. He seemed to be very honest and scrupulous in the way he detected his evasiveness, his holding back, his tendency to appease me. In a relatively short time he seemed to have formed a good working alliance with me and over the next several years he was able to let himself develop an intense transference neurosis with strong positive and negative oedipal and preoedipal aspects. Yet after three years of work with me, which followed the many years of earlier analysis, there was no significant change in his behavior outside of the analytic situation. He had a great many insights and he changed markedly in his reactions and behavior toward me, but he was not able to change in any effective way in his outside life. I reviewed my work with this man in order to see whether I had overlooked certain important dynamics, some obscure historical determinants in his history, or some form of transference resistance, but I could find nothing. Yet, I was certain there was a subtle resistance at work which was responsible for the lack of therapeutic progress. From a diagnostic standpoint, I considered the patient to be suffering essentially from a neurotic depression with hysterical and compulsive-obsessive symptoms. There was nothing to indicate any "borderline" qualities. Let me review some essentials of the case.

The outstanding psychopathology in this patient revolved around his extremely strong and tenacious attachment to his mother and his homosexual conflict with his stepfather. There was a great deal of material concerning his deep sense of deprivation and abandonment by his mother. On the one hand, he had a constant yearning for closeness, for fusion with her, along with a terribly destructive rage toward her for neglecting him. He had a deep mistrust of all her motives, despised her values, and yet was tempted to beg her for crumbs of interest. Some of his hatred was turned upon his own self, in the form of feelings of unworthiness and self-reproach. Other aspects of his hostility were projected onto the external world and he lived in constant expectation of rejection. Furthermore, the patient also had a strong positive oedipus complex with masturbation activities containing disguised incestuous impulses and fantasies along with terrible jealousy toward his stepfather and grandfather. The mother was the most exciting of women and also a loathsome creature who revulsed him. These reactions he reenacted with young women in his current life. He demanded that every attractive woman was to love him exclusively and even more than that—they were never to have loved anyone or anything in their lives previously. He hoped they would undo the traumatic deprivations his mother had inflicted upon him. If they showed any liking for anyone or anything else, they were whores and he wanted not just to destroy them, but to obliterate them from his memory. Yet he clung tenaciously to the unreliable and rejecting mother because she was a protection against his homosexuality. These conflicts were defended against by a partial regression to the anal-sadistic level with intense conflicts concerning retention versus expulsion, passivity versus activity, masochism versus sadism.

This fixation to the mother was complicated by the patient's struggle with his homosexual impulses toward his stepfather. During the analysis it was possible to reconstruct from a few screen memories and from his repetitive dreams that at age two, while the patient's mother was away, he had been homosexually seduced by the chauffeur. Thus when the warmhearted stepfather entered the family and when his mother gave birth to another baby and left him alone with the stepfather at age five, the boy was strongly predisposed to develop an intense love and sexual longing for the stepfather. This was further stimulated and prolonged by the stepfather's tendency to parade in the nude before the boy while performing his various toilet activities. The homosexual attachment to the stepfather was vividly reexperienced in the transference situation in different ways from the beginning of the analysis. At first the resistances against oral and anal homosexual fantasies were in the foreground; at other times the homosexuality served as a defense against the oedipal and preoedipal mother. In any case, the homosexuality was the most persistent and painful part of the patient's trans-

ference resistances. The danger of being rejected was the patient's rationalization for his conscious and unconscious holding
back. He considered his first analyst "austere" and me "warmhearted," which was an advantage in the beginning of the
analysis, but became a grave threat later when the patient
became aware of his homosexual impulses.

I can best illustrate the quality of the homosexual material
by some brief clinical excerpts. The patient could not directly say
to me: "I like you." That was equivalent of saying, I want a
homosexual affair, or more exactly, please fuck me. Crying in
my presence had the same meaning and was warded off for two
years. It became apparent that the homosexual seduction at age
two had left him almost unable to discriminate between liking,
loving, and having a sexual relationship with a man. There was
a similar difficulty in differentiating between annoyance,
hatred, and murderous rage. At various times when he struggled
against his homosexual feelings, he would lie on the couch with
teeth gritted, fists clenched, body taut, and say: "I am not going
to let myself feel anything for you; I will be impervious to you;
nothing you say will touch me." Yet, despite the anxiety and
hostility the patient worked with this material, and during the
first two years of his analysis we were slowly able to uncover the
different homosexual experiences in his history. At age twelve in
camp he suddenly one night sucked the penis of an eight-year-
old boy who was half asleep. This was an isolated event and was
connected by us to fantasies of what (between five and nine
years) he wanted to enact with his nude stepfather, and to the
reconstructed seduction by the chauffeur (age two). At the age of
thirteen he was taught masturbation by a slightly older boy who
later twice performed mutual masturbation with him. At the
ages of fourteen to sixteen he occasionally put on his mother's
undergarments in the bathroom and masturbated while looking
at himself in the mirror. At age seventeen he permitted a prosti-
tute to perform fellatio upon him in a dark alley only to realize
afterward that "she" was a man masquerading as a woman.
Recall of this material was usually preceded by strong transference resistances the surface of which was his fear of being

attacked by me while he was in a defensive anal position. Then a dream would indicate that there was a passive wish hidden behind the fear and then one of the homosexual memories would appear.

All of the material I have condensed in this presentation *seemed* to have been satisfactorily worked through with the patient. The insights concerning his major conflicts were repeated, deepened, and broadened. Reconstructions had traced the complicated interrelationship between the ambivalent mother fixation and the struggle with the homosexual impulses. The patient recognized how his self image was distorted under certain conditions of stress. His anxiety in the analytic hour lessened; he dared to feel more and there was less defensiveness and more directness in his transference reactions. Yet, despite what seemed to be a satisfactory working through, the patient remained essentially unchanged in his outside life. Then, in one analytic hour, a new insight was arrived at which proved to be the turning point in the therapeutic stalemate.

One day the patient told me that at a party he had met an attractive young woman and again found himself reacting in his typically neurotic way: he felt hostile to her, had the obsessive thought she was a whore, and became miserably silent and withdrawn. Then he added: "I had no idea why this should have happened." I was struck by this last sentence, since it seemed obvious to me from the way he described the girl, and his reactions to her, that she must have reminded him of his mother. I was amazed that he had no idea of what had happened since we had talked on countless occasions about how he had "oedipalized" his relationship to women. Pursuing his remark "I had no idea why this should have happened," I discovered that he had a strange and specific inhibition in doing analytic work *outside* of the analytic hour. He described to me how he would try to do a piece of self-analysis. When he was upset, he would ask himself what had upset him. He would usually succeed in recalling, via free association, the event which had triggered his reaction as well as other associatively connected occurrences. Sometimes he could even recall an interpretation that I had given him about the point in question. But the insight he would arrive at in this way was meaningless; it felt foreign, artificial, and remembered by rote. It was not *his* insight; it was *my* insight and had no living significance for him. He was therefore blank about the meaning of the event which upset him.

In analyzing this inhibition in identification, it slowly became clear that the patient did not allow himself to assume, outside of the analytic hour, any attitude or point of view that was like mine. He felt that to permit himself to do that would be tantamount to admitting that I had entered into him. This was intolerable because he felt this as a homosexual assault, a repetition of his childhood trauma. By dint of some additional analytic work we were able to uncover how the patient had sexualized and aggressivized the process of introjection. This interfered with his identification with me in the analysis just as it had with his identification with other men in his outside life. He unconsciously would not let himself feel like another man among men. He had to hold on to a self image of a boy, or of a person apart, "unentered." This persistent need to maintain an inviolate, "uncontaminated" self image prompted him to behave again and again in strangely childish ways in all sexual situations with women, and in competitive situations with men. The struggle against identification with a man was another determinant for his fixation to his mother (chapter 6).

Apparently as long as the patient could see me as an external object in the analytic hour, he was able temporarily and partially to identify with me. However, when he could not reassure himself by my physical presence of my separateness, he reacted to the identification as a homosexual and aggressive intrusion. Perhaps it is more precise to say that as long as the identification was limited to a more conscious imitation, he was able to do this, but he could not let the introjection become an identification. It remobilized the dangerous homosexual seductions of the past. The patient could remember what I said, he could *consciously* assume an attitude I had assumed, but it had to remain distinct from his own. It remained ego-alien and ineffectual. He remained uninfluenced and unchanged.

With this new insight, the patient became eager to over-come this inhibition. He felt he might do better at this point if he sat up and could face me. I agreed and the patient did this for three weeks. During this time I reviewed with him the situation at the party which had brought his "identification phobia" to our attention. Just as with a phobic patient, I encouraged him to revisit the old phobic situation (in fantasy). I helped him see how he might have reacted had he dared to identify with the analytic point of view in the situation. It took many hours to review in great detail the happenings at the party and to get the patient to see how he might have felt and behaved. But this was only possible after he recognized the distortions involved in his terror of identifying with me, of taking in, assimilating, and retaining my attitudes and my interpretations. He had to be helped to desexualize and deaggressivize his listening to me, his under-standing of me, his recollecting of me, i.e., introjection of me and of the analytic point of view I represented. Just as the patient had previously learned to discriminate among liking, loving, or having sensual feelings, so he now had to learn to discriminate among the varieties of taking in. He had to learn that you could allow yourself to be influenced, to let another person's ideas enter you and merge with your ideas, and that this was neither destructive nor sexual. I helped him discover how he could have thought analytically at the party and yet completely in accordance with his own standards and preferences. He was shown that he could utilize analytic insights in his own way and for his own purposes; he could take them or leave them; he could make them his own or let them remain mine. Above all, he had a choice just as long as he did not confuse letting himself be recep-tive to the analytic point of view with letting himself be homo-sexually intruded upon. As we slowly and repeatedly reviewed the events at the party, the patient gradually grasped the notion of a homosexual-free introjection and identification with me.

The patient spontaneously resumed lying on the couch after three weeks. He again worked in his customary way, diligently and studiously. This ability to identify with the analyst now made him aware of insights which had previously been unrecog-

nized as incomplete or partially incorrect. Insights which had
been remembered but had remained isolated from the self now
became assimilated and integrated and the patient's way of life
began to change. In a few months' time he became a partner in a
law firm where he had worked on salary. A longstanding ac-
quaintanceship with a man gradually became more intimate
and changed markedly in character. His relationship to women
lost its hostile façade and he became demonstrative and tender
as well as sexual. The analysis was terminated shortly thereafter.[3]

I believe that the clinical material from an atypical case
demonstrates some of the special problems of working through
and also amplifies some of the silent processes which go on in the
more usual analytic patient. If we compare the psychopathology
in the two cases described, it is my impression that the young
woman had a more severe neurosis; there were indications of
some ego deviations, poor impulse control, strong oral fixation,
almost total lack of a father representative, and a highly
unstable mother for purposes of identification. Yet in her analysis, the course of working through went smoothly. In both
patients the crucial conflicts revolved around orality and homosexuality. Both had undergone some traumatic experiences in
this regard; but the young man had come closer to developing a
homosexual perversion than the young lady. The warmhearted
seductive stepfather was a longstanding temptation for the
young man and several times in latency and early adolescence he
actually acted out his homosexual desires. In late adolescence he
attempted to ward off this danger by avoiding all intimate
relations with men. However, his tendency to explosive rage
with women forced him to renounce closeness to them as well.
As a consequence, despite his many attractive qualities and his
yearning for companionship, he lived essentially alone for many
years before and during the first years of his analysis.

In the course of the analysis the patient reexperienced in the

[3] At that time I had the impression that the major objectives had been
obtained. However, he returned for analysis about five years later. What had
not been worked through was the early engulfing relationship to his mother.

transference the oedipal and pregenital libidinal and destructive impulses he had felt toward his mother and stepfather. However, the working through was blocked as long as he felt that to identify with me was tantamount to being homosexually attacked by me. Therefore, no genuine working alliance was possible. Furthermore, he could not permit his self image to change via identification with a man and he remained a boy who could not mature. All the knowledge gained from the analysis did not alter his picture of himself or his perspective in regard to the significant people around him. Insights and knowledge were not assimilated but were retained as interesting foreign bodies. The homosexual traumas had impaired his capacity to introject and to identify (Greenacre, 1956). This inability to identify with a man also interfered with his ego's synthetic function (Nunberg, 1932). Analytic insights and attitudes were not integrated. As a consequence there did not take place any of the circular processes such as: insight leads to changes in one's biography, which leads to changes in one's self image, which leads to new memories, which leads to new insights, etc. Working through was blocked and the therapeutic process stalemated. Only the detection and successful analysis of the specific transference resistance made the working through possible. For the sake of completion, I ought to add that the patient and I had often discussed the possibility of his changing to a woman analyst, but the patient emphatically rejected this idea. He felt he *had* to work out his problem with a man and not a woman.

Conclusions

I shall now reexamine the clinical material presented here, with the view of determining how it corresponds to the theoretical ideas put forth by Freud and the other contributors to the subject of working through. At first glance, it seemed apparent that the young man presented clinical evidence that would fit in with Freud's speculations (1937a) about the special resistances of the id, the psychical inertia, and the repetition compulsion. The patient's tenacious and seemingly unchangeable clinging to his rejecting mother, the inability to find new objects or new modes of instinctual expression, the repetitious, destructive reenactments, all would seem to confirm Freud's point of view. However, this same clinical material can be approached and understood differently, without having to resort to the notion of special resistances of the id, about which Freud himself had misgivings.

The young man's fixation to the rejecting mother of his childhood was so difficult to overcome not only because of the early traumatic deprivations but also because the homosexual attack and the seductive stepfather forced him to retreat to this relatively safe fixation point. The repetitious neurotic reenactments were not only manifestations of unconscious guilt, but were belated attempts to master the old traumas as well as futile attempts to gain some satisfaction. It was the combination of unconscious infantile gratifications and the simultaneous defense against homosexuality (Fenichel, 1945, p. 66; Greenacre, 1956).

It seems particularly instructive to review the clinical material from the standpoint of the therapeutic process. The course of this patient's analysis was stalemated by his inability to develop an adequate working alliance, which *seemed* to be effective but was gravely impaired. His inability to permit himself to form a partial and transitory identification with me prevented the insights he was given from becoming his own and effective. It is clear that working through will always suffer when an essential therapeutic process becomes impossible. This will occur when a traumatic event of the patient's past is equated with one of the necessary processes of the psychoanalytic therapy. Here we seem to come upon an important point of differentiation between the routine and special problems of working through. The analytic situation is arranged so that it facilitates the repetition of the patient's traumatic past in the transference neurosis. The patient's resistances are always indications that the analytic work has touched upon some past anxiety-producing event. However, in the analyzable patient the resistances do not interfere with the working alliance for any considerable length of time or to any considerable extent. The treatable patient may have great difficulties in working through the different aspects of his transference neurosis, but he can do so because *he becomes able to maintain a working alliance even during the height of the transference neurosis.* The first patient is a good example of this. The situation becomes much more difficult and even intractable when a patient is unable to establish and maintain a good working alliance. The second patient is a case in point. The defect in the working alliance made him unable to work effectively with his transference neurosis. He became a terminable patient when, after three and a half years of analysis with me, we were able to recognize and to handle the silent but important limitation of his working relationship. I believe this distinction may help clarify the differences between cases which are analyzable, cases which are unanalyzable, and those which seem to be analyzable but turn out to be interminable.

In addition to the defect in the working alliance, it is essential to focus on the impaired ego functions in this patient. Here I agree with some of Greenacre's (1956) formulations about the decisive importance of working through, of thoroughly analyzing, the original traumatic events and their later reinforcements. Such traumatic events always lead to a deficiency in ego functioning in such areas and situations which are reminiscent of that event. Inherent in the definition of trauma is an overwhelming of the ego with loss of some of its functions. Specifically, the ego's capacity to discriminate and to integrate is almost always impaired. As a consequence it is necessary for such patients to get back to this original situation repeatedly in order to master the trauma and to reestablish and repair those damaged ego functions. Sometimes, as in the case of the young man, the analyst may have to do for the patient what a good mother would have done in early childhood when traumata are frequent: he may have to serve *temporarily* as an auxiliary ego of the patient, helping him to learn how to discriminate, integrate, and master the overwhelming anxiety of these events (Winnicott, 1956; Loewald, 1960). In the second patient, I tried to do so by repeat-

edly going back to the situation at the party and showing him
how he might assume an analytic attitude without experiencing
this as a homosexual assault. Furthermore, I demonstrated to
him how he could permit changes in his self image to take place
in accordance with the new historical material without this also
becoming a sexualized and aggressivized intrusion. Once the
integrative function of his ego had been reestablished, it was
possible for the insights and the new memories to produce
changes in his self image, which then made possible new per-
spectives in relation to the significant people around him. Only
then could the patient experience the constructive circular processes which make for therapeutic change (Kris, 1956a, 1956b).

In his paper "Lines of Advance in Psycho-Analytic Therapy" Freud (1919) made an unusually strong attack on the
concept of psychosynthesis, which I believe I have been describing. He said at that time that it was unnecessary because
"Whenever we succeed in analyzing a symptom . . ., in freeing
an instinctual impulse from one nexus, it does not remain in
isolation, but immediately enters into a new one.... The
psycho-synthesis is thus achieved during analytic treatment
without our intervention, automatically and inevitably"
(p. 161). Yet in the same paper Freud talked about the need for
activity in helping a phobic patient overcome a phobia or in
helping obsessive patients overcome their obsessiveness. I believe
he is right in criticizing psychosynthesis insofar as it is per se not
an analytic procedure. The same is true of setting a time limit or
other active techniques psychoanalysts sometimes perform.
Nevertheless it seems to me that psychosynthesis is indicated
when we have to overcome an ego defect which blocks the ego's
integrative function. If this is successful, it is possible to resume
the analysis in accordance with traditional psychoanalytic procedure (Eissler, 1953, 1958).

If we turn now to other theoretical considerations, it seems
that the patients described above validate Fenichel's (1941b) and
Greenacre's (1956) contention that working through is essentially the repetition, deepening, and extension of the analysis of
the resistances. When this is not possible, we have the special

problems with which Freud was concerned. Kris's views (1956a, 1956b) on the particular importance of reconstructive interpretations, the need for changes in the self image as well as his formulations about the different circular processes are also borne out by the clinical examples. The two patients described above also demonstrate clearly that the patient himself has to contribute to the work of working through, which Freud (1914a), Novey (1962), and Stewart (1963) pointed out. However, it is very clear that when the patient is unable to perform his share of the work, it is up to the analyst to recognize, analyze, and otherwise handle this difficulty in the patient.

The resemblance between the work of mourning and the work of working through also seems to be confirmed, especially in the case of the young man. He clung to his lost love object, his mother, unable to detach his libido from her or to modify his instinctual aims. She lived on in his unconscious, unchanged by reality because the patient was unable to replace her by means of the identificatory processes he could not perform. He was chronically depressed until the transference resistances were properly handled. Only then could he turn toward new objects in reality and permit new instinctual aims to mature. In the first patient, her clinging to the lost and idealized father was slowly and painfully worked through in the transference relationship. This parallel between the work of mourning and working through seems very pertinent, as pointed out by Fenichel (1941b), Lewin (1950), Kris (1956b) and Stewart (1963).

In summary, I have attempted to clarify and extend our understanding of working through by singling out some of the essential procedures which occur in this phase of the analysis. I have attempted to focus attention on the special problems which arise when the working alliance is impaired because of defects in ego functioning. The essential prerequisite for a successful therapeutic analysis is the patient's capacity to form a working alliance *and* a transference neurosis. The insights gained from the transference neurosis cannot be properly worked through, i.e., integrated and assimilated, unless the working alliance can be established and maintained.

17

That "Impossible" Profession

(1966)

HE TITLE FOR THIS TALK occurred to me at the end of one of
those working days when all my clever insights turned out
to be wrong, when I discovered the right interpretation
only after the patient had left, when what I considered profound
insight was revealed as complicated confusion, and when my
kindly passivity was felt by my patients merely as inattentive-
ness. On such days I have attempted to reassure myself by
recalling that such feelings pass and that I might be exaggerating
the difficulties in practicing psychoanalysis. But even sober
reflection leaves no doubt that the practice of psychoanalysis
makes arduous demands on the psychoanalyst. I should like to
address myself to the following questions: what are the extraordinary difficulties that seem to be inherent in the profession?
Are there any factors that might play a mitigating role?

Freud himself seemed to be of a pessimistic frame of mind in
this regard and I want to quote part of a paragraph from "Analysis Terminable and Interminable" (1937a):

Here let us pause for a moment to assure the analyst that he
has our sincere sympathy in the very exacting demands he

Presented at the Plenary Session of the Annual Meeting of the American
Psychoanalytic Association, May 2, 1965, New York City. First published in
Journal of the American Psychoanalytic Association, 14:9-27, 1966.

has to fulfil in carrying out his activities. It almost looks as if analysis were the third of those 'impossible' professions in which one can be sure beforehand of achieving unsatisfying results. The other two, which have been known much longer, are education and government. Obviously we cannot demand that the prospective analyst should be a perfect being before he takes up analysis, in other words that only persons of such high and rare perfection should enter the profession. But where and how is the poor wretch [Freud's words] to acquire the ideal qualifications which he will need in his profession? The answer is, in an analysis of himself, with which his preparation for his future activity begins. For practical reasons the analysis can only be short and incomplete [p. 248].

Today I believe we would modify the last sentence and say that for practical reasons the analysis can only be long and incomplete.

In order to pursue the question: what makes the practice of psychoanalysis so arduous? we have to examine the various skills that the analytic situation demands of the psychoanalyst. Facility in gaining insight into the mind of another human being is inextricably tied up with the analyst's unconscious mind and the degree to which it is accessible for use by his conscious ego. The analyst's personal analysis has the ultimate aim of increasing the analyst's ability to utilize his insight into the important drives, defenses, fantasies, and conflicts of his own infantile life and their later derivatives. The psychological processes which the analyst has to employ in his technical procedures are also decisively involved in the formation of his character and personality. Even his knowledge and intelligence are influenced by the degree and kind of resolution of his neurotic conflicts. I would go still further and add that the motivations which led him into the field of psychoanalysis also play a role in how he works with patients.

Skills, traits, and motivations are the crucial elements in the analyst's armamentarium. They are interdependent and interrelated and bound up with the conscious and unconscious emotions, drives, defenses, fantasies, attitudes, and values of the analyst. Nevertheless, for purposes of clarification I shall artificially separate these factors—skills, traits, and motivations—in order to highlight those factors which cause the most difficulty.

Skills

The primary task of the psychoanalyst is to gain a detailed understanding of the patient's emotions, attitudes, and actions. The most difficult part of this job is to comprehend the unconscious processes which go on in his patient's mind. This depends on his skill in being able to translate the patient's conscious material into its unconscious and preconscious antecedents. While he listens to the patient precisely and carefully, he also has to sense what lies behind the various subjects the patient is expounding. While he listens to the melody, he must also listen to the hidden themes, the "left hand," the counterpart. This is possible only if he listens with the so-called evenly suspended attention that Freud (1912a) described. He listens consciously, intellectually, and detachedly, and at the same time from the inside as a participant. This kind of listening requires that the analyst have the capacity to shift from participant to observer, from introspection to empathy, from intuition to problem-solving thinking, from a more involved to a more detached position. It is necessary to oscillate, make transitions and blendings of these different positions (Ferenczi, 1928; Sterba, 1929; Sharpe, 1930; Reik, 1948; Fliess, 1953a).

The ability to empathize with the patient is an absolute prerequisite for psychoanalytic practice. It is our best method for comprehending the complex, subtle, and hidden emotions in another human being (Fliess, 1953a; Schafer, 1959; see also chapter 11). Empathy means to share, to experience partially and temporarily, the emotions of another person. It is essentially a preconscious phenomenon. It can be consciously instigated or interrupted and it can occur silently and automatically, alternating with other forms of relating to people. The essential mechanism in empathy is a partial and temporary identification with the patient. In order to accomplish this it is necessary to regress from the position of detached, intellectual observer to a more primitive kind of relationship in which the analyst becomes one with the person he is listening to. It requires the capacity for controlled and reversible regression (Kris, 1950).

Empathy is a special variety of intimacy with another human being. In order to empathize the analyst must be willing to become emotionally involved with his patient. He cannot empathize coldly; he can only empathize out of some wish or willingness to become close. Then he must be able to give this up and become the observer, the thinker, and analyzer again. Empathy is most likely to come into play when the analyst feels lost or out of touch. Empathy becomes a means of regaining contact with the ununderstood patient. It resembles other identificatory processes which occur when one is attempting to re-establish contact with a lost love object. One must be able to do this again and again and yet retain the ability to return to the detached and uninvolved position of analyzer. This is one of the important antithetical, bipolar demands of psychoanalytic practice.

Another skill of vital importance to the analyst is the ability to communicate meaningfully to the patient. We gather the data from the patient by detached or involved listening and understanding. Then we are faced with what to say, how to say it, and when to say it. This again depends to a great extent on our capacity to feel in empathic contact with the patient. We must be in intimate touch and yet not that close that we lose our independent judgment. If we want to make contact with and have an impact on the patient, we must be clear and precise and the words we use should usually be from the living language of the patient and not from our own private vocabulary. If our language is too distant, what we say will seem unreal. If our language is too much like the patient's, then there is the danger of having too much impact, which may be traumatic. Intonation, tone, force, rhythm are often more important than the precise words we use because the tone of what we say indicates the nonverbal, the preverbal relationship we have to the patient and is apt to stir up reactions derived from the early mother-child relationship (Sharpe, 1940; Loewenstein, 1956; Rycroft, 1956; Loewald, 1960; Stone, 1961; see also chapter 3).

Matters become more complicated because the analyst has to be skillful in communicating not only with words and with tone but also with silence, which is very different. He has to know when to be silent and how to be silent, and he has to understand the many meanings of silence to the patient—when it is comforting and reassuring, and when it is distant and hostile. He must sense when silence is warm and when it is cold; when it is probing, questioning, and demanding; and when it is apt to be felt as a terrible stress and a criticism. The analyst cannot perform these delicate deliberations only with his conscious intellect. He has to do this also preconsciously, unconsciously, with empathy. And again this has to be reversible. One must be able to make oscillations, transitions, and combinations of these various methods of communicating. These skills also have complicated antithetical properties and are a severe demand on the psychoanalyst.

The psychoanalytic situation demands of the psychoanalyst that he possess the ability to relate to his patient in such a way that the patient will develop a transference neurosis and also a working alliance. This is another instance when the analyst is required to have proficiency in maintaining two conflicting positions, for the attitudes and techniques which further the transference neurosis are often in opposition to those which facilitate the working alliance (Zetzel, 1956b; Stone, 1961; see also chapter 15).

Stated in a condensed form, in order to facilitate the development of a transference neurosis, we must frustrate the patient's search for neurotic gratifications and reassurance. Only in this way do we induce him to regress in his quest for satisfaction and security (Freud, 1919). Furthermore, we must try to comport ourselves so as to present ourselves to the patient as a rela-

tively blank screen for his fantasies, displacements, and projections (Freud, 1912a; Greenacre, 1954).

On the other hand, we must work with the patient in such a
way that he can also become our co-worker part of the time and
work along with us on understanding and integrating his insights. We must mobilize his relatively nonneurotic capacity for
object relationships and induce him partially and temporarily to
identify with our psychoanalytic point of view. In order to
promote the working alliance we must demonstrate to the
patient our unwavering pursuit of insight and understanding in
our daily work. No matter what he presents to us, be it ugly or
beautiful, delicate or brutal, sensitive or crude, loving or
hateful, we are concerned only with why, how, when, and with
whom did this happen. To the analyst each hour is important,
and he is willing to devote years in his attempt to understand the
patient.

The analyst must also safeguard the rights of the patient if
he hopes to maintain a working alliance. The patient is in a
relatively helpless position when he comes for help and will
therefore tend to accept uncritically and submissively what the
analyst offers him. This forms part of the uneven and tilted
relationship Greenacre (1954) has described. The analyst must
be sure not to demean the patient unwittingly and to take
advantage of his helplessness by treating him with imperious
attitudes and expectations. The procedures of psychoanalysis are
strange, unique, and artificial, and the patient has a right to
know, at the proper time, why we ask him to use the couch, do
free association, refuse to answer his questions, etc. By protecting his rights as an adult we nurture his self-esteem, so that one
day he can become a truly independent human being and not
just a submissive, masochistic patient.

Again we have two sets of demands on the analyst which
are in opposition to each other—the deprivational incognito
required for the development of the transference neurosis and
the reasonable co-worker of the working alliance. These two
positions do not nullify each other or neutralize one another.
Each has to exist at the proper time and there must be oscil-

lations, transitions, and blendings of them. Only a strong, consistent therapeutic commitment to the patient (within limits that are controllable) makes this contradictory combination of attitudes possible. It is for this reason that I consider the therapeutic commitment mandatory and not optional (Stone, 1961; chapter 15).

Traits

To perform the complex, subtle, and conflicting skills I have outlined requires persons of a certain sensitivity, personality, and character. Yet, all that is not sufficient. No one is a born psychoanalyst or suddenly blossoms into one. The psychoanalytic situation makes such arduous demands that the talents and abilities a person brings with him to the field have to be supported by an analyzed character structure. And here I want to quote Freud (1937a) again:

> But where and how is the poor wretch to acquire the ideal qualifications which he will need in his profession? The answer is, in an analysis of himself, with which his preparation for his future activity begins.... This alone would not suffice for his instruction; but we reckon on the stimuli that he has received in his own analysis not ceasing when it ends and on the processes of remodelling the ego continuing spontaneously in the analysed subject and making use of all subsequent experiences in this newly-acquired sense [pp. 248-249].

The experience of having undergone a therapeutic psychoanalysis (as well as a continuing self-analysis) is a prerequisite for the practice of psychoanalysis. However, certain traits of personality and character are necessary for reaching a high level of professional competence in the field. I realize that the selection of only a few qualities as being of special importance for psychoanalysts is apt to be highly subjective. I therefore recommend the works of Ella Sharpe (1930, chapt. 2; 1947), Ernest Jones

(1953-57), and Leo Stone (1961), who have written more extensively on this subject.

The relationship between analytic skills and personality traits is a complex one, and the origins of skills and traits vary from individual to individual. Here I shall pick out only what I consider to be the major faculties and outline the most typical antecedents. A single source may be the fountainhead for many traits and skills; although they share the same source, the traits or skills may be uneven in quality. On the other hand, a single trait or skill may have multiple origins.

The analyst should possess a lively interest in people, their way of life, emotions, fantasies, and thoughts. He should have an inquiring mind, an impelling but benevolent curiosity. Too little curiosity makes for a bored analyst. Too harsh a curiosity will cause the patient to suffer unnecessary pain. There should be a pleasure in discovering things and in bringing insight to the patient; yet this should not be a scoptophilic or sadistic gratification. This is possible only when curiosity has become a relatively deinstinctualized and neutralized activity. I want to stress the term relatively, because sublimations are rarely absolute and final. Partially and occasionally such activities do become reinstinctualized, and one has to be aware of this occurrence. Hartmann's (1955) ideas on sublimation are valuable for understanding this problem.

An analyst should meet the unknown in the patient, the strange and the bizarre, with an open mind and not with aversion and anxiety. One has to be free of the usual restricting conventionality of society and relatively indifferent to the superficialities of everyday life. In order to be initially receptive and accepting, it is necessary for the analyst to be credulous and gullible. Only in this way is it possible to do full justice to what the patient might be feeling. Although I maintain that this is a necessary character trait, I would state the opposite as well. The analyst must also be somewhat skeptical, knowing how people distort, twist, and change things to make themselves appear virtuous or innocent. On the other hand, a hawklike, detective-like suspiciousness about everything the patient says may make the analyst appear clever but may estrange him forever from the patient because an analyst cannot empathize properly with a patient when he is trying to entrap him. Once again you see the antithetical and complicated combination of traits that one needs in order to understand another human being.

I have already mentioned the central importance of empathy, and I want to add that I believe that the capacity to empathize requires a willingness temporarily and partially to give up one's own identity. People with a rather narrow sense of identity, rigid and fixed, are unwilling or unable to empathize. The analyst's self image has to be flexible and loose; yet he may not lose his identity. At the end of the hour he has to end up being the analyst. Furthermore, I am not referring to consciously playing a role, which implies conscious deception. When I talk about empathizing and letting oneself be carried away temporarily by the patient, I have in mind something similar to what Beres (1960) and Rosen (1960) have described about what happens when one lets oneself be carried away temporarily by a piece of music or art. This is also what is required in empathizing. Yet, one cannot have multiple identities. Empathy—and I dwell on it because it is so crucial—is a special kind of nonverbal, preverbal closeness which has a feminine cast; it comes from one's motherliness, and men (and women too) must have made peace with their motherliness in order to be willing to empathize. This is derived from the mental bisexuality of the analyst, a trait that Jones (1953-57, vol. 2) pointed out in Freud. People who are empathizers are always trying to reestablish contact, like people who are depressed. I believe that analysts who have been depressed and have overcome their depression make the best empathizers (see chapter 11). One must be able to regress to the empathic contact with the patient and then be able to rebound from it in order to check on the validity of the data so gathered.

The skill in communicating to a patient is very different from ordinary social talking, history-taking, cross-examination, or lecturing. Eloquence, erudition, and logic are not of primary importance in the art of talking to a patient. The essential element is a therapeutic attitude with an empathic undertone. I want to stress the point about the therapeutic attitude because I know it is controversial. This commitment to help the patient should be manifest or latent in all interactions with the patient from the first interview to the last. I want to state my position about this clearly and emphatically. I believe only sick people— patients who suffer from neurotic miseries—can be successfully treated by psychoanalysis. Candidates, research workers, investigators cannot undergo a deep analytic experience unless they are able and willing to become patients. And parallel to that statement, I believe that deep psychoanalysis is first and foremost a method of treatment and therefore can be carried out effectively only by therapists—people trained and dedicated to helping or curing the emotionally ill. A medical degree does not automatically make one a therapist, nor does the lack of an M.D. degree prevent a therapeutic attitude. It is my conviction that the analyst's commitment to help the patient—ever present but under control—is an essential ingredient which enables the analyst to develop the subtle skill of communicating meaningfully and effectively with the patient (Gill, Newman, and Redlich, 1954; Jones, 1953-57; Sharpe, 1930; Stone, 1961).

Other skills play a role in communicating but are secondary. Literary skill is of little value. Verbal dexterity can be the difference between a more deft therapist or a more clumsy one, but I do not believe that it is ever of decisive importance. Analysts who tend to remember the brilliant things they say to their patients may sound good at meetings, but I sometimes wonder how it felt to the patient. What appears brilliant to the patient usually comes from the patient's dynamics at the moment and not from the analyst's cerebration.

I want to return to another skill in communicating—the silent part—which requires a very different set of traits: patience, the ability to wait, to suspend judgment. Here too one must be careful because what looks like a virtue may turn out to be something quite different. Patience—or what looks like patience—in the very silent analyst may really be hidden passive, sadistic, aggressive impulses. Or patience may be a screen for professional indecisiveness or timidity. Here too the important question is whether the capacity to wait and be patient is or is not a relatively conflict-free ego function.

I stated earlier that to facilitate the development of a transference neurosis in the patient, the analyst has to maintain attitudes suggested in the term "deprivational incognito." In order to achieve this the analyst must be able to stand aloof from his patient, restrain his therapeutic intentions, and blanket his normal, humane responses. In part this stems from the analyst's ability to control his loving and reparative tendencies. Partially, however, this is derived from the analyst's ability to inflict pain on his patient, which in turn stems from some aspect of hatred for his patient. I realize this may be a shocking way of putting it—hating one's patient—but I see no reason to camouflage reality. Just as the analyst must be able to love his patient, within limits, so must he be able to hate his patient, also within limits. Inflicting pain, be it in the form of aloofness, silence, making interpretations, or charging fees, are all ultimately derived from hatred. It is important that the analyst be able to do this without unconscious anxiety or guilt and for the patient's therapeutic benefit (Winnicott, 1949).

On the other hand, the working alliance requires an ever-ready willingness on the analyst's part, no matter how offensive a façade the patient may be presenting, to keep in mind that this is a sick and relatively helpless human being, a child. This brings with it the danger that we become overly concerned and then tend to overprotect and indulge the patient. And yet one may not remain wooden and untouched. The analyst has to be reliable in human terms, not rigid, and predictable by starting every hour exactly on the hour and ending every hour exactly in fifty minutes, come hell or high water. This kind of reliability is valueless. The patient needs the knowledge that his analyst is a human being who is both concerned and expert, who is trying to help him by providing an atmosphere where he can gain insight and understanding. The corollary danger is that of showing sympathy and loving kindness too early and too copiously. The analyst who does so is as bad as the one with the wooden face.

Instant warmth has no place in psychoanalysis, which cannot be done in a hale and hearty manner, cheerfully or lightheartedly. Neither can it be effective if it is essentially grim, gloomy, or agonizing. The analyst must be able to feel a genuine liking, compassion, and acceptance for his patient while establishing an atmosphere in which the patient can develop the various transference reactions. Then he must be able to communicate insights within the patient's ability to bear them.

The wish to cure the patient should not be confused with pathological therapeutic zeal. It should be apparent in the analyst's seriousness of purpose, his rigorous pursuit of insight, his respect for the various instrumentalities of his profession, and his willingness to struggle for years toward the long-range goals. The analyst's ability to administer painful insights is as much a sign of his therapeutic intent as his concern for the patient's dignity and self-respect. Bearing the hostile and humiliating outbursts of his patients without retaliation is as important as remaining unperturbed by their sexual provocations. This does not mean that the analyst should not have feelings and fantasies in response to his patients, but their degree and quantity ought to be within limits that enable him to control his responses so that what comes into the open is only as much as the patient requires.

The analyst must permit the patient's transference feelings to reach their optimal intensity without intervening. This calls for his ability to endure stress, anxiety, or depression quietly and patiently. The analyst is the bearer of insight, which is usually painful, and which must be conveyed in an atmosphere of straightforwardness, compassion, and concern. How to resolve the conflict between creating an atmosphere of deprivation and concern and maintaining closeness to the patient and also distance is an extremely personal matter and I do not think there is a single, exact prescription. However, I do maintain that despite individual variations, analysts who do deep psychoanalysis for therapeutic purposes must be able to reconcile these two antithetical tasks, and they must have the character traits which enable them to make this possible.

Motivations

The motivations which lie behind the skills and character traits that I believe are necessary for practicing psychoanalysis are the most difficult to dissect, because some of the motivations originate in the most primitive unconscious instinctual drives related to the earliest forms of object relations. This makes them hard to verbalize and almost impossible to verify. I also want to make the point that later maturational processes in the ego, id, and superego, as well as experiential factors modify these motivations so that an early motivation may then be transformed into newer forms of motivation. Furthermore, there are complex hierarchies of instinct and defense which may present a similar surface, so that it is hard to judge from the external appearance what the motives are. I shall limit this discussion of motives to the three main tasks of the analyst: (1) the analyst as the gatherer and transmitter of insight and understanding; (2) the analyst as the target of the transference neurosis; and (3) the analyst as the treater of the sick and the suffering.

The origin of the urge to understand a patient can be traced back to the propensity to get inside another human being (Sharpe, 1930). This is related to the infantile wish and need to get inside the mind and body of another human being, and has primitive libidinal and aggressive beginnings. It seems to start with the urge for symbiotic fusion with the mother. Secondly, it may also be derived from strivings for omnipotence and the overcoming of fear toward the stranger. Later libidinal and aggressive strivings may also play a role. For example, gathering, acquiring, and gaining insight may indicate anal components; curiosity about sexual matters may be derived from oedipal peeping, etc.

The transmitting of insight, the giving of an interpretation may stem from impulses of feeding, nurturing, teaching, protecting, mothering, fertilizing, and impregnating. It can also be used as a means of reparation for past unconscious guilt feelings and counterphobic activities. Nor should we forget that every analysis we do also serves in some way or another as a continuation of our own analysis. I believe that the analyst will always learn something about himself from every patient he helps, because if he helps them, it means that he has made mistakes with them which they were able to bring to his attention. He learns about himself from the mistakes because they derive in part from unconscious feelings within himself.

In my opinion, the point of origin of a given motivation is not the decisive factor in determining its value or harm. What is significant is the degree of deinstinctualization or neutralization that has taken place. The gradations of neutralization will decide to what extent the function of serving as the bearer of understanding has become relatively conflict-free, and an autonomous, reliable ego function. I do not believe it matters, for example, whether giving a patient insight means feeding, nurturing, protecting, or teaching. What is important is that the feeding, nurturing, protecting, or teaching should be free of its sexual and aggressive undertones, and is therefore neither unduly exciting nor guilt-producing to the analyst and the patient.

Similarly, the fantasies associated with getting inside the patient in order to obtain insight are not the crucial factor; the real issue is whether this activity is still associated with anxiety and guilt-producing fantasies. However, it must be borne in mind that this is never established once and for all since pressures from the id, superego, and external world do make for regressions and progressions. Another important consideration, therefore, is how readily accessible to the analyst's conscious and reasonable ego are these aggressive and libidinal fantasies. Awareness of the countertransference may set other adaptive measures in motion in the psychoanalyst; these may supplement the safeguarding function which the neutralization has failed to handle (Hartmann, 1955; Winnicott, 1955; Spitz, 1956b; Khan, 1963).

It does not do justice to the complexity of the human mind or to the arduous demands of the analyst's profession to expect that the obtaining and delivering of insight might be completely or permanently free from conflict, guilt, and anxiety. Yet I would like to go further and suggest that these activities not only should be free from guilt and anxiety, but they should be pleasurable. The daily work of therapeutic psychoanalysis is difficult and often painful for the analyst. He needs a certain amount of positive pleasure in the performance of his duties to enable him to sustain a lively interest and concern for the goings-on in his patients. The pleasure in listening, looking, exploring, imagining, and comprehending is not only permissible but necessary for the optimal efficiency of the analyst (Sharpe, 1947; Szasz, 1956).

I now turn to the motives for comporting oneself as a relatively nonresponsive blank screen so that the patient can displace and project onto that screen the unresolved, warded-off imagos of his past. What would make someone want to go into a profession where he or she has to be a blank screen so much of the time? And yet it seems that many analysts find the blank screen requirement very easy. If the ease stems from a tendency to be withdrawn, emotionally isolated, or uninvolved with other human beings, it is a serious drawback. The mature variety of this willingness and readiness to be the blank screen is dependent on one's capacity to be alone. Analysts must be able to be alone, to be quiet, to be contemplative, introspective, to have a sense of privacy about themselves and even about their patients. They work with the most intimate details of another person's life, and yet the patient has a right, even in analysis, to a certain sense of privacy.

Again, the ability to be quiet physically and to assume the role of the blank screen must be controllable and reversible. The analyst must have the ability to bear the roles the patient casts on him in his transference reactions, to endure being the hated enemy or rival, or the dearly beloved or the frightening father, or the seductive loving mother, etc. Not only does the analyst have to endure it and allow it to happen, he must help the patient embellish and refine the character type that he has displaced onto the analyst at the moment so that the patient can better understand what he is experiencing. The analyst becomes in a way a silent actor in a play that the patient is creating. The analyst does not act in this drama. He tries to maintain himself as the shadowy figure the patient needs for his fantasies, but he helps the patient work out the details of the character that the patient is creating. He becomes in a sense the stage director. Or he is like the conductor of a symphony. He does not write the music, but he clarifies and interprets it. The interpretive work of the analyst as he listens to what the patient fantasies is at its best related to the creative process in literature, music, and art (Kris, 1952; Loewald, 1960).

Finally, let us examine the analyst as the treater of the sick and suffering. Freud was, to say the least, highly ambivalent about this point. I shall quote him because what I want to say is very different. This is Freud (1926b):

> After forty-one years of medical activity, my self-knowledge tells me that I have never really been a doctor in the proper sense. . . . I have no knowledge of having had any craving in my early childhood to help suffering humanity. . . . I scarcely think, however, that my lack of a genuine medical temperament has done much damage to my patients. For it is not greatly to the advantage of patients if their doctor's therapeutic interest has too marked an emotional emphasis. They are best helped if he carries out his task coolly and keeping as closely as possible to the rules [pp. 253-254].

I do not believe Freud was accurate in his evaluation of himself on this point, which may be presumptuous of me or perhaps defensive of my ideals (see also Stone [1961] on this issue). Be that as it may, I do not agree with his point of view because I do feel that the physicianly attitude toward the patient is a basic prerequisite for an analyst. This issue is complicated, and also contains several opposing elements. The physician is the activator of highly charged and diverse fantasies in the patient. The physician is the one who comes when the parents are frightened, when the parents are confused, when the parents are worried; he is even stronger than father. It is the physician who may look upon everyone's nakedness, including that of the parents and that too had been the sole prerogative of the parents. He alone is not afraid of or disgusted by vomit, feces, urine, pus, or blood. In some ways he is like a powerful and awesome father, and in others like the mother. The physician is involved in many aspects of the patient's bodily intimacy and in the nursing care of the sick human being, which resembles the mother's role.

Furthermore, he is also a scientist; he observes, he gathers data, thinks, and remains overtly unmoved. In a sense he is a researcher. Yet the analyst is neither a researcher nor a parent, but he is a peculiar and unique blend of the two which is the psychoanalytic therapist.

All of this leads us to the analyst's motivations in becoming a therapist. Freud (1926b) said, "My innate sadistic disposition was not a very strong one, so that I had no need to develop this one of its derivatives. Nor did I ever play the 'doctor game'; my infantile curiosity evidently chose other paths" (p. 253). He indicated that the urge to become a physician originates in sadistic pregenital strivings and sexual curiosity. Ernst Simmel (1926) wrote a very remarkable paper on the doctor game and its pregenital antecedents and later derivatives. Such urges as the need to mutilate and inflict pain upon the body of another produces sadistic doctors, whereas reaction formations in this regard make for the indecisive, passive, and inhibited ones. Restitution and reparation phenomena are responsible for the compulsive rescuers and masochists among physicians.

I have already mentioned the urge for fusion blended with destructive aims, the anal-sadistic and phallic strivings which may lie underneath the wish to be a doctor. The physician may unconsciously fantasy himself as the sadistic father torturing the victim-patient, he may be the oedipal father, the impregnating father, or the suckling mother with her infant-patient (Simmel, 1926). On the other hand, defensive maneuvers may decisively color the picture which may shade into the realm of sublimation and neutralization. The search for knowledge may be a conflict-free derivative of the urge to gain access to the unknown and dangerous body and mind. A feeling of kinship with suffering humanity may lead to the wish to fight against the tyranny of unnecessary sickness and pain. Once again it is impressive to note the diversity and the antitheses among the different elements that make up the motivations.

Conclusion

Perhaps I have now convinced you that psychoanalysis is truly an impossible profession. It seems to spring from such primitive motives; it is related to such infantile object relations. The traits required are so varied and so contradictory and the skills so complex and antithetical. Yet psychoanalysis cannot be altogether an impossible profession since it is sometimes practiced with success and even with pleasure. However, certain conditions have to be fulfilled.

I should place in the primary position the fact that the psychoanalyst has experienced a deep personal analytic experience. Preferably this should include some analysis outside of the confines of a training situation. In addition, he should be able and willing to do some continuing self-analysis. The analyst should be able to recognize that the occurrence of some neurotic conflicts within himself is inevitable and requires constant self-scrutiny. I mean not an obsessive search for perfection but a willingness to recognize the coming to light of blind spots which he will have the humility to recognize as such and be willing to explore. I believe if these factors are adhered to, the psychoanalytic work will give pleasure and a sense of accomplishment which compensate for the many hours of frustration and disappointment.

It is no doubt also true that a good personal life outside one's work is an essential prerequisite for making psychoanalysis a rewarding profession. This means that the psychoanalyst must have the opportunity to stop being a psychoanalyst when he comes home. He should feel free to react as a spontaneous, wholehearted, whole person when he leaves the office. If he has to be right and rational in the analytic hours, he needs a place to be wrong and to be irrational at times. He needs a place where he can expose his frailties and not only not be punished for it, but even have them looked upon as endearing qualities. It is easy to love and admire a bright man, but only a truly loving wife can love one who is a fool at times. And the psychoanalyst needs this. His work takes so much out of him emotionally that if he really is wholehearted in his work, he becomes depleted. The analyst needs some emotional sustenance when he comes home.

With these requirements fulfilled, it is possible to enjoy psychoanalytic work. It is certainly in many ways terribly rewarding. It is one of the few places where science and art and creativity all come together. Analysts work with some of the most interesting people in the world, probably the most creative people in the world, and every patient that we work with offers us a new world to explore. More than that, the analyst's work is needed. He does good for the most part, and is well rewarded for what he does. Despite all the difficulties, how fortunate is the psychoanalyst!

18

A Transsexual Boy
and a Hypothesis

(1966)

IN THIS PRESENTATION I shall describe the treatment of a five-year-old boy, Lance, the first child I have ever attempted to treat psychoanalytically. I am not sure that my method of treatment would meet with the approval of the child analysts. Nevertheless, the clinical material is unusually interesting and the simultaneous analysis of the mother, carried out and described by Stoller (1966), offers an added dimension for study. Stoller and I worked independently and did not discuss our findings until shortly before this Congress. I shall report the first fourteen months of treatment, during which time I have been seeing the boy four times weekly, have seen his mother about once a month, and his father on two occasions.

Historical Data

The pertinent history given by the parents before the Gender Identity Research Committee is as follows. Their main

Presented at the 24th International Psycho-Analytical Congress, Amsterdam, July 1965. First published in *International Journal of Psycho-Analysis*, 47:396-403, 1966.

reason for seeking help for Lance was his compulsion to wear his mother's or his older sister's clothes. This had begun when Lance was a little over one year old and barely able to walk. He seemed to want to put on his sister's or mother's shoes. He very quickly seemed to prefer above all to walk around in his mother's high-heeled shoes and wept furiously when she tried to remove them. Since he seemed remarkably adept at this and since he was so young and looked so "cute," he was permitted to continue doing this. Later on he was able to run up and down stairs in these shoes, to climb trees in them, ride his bicycle, etc. He gradually put on other items of clothing—blouse, stockings, purse, hats—until he began to insist on dressing as a girl. Since all attempts to stop this were met by tears, rage, or temper tantrums, the parents decided not to interfere. When questioned about it, Lance said he liked to "dress up" because it made him feel good. The parents believed this was a "phase" and that he would eventually outgrow it.

When Lance was three and a half years old, a neighbor became indignant with the mother for allowing the boy to dress as a girl. This upset the mother, who then consulted the nursery school teacher. The latter told her that Lance was a worry in school as well since he played with the girls and put on girls' clothes and played house with the boys. He often tried to get the boys to put on girls' clothes as well. This was disturbing to the other boys' parents and they asked the teacher to keep Lance away from their offspring.

This information came as an unexpected blow to Lance's parents; they inquired where to go for help and, after a considerable delay, were directed to the Gender Identity Research Clinic. Soon thereafter Lance's mother began psychoanalytic treatment, as Stoller (1966) described.

A few months later the boy was seen twice weekly in psychotherapy by one of the psychiatric residents. When the resident was called into military service some six months later, I decided to undertake the treatment.

I interviewed the mother for several hours before I saw Lance and obtained the following additional information. The boy had always been a prodigious eater. He cried a great deal as an infant because he was hungry. He was breast-fed for a few weeks, but the mother's milk was woefully inadequate and he was changed to the bottle. Lance needed to be fed every hour and a half as a baby and up to the present "ate enough food for a grown man." For example, he would have a hamburger, two eggs, and cereal for breakfast. He was not overweight and there was no history of colic or any other gastrointestinal disorder. Lance insisted on a bottle at night until he was five and gave it up only when he realized he could not have a friend stay overnight if he needed the bottle. In addition, he had a blanket he nuzzled, also until about five years of age.

The mother was unhappily married to an artistic, but weak man, who was strongly attached to his mother and afraid of his wife. He had given up a failing career as a painter a few years ago and worked frantically at the insurance business in an attempt to straighten out the family's miserable financial situation. He worked day and night and was rarely at home. Their sexual life was practically nonexistent. When they quarreled, he would leave the house and stay away for long periods of time, often at his mother's home.[1]

The mother claimed that her relationship with her daughter was a mutually happy one, and the daughter seemed to have developed without any special problems. It was evident that the mother was enormously concerned with Lance's problem. She felt guilty for not having recognized the dressing in women's clothes as a symptom. Furthermore, she indicated a strong love for the boy which far outweighed her feelings for her husband and daughter. In addition, she spoke of Lance's various qualities with great pride and great discernment. I had the clinical impression that she felt as if the boy were her personal creation, her prized possession, and also herself. When I agreed to take the boy into treatment, she reacted as though I had agreed to become the boy's father as well as the head of their household.

[1] See Stoller (1966) for more details of the family history.

Clinical Data

Lance began treatment with me when he was five and a half years old. He was a bright-eyed, alert, warm, quick, charming, lively, unusually good-looking little boy. He was somewhat apprehensive at coming to see me at my home and timorously took my hand when I asked him if he wanted to look at the house. He was intrigued with the grand piano, and after I played a few notes, I was struck that he immediately played the same few notes for me. Although he rarely touched the piano again in the following year, whenever he did he always played those same notes.

He was delighted with the balcony in the living room and happily exclaimed that it reminded him of a cinema. From the balcony he saw out into the garden and joyously discovered the swimming pool. He ran outside and asked me if I would teach him to swim, which I impulsively promised to do. Since his problem was a form of transvestitism, I felt that a manly activity like teaching him to swim would be beneficial. The discovery of the swimming pool made Lance feel quite happy about coming to see me, and as he and his mother left that first hour, hand in hand, he turned around in the middle of the street and shouted gleefully to me, "Good-bye Dr. Greenson, we are your customers, we are your customers." (I mention this point because of the use of the word "we," which I believe is central to his pathology.)

The next day Lance came with his bathing suit and I had prepared life-preserving equipment for beginners to put on him. However, he tearfully said that he did not want to put this on; he just wanted to jump in the water and swim, although he admitted that he did not know how to swim. I was attempting to explain that first he had to learn how to swim, when he burst from my arms, ran to the deep end of the swimming pool, and jumped in. I rushed after him and plunged in half-clothed. As I came to the surface, I saw to my amazement that the boy was swimming. After I had caught my breath, I swam alongside him and asked him where he had learned to swim and to use that peculiar stroke. He gasped, "That's how you are swimming." I was unwittingly using a peculiar mixture of crawl and breast stroke which the boy had apparently noticed in the few strokes I took and was copying me. When we reached the shallow end, I asked him again when he had learned to swim and he told me he had watched other boys swim and he knew he could do it.

This brings me to the first outstanding clinical finding, the hunger for identification and imitation—already indicated in his piano-playing and his "*we* are your customers." Lance did the same with all games or sports like darts, skate-board, or croquet, at which he became quickly proficient. When he played with a truck or car he became the truck or car. When we built a tunnel for the truck to go through and I asked him to send the truck through to me, he would say, "O.K.," and then go with the truck through the tunnel. Once I introduced him to my mother who was visiting; and when we left a few moments later he said to her, "Good-bye, Mommy." He would imitate different dancers and singers he saw on television.

It was noticeable, however, that Lance preferred to identify with feminine objects and activities. He loved to play with a Barbie doll, a very popular doll in America, for whom one can buy many different wardrobes, jewelry, wigs, etc. For months, no matter what he did with Barbie, he was Barbie. If Barbie fell into the pool, he fell into the pool; if Barbie fainted, he fainted. Sometimes he did the activity along with the doll and then alone, after the doll. When the weather got too cool to be outdoors, he as Barbie would sweep the dollhouse, bathe children, wash the clothes, etc. The father doll or other male dolls were essentially ignored.

Once, in the first weeks of treatment, while we were walking outdoors, we passed some older girls playing on a lawn with a dollhouse and some of these Barbie dolls. Lance became feverishly excited and hesitantly asked me if he might "watch" them play. When I consented he walked over to them and, despite their taunts, joined their play. In a few moments he had captivated them and was a fully accepted member of their group. Later he begged me to buy him such a Barbie doll. I agreed, because I felt it might offer the possibility of bringing a great deal of material into the treatment, but stipulated that he should leave the doll in my house and only play with the dolls when he was with me. When we got home after buying the doll I was impressed by Lance's excitement. His face was flushed and sweaty and his hands trembled as he began to take the doll out of its box and dress it. He was completely uninterested in the Ken doll I had also bought at the same time. (Ken is Barbie's boyfriend.) It is worth noting that shortly after I had bought the Barbie doll, Lance put on female clothing only on rare occasions.

Related to this tendency to feminine identification was Lance's great interest in clothes, jewelry, and appearance. Even after he stopped wearing his mother's and sister's clothes, he noticed women's apparel, jewelry, earrings, hair styles, shade of lipstick, etc. He would often comment on a new dress my wife or daughter or housekeeper was wearing, or stop to admire a dress in a store window or the jewelry which a visitor or passerby was wearing. He was aware of his own appearance and took pride in keeping his hair combed. His own clothing when he came to the hour was in good taste but unremarkable. In the early months of treatment he carefully and lovingly dressed Barbie down to the last detail, including scarf, bracelet, and gloves. He often changed the outfits and sometimes made scarves or shawls or stoles for the doll from pieces of materials he would obtain from my wife. He seemed completely uninterested in the doll's nakedness and also uninterested in the clothes of the boy doll, Ken. Lance had a keen appreciation of color and form, and dressed Barbie in aesthetically fastidious combinations. His feeling for art extended also to classical music, opera, and Shakespeare's plays.

There was a decidedly feminine cast to all of this. Once, when we played cops and robbers and I was a detective asking him to describe the thief who robbed him, he could recall only one detail, that "he had very long eyelashes." I told him this description was not a great help and next time he ought to pay more attention. The next time we played the game I questioned him and Lance said: "The robber wore beige pants and a yellow shirt, white and tan shoes and he had blue eyes with long eyelashes."

Another outstanding clinical feature was Lance's love of water. He not only used the swimming pool every chance he had for swimming, diving, and playing under water with and without Barbie, but he would go home afterward and play for hours with water from the garden hose. His mother reported that he had shown this love of water since infancy. He loved to be bathed, would play in the tub for hours if she permitted it, loved the sea, etc. He was never a problem in toilet training and toilet trained himself at about thirteen months. He wet his bed occasionally until the age of two and a half.

During his treatment with me, Lance would play with water in the cold weather, dirtying toy cars and dolls and washing them off with the hose. It did not appear to be a joy in cleansing but was a joy in wetting and dirtying. As mentioned above, he enjoyed dressing Barbie and throwing her into the pool when dressed. In the pool he was happy and fearless. He once drew a picture of the happiest day in his life, which showed a boy in a swimming pool and a man standing outside watching him. Lance rarely touched me physically and seemed afraid of bodily contact with me when we played together. This was in marked contrast to the constant touching he did with his mother, which I observed when he waited for me to begin the hour. The first time he ever grabbed hold of me physically occurred in the fifth month of treatment when we were playing together in the pool.

The last clinical feature I want to note before going on to the developments arising from the treatment is the apparent lack of active, phallic oedipal activities: for the first half year of treatment he showed no interest in guns, shooting, knives, or fighting. (This is remarkable for an American boy.) He appeared uninterested and without curiosity in regard to nakedness or sex. He urinated sitting down until the age of three and a half, despite his mother's urging that he urinate like daddy did. He seemed afraid of ordinary roughhouse play, yet he showed an amazing lack of anxiety in other ways. At fifteen months, he jumped out of a window because he wanted to fly. He was decidedly accident-prone and often had stitches taken in his scalp for rather serious falls. At four years, Lance was overheard saying to his sister, when both were naked: "I see your penis." She answered: "I see your penis." He answered: "I don't have a penis." The mother reported that he asked her at four years of age, "What will I be when I grow up?" When she replied, "You will be a man," he cried and said, "I don't want to be a man, I want to be a girl."

In appearance Lance seemed to be an unusual combination of boy and girl. He had fine features, with big brown eyes and long, dark eyelashes. He was short but sturdily built, active, quick, dexterous, and agile. Yet he was also unusually graceful, handsome, gentle, and charming. He related easily to grownups, in fact too readily, as though he were trying to ingratiate himself. This was true particularly in regard to adult women. He was shy and timid with boys above all and less so with grown men. He preferred to play with girls and had no boyfriends when he began treatment.

Course of Treatment

The following are some of the highlights taken from my notes during his fourteen months of treatment.

SUMMER 1964

After the first two hours, I do not go into the pool with Lance, but watch and talk to him as he swims, dives, or plays with some dolls. His favorite game is to make the doll walk up to the edge of the pool, slip, scream, and fall in. Then he falls in and shouts "I'm drowning." He repeats this endlessly. Sometimes he plays with little cars and they also have accidents and fall into the water and he does the same. If he becomes aggressive, he becomes wild and scatters the cars all around in a disorganized temper tantrumlike way. If I play with the cars with him, he bangs into my car, and if I pretend to be angry, he becomes frightened.

Now that he has Barbie, he plays with her fully clothed at the side of the pool so that she falls in and is drowning, fainting, or getting murdered. After a few days he undresses her and says, "Let's imagine she's dressed." In these games I am usually Ken, and am usually ignored or bumped into. When I ask to be Barbie, Lance refuses. He only talks of his mother and sister and never about his father. He tells me spontaneously about some accidents he has had and listens intently when I bring up the subject that sometimes mothers can get angry. He ignores my comment that sometimes boys get angry with their mothers or fathers or sisters. When I tell him I can remember getting angry with my mother, he blandly says: "You're nutty."

Lance gradually wants me to participate more in his play. At first, he wants me to play with the dolls or cars. Then at times he wants to play with me alone. He is the king floating on a raft and I should pull him. He reluctantly agrees to change roles when I claim to be tired. Lance asks me to teach him how to swim underwater and to dive, which I do. On one occasion he lets the air out of the rubber raft and gleefully says, "That was your air, now I'll put in mine," and he does. He shows me he can ride a skate-board and also a bicycle, which he does exceedingly well. I tell him I am impressed and also try to ride his bicycle and skate-board, which I don't do nearly as well. At this point, his mother reported that he has lately taken to prancing about the garden urinating proudly. When he develops a cold, he goes back to playing with Barbie, and sometimes he calls her Barbie and not I.

AUTUMN 1964

After five months of treatment, it is too cold to play in the pool and we play with trucks and dolls. At first Lance covers them with mud and then waters them clean with the hose. Gradually, he becomes more aggressive and slams Barbie in the

face with mud, shouting, "Shut up" or "Take this, Barbie," or
some other girl's name. He refers to Barbie as "she" in this
activity. He brings a Chinese girl to the hour to see "our" house.
They had been in a play together at school and Lance is proud
and delighted to show off "our house." They talk about other
plays they were in and Lance exuberantly says that sometimes he
used to dress up as a girl. His schoolmate laughs at him, and
Lance blushes and quickly says, "That was when I was three."

For Christmas I give him a Marine uniform, which he loves
and wears proudly for days. His mother reports that he has been
hitting her and his sister of late. His play with the dolls gets more
aggressive, but mainly with Barbie. Once, after covering Barbie
with mud, he cooks her and makes a witches' brew out of her.
As he leaves, Lance mimics me, saying, "Good-bye, Barbie, I
will see you at nothing o'clock," and laughs. One day as we leave
my house and I accompany him to his car, he suggests that we
march out together, walking stiffly in step, as Marines. He puts
a stick of licorice in his mouth to imitate my cigar. His mother
reports that he keeps lifting up her skirts to peek at her underwear. When I ask him about this he laughingly retorts, "Liar,
liar, pants on fire, Hang it on a telephone wire."

WINTER 1964-65

We draw moving pictures, i.e., pictures in sequence telling
a story. A man and woman are in bed and they are scared by
Frankenstein, a little devil. A girl falls in a swimming pool and a
boy rescues her. They go to live together on a boat. His mother
finds him in the mornings without pajama bottoms. He wants
his hair cut shorter. We play lots of hide-and-seek games. In one
hour Lance falls asleep and I cannot awaken him. In the next
hour he tells me that his friend's father had died and the boy had
almost cried and so had Lance. Later, when we talk about
dying, Lance says that he knows that means he is sleeping
forever.

Sometime later Lance sees a picture on the cover of a
murder mystery showing a half-naked female corpse and a man

with a gun. Lance wants to play murder with Barbie, Ken, and me. Barbie falls down and her skirts fly up over her knees. He denies any knowledge of how babies are made, but seems anxious so I explain it to him. He listens with rapt attention, face flushed, biting his nails. When I finish, he asks, "Can you do it if you are divorced? Can bachelors do it? How old do you have to be to do it? Can you do it at fourteen? How does the penis get in?" When I explain, he asks me, "Please, Dr. Greenson, tell me it all over again," and I comply. The next day he points to Barbie's pubic area and asks me if that is where the penis goes in.

Lance asks me to buy Barbie a wedding gown. I am reluctant and he says he knows I don't like beautiful dresses. I tell him that I do, that I think women's clothes are beautiful, but I am glad to be a man and be able to wear simple clothes which are much easier to put on. He seems puzzled by this remark. I explain to him again that I like beautiful women and beautiful clothes, but I am glad that I am a man. He does not seem to comprehend this. In the next hour, I go with him to buy Barbie a beautiful evening gown. Lance is excited and suggests that we play that we are going to a ball in a castle, by which he means he is going as Barbie, who is a princess. Then he adds that at the ball we would meet a prince and I should be the prince. I agree, and as he dances around the room making Barbie do the dancing steps, I enter the room as the prince and say, "Barbie, how beautiful you look. I love you. I want to dance with you." Lance is startled and pleased. I repeat this and take the Barbie doll from his hand to dance with her. He refuses to give her up. I repeat, "Oh, you are so beautiful, Princess, I want to dance with you. I like you. I want to kiss you." Lance hesitantly says, "Oh, do you want to be the princess? Go ahead, you can be the princess." I repeat, "No, I don't want to *be* the princess, I like her, I want to dance with her." The boy is baffled. Once again he says, "Go ahead, you can be the princess," and I say, "No, I like her, I don't want to *be* the princess. I want to dance with her and hold her." Finally, Lance allows me to and I dance joyously with the princess, telling her she is beautiful and I love her and I want to kiss her.

In a later hour he asks me, "Do you like your wife? Do you go dancing with your wife?" I answer, "Yes, I often do dance with my wife and I do love her." This remark makes him very thoughtful.

Thereafter Lance is able to play with Barbie, but no longer refers to her as "I" or "we," but only as "she." Soon after that he rarely plays with Barbie alone. Most of the time he plays with me and Ken and we play murder. It always concerns a man and woman sleeping together and someone comes in and kills the woman or the man. The murderer is often an old witch. His mother reports that he keeps pulling up her sweater. If we play in the pool with dolls, Barbie's dress always flies up above her knees and her bosom is exposed. Lance asks me to teach him how to box with boxing gloves and I do. He fights a great deal with his sister and then with a boy who hits him in the eye, but Lance keeps on fighting. The other boy runs away and Lance taunts him, "You use that greasy kid's stuff." (This is in reference to a popular advertisement.) He opens up one of my medical books and sees a picture of a dissection of a penis. The next few days Lance again plays alone with Barbie. I tell him I once got scared when I saw a picture in my father's medical book, but my father told me that those penises were not of boys, but of old men who were already dead. He asks me to tell him again of the time I was scared by pictures. Lance brings me a book from home to read to him. It is about where babies come from. On a foggy day he runs happily about as the fog rolls in, shouting, "Oh, Dr. Greenson, I can touch a cloud with my fingertips, I can touch a cloud with my fingertips!"

SPRING 1965

On Sundays, Lance and his father spend the morning together. They go to the beach and one day Lance tells me proudly and excitedly how his father saved a girl from drowning (a true story). His mother reports he wakes up at night sometimes, comes into her room, and tries to get into her side of the bed. In the pool, I notice he sometimes presses Barbie against his penis. He puts her dress on, but leaves off her underwear. He begs me to let him swim nude and I permit it, but tell him to be careful not to expose himself to the neighbors. Once he asks me how does a penis get hard. I tell him it will if he rubs it. Lance proudly replies that his can get hard just by thinking. I tell him that is pretty good, but am careful not to show too much interest. His mother reports for the first time he is truly affectionate to his father, who seems to enjoy it. He is working well in school and has a boyfriend for the first time. In the pool we have a "secret" rendezvous under water, where we meet and shake hands. That is only to be used if there are strangers about. After swimming, he insists that I comb my hair as he does. It was at this time that Lance exclaimed, "Think of all the time I wasted in my mother's belly!"

One day Lance comes into my house and says, "Let's not swim today, let's go upstairs and play with Barbie." I follow him and he plays silently that Barbie falls and faints and sleeps and bangs Ken. He volunteers that he likes to play with Barbie when he does not feel well. I ask repeatedly what went wrong and he says nothing is wrong, or refuses to answer. The next day, as he continues to play with Barbie, he tells me mournfully and tearfully that his dog Muffet was killed by a car yesterday and he saw it. He keeps on repeating, "But she was so young, she was so young!" I tell him that it is hard for dogs to learn about cars, but boys can and they can be careful and they do not die young, etc. We draw the accident, and Lance draws a picture of himself crying. At home he dictates a letter to me: "I love my cat and my mom and dad and sis and my dog Muffet got dead and I loved Muffet and that is the end of Muffet." His mother reports he cries at night about Muffet. He tells me he dreamed his mother and father were dead and they were buried right next to Muffet in the garden. He went to see how they were, so he dug them up and there they were, playing checkers!

For ten days he plays a great deal with Barbie again. His mother tells me that once when he cried he said he wished he was inside her as when he was a little baby. His mother is quite worried about his regression and remarks that he has again been noticing the shade of lipstick and earrings she has been wearing. She also admits to me that she always felt sorry for boys because they seemed frailer than girls. Suddenly one day Lance runs off to the garden, undresses, and dives into the pool. He asks me to give him a "bronco-buster" ride on the rubber raft, "but don't be dangerous, Dr. Greenson." This is soon forgotten and he is a happy little seal again.

Lance starts to go to a day summer camp for boys and girls and loves it. He likes to hike and shoot guns and play darts and do "artistry." He is delighted to be in the seven-year-old group of boys, even though he is six and a half. We talk about the anatomical differences between men and boys and women and girls. (He sees lots of nakedness in the camp.) After our discussion he says, "You forgot one thing. Girls and ladies have one extra rib." His mother reports he hit her one day and for the first time said, "I hate you." She replied, "Go ahead and hate me, but don't hit." Lance appears for his last hour before the summer break all dressed up and proud, in a cowboy suit, complete with cowboy hat and high cowboy boots, which he loves to stamp about in. We spend the hour practicing all our "special" water tricks. As he dresses, Lance asks me how many days there are in a month and will I write to him; and he bashfully gives me a photo of himself which I can keep. He says he hopes I shall not forget how to swim, and I tell him not to worry, that I shall not change. We march out to the car together like Marine cowboys, and Lance stamps his cowboy boots much louder than I.

Summary and Formulations

Lance lived in a family constellation which can be condensed to the following: his mother loved him possessively and was in overly close contact with him in a tactile sense, visually and emotionally. She hated and disrespected her husband and men in general. Lance's father was unloved and despised by his wife; he was afraid of her, was a failure in his work which he disliked, and was absent from home a great deal. Lance's sister was no serious rival for his mother and was more attached to the father.

This situation led to problems in Lance's development which can best be understood by following some of the ideas of Jacobson (1964), Greenacre (1958), Mahler (1958), and Winnicott (1953). Lance developed difficulty in certain aspects of the process of individuating himself from his mother. Although he could develop a self representation as distinct from object representations, this broke down in his attempt to establish a realistic gender identity. For Lance, loving was equated with becoming, with some primitive form of identification and imitation. Some of his activities had the quality of "as if" activities, magical fantasies based on the idea that if I imitate mother, I will become her (Jacobson, 1964, p. 43). The overgratification by the mother kept Lance fixated to oral pleasures derived from eating, tactile, temperature, muscle, visual, auditory, and kinesthetic stimuli. The relative absence of frustration and rivalry helped keep obscure the boundaries between himself and his mother. The lack of a loving and loved father interfered with his opportunity for identification and identity formation. The tactile and visual overexposure to his mother's body helped confuse his gender identity (Greenacre, 1958, p. 617). It seems to me that just as the girl has a special problem in establishing object relations by having to change the gender of her love object, so the boy has a special problem in building a gender identity by having to change the original object of his identification.

Lance's transvestite behavior was a means of preserving a tie to his mother and in conflict with the reality testing he was capable of in other areas of his life. He shifted his oral desires from his mother's body to her clothes, to a partial identification (A. Freud, 1965, p. 206). It was a failure of individuation and a defense against separation anxiety. The wearing of women's clothes was a transitional activity, a compromise between narcissism and reality testing, between inside and outside (Winnicott, 1953). The play with the girl doll is a similar phenomenon —the doll is partly mother and partly himself. Only when Lance progressed did the doll become Barbie, a completely external object.

It seemed to me that the transvestite behavior can be best understood in this child if we regard the clothes as representing the mother's skin. His loving concern, touching, caressing, and looking at women's clothes indicates this clearly. It fits in with the mother's constant tactile contact with the boy. Lance was reluctant to give up this source of satisfaction and security because he was permitted to indulge himself on this level far too long and he had difficulty in finding the path to satisfactions on higher maturational levels. Whenever he became instinctually excited or anxious, he retreated to this haven. The mother's clothes were to him what the pouch of the mother kangaroo is to the baby kangaroo. He runs back under the warm skin covering which protects him from harm and gives tactile and temperature pleasures. Furthermore, he can keep his head outside so that he can be oriented to reality and leave when he is satisfied and safe. I would speculate that a pouch fantasy is also present in Lance's mother.

Thus far the therapy seems to be successful because I presented myself to the boy as a male figure who obviously liked him and also liked being male. Since I was liked and respected by the mother, I became a figure worthy of identification as well as a rival to contend with by identification.[2] I was apparently not afraid of women nor of instincts, and Lance gradually dared to learn belatedly the difference between loving and becoming. I taught him things which were illuminating, pleasurable, and security-giving, all of which seems to have encouraged his identification with me and then with his father. It should be noted that as the therapies of the mother and son have progressed, Lance's father has achieved a more respected and active place in the family, which has also given the boy a further incentive for becoming male.

[2] For a somewhat different formulation, see chapter 19, where the case of Lance is discussed further.

19

Disidentifying from Mother

Its Special Importance for the Boy

(1968)

THE EARLY PSYCHOANALYTIC LITERATURE stressed the special problems the little girl has to overcome in order to achieve a satisfactory sex life and the capacity to love. The female child must work through two important conflictual areas from which the male is spared. She must shift her major erogenous zone from the clitoris to the vagina and must renounce the mothering person as her primary love object and turn to the father and men (Freud, 1925c, 1931, 1933, 1940). The purpose of this presentation is to focus attention on a special vicissitude in the normal psychological development of the boy which occurs in the preoedipal years. I am referring to the fact that the male child, in order to attain a healthy sense of maleness, must replace the primary object of his identification, the mother, and must

---

Presented at the 25th International Psycho-Analytical Congress, Copenhagen, July 1967. First published in *International Journal of Psycho-Analysis*, 49:370-374, 1968.

identify instead with the father. I believe the difficulties inherent in this additional step of development, from which girls are exempt, are responsible for certain special problems in the man's gender identity, his sense of belonging to the male sex.[1]

The girl, too, must disidentify from mother if she is to develop her own unique sense of self, but her identification with mother *helps* her establish her femininity. It is my contention that men are far more uncertain about their maleness than women are about their femaleness. I believe women's certainty about their gender identity and men's insecurity about theirs are rooted in their early identification with the mother.

I am using the term "disidentify" in order to sharpen my discussion about the complex and interrelated processes which occur in the boy's struggle to free himself from the early symbiotic fusion with mother. It plays a part in the development of his capacity for separation-individuation (Mahler, 1963, 1965). The male child's ability to disidentify will determine the success or failure of his later identification with his father. These two phenomena, disidentifying with mother and counteridentifying with father, are interdependent and form a complementary series. The personality and behavior of mother and father play an important and circular role in the outcome of these developments (Mahler and La Perriere, 1965).

I became alerted to the possibility of some special difficulty in the formation of the male's gender identity from a variety of clinical experiences. I have been working for some years in a research project at the University of California at Los Angeles studying transsexuals, people who wish to undergo surgery in order to change their anatomical sex. These patients are normal biologically, and are not psychotic; but they are convinced that they belong mentally and emotionally to the opposite sex. (Incidentally, they abhor homosexuality.[2]) On the basis of the prevalence of women's penis envy and men's contempt of women in

[1] For a more detailed discussion of the sexual development of boys and girls, especially as it relates to the concepts of masculinity and femininity, see Greenson (1966e, 1967c).

[2] See chapter 14 for a striking example.

our society, I had expected that most of the transsexual patients would be women wanting to become men. Instead, the study of 100 cases over a nine-year period revealed that between two-thirds and three-quarters were men hoping to become women (Stoller, 1964b). Similar studies by others indicate an even higher ratio (Pauly, 1965; Benjamin, 1966).

These patients are a very select and small group and perhaps not a reliable indicator of the male's greater discontent with his gender identity. The fact that transvestism is almost exclusively a male disease and more widespread then commonly believed is a more impressive testimonial for man's dissatisfaction with maleness and his wish to be a female. Furthermore, my own clinical experience with relatively healthy neurotics in psychoanalysis also points in the same direction. It is true that my female patients envy men in a variety of ways, particularly their possession of a penis, as well as their greater social, economic, and political advantages. However, I am impressed by the fact that on an earlier, more deeply unconscious level, my male patients harbor an intense envy of the female, particularly the mother (see also Jacobson, 1950). Each sex is envious of the opposite sex; but the male's more covert envy underneath his external façade of contempt seems to be particularly destructive in regard to his gender identity (Bettelheim, 1954; Greenson, 1966e, 1967c, 1968).

I can illustrate this point by the following material. My men patients frequently reveal a history of putting on some female undergarment in their masturbatory activities as a sign of their fantasy of being a woman. I do not recall any female patient describing anything analogous. This may well be related to the fact that fetishism is also almost 100 percent a male disease. Even neurotic women who imagine they are enacting male, phallic activities in the sexual act usually visualize themselves as women with a penis, not as men. (The overt "butch" homosexual is a special problem and beyond the limits of this paper.)

It is my clinical impression that the dread of homosexuality in the neurotic, which is at bottom the fear of losing one's gender identity, is stronger and more persistent in men than in women (chapter 14). Observations of the current social scene[3] also demonstrate that men are far more uncertain about their sense of maleness than women are of their femininity. Women may doubt their attractiveness, but they are quite sure of their femaleness (Mead, 1949). Women feel at their most feminine in the company of the opposite sex, whereas men feel at their most masculine in the presence of men.

I believe that envy is one of the main driving forces in man's wish to be a woman and originates in the early envy all children feel toward the mother. The Kleinians have attempted to explain this on the basis of the infant's envy of the mother's joy- and security-giving breast (Klein, 1957). Although I do not deny that this occurs, this explanation neglects other important factors which contribute to the *difference* in the envy of men and women.

The general clinical findings sketched above were the starting point for my speculations about the role of the boy's early identification with the mother and the importance of his ability to disidentify from her. In my work with a "transsexual-transvestite" five-and-a-half year old boy, Lance, I had an opportunity to observe the problem of disidentifying at first hand (chapter 18).

This lively, intelligent, well-oriented boy was highly disturbed in two major interrelated areas of his development. In the first place, he had not made that step in the maturational process which enables one to distinguish loving someone from identifying with someone. As a consequence, he was consumed by the wish to be a girl, he acted and dressed as a girl. I have

---

[3] One of the most striking changes consists in the blurring of the differences between the two sexes. This is apparent in dress, behavior, and the pursuit of careers. Such changes are rooted in historical and cultural influences. Borgese (1963) has pointed out that in collectivist states, in industrial areas, there is a definite decrease in the differences between men and women. Socialization seems to feminize men and masculinize women. Collectivist states like Russia, China, and Israel (in the kibbutz) play down the differences between the sexes and tend to treat them as equals. Whatever the cultural and social causes of such changing roles, they invariably have an impact on the psychological life of both sexes (Greenson, 1966e).

previously described how Lance dressed up his Barbie doll as a princess and went to a ball. When I followed the princess and told her how beautiful she was and that I wanted to dance with her, etc., Lance finally said to me, "Go ahead, you can be the princess." I replied, "I don't want to *be* the princess, I want to dance with her." Lance was baffled. I repeated this several times until he permitted me to dance with the princess. He watched this, puzzled and upset.

Shortly after this episode, Lance no longer referred to the Barbie doll as "I" or "we" but only as "she." Soon thereafter he rarely played with Barbie and when he did, there was a sexual element in the play which had not been present before. He then developed a strong identification with me and later with his father. For the first time he manifested behavior which indicated he was unmistakeably in the phallic oedipal phase.

I believe that Lance's central problem was his inability to complete his separation-individuation from his mother in certain respects. Lance's mother was extremely possessive of him and gratified him excessively in terms of tactile and visual contact. In addition, the mother hated and disrespected her husband and men in general. (I was an exception.) The father was afraid of his wife and a failure in his work. He was absent from the home a great deal and had little if any pleasurable contact with the boy. As a result, although Lance was able to develop a self representation as distinct from object representations, this failed when it came to establishing a realistic gender identity.

It is precisely in this area that I believe the boy's capacity to disidentify himself from his mother is of paramount importance. The girl can acquire feminine characteristics by means of her identification with the mother. Her femaleness is practically assured if she is raised by a female mothering person. The boy has a more difficult and far less certain path to pursue. He must disidentify with mother and identify with a male figure if he is to develop a male gender identity. Greenacre (1958, p. 618) hints at this point when she states that women seem to show more frequent but *less gross disturbances* in this area. Jacobson (1964) also raises the question of why women do not develop more identity problems than men. I believe that both authors are touching on the same issues I am trying to delineate—the boy's special problem of disidentifying from mother and forming a counteridentification with father.

I would like to pursue this last issue in a little more detail. I believe that we would all agree that in early infancy both girls and boys form a primitive symbiotic identification with the mothering person on the basis of the fusion of early visual and tactile perception, motor activity, introjection, and imitation (Freud, 1914d, 1921, 1923a, 1925c; Fenichel, 1945; Jacobson, 1964). This results in the formation of a symbiotic relationship to the mother (Mahler, 1963). The next step in the development of ego functions and object relations is the differentiation of self representation from object representations. Mahler (1957), Greenacre (1958), Jacobson (1964), and others have elucidated how different forms of identification play a central role in this transition as maturation makes it possible to progress from total identification to selective identifications. The capacity to differentiate between similarities and contrasts results in the capacity to discriminate between inside and outside and ultimately the self and the nonself. In this process, the child learns he is a distinct entity, different from mother, dog, table, etc. However, he also gradually learns by identification to behave and perform certain activities like the mothering person, such as speaking, walking, eating with a spoon, etc. These activities are not duplications, but are modified in accordance with the child's constitution and his mental and physical endowment. The style of his behavior and activities are further changed by his later identifications with others in the environment. What we call identity seems to be the result of the synthesis and integration of different isolated self representations (Jacobson, 1964; Spiegel, 1959).

I would now like to focus on one aspect of these developments—the development of the gender identity. In chapter 14 I suggested three factors which play a role in this process: (a) awareness of the anatomical and physiological structures in oneself, according to Greenacre (1958), primarily the face and the genitals; (b) the assignment to a specific gender, done by the parents and other important social figures, in accordance with the overt sexual structures; (c) a biological force which seems to be present at birth. To verify these points, I can state that in our Gender Identity Clinic, I have seen boys who behaved completely boyishly despite the fact that they were born without a penis and no visible testes. They were treated like boys by their parents and this seemed to be decisive. We have seen many pseudohermaphrodites in this clinic who live their life in a biologically false gender role without any manifest doubts about their identity. Yet we also know that in some children there seems to be a biological force which is strong enough to counteract their overt anatomy and the parents' assignment of sex (Stoller, 1964b). This is rare and does not represent a typical outcome. Clinically, all three factors interact to establish one's sense of gender.

I believe that a fourth factor must be added, in the boy, to those already mentioned. I am referring to the disidentifying from mother and his developing a new identification with the father. This is a special problem because the boy must attempt to renounce the pleasure and security-giving closeness that identification with the mothering person affords, and he must form an identification with the less accessible father. The outcome will be determined by several elements. The mother must be willing to allow the boy to identify with the father figure. She can facilitate this by genuinely enjoying and admiring the boy's boyish features and skills and must look forward to his further development along this line (A. Freud, 1965).

The other vital component in this switch of identification in the boy consists of the motives the father offers for identifying with him. Lance did not identify with his father because his father was a frightened, joyless man. There was little motive for identifying with him. The essential therapeutic part of his work with me was his eagerness to identify with me because I seemed to him to enjoy life and to be unafraid. Later on, when his father improved as a result of his own psychotherapy, Lance did identify with the father. I should add that part of the motivation to identify with the father stems from the mother's love and respect for the father. Identification based on other grounds seems to be less reliable (A. Freud, 1965).

The questions which now arise are the following: What happens to the original identification with mother, after the boy has identified with father? Does the identification with mother disappear, its place taken by the new identification? Does it remain but become latent because it is superseded in importance by the identification with father? How much of the boy's identification with the father is a counteridentification, actually a "contra"-identification, a means of counteracting the earlier identification? Is it not in this area where we can find an answer to why so many men are uncertain about their maleness? Perhaps it is the shaky basis of their identification with the father, their contraidentification, which makes them so reactively contemptuous of women and so envious, unconsciously. Perhaps the mothers of fifty years ago who dressed their boys in girls' clothes intuitively recognized that one had to gratify each phase of the child's development in order to insure his future maturation. By satisfying the boy's early need to identify with mother, he was better able to make the later step of identifying with father.

I realize I have raised more questions than I have answered, but I hope future work and discussion will bring greater clarification to this important area.

20

The Use of Dream Sequences for Detecting Errors of Technique

A Clinical Study

(1968)

QUITE RECENTLY I was chairman of a workshop dealing with errors in technique and how one deals with them. I asked the fifteen participants to come prepared for discussion of a recent error in their own technique. When the meeting was called to order, I asked if anyone would like to start. Complete silence followed. I tried to encourage someone to start by stating that I make some kind of error in technique practically every day. Again, complete silence followed. So I decided I would describe the most recent error I had made, which was the day before the meeting. This was followed by a brisk discussion, after which I again asked whether anyone would like to recall their own errors. At least half the persons were now ready to present their own errors. Most analysts are

Presented to the Western New England Psychoanalytic Society and Institute in 1968 and to the Washington Psychoanalytic Society in 1971. This paper is here published for the first time.

reluctant not only to present their own case material but seem to be afraid to reveal any errors they might have made. Once they are assured that all competent analysts make mistakes, then they admit it verbally, but rarely will they do it in writing.

Freud, on the other hand, used the Dora case (1905a) to illustrate that his failure to pick up the transference was the main reason for Dora's abrupt and premature termination. Ferenczi, too, was one of the few pioneers who had no trouble in revealing his errors (1919a, 1925). Later, Little (1951), Gitelson (1954), Glover (1955), and Winnicott (1955) began to write about errors of their own.

I have found that recognition of my own errors, no matter what the source, was immeasurably helpful in getting over stubborn resistances and stalemates. In fact, I would say that if, over a long period of time, a patient has not perceived and mentioned *my* errors in technique, then I believe a subtle resistance is going on undetected by the patient and me. Once the error or errors are detected and handled effectively, it lends a fresh impetus to stalemated situations. Also, it sheds new light on repetitious behavior of analyst and patient, and it reveals, above all, an undiscovered part of the patient-therapist relationship. I would like to demonstrate how dream interpretations, especially dreams on successive nights, can highlight those errors.

Clinical Material

Mr. Z. is one of the patients I have mentioned many times in my book, *The Technique and Practice of Psychoanalysis* (1967a), and also in chapter 16. I shall give only a brief history in order to make the clinical material understandable.

Mr. Z.'s original complaints were difficulty in sustaining an intimate relationship to a woman despite good sexual potency, no friendships with men of any real depth, a vague but persistent feeling of sadness and inadequacy, and a sleeping problem. Mr. Z. worked hard in his analysis with me. He was an intelligent and cultured man, was emotionally involved in the analysis, cooperative despite stubborn resistances, imaginative and unusually honest. He found free association very difficult, admitted skipping certain painful associations, struggled to analyze his resistances and to understand and work with interpretations. He was also a good dreamer and, I believe, we both enjoyed working together despite many painful periods of analysis.

The essential history in Mr. Z.'s case was that his mother and father divorced when he was about two and a half years old, at which time his mother left him for some six months to take a trip around the world. The mother remarried when the patient was three and a half years old and gave birth to three children. The stepfather was a warm, intelligent, but ineffectual man who eventually came to be despised by the patient's mother and her entire family.

Mr. Z. was in analysis for almost four years when we decided, by mutual consent, to interrupt his analysis. On the surface most of his symptoms had improved somewhat and Mr. Z. had a rare opportunity to go into a business partnership which would require traveling for long periods of time. Later on, in his second analysis, we both realized that an unconscious and unresolved stalemate had developed in the psychoanalytic situation. The fact that I had agreed to the interruption played an important part in our subsequent difficulties. I had replicated what his parents had done, that is, emotional and physical abandonment.

During his separation from the analysis, he fell into the habit of regularly taking a strong barbiturate, even though it proved to be relatively ineffectual. While he could easily fall asleep, he would awaken after two or three hours and then would remain awake the rest of the night. On good nights or with the sleeping pills, he might doze off an hour or two around daybreak. During the waking intervals he was obsessed by two sets of fantasies of self-destruction which he imagined in great detail. The most prevalent was the fantasy of being hanged and the other of being shot. These two fantasies recurred regularly with no variation in the sleepless interval. They were unpleasant but were not accompanied by consciously felt great anxiety. He awoke tired, exhausted, thickheaded, irritable, and depressed after a sleepless night.

I had been able to point out that he dated the onset of his insomnia to shortly after he had completed a tour of duty as a Naval officer and returned to civilian life. It was then that he realized his mother would not take him back into their home, nor would his uncles take him into the family business.

In the first analysis, we had come to understand that one of his basic neurotic conflicts stemmed from his reactions to the divorce of his parents. On the one hand he felt he now had his mother all to himself, he was rid of a hated rival; but he also felt he had been the cause of the divorce, an intruder who had destroyed his parents' marriage. On the other hand, he felt responsible for getting rid of his beloved father, and that it was his innate badness which had made his mother leave him for her long journey. Throughout his life, Mr. Z. suffered from enormous envy of his grandfather's sons, his uncles, and he was also jealous and envious of his mother's attachment to her father. As a boy, Mr. Z. felt warmly toward his stepfather, but later jealousy and contempt predominated. In recent years, the patient had become aware of great love and hatred for his mother. Above all, he could not bear his irrational dependence on this extremely narcissistic woman.

The hours which I shall report occurred five months after we had resumed analysis. I had repeatedly interpreted to the patient, in the hours preceding the ones I shall describe in detail, that the taking of the sleeping pills was a resistance to the analysis. On the one hand, these pills were a form of magic which would dispel the insomnia without analysis; on the other, they were a means of blotting out my interpretations. The sleeping pills were an attempt to circumvent thoughts and feelings which he had when he lay awake, apart from his usual obsessions. They hid his fantasies both hateful and loving concerning, above all, his mother and me, who he believed were the bringers or the disturbers of his sleep.

The patient began the hour by telling me that he had not

taken any sleeping pills. He did not sleep and he agreed that when he did not take the sleeping pills he was more aware of his fantasies. He had slept from about 10 o'clock until midnight and was more or less awake from then until 6 in the morning. Then he dozed off and he did dream. He felt exhausted and found it very difficult to work. It had been a most unpleasant night. During the night, he had felt great anger and resentment toward me and wondered, "Why, in the world, do I listen to this man?" This went on in various forms all through the night. (This was something new because ordinarily he had self-destructive fantasies at night.) At 6 o'clock in the morning he was tempted to take a sleeping pill, but did not. At any rate, his workday was all but wasted from extreme fatigue.

Mr. Z. now reported the following dreams, or parts of dreams, he was not sure which:

> I was in an apartment and my mother was some place around. I opened a closet and found a hatbox and in it was a man's Borsolino hat. It was odd. It was too large for me and had a very big brim and a very high crown. I fiddled with it to get it into shape, but it still did not fit me. In the next part of the dream there was also a hat, but this was a kind of old-fashioned stovepipe hat. Strangely enough, from the rear there was a capelike fabric hanging down . . . like they wear in the Foreign Legion. . . . I put it on and it changed its form. Now it became an overseas cap, like they wore during World War II, made of soft material. . . . Somewhere in all of this there is reference made to a man who was the biggest manufacturer of artificial food that he sends to Europe or Africa.

I was silent, which is my customary way of dealing with dreams when a patient has been in treatment a long time. Mr. Z. then began to associate:

> The hat immediately reminds me of something sexual and probably has to do with penises or something like that. The Borsolino hat, I recall, my grandfather once came back

from Europe with one. I remember that my stepfather was so pleased that it could be crumpled but never lose its shape. . . . Last night I thought about the Navy. All those years I lived with my mother and stepfather were unpleasant. The only time I ever had a good time in my life was when I went to college in Illinois and the years I spent in the Navy. [Pause.] I am annoyed with you. I have a feeling that you are responsible for my not sleeping. You made me give up the sleeping pills and that makes me worse. I am prepared not to sleep, but I am also prepared not to do free association. I would rather do no talking and no associating. [Pause.]

I'd rather do anything than relate to you. . . . During the night I did not get any indication as to why I do not sleep. Nothing comes to my mind during the night. In the first analysis, I felt I had sacrificed everything and now I just don't want to do it. I know it is irrational. This was one of the first nights in years of my not taking sleeping pills. They do help, those pills. I have such hostility now. You took something away and I get nothing back. That's what I think. Also, you don't know what you are doing. I thought I would work a few hours and then come home during the day for a nap, but I didn't. I just can't sit at my desk. I did go out and talk to some customers but all I felt was irritability, anger, and depression. [Pause.]

At this point I intervened and said the following: "You are enraged with me for suggesting that your analysis would go better if you gave up taking sleeping pills. You question the correctness of this decision and, in general, you wonder if I know what I am doing. In some way your dream seems to talk of something similar. You are trying on a hat that does not fit you. It does not even seem to belong to you. What occurs to you to that?" (I was thinking that sleeping without the sleeping pills meant sleeping like a grown man, not like a little boy who needs pills or milk, etc. On a phallic level it could mean: I am too small to get sexual satisfaction, etc.)

The patient associates:

This makes me think of European hats. My stepfather had
eight or nine of them. The whole closet was full of them. In
later years, he had one made for him with a low crown and
a very narrow brim. He looked crazy and he kept getting
worse all the time. You know, I eventually hated that man.
After adolescence I couldn't stand him. There was his constant invasion of my privacy with his nudity. [The stepfather had the habit of entering the living room completely
naked, at odd times, which repulsed his wife and enraged
the siblings.] I couldn't stand him. He also once had a high
hat that folded up which he wore with tails. I think he wore
that two or three times. I don't remember. I liked to play
with it when I was a kid. That I do remember. The other
hat with the fabric hanging down reminds me of the French
Foreign Legion. I was stationed in Morocco for a time
during World War II and I met a French army captain
while there. I befriended him. I became an Honorary
Private First Class in the French Colonial Army. This captain and I became very friendly. Once when I went to visit
him I found everyone with a long face. He had been shot;
killed, instantly, by a Senegalese guard. There was a big
funeral. I liked him. He was a quiet man; silent but warm
and friendly. [The patient was quiet.]

At this point, I felt there was too much material and I did
not know which path to pursue. First, there was his resentment
of me for taking away his sleeping pills; then the dream saying
he tried using his stepfather's "sexual" hats; and now there was
the issue of a friendly captain being killed by a guard who was
supposed to have been guarding him. Actually, in retrospect, I
believe I was unconsciously upset by the notion of the Senegalese
guard who killed the captain. I then asked the patient, "A
manufacturer of artificial food which is sent to the underdeveloped countries?" I always make a point of bringing up a
bizarre issue in a dream which does not seem to fit in with the

major context of the dream. Perhaps this may clarify a complex and complicated situation.

Mr. Z. associated about a man who used to be a former boss of his. He had read something recently about artificial food being manufactured for the underdeveloped countries of the world. It suddenly occurred to him that there was a company that did this in Santa Monica. Pause. (I live in Santa Monica and he came to see me at my home where I work in the late afternoon.)

I intervened and said something like this: "You are furious with me because I take away the synthetic sleeping pills. Your anger with *me* keeps you awake and this is something new. Usually, when you don't sleep, you are full of self-destructive fantasies. This time you are loaded with hostility toward me, even going so far as to question if I know what I am doing. I took something valuable away from you and all you get is sleeplessness and an irritability which lasts all day. It is new for you to feel and express verbally your hatred for me. I wonder if you don't feel that I have become a dangerous person to you? By getting you to stop taking the sleeping pills, I may get to know too much about you. Perhaps I may hurt you like the Senegalese guard who killed the French captain he was supposed to take care of."

The patient responded to this by saying: "I am not listening to you. I just feel angry. I am not really listening. [Pause.] I just have the feeling that I would like to leave. I don't want to work with the dream. I don't want to be here. I just want to leave!"

I said: "It seems clear to me that at this point you don't really want to work in the analysis. You don't really want to do free association, to expose the real fears and desires which you have and which you have hidden from yourself and me for so many years with the sleeping pills. You have the feeling that I am going to betray and destroy you. I ask for something new. For you to give up taking the sleeping pills. You react as though I took something valuable away from you."

Mr. Z. responded, sarcastically, "You always have such explanations! They seem so intelligent, but, I must tell you, I don't understand what you are saying. You can repeat it again and again, but I still won't listen and I won't comprehend. Maybe you are right, but you just don't touch me." Silence. End of hour.

Since this was my last hour of the day, I had time to notice my reactions and reflections. I felt dissatisfied and disgruntled toward the end of the hour, and after the hour. The dream and the associations had seemed so promising that I was annoyed with him and myself for not getting more out of the hour. I was so eager to pursue the unconscious contents, the latent dream thoughts, I had failed to recognize that perhaps he wanted to provoke my anger. I only felt discontented and angry with myself.

The next day Mr. Z. came a few minutes early. He started the hour by saying:

Last night was just the same as the night before. I slept until 2 in the morning and then I didn't sleep at all after that. In addition, I felt irritable. I think you were saying to me, yesterday, that I am a fraud. There was an irritability in your voice. I feel that I am being jabbed hostilely not just helpfully. You argue with me when you make an interpretation. You try to degrade and to humiliate me. I know this is not quite true. At least, now I feel it isn't true. But then, while you were talking to me, I felt, "Who needs you. The hell with you. Good-bye!" [Pause.]

By the way, I had a dream last night or early this morning. I was walking outside a building. It was an odd combination of a residence and barn and it wasn't well maintained. It was kind of shabby. Through the window I could hear someone talking inside. I was outside. It lasted for several minutes. I thought to myself, "That man should be aware he is being overheard!"

[I kept quiet and the patient associated as follows:] The voice in the dream was like a man I visited yesterday afternoon, a manager of a company with whom I used to do business, but I don't anymore. [Me?] While I was there he had to speak on the phone and I noted his false laughter. "Such fraudulent behavior that goes on in business," I thought to myself. [Does this refer to me, him, and our psychoanalytic situation?] This reminds me of what you said yesterday. By taking the sleeping pills I am hiding certain wishes and fears of my own. In a sense, I am fraudulent. [Pause.] I suppose the overhearing of the man must have to do with my mother and stepfather quarreling. [Notice how he tries to skip over his angry feelings toward me.] Especially that one quarrel when I heard them talk about divorce. After the last hour I was very upset and distraught. It's hard to tell what is real in my feelings and what isn't. But I do feel that when I get angry with you and resistant, you get annoyed with me. I do feel that you are trying to degrade me, although later, I know this isn't true. [Now he became more courageous.] I was thinking about this when I couldn't sleep last night. When I don't take the sleeping pills, I must admit, I do have more thoughts. I do want to remind you, though, that when I did take the pills, I was able to remember my dreams. But it is getting very hard for me to do my work at business. I just can't go on being a failure in business! [Pause.]

I intervened: "You are full of resentment toward me and you are aware of it. There is also a part of you that recognized I *was* angry with you yesterday. Many times before, you have felt I was annoyed with you or that I had humiliated you with an interpretation. Yesterday, I think you were right! I did feel some annoyance with you when you told me you weren't listening to me, you found me incomprehensible, etc. Now, interestingly enough, in the dream you felt the man should have been aware he was being overheard. You were overhearing my anger and you retaliated by changing my office at home into a shabby combination of house and barn."

Mr. Z. burst into laughter and, after a slight pause, went on:

I must say that I have changed! I was never able to tell you so openly how angry I felt and, also, that I felt you were angry. I know that when I get angry I develop a cutting edge to my voice. I know you don't intend to humiliate me, but, the point is, it does feel humiliating to me. [We are similar?] Your interpretations are of no help to me when I am so angry. I have the feeling that until I straighten out my relationship with you I am never going to make any improvement by interpretations alone, or am I contradicting myself? I just have the feeling that your interpretations are of no meaning when I have such hostility. [Pause.]

I said, "I think there is something true in this. I said too much to you yesterday. I should have pointed out how resentful and afraid you are of my asking you to stop taking the sleeping pills, and let it go at that. I tried to tell you more and then I became annoyed when you refused to listen and this complicated everything. In some way you realized that I tried to explain too much and then, I think, you started to degrade me by not listening."

Mr. Z. responded: "I am not at all aware of degrading you. I admit, though, at times I had the feeling that you didn't know what you were doing."

I added: "The dream you had about the combination house-and-barn, which was shabby, was my house which is a combination of home and office. Furthermore, you felt it was shabby and in bad repair—all of which I think is your attempt to degrade me in retaliation for your fantasy of being humiliated by me. All of this began when I suggested to you it might be helpful if you gave up the sleeping pills. You felt I was taking something valuable from you."

The patient went on:

Yes, the sleeping problem is a bitch! [Notice the gender of the word bitch.] I do believe you are right about the sleeping pills. I am aware of things coming up. You used to tell me I don't just have self-destructive impulses but murderous impulses in my fantasies when I don't sleep. Now I think you must be right! I also notice that at night I tend to think about all the errors I have committed during the day, and then I get frightened. What will the bank do to me; or my grandfather who looks after my financial affairs; or the accountant; and so it goes, on and on. I imagine I have a similar feeling to them as I have to you.

I intervened and said: "Yes. I think you are full of hostility and self-reproach which you project onto me and which makes me untrustworthy and unreliable. Then you feel I am going to hurt you, kill you, humiliate you, or treat you poorly in some form or other, which then interferes with your ability to relate openly to me and to do free association."
Mr. Z. said:

Yes. I do have the feeling that if I am going to be completely open with you, you will abandon or humiliate me. It is probably related to this whole business of not being able to sleep, that is, to give in as you say, to let something happen, to do free association. It always means I am going to be abandoned or I am going to lose somebody. I can't imagine liking someone without the fear of losing them. I must have a feeling of liking you and then I get the fear of loss and abandonment, but I have never been so miserable before as I have been lately. You told me once that I would have to go through a depression to get well. I couldn't go on avoiding it. Maybe that's what you mean. [He paused and said:] By the way, when I came early one day I did overhear your wife on the phone. She spoke very loudly and I wondered why she did. She has a very nice voice, though, not a harsh voice like some women have. I hate coming early and over-hearing things in your house. It is terribly embarrassing to me. [I have no waiting room in my house and if the patient comes early the housekeeper opens the door and he is invited to sit in the living room which is adjacent to my treatment room.]

I said: "Yes. I know you hate it on the one hand, yet, I do think you also like it. After all, the manufacturer of the artificial food is me. I am manufacturing some kind of artificial food which I am trying to feed you and my home is in Santa Monica. Although you may resent hearing my wife's voice, I think you do like to look into the living room and see what's going on in there."

The patient laughed and said:

You never can tell what lies under the rocks. Yes. I do like your wife's voice. Although it was loud it was very musical. I also like your living room. I think it is done in good taste. I admit it is not the neatest room in the world, but it looks like a room in which people enjoy themselves. The man's voice that I overheard in the dream was like your voice. It was a loud but not a raucous voice.

I intervened at this time and said: "Yes. Your first association to that voice was the businessman you had visited the day before who, you felt, was hypocritical. Again, I think I see how mixed your feelings are toward me. On the one hand, I am the kindly, good, father figure, and then I am also the harsh, raucous, fraudulent businessman. It seems we alternate who is good and who is bad, who is true or fraudulent, and who is competent or incompetent. I think a good deal of it came about because you felt I was annoyed with you yesterday and then came these feelings of degradation and your retaliation against me."

To this, the patient said: "I guess I must give up those sleeping pills. I don't like to do it, but I have to give it up if I am ever going to get anywhere in this analysis. I suppose I must trust you or . . . ."

I interrupted: "It isn't that you *must* give up the sleeping pills or that you *must* trust me. All I can ask of you is to try to analyze what it is that keeps you from free associating, from trusting me, or from sleeping. These are all related and all of this is related to the feeling that somebody is false, fraudulent, a betrayer, like the Senegalese guard who murdered the captain he was supposed to look after. I think this was really the crucial part of the dream in the last hour."

Mr. Z. said: "Yes. It is true. You cannot sleep when you have to be on guard. I suppose you can't sleep when you are in enemy territory."

That was the end of that hour. I felt better after it. I felt it was correct and necessary to acknowledge my inappropriate anger, but I felt that perhaps I was misusing the analytic situation to confess so explicitly, and that I had made too many interpretations. I recovered from this quickly, however, by focusing on the central issue and I talked less. Toward the end of the hour, the patient and I were working effectively.

The next hours I will only present in shorter form, with the aim of demonstrating how the detection and working with errors can uncover new material which can be worked through very effectively.

The next session was a Friday hour. The patient told me that he could not sleep from 2:30 A.M. on, so he did take a pill and wondered if I would be angry. He then told me that he had difficulty in talking and wondered if it was because he had taken pills and I would be disappointed and perhaps angry with him, or whether it was because this was his "Friday hour depression." Right now he was beginning to realize that he had to concentrate more on the analysis and less on his business. He went on talking about his difficulty in talking. Then he continued with what a warm living room I have and that in order to have a good life one must be able to free associate in real life, not just in analysis. This led him to talk about his desire for a relationship with me and how alone he really was. He then talked about his anticipation of rejection which by now he knew was a projection of his own hostilities, in addition to his history of having been rejected in the past.

He cannot really visualize himself married, with a wife and children. It is so hard for him actually to imagine it. "I can't imagine being accepted by a woman. I also can't imagine loving one. No," he corrected himself, "that's not so hard. It's more that I can't imagine a woman loving and accepting me for over a long period of time." This then led him to talk about his mother and the very unsatisfactory relationship he had with her. Then he went on to his fear of doing real association—his fears that I would not or could not accept everything that would come out of him. This led to his idea that what comes out of him is repellent and his recognition that these were his feelings and not mine. "If anything at all comes out of me that is ugly or harmful or hateful, then it seems to me that it will cancel out all your good feelings for me. This is how I felt my mother treated me and I guess I expect the same treatment from you."

This brought him to a new association; namely, that in a previous analysis he used to read a great deal of Kafka which he enjoyed enormously then. He sensed, correctly I might add, that I have never liked Kafka. I had mentioned something to him, probably, that Kafka made me feel uneasy. (There was almost a four-year interval between the two analyses.) He now found reading Kafka to be upsetting and did not like to read him anymore. However, he did want to bring a letter of Kafka's, written to Kafka's father, since it shows very clearly the disturbance in the relationship between the son and father.

I submit this hour as an indication that I had temporarily repaired the error in technique and the patient is once more in a good therapeutic alliance with me, and *we* are working through this material once more.

On the following Monday, Mr. Z. said that he had slept badly in anticipation of having to see me on Monday. After a pause he recalled a dream. He is carrying a dictating machine, one you can use by hand. Somebody was trying to taunt him and tease him by manhandling this machine, but the patient took it away and got it to work. The patient's first association to this was that the dictating machine was one he has in his office, which is very much like the one he sees on my desk. This and other associations led to the idea that I was a dictating machine as well as a dictator. He has to receive my interpretations passively. However, the roles can be reversed in the sense that he has the power to receive or reject my interpretations.

This indicates the continuing struggle with his ambivalence toward me and our therapeutic alliance, which is an essential part of this man's disturbance. Obviously, it has to be worked with. The teasing, taunting, is what he does to me and which, at

times, he feels I do to him. Once again, I believe that these
emotions are essentially a projection and an internalization. The
teasing and taunting are connected with pleasurable and sadistic
feelings, as well as heterosexual and homosexual impulses.
Mother, father and child, and with the room with the dictating
machine.

Wednesday was an important hour, which occurred one
week after the "angry" hour. I believe the patient's ability to
recall his dream, and our working with the dream, indicates that
we have more than made up for the error.

Mr. Z.'s dream: He is in a small room, the size of this room
(pointing to the room in which I see him). It is in an old part of
the city. In order to go to the bathroom, he goes into another
part of the room to lock the door. It has frosted glass and it is
opaque. Just as he is about to do this, a husky Negro working
man enters the room in order to use the phone. The patient lets
him do this. The Negro man makes eight or nine phone calls for
which he paid. This kind of intrusion occurs two or three times.

The associations to this dream are very important because
they repeat themes which were important in Mr. Z.'s analysis.

The patient's associations: "Psychoanalysis and the psychoanalyst are like being seen on the toilet. I would like to shut the
door on every intruder. I feel we should be separated by some
kind of opaque material and perhaps I might find some privacy." (A typical sign of resistance from early in his analysis.)
"The Negro reminds me of my grandfather's chauffeur who was
kind to me when my mother left me when I was two and a half
years old. This also recalls the Senegalese guard who killed when
he should have been guarding. Strange, the Negro had to make
eight or nine calls. . . . And pays for them." (Pause.)

I intervene: "The man who has many calls to make is me."
The patient continues: "Oh, my God! I suppose I am still
envious and jealous of all your other patients. It embarrasses me.
I don't want you in my bathroom. Yet, psychoanalysis demands
it, to be seen on the toilet. . . . You don't demand it, but it is
expected from a grownup. I know I want to run and, yet, I also
want to comply."

My response: "You have two sets of feelings which contradict each other. The last several hours, after giving up the sleeping pills and after recalling the Senegalese guard who killed the captain he was supposed to guard, you have been more ambivalent about doing the analysis and working with me."

Mr. Z. associates: "I really wanted to quit. I would like to show you that I don't need you; but I know better."

I replied: "True. You are no longer the helpless little boy who had to be given enemas and who believed that grownups could read your mind. You are old enough to leave the toilet and the analysis. You can act out your spite or you can realize I want to help you to get rid of the past tortuous fantasies."

The patient associates: "Yes, I have to face the fact that to do analysis properly I have to expose all my toilet fantasies but, and this is a big 'butt' [that's a pun!], I am doing this to help myself; not to torture myself, nor to please you. [Pause.] You cannot make me sleep well when I am on guard or on guard duty. I am no longer in enemy territory. [Pause.] The blacks have their shortcomings, but they also can be very effective, like Ralph Bunche." (Pause.)

I interrupt: "Or like Ralph Greenson."

Summary and Conclusions

I have tried to demonstrate that the detection of errors in my handling of the patient's dreams helped me to understand certain of his chronic and stubborn resistances which interfered with the progress of the analysis. In this instance, the patient and I more or less simultaneously discovered the errors. I am using the word "errors" to include those unfortunate lapses of an analyst's behavior that, if undetected, can play havoc with the psychoanalytic process (see chapter 22 and Greenson, 1967a).

I have tried to show how my subtle but uncontrolled anger, and my making excessive interpretations, could have been damaging. Fortunately, I was disgruntled with my work and on the next day the patient brought in a dream which confirmed my discomfiture. Once I was able to confirm my mistakes, the patient and I began to work enthusiastically on the multiple meanings of such behavior. The two subsequent dreams not only confirmed that we had reestablished a good working alliance, but, I had the distinct impression, that using the mistakes helped us to penetrate the patient's basic neurosis in greater depth than heretofore.

I want to speak briefly about the general area of errors in technique. In order to detect our flaws, we have to rid ourselves of the notion that the "ideal" or "perfect" analyst makes no errors. I believe that every analyst makes errors, be he young or old, a beginner or an experienced training analyst. We need to keep an open mind with no hero and theory worship. We have to accept the fact that every analysis is unfinished and no one knows what is going on within the patient at all times. We are prone to lapses in proper analytic behavior at times as, for example, my anger at Mr. Z. Unrecognized or uncontrolled countertransference reactions are another important source of errors.

I have found it useful frankly to admit all errors, whether they be due to countertransference reactions, faulty interpretations, or shortcomings in my personality and character. I believe it is right to apologize to a patient when the analyst's behavior has been unnecessarily hurtful. I believe the apology for behaving badly should be made before attempting any interpretations. Analyzing before apologizing may be perceived correctly by the patient as an attempt to minimize the analyst's responsibility. Apologizing does not interfere with the therapeutic process.

When I have made errors or lapses in behavior, and either the patient detects them or I have pointed them out, the patient frequently asks about their origin. I do not agree with Little (1951) or Searles (1965) that the patient has a right to know the sources of the analyst's lapses in behavior or other errors. I am willing to apologize for my irrational behavior or my lack of perceptiveness, but their sources are my business. Under such circumstances, I always tell the patient that the analytic situation is unequal. I also add that his knowing too much about my private life would become a burden. I would not misuse my patient as a confessor to expiate my guilt.

There is much more to be said about the detection, source, and management of errors. I wanted to demonstrate in this clinical study how the use of my errors, together with the help of the patient's dreams, not only caused no harm but helped greatly by adding fresh impetus to the working through of the analytic process.

21

The Origin and Fate of New Ideas in Psychoanalysis

(1969)

I N THE FIRST ISSUE of the *International Journal of Psycho-Analysis*, Freud (1917b) contributed a paper, "A Difficulty in the Path of Psycho-Analysis," which I believe is particularly relevant today in understanding the developments in psychoanalysis in the past fifty years. In that essay Freud attempted to demonstrate how psychoanalysis, like other scientific research, has alienated most men by hurting their narcissism, their self-love. He described the three most hurtful blows to human narcissism as follows:

> In the early stages of his researches, man believed at first that his dwelling-place, the earth, was the stationary centre of the universe, with the sun, moon and planets circling around it. In this he was naively following the dictates of his sense-perceptions, for he felt no movement of the earth, and

Presented as the Fourth Freud Anniversary Lecture, the Psychoanalytic Association of New York, May 19, 1969. First published in *International Journal of Psycho-Analysis*, 50:503-515, 1969.

I am very much indebted to Milton Wexler, with whom I discussed many of these ideas. I am also indebted to the generosity of Max Schur, who pointed out pertinent passages in some of Freud's unpublished correspondence.

wherever he had an unimpeded view he found himself in the centre of a circle that enclosed the external world. The central position of the earth, moreover, was a token to him of the dominating part played by it in the universe and appeared to fit in very well with his inclination to regard himself as lord of the world [p. 139f.].

Copernicus and his forerunners put an end to this illusion and proved the earth was much smaller than the sun and moved around that celestial body. That was the *cosmological* blow to man's narcissism.

Freud then went on to define the second narcissistic wound, the *biological* one:

We all know that little more than half a century ago the researches of Charles Darwin and his collaborators and forerunners put an end to this presumption on the part of man. Man is not a being different from animals or superior to them; he himself is of animal descent, being more closely related to some species and more distantly to others [p. 140f.].

The third blow to man's self-love, the *psychological*, Freud considered the most wounding:

Although thus humbled in his external relations, man feels himself to be supreme within his own mind. Somewhere in the core of his ego he has developed an organ of observation to keep a watch on his impulses and actions and see whether they harmonize with its demands. If they do not, they are ruthlessly inhibited and withdrawn [p. 141].

Freud portrayed how illusory this strength was. It is in his neuroses that man is forced to recognize the limits of his ego's powers. Freud then describes for us an imaginary talk to the ego:

You over-estimated your strength when you thought you could treat your sexual instincts as you liked and could utterly ignore their intentions. The result is that they have rebelled and have taken their own obscure paths to escape this suppression; they have established their rights in a manner you cannot approve.... What is in your mind does not coincide with what you are conscious of; whether something is going on in your mind and whether you hear of it, are two different things.... You behave like an absolute ruler who is content with the information supplied him by his highest officials and never goes among the people to hear their voice. Turn your eyes inward, look into your own depths, learn first to know yourself! [p. 142f.]

Freud concludes this paper with the following:

It is thus that psycho-analysis has sought to educate the ego. But these two discoveries—that the life of our sexual instincts cannot be wholly tamed, and that mental processes are in themselves unconscious and only reach the ego and come under its control through incomplete and untrustworthy perceptions—these two discoveries amount to a statement that *the ego is not master in its own house* [p. 143].

Ernest Jones (1920), in an editorial in that same first issue, depicts how mankind uses two main methods of defense against disagreeable truths:

... the first, more obvious, and therefore less dangerous one is direct opposition, the new truths being denied as false and decried as obnoxious; the second, more insidious, and much more formidable one is to acquiesce in the new ideas on condition that their value is discounted, the logical consequences not drawn from them, and their meaning diluted until it may be regarded as 'harmless'.

Jones also mentions that this opposition may not only be displayed by outside antagonists, but may assume subtle forms within psychoanalysis itself.

Reviewing the developments in psychoanalysis during the last fifty years, I have the impression there is much evidence which indicates that similar conflicts concerning their narcissism

have influenced psychoanalysts and have become an important
factor impeding the progress of psychoanalysis. I believe that
unresolved problems with narcissism have resulted in a dearth of
creativity in psychoanalysts and also in the establishment of
separate psychoanalytic "schools." I believe that both of these
developments are interrelated and are obstacles to the further-
ance of new ideas and the advancement of psychoanalytic
knowledge.

Anna Freud (1969) apparently had something similar in
mind when she referred to an *ad hoc* committee of the International Psycho-Analytical Association that was examining the
lack of creativity among analysts today. She also said, "The
analyst's task is not to create ... but to observe, to explore, to
understand, and to explain" (p. 153). I myself have noted how
few new faces appear on our scientific program and that many
papers do not contain new ideas. Above all, I have been impressed and depressed by the observation that applicants for
training often seem to be more creative than the psychoanalysts
who graduate from our training institutes. Perhaps our method
for selecting candidates is faulty, but in all candor, we must also
face the possibility that our training programs and the atmosphere of our institutes may stultify the creative imagination of
our students.

It has often been said by certain enemies of psychoanalysis
that psychoanalysis is dead, but that is the tongue of ignorance
being wagged by envy and wishful thinking. It does seem to be
true, however, that the psychoanalytic movement is no longer
moving very quickly; it is not very lively. I believe that some of
the reasons for this relative inertia are related to factors which
are involved in the origin and fate of new ideas.

In this presentation I shall try to explore some of the rudi-
ments which seem to serve as the source and stimulus for new
ideas in the psychoanalyst. Then I shall attempt to describe what
may happen to the innovation in the psychoanalyst himself and
also in the psychoanalytic community. I shall try to demonstrate
that the forces which make for new ideas contain elements
which may lead to both constructive and destructive develop-

ments in the analyst and in psychoanalytic groups. It should be emphasized that this paper deals in the main with new ideas, not great ideas or the ideas of geniuses. And while I do touch on the origin of such ideas, in the end I shall be more concerned with their ultimate fate.

The Origin of New Ideas

I always prefer to begin a psychoanalytic paper by presenting clinical material, because I have found that clinical data offer the presenter and the reader the clearest basis for understanding and discussion. In this instance, however, there is a dilemma. My major embarrassment is that of necessity I must use my own personal experiences in the analysis of a patient as my source material. I find myself having to reveal my immodesty publicly, for the sake of providing clinical data. I shall present some pertinent highlights from a patient previously described in chapter 3.

In 1946 I began the psychoanalytic treatment of an intelligent and attractive 35-year-old married woman, who sought help primarily because of a sleep disturbance. She was born and raised in Vienna until the age of 18, when she moved to the United States. The first year of psychoanalytic therapy proceeded relatively smoothly and seemed to follow the course one would expect in a hysterical phobic patient who seemed to be fixated to the oedipal, phallic phase of development. Pregenital elements also appeared, but they were fleeting and very much in the background.

In the second year of her treatment, the analysis became stalemated when she fell in love with a young married man. My consistent interpretations of how she was acting out her transference feelings in terms of both libidinal and aggressive oedipal as well as preoedipal strivings did not influence either the patient's material or her behavior. The stalemate was broken one day when the young woman told me a dream and, after a few desultory associations, added almost as an afterthought that she had dreamed the dream in German. She then became silent. Up until this time in the analysis, the patient would often use a German word or phrase when she had difficulty in expressing herself in English. I therefore rather impulsively asked her to tell me the dream again, but this time in German. She balked at this and I tried briefly to analyze this new resistance. This procedure was at best only partially successful, but I told her nevertheless that I wanted to conduct the analysis from now on in German. The patient reluctantly submitted to my request, and to my surprise, the whole course and content of the analysis changed remarkably.

I must add that I myself was somewhat taken aback by my own behavior. I do not ordinarily act so impulsively, not do I make requests of patients before I try thoroughly to analyze their resistances. I had vague misgivings that I was breaking some rule and yet at the same time I felt I was pursuing the right course. For three months we spoke only in German and the patient complied by even dreaming in German. During the first weeks I alternated between feeling that I was making a significant discovery and that I was recklessly pursuing a whim of mine based on some countertransference reaction. I had constantly to battle against a resistance in myself to continue working with her in German. I was often tempted to retreat to the safe and familiar method of working in English, because I felt more comfortable doing so and also the patient was extremely articulate in English. As our work proceeded, however, I became convinced that the patient's material and behavior proved that my new idea was essentially constructive, even if it had originated from my frustration in not being able to influence her addictionlike relationship to her lover.

Let me briefly use some of the changes in the clinical material during the German-speaking phase of the analysis, in order to demonstrate what went on in me. For the patient, in English, a chamber-pot was clean but in German a *Nachttopf* was dirty; it stank and was disgusting to her. I had to translate the clean German *Nachttopf* in me to the dirty *teppelle* (Yiddish) of my childhood. The patient could hardly bring herself to speak of her mother as *Mutti* or, even worse, to say the word *Busen* (bosom). I had to translate these words which, as words, were innocuous to me, into my childhood equivalents, in order to realize that for the patient these words when spoken were felt concretely as things in her mouth. In this way we discovered that she habitually experienced her mother as an *unappetizing* creature.

The patient's material was now predominantly preoedipal and pregenital. This was manifested in a marked change in the transference and I was transformed from primarily a sexual father into a most ambivalent mother figure. Her obsession with her lover shifted to his wife, her fascination with his erect penis changed to an obsessive curiosity about his limp penis and then to women's breasts and their large shiny nipples. As the patient's oral preoccupations were pouring out in German, her interest in her lover and his wife slowly dwindled away. We continued to work further, on breaking down the barrier between her German preoedipal identity and her English oedipal self image. The patient herself had said, "In German I am a scared, dirty child; in English I am a nervous, refined woman." Eventually we were able to speak either language without the language determining the patient's material or behavior.

Using these clinical data from the analysis, I now propose to turn to my subjective reactions, which seem to be of value for studying the origin of new ideas. The first major finding is that the innovation arose when I was in a depressive state of frustration. The analysis was stalemated, my interpretations were futile, and I felt out of touch with what was vital in the goings-on in the patient. If I reconstruct the situation in myself (and I have had many repetitions of it over the ensuing years), I was frequently aware of feeling a mixture of mild depression, anxiety and annoyance. I had felt compelled to go on repeating my interpretations, partly because I knew of nothing better to do. Probably I also felt stubborn because I sensed the patient knew she was frustrating me. I interpreted this to the patient, to no avail. At the same time I kept hoping and searching for some clue that would lead me to a new insight and might rescue both of us from the unhappy impasse.

The patient offered me this clue when, after telling me the dream, she added that she dreamed it in German. My behavior indicates that I was ready for this opening; if anything, too eager. I leaped upon speaking German before I understood what its implications were. I seized upon it because I was tired of repeating my old interpretations. I sensed something was lacking and I was ready to risk doing something new. Yet I was in conflict about it; I had my own resistances to overcome. I could have played it safe and just waited, but the more adventuresome part of me won out.

The change in the patient's material, the alteration in her relationship to me, her ability to work and change despite her hostile feelings, proved to me that the innovation was valuable. As time went on I learned a great many new things, not only about this patient and her mother tongue but also about the origin and function of language in early childhood. I became very preoccupied about the meanings of language and its derivation from the experiences between the mother, the breast, the mouth, and the baby. During this interval many news ideas began to "cook" and to "percolate" in my head, ideas which would rise to the surface as a glimmer or a flash. If I pursued them, however, they turned out to be only "half-baked." I would push them away because they were exciting and distracting and I did not want them to interfere with my therapeutic work with my patient. Left to germinate, these ideas would pop up later, usually clearer and more meaningful, but the newer formulations again produced excitement and elation in me and I often found myself pursuing the validation or elaboration of the new idea instead of focusing on the patient's therapeutic needs. It was necessary to discipline myself to keep what went on in the patient in the center of my attention and to insert new ideas only when they seemed likely to add insight which would benefit the patient therapeutically. This was a difficult period for me because I was constantly torn between indulging myself in the joys of discovery and sticking to my therapeutic task. I experienced varying moods of excitement, exuberance, depression, apathy, and annoyance. Fortunately, some of my new formulations occurred during weekends and holidays or after I had completed the treatment and had begun to write the paper.

I was later surprised to find that my discoveries turned out to contain elements described by other authors. When I began to write "Mother Tongue and the Mother," I began to reread the literature that I felt might be helpful and pertinent. I found that Freud (1905c), Ferenczi (1911), Fenichel (1930), Stengel (1939), Brunswick (1940), Erikson (1946), and Buxbaum (1949) had already touched on many of the ideas I thought I had discovered.

Thus, much of what I had considered a discovery was actually a rediscovery. In a sense while I was making my "discoveries," I was guilty of some unconscious plagiarism, by temporarily repressing other people's ideas. What was new was my particular way of using and formulating what I had found and the way in which I tried to integrate it into the existing framework of my psychoanalytic knowledge. The joyous excitement I had experienced in first making my discoveries and formulations was dampened by recognizing the original sources of my ideas, but, fortunately, it also kept me from overevaluating the importance of my paper. However, many of the ideas that began to percolate in my head during that period eventually led to a series of related papers (see chapters 7, 8, 9, and 11). All of these papers were derived from ideas which arose during my work with the "mother tongue" lady.

At this point I believe it would be valuable to compare the clinical material described above with the observations of other authors on the subject of the origin of new ideas in psychoanalysis. In some respects what I have experienced can be seen taking place in the personality of a genius, when one studies Ernest Jones's (1953-57) volumes on Sigmund Freud. I am referring to similarities in feelings, attitudes, and moods, *not* in accomplishments.

Earlier I pointed out that the new idea, asking the patient to speak in German, occurred when I was in a state of frustration, puzzlement, and discontent, along with feelings of mild depression, anxiety, and irritability. Referring to the flow of Freud's creativity, Jones stated:

The significant point is, however, that happiness and well-being were not conducive to the best work.... [Freud] himself remarked: 'I have been very idle because the moderate amount of discomfort necessary for intensive work has not set in' [2:345].

The term "discomfort" Jones had translated from the German word *Mittelelend*, a term Max Schur believes implies more pain and suffering than "moderate discomfort." Later, in the same letter, Freud referred to being in a kind of *Zwischenreich*, an in-between state of dawning recognition. I believe all of this indicates the relationship of pain and adversity and self-analysis (which Freud was undergoing at that time) to the new burst of Freud's creativity.

Related to this state of mind is the willingness to admit to oneself the possibility that one may have been pursuing the wrong path, the wrong material, or using a faulty theoretical and technical approach. If one is sure that one is right, that one has all the answers, there will be no doubt, no conflict, no discontent, but also no new ideas.

One becomes strikingly convinced that this is true if one reads Freud's *Studies on Hysteria* (1893-95), which demonstrates how he changed his theories and his technique between the "Preliminary Communication" in 1893 and the later (1895) chapter on the "Psychotherapy of Hysteria" in the same book. In the "Preliminary Communication" Freud believed that he could *permanently* remove a hysterical symptom by hypnotizing the patient and getting her to abreact the emotions connected to the traumatic memories (p. 6). The memories and affects could not be discharged spontaneously because they were repressed and had been denied the normal "wearing-away processes" (pp. 10-11).

Freud begins the last chapter of that book by stating that although he still stands by what he wrote in the "Preliminary Communication," fresh points of view have forced themselves upon his mind (p. 255). In treating a number of cases he came up against two difficulties which led to alterations in his technique and his views of the facts. First of all, not everyone was hypnotizable who had hysterical symptoms (p. 256). Secondly, the cathartic method cannot affect the underlying causes of hysteria; thus it cannot prevent fresh symptoms from taking the place of the ones got rid of (p. 261). In other words, the abreaction of affects was no longer the major therapeutic tool, but it remained in a lower hierarchical position after he discovered the importance of resistance and transference analysis.

Freud slowly abandoned hypnosis, turned to suggestion and persuasion, and eventually to free association. In that process of change, Freud realized that the resistance to hypnosis was the result of a psychic force against remembering and this same force must be responsible for producing the symptom. He gave up hypnosis and the attempt to gain direct access to the symptoms and began to work from the periphery of the symptoms and saw how the pathogenic material could not be excised but had to be handled as an infiltrate. Finally, Freud discovered that the patient's relationship to the physician, the transference, the "false connection," could be a major obstacle to recovery, but if properly handled, it could become the most valuable vehicle for success. All of this occurred during Freud's self-analysis (Max Schur, personal communication; see also Schur, 1972).

No preconceived idea precluded the possibility of discovering new insights, new techniques, and new theories. Obstacles and adversities prompted him to try new approaches and led to new discoveries, new formulations, and new theories. Just as dramatically, new discoveries did not lead automatically to the elimination of old ideas. I believe one can here see the advantage of an open mind at work. *Creativity is not the antithesis of conservation.*

If we now return to the clinical material I presented, we see, on a minor scale, an example of some willingness in me to risk doing or thinking something new. I like to think this shares in some way the quality of adventuresomeness that Freud recognized in himself. Jones quotes Freud as follows:

> You often estimate me too highly. For I am not really a man of science, not an observer, not an experimenter, and not a

thinker. I am nothing but by temperament a *conquistador* —an adventurer, if you want to translate the word—with the curiosity, the boldness, and the tenacity that belongs to that type of being [2:348].

Jones says this letter was written in a half-serious tone. Actually, later passages from that same letter reveal the sadness as well as the creativity of freeing himself from Fliess: "I am always alone . . . so it is out of what is most intimately our own that we are growing apart" (Max Schur, personal communication).

The *conquistadors* are in complete opposition to those who "play it safe." They only repeat what they have learned and what seemed at one time to be successful. They do not dare to risk leaving the safety of the old and familiar. If one extends this line of inquiry further, one comes to three new, but related elements in the origin of new ideas. The adventurer is tempted to rebel against the traditional and conventional. His curiosity impels him to explore new, virgin territory; to trespass. In the creative mind there is also a playful joy in "juggling" ideas around, in finding new sequences and new arrangements and forms for conventional ideas (Greenacre, 1957, 1959a).

Kris (1952) and Greenacre (1959a) have stressed that the psychic energies utilized for creative work are not well neutralized or sublimated. Both libidinal and aggressive drives are used in such activity, which is often plainly observable in the agitation and drivenness during the creative period. In some creative people the sexual and aggressive strivings are often very conspicuous in their overt behavior during such periods. In others it is discernible in the products of their creativity. Greenacre goes so far as to state that people who sublimate very well may be very capable, but do not turn out to be creative. She also points out that creative people have a lower tolerance for repetitive work than do noncreative ones. She relates this to the idea that children first play repetitious games until they gain a sense of mastery. After that, the child who is free of anxiety or who is unusually gifted or talented will experiment playfully and will change his activity. This train of thought demonstrates the connection between freedom and anxiety, adventuresomeness, rebelliousness, and playfulness. Greenacre finds these characteristics typical for people who show a great deal of creative imagination.

Another issue I wish to bring up is the uneven flow of creative activity. In my clinical material I tried to show how the new ideas arose impulsively or first broke through as glimmerings or half-baked ideas. They became distractions, then they went underground, and only later did they become clear enough to be worked into a coherent paper. Jones quotes Freud on this as follows:

> There is a curious alternation of flood and ebb. Sometimes I am carried up to a state in which I feel certain, and then everything flows back and I am left high and dry. But I believe the tide is gaining on the land [1:345].

Kris (1952) stated that the mind involved in research does not work in continuous application, but there are alternations between sudden advances and quiet periods of preconscious elaboration. Székely (1967) describes something similar in what he calls creative pauses.

A further point I want to mention is the "love affair" quality, the infatuation with the creative work or with the fantasied audience, which Greenacre (1957) alludes to in the artist. I believe I have indicated how, at times, the new ideas threatened to overwhelm the rest of my interests. This was true even for my nonworking activities. During the psychoanalytic sessions I had consciously to discipline my thinking and imagination or I would have forsaken the welfare of my patients for the allure of the new ideas.

I would like to conclude this discussion of the origin of new ideas by stating that a favorable predisposition would seem to consist of allowing one's self to recognize frustrating, stalemated situations in one's work and to use adversity and discontent with one's progress as an incentive for accepting new associative ideas. In a later phase of his work Freud wrote that he now went out to meet a new idea half-way (Jones, 1:345). The inspiration Kris (1952) refers to seems to me to consist of allowing one's self to permit free associations to break into consciousness. Such associations are closer to unconscious primary process thinking, closer to the repressed and the id. Kris considers this to be a form of regression in the service of the ego. Greenacre (1959a) has pointed out that markedly creative people are restless and responsive to the new to a high degree (p. 74). She further suggested that not only is the creative individual a poor sublimator, but he is able to split his identity into a creative self and a conventional self. Weissman (1967) believes this and similar dissociative phenomena are not indications of regression in the service of the ego in creative people, but are dissociations utilized by the ego's synthesizing function. I have the impression that the ego in creative people not only tolerates, but even enjoys or needs regressing; thus the ego has less control in the initial stages over this than the concept "regression in the service of the ego" implies.

From this clinical material on the origin of new ideas, which I have sketched above from my work and the findings Jones and Schur described on Freud's creativity, plus the contributions I have used from Kris, Greenacre, and Weissman, I believe we now have a background for pursuing the question of what may happen to new ideas in the psychoanalyst, the fate of new ideas.

The innovator psychoanalyst is an adventurer, a risk-taker, an explorer. His curiosity leads him to investigate the unknown. This may indicate a freedom from anxiety or a counterphobic attitude. In any event, the anxiety is overridden by the urge to know, to explore. Innovators are not awed by tradition, nor are they lovers of conformity. They are willing to risk being wrong and to expose themselves to the attacks of their colleagues. But there is also an important aggressive component in putting forth a new idea. There is a quality of invading a hitherto uncharted territory and claiming it as one's own. Innovators are rebelling against the old and the familiar, and they are willing to endure being alone. The creative psychoanalyst whose aggression is not under control may use his innovations to destroy the old and traditional ideas. He will discard them as valueless. As I have already indicated, this is in marked contrast to Freud's way of working.

The creation of a new idea, particularly if it is more than a modest innovation, tends to mobilize old narcissistic feelings and attitudes that I believe to be akin to giving birth to a baby by parthenogenesis. Freud, in an unpublished letter (19 November 1899), wrote to Fliess: "I still want to hold back with the sexual theory. There is still an unborn piece of what has already been born" (E. Freud, 1960; see also Hitschmann, 1956). This may explain the postpartumlike depression after finishing a paper or any creative work. Any creation may also be felt as a re-creation of the self, an ideal self. The new idea can, in addition, serve as a means of reparation or as a restitution of the self (Kris, 1952). For these diverse reasons, there is a tendency to overestimate its merits, to consider it unique, to insist upon being its one and only creator, and to control and possess the idea as mine. The new idea is considered "it," the center of the universe. This is reminiscent of Freud's description of pre-Copernican man.

It is astonishing that a psychoanalyst can allow himself to feel that this or that idea or set of ideas can explain everything. It seems as though he invests the new idea with the magical omnipotence the psychoanalyst once felt in himself in his childhood and has now projected into his new system. It becomes a magical formula which can unravel all the hitherto inaccessible secrets of human behavior. I have already mentioned that there is a love affair quality to creativity, but some psychoanalysts seem to have turned the love affair into a regressive form of love, where love really becomes total possession, control, and omnipotence.

Again, all such authors seem to me to be in marked contrast to Freud's way of working and different also from the ways of

other creative analysts. Freud constantly recognized the limitations of his knowledge and was constantly at work revising,
changing, and amplifying his ideas. I believe I have convincingly
demonstrated this in the *Studies on Hysteria*, but it can also be
readily shown in the changes he made in his theory of anxiety,
his major change in the instinct theory when he introduced the
hypothesis of an aggressive instinct in man, and in many other
areas of his thinking. Some analysts, other than Freud, also work
in this way. What is characteristic for them is that they do not
destroy all the old theories when they conceive of a new idea.
They conserve the parts they consider useful, add their innovations, and try to integrate them into a cohesive framework which
is not closed off from further elaboration and emendation.

I find it particularly helpful or fruitful to look upon a
creative idea, or system of ideas, as though it were a baby. The
scientific psychoanalyst will allow his baby to grow and mature,
to learn and have new experiences with others besides the
creator and his family. The creator will even allow his children
to marry, to become part of another family and have children of
their own. This analogy may seem maudlin and personal, but it
does seem to point up a shortcoming in the behavior of many
analysts in regard to their new ideas. They want exclusive and
total possession of this valuable treasure and refuse to let it be
integrated into the mainstream of psychoanalytic developments.
I have also seen similar reactions in me, in regard to a new interpretation I have made. If, a week later, the patient brings it up
as his idea, I find myself tempted to say: "It was my idea, I
thought of it, not you." Fortunately, I have learned not only to
restrain myself, but to realize that his taking the interpretation
over as his own insight indicates he has listened and heard me,
and hopefully he has now integrated it into his own thinking.

One can even carry on a love affair with psychoanalysis
constructively as long as one is willing to relinquish the wish for
total and exclusive possession of her love, and one is willing to
give up the fantasy of being her favorite child or sole heir. Then,
one would be eager to defend her against her enemies, to give
her constructive criticism without being carried away by the

more infantile, grandiose, and intoxicating aspects of love. One would then be willing to allow others to be in her favor and receive rewards without becoming destructively jealous and rivalrous. This is the kind of love one has toward a good mother, one who has raised you, educated you, protected you, and rewarded you well. For such a mother it is only natural to feel love and gratitude. Some psychoanalysts show this by continuing to support her by learning and working hard, and by occasionally bringing her a gift, a new idea. Such analysts retain their individual independence and still remain devoted to psychoanalysis and to the pursuit of knowledge for her enrichment.

What is striking and particularly notable about Freud was his capacity to hang on to what was valuable in his own past thinking, to synthesize seemingly irreconcilable elements, and to make new creative formulations from seemingly diverse elements. Freud not only did this with his own work but he could also do it with the work of others. He used Abraham's (1908) paper to help him with the Schreber case (Freud, 1911a). He utilized another of Abraham's papers (1911) for his "Mourning and Melancholia" (1917a). But Freud went even beyond this. He integrated some of the ideas of Rank, Jung, and Adler in formulating his paper "On Narcissism" (1914d). Strachey's introductory comments make this abundantly clear (1957, pp. 69-70). In other words, Freud was no Freudian in its narrow sense. He was even willing and able to use the works of his opponents if their ideas served a useful purpose. In addition, Freud constantly used his own self-analysis to help with his new formulations.

The Fate of New Ideas
in Psychoanalytic Groups

This desirable creative synthesis is not found in the history of the psychoanalytic movement as it relates to the development of different "schools" of psychoanalysis. A school of psychoanalysis refers to a group of analysts all of whom adhere publicly to a set of ideas concerning psychoanalysis which conflict in important ways with the central ideas of other groups. In its earliest days, there was only a Freudian school and then there evolved Adlerian, Jungian, and Rankian schools. Today it is possible to distinguish an orthodox Freudian school, a classical Freudian school, a Kleinian Freudian school, and a neo-Freudian school. What is remarkable about the more recent schools is that each of them considers itself to be a devotee of psychoanalysis and Freudian to boot. If one studies the underlying concepts and techniques of each, it becomes clear that they differ markedly from one another in what they consider to be Freud's basic principles and also in how they deal with the new discoveries in clinical findings and the resultant new theories and techniques. The history of the different schools is inseparable from the origin and fate of new ideas in psychoanalysis. Differences in attitude toward adversity, the ability to endure uncertainty, to take risks, the quality of their libidinal and aggressive strivings, the ability to stand alone, all play a part in the formation of schools of psychoanalysis.

I think it is important to describe briefly the various schools because they all parade under the banner of psychoanalysis. I shall not discuss the older deviant schools because their beliefs are well known and they no longer consider themselves Freudian psychoanalysts. I do want to touch briefly on the newer schools because, to the public at large, they represent psychoanalysis today and we do meet one another, at least physically, at international meetings. My opinions are subjective ones and may not be shared by many, but they are derived from my readings, observations, and personal discussions with the adherents of these different groups.

I would classify as orthodox Freudians those psychoanalysts who consider the oedipus complex as the nuclear conflictual source of all neuroses, who consider castration anxiety as the major anxiety in neurotic patients, and who believe that the optimal behavior of the psychoanalyst in the analytic situation is to behave as nearly as possible as an anonymous dispenser of interpretations. They reject or ignore or deprecate any clinical findings or hypotheses which were not stressed by Freud or by his most devout followers. For example, they do not *study* the ideas of Erikson on the concept of identity, nor Klein's view on the early mother-child relationship and her theory of a normal preoedipal, paranoid and depressive phase of development. In addition, they are mistrustful of Hartmann's (1939) ideas concerning autonomous ego functions and conflict-free spheres. In general, they are more id-oriented than ego-oriented, although they do recognize the importance of analyzing the ego's resistances. The orthodox analysts look askance at such notions as "handling" transference phenomena or building a working alliance. They believe they are followers of Freud, and they are, but only in their worship of Freud's findings. They do not emulate him in his constant search for new knowledge.

The classical school differs from the orthodox insofar as it does accept certain modifications and amplifications of Freud's original ideas. It endorses the importance of Hartmann's ideas— in fact, it has extended the influence and power of the early ego and downgraded the potency of the id. Its adherents seem to object to Freud's (1917b) idea that the ego is not the master of its own house and support Rapaport's (1967) view that the id is not a seething cauldron.

They write, in Waelder's opinion (1967), as though Freud's psychoanalysis was essentially a drive psychology, an assumption Waelder believes is a myth, containing an element of truth covered by a thick layer of error. Their model of psychoanalysis is much more schematic with its greater emphasis on psychic structure, than it was in Freud's day (Waelder, 1967, p. 21). The classical psychoanalysts accept many of Erikson's ideas and they recognize the importance of the preoedipal phases of development. At the same time, they reject Kleinian ideas almost totally, as well as the ideas of Fairbairn (1954). They analyze transference and resistance consistently, but are loath to differentiate what is real from what is distorted in the patient's reactions to the psychoanalyst and ignore the technical and theoretical problems this differentiation implies. The classical analysts are creative, but their creativity is limited because they dare not

352 RALPH R. GREENSON

contend with the valuable ideas of those they consider to be outside the mainstream of Freudian psychoanalysis.

Whereas the classical school makes its major contributions to the ego functions, the Kleinians write about psychoanalysis almost exclusively from the standpoint of the analysis of the id, as they see it, its derivatives, and its relationship to split objects. The term resistance is almost completely absent in their writings; and when they interpret defenses, they only stress the instinctual components which are used for defensive purposes. The Kleinians believe that by focusing on the fantasy life of earliest childhood (which they believe to be nearly identical in all children) and by interpreting all the patient's reactions to people and the analyst as transference reactions, they can, by these two procedures alone, completely understand and treat all forms of neuroses, perversions, and psychoses. Concepts such as the therapeutic alliance and the real relationship between the patient and the analyst are never mentioned. Segal (1964) and Rosenfeld (1965) are the most lucid exponents of these views.

What is impressive in the Kleinian school, in addition to their almost total disregard for ego functions, is their relegating the oedipus complex, phallic sexuality, and sexual passion to a minor role. Furthermore, they tend to disregard the importance of historical events after earliest childhood. I am impressed by their closed system of thinking and their neglect of the ideas of other than Kleinian psychoanalysts.

They even overlook one of Freud's most important hypotheses concerning the psychoses, which they treat by interpretation alone. For example, Freud's basic differentiation between neuroses and psychoses, which he first described in the beginning of section 7 of his paper "The Unconscious" (1915c), is disregarded in their thinking and in their technique. Neurotics, said Freud, withdraw libido from real objects and divert it on to fantasied objects. Schizophrenics, on the other hand, withdraw libido from external objects and *also* withdraw it from internal object representations, displacing it onto fragments of the self representation. The orthodox Kleinians disregard this hypothesis in theory and practice. Federn (1952), Eissler (1953), Winnicott (1955), and Searles (1965) seem to treat psychotic patients in accordance with Freud's views, but, as far as I know, only Wexler (1960) states Freud's theories as a basis for his technique.

In the Kleinian analysts, I believe one can observe a group of followers who are united in downgrading the importance of many of Freud's basic ideas and at the same time are united in deifying the belief that putting preverbal fantasies into words gives them the very omnipotent control they seem constantly to find in their patients. The Kleinians are creative, but again, I find their new ideas are narrow and are reacted to by their adherents with the same contagion one sees in fads. All Kleinians see projective identifications in all patients most of the time and recently they are enthusiastic about the notion of people searching for "containers."

The neo-Freudians are a more heterogeneous group whose original leaders were Horney (1939), Kardiner (1939), and Fromm (1941). They stress, I believe correctly, the importance of cultural factors in character development, the importance of the striving for security, and the ego's building of unified defensive systems. At the same time, however, they discarded as valueless the libido theory, the oedipus complex, the theory of instinctual drives, the overriding importance of childhood experiences, and Freud's concept of the origin of the superego (Fenichel, 1940). The later adherents to this school of thought, e.g., Salzman (1962), Kelman (1964), Marmor (1968), and a host of others, are essentially anti-id, but pro-ego, pro-object relations and culturistic in their orientation.

I believe that Fairbairn (1954) and Guntrip (1968) also share much of their thinking, particularly in the concept of the human newborn being a unified self who begins life seeking human togetherness. The latter two see sexuality essentially as a defense. Their views smack of theology, moralism, and utopianism, harking back to the belief in the newborn babe as innately pure and noble (Schaar, 1961). They do not seem to question what drives, what impels a baby to seek the breast. If they do, their answer seems to be not hunger for milk, but togetherness.

354 RALPH R. GREENSON

This is reminiscent of the notion of human supremacy of the pre-Darwinian man Freud described.

The beliefs of the neo-Freudians illustrate how the aggressive and narcissistic component in creativity can lead to the formation of new ideas which are idealized and simultaneously lead to the destruction of the essential components of psychoanalysis. For a more comprehensive review of this school the reader is urged to read the careful and penetrating views by Tartakoff (1956) and Levine (1967). Here one can see how some valuable new ideas are vitiated by a destructive attack upon the basic concepts of psychoanalysis.

The *anti-id* tendency can also be seen, to a lesser degree, in some of the classical Freudians. The ego school, or American school, with its emphasis on such concepts as autonomous ego functions, conflict-free spheres, adaptation, the undifferentiated ego-id, etc., all seem to claim more inherent power for the ego and belittle the strength of the id (Zelmanowits, 1968).

This brief description of "schools" does not exhaust all the practitioners of deviant views of psychoanalysis. For example, I have mentioned Alexander and his followers (1946), who believe in manipulating the transference and who consider the regressive transference neurosis an unnecessary development and a waste of time. At this point, however, I want to turn to certain general characteristics which are typical of all schools.

The disappointing and destructive consequences of school formation are that they all tend to become *establishments*. To a lesser or greater degree every one of them becomes parochial and insular. In all of them, the majority of members are followers, true believers, and purists. The very need to belong to a school, the need to be "in," seems to me to indicate a need for protection or a need to obey the dictates of a leader, or of an "ideal analyst." In my opinion, the concept of the "ideal analyst" or the belief in a perfect or complete system excludes doubt, criticism, and rejects new and different ideas. This is incompatible with a scientific approach. If I imagine an analytic session with a "true believer" analyst repeating the catechism of his school, it is hard to see this as a living creative experience for either the patient or the therapist.

Followers of a school react to new ideas from a different school as though they were a danger, a threat to the very foundation of their professional beliefs. They seem to react as though the new and different idea would destroy their professional identity. As a result, they tend to overidentify, to overestimate, and even to deify the ideas of their leaders and reject out of hand all dissenting points of view. All followers of a school are, in my opinion, orthodox, which leads to dogma and bigotry. The purist and the "ideal analysts" to not tolerate change and seem unable to endure uncertainty and the unknown. They seem to prefer sterile certainty to the risk-taking of discovery.

The insularity of the various schools can be seen in the curricula of the various training institutes in which new ideas, particularly if controversial, are rarely if ever given a thorough discussion. As a consequence, the bibliographies of authors from these schools omit any references to authors of divergent views even where the particular idea under discussion touches directly on the controversial author's work. A good example is to be found in my own paper "The Mother Tongue and the Mother." Although I referred to the decisive importance of the early mother-child-breast relationship, I made no reference to the work of Melanie Klein (1932).

It seems to me to be apparent that in each school there is a resistance to integrate the new and different ideas with the old. There is thesis and antithesis, but not synthesis. Symptomatic of this trend is the fact that the term "synthesizing ego function" has been denigrated to *synthetic ego* function. What is happening in our various psychoanalytic institutes seems analogous to what is going on in our universities and other establishments. The new and the different are excluded or segregated from the old and familiar. There is no true integration. The faculty and administration tend to think that only the students are at fault and the institution is being unfairly attacked or improperly used. They want to protect the establishment and their jobs and not the search for knowledge.

This state of affairs has grave implications for the psychoanalytic movement. It is my belief that there is a lack of progress, a lack of creativity, because there is a lack of free and open discussion, as well as a reluctance to study differing points of view. It may well be that the distress and even the outrage which confrontation arouses are important antecedents to creativity in our psychoanalytic institutes and universities.

Certainly, placidity, contentment, and self-satisfaction are not the breeding ground for new ideas. I have the impression at the International Congresses that members of different schools talk at each other and not to and with each other. Each school seems to avoid serious open discussion of their different ways of working and understanding. The young are too timid or brash, the old are too protective of their special views and of their high position. It is true that it is a most painful experience to realize that, after more than twenty-five years of practice, one's work was deficient because one neglected some of the ideas of another school. I have had this happen to me and I can attest to its earth-shaking effects. Yet humility and honesty are essential for a scientific psychoanalyst. Shortly after Freud's sixty-ninth birthday, he wrote to Lou Andreas Salomé:

> I even think I have discovered something of fundamental importance for our work ... a discovery of which one ought almost to be ashamed for one should have divined these connections from the beginning and not after 30 years [E. Freud, 1960, p. 361].

One month later he wrote *Inhibitions, Symptoms and Anxiety* (1926a) (Max Schur, personal communication).

There are many areas in psychoanalysis which I believe urgently need clarification and further exploration. For example, the conflict theory is central for explaining the development of neuroses, but it is insufficient for our understanding of the psychoses and the perversions. It is important not to leave to a few to explore further the theory of ego deficiency, the failure in building early internal object representations. The oedipus complex is crucial for understanding full-fledged neurotic symptom formation, but the importance of preoedipal and early ego developments must be reevaluated, clarified, and integrated into our theory if we want to understand more completely all forms of psychopathology. Interpretation is a major instrument for giving insight, but something more is needed in patients with severe maturational deficiencies in their early object relations. Milton Wexler recently made the point that healthy children mature without interpretations. Does not this indicate the importance of the real relationship in the psychoanalytic situation for patients who have signs of early maturational defects?

I have selected these few areas where the psychoanalytic movement needs to make progress as a plea for a real interchange of ideas *among and within* "schools." I have emphasized the stultifying effects of institutes and schools, but I want to end on a positive note. Training institutes are needed, even "establishments" can serve a useful purpose. It is true that institutions tend to ossify, but the institution also provides a holding, structuring function. In a personal communication, Masud Khan wrote that "paradoxically, the institution is the one enemy one must keep to define the rigor and boundaries of one's own freedom. The question is, how *not* to let this enemy become one's master."

Psychoanalysts who belong to no institute or society usually end up as "wild analysts," existentialists, or evangelists, or in some way manifest the effects of the return of the repressing forces that led them originally into psychoanalytic treatment. Perhaps Laing (1967) and J. N. Rosen (1947), among others, are examples of this development. What we need is to study seriously the views of those we disagree with, exchange views openly based on clinical material described in detail. Our curricula must be more flexible and heterogeneous, our students should be given more freedom, and we teachers should have the humility to be dedicated to the pursuit of knowledge and not in selling our particular brand of psychoanalysis.

I believe it is no longer necessary for us to spend our lives defending or attacking Freud's major discoveries. Our task is to pursue further knowledge and to be willing to modify and amplify what we have learned from him. To my mind that is in the true spirit of Freud—not in being an orthodox or classical or Kleinian Freudian—but in being a psychoanalyst.

22

The Nontransference Relationship in the Psychoanalytic Situation

(1969)

E VER SINCE FREUD'S DORA CASE (1905a), psychoanalysts in
general have made the analysis of transference the major
focus of psychoanalytic technique. This development has
reached such proportions that Kleinian psychoanalysts consider
all interactions between the patient and his analyst as transference or countertransference and would make interpretation the
only correct intervention. "Orthodox" Freudians often recognize
that personal interactions other than transference may occur,

This paper was written jointly with Milton Wexler, whom I thank for his
permission to include it in this volume. It was presented at the 26th International Psycho-Analytical Congress, Rome, 1969. First published in *International Journal of Psycho-Analysis*, 50:27-39, 1969. Also as: Il rapporto non
transferenziale nella situazione analitica. *Rivista di Psicoanalisi*, 15:49-71,
1969. Die übertragungsfreie Beziehung in der psychoanalytischen Situation.
Psyche, 25:206-230, 1971.

but tend to treat them as irrelevant or trivial, at least in their
writings. They even acknowledge that interventions other than
strictly defined interpretations may at times be necessary, but
these are mainly considered "parameters" and are to be used
sparingly and then eliminated (Eissler, 1953, 1958). On the
whole both groups ignore the subject.

Over the years, however, a number of psychoanalysts, too
heterogeneous to be classified, have taken a growing interest in
what may be broadly termed the nontransference or "real"
interactions that take place in the course of psychoanalytic treatment. The sensitive nature of the problem raised becomes readily
apparent. For example, while acknowledging the importance of
the inevitable nontransference interactions which take place,
they tend to be more impressed by the possibility that any non-
interpretive measure may become a dangerous parameter. Some
raise the issue, but then there is a discreet silence as to how such
material is to be handled. Or their concern is limited to the
exceptional case and by implication eliminated from the mainstream of psychoanalytic technique. None of these approaches
seems very satisfactory.

Sigmund Freud (1937a) wrote about the treatment of a
former colleague: "not every good relation between an analyst
and his subject during and after analysis was to be regarded as a
transference; there were also friendly relations which were based
on reality and which proved to be viable" (p. 222).

One of the earliest and clearest discussions of the problem
came from Anna Freud in 1954. In commenting on a paper by
Leo Stone (1954) concerning "The Widening Scope of Indications for Psychoanalysis" she said:

> I refer briefly to Dr. Stone's remarks concerning the "real
> personal relationship" between analyst and patient versus
> the "true transference reactions." To make such a distinc-
> tion coincides with ideas which I have always held on this
> subject.... We see the patient enter into analysis with a
> reality attitude to the analyst; then the transference gains
> momentum until it reaches its peak in the full-blown trans-

ference neurosis, which has to be worked off analytically until the figure of the analyst emerges again, reduced to its true status. But—and this seems important to me—to the extent to which the patient has a healthy part of his personality, his real relationship to the analyst is never wholly submerged. With due respect for the necessary strictest handling and interpretation of the transference, I still feel that somewhere we should leave room for the realization that analyst and patient are also two real people, of equal adult status, in a real personal relationship to each other. I wonder whether our—at times complete—neglect of this side of the matter is not responsible for some of the hostile reactions which we get from our patients and which we are apt to ascribe to "true transference" only. But these are technically subversive thoughts and ought to be "handled with care" [p. 372f.].

It is precisely such thoughts that we propose to handle with both care and boldness, for there is the greatest need to explore these matters openly and in depth. It seems to us that what is technically subversive is to continue the evasion of the difficult problems posed by Anna Freud.

With this in mind, we want to state our basic propositions: to facilitate the full flowering and ultimate resolution of the patient's transference reactions, it is essential in all cases to recognize, acknowledge, clarify, differentiate, and even nurture the nontransference or relatively transference-free reactions between patient and analyst. The technique of "only analyzing" or "only interpreting" transference phenomena may stifle the development and clarification of the transference neurosis and act as an obstacle to the maturation of the transference-free or "real" reactions of the patient. As central as the interpretation of transference is to psychoanalytic therapy, and about this there can be no question, it is also important to deal with the nontransference interactions between patient and analyst. This may require noninterpretive or nonanalytic interventions, but these approaches are vastly different from antianalytic procedures.

Working Definitions

Transference is the experiencing of impulses, feelings, fantasies, attitudes, and defenses with respect to a person in the present which do not appropriately fit that person but are a repetition of responses originating in regard to significant persons of early childhood, unconsciously displaced onto persons in the present. The two outstanding characteristics of transference phenomena are: (1) transference is an indiscriminate, nonselective repetition of the past; and (2) it ignores or distorts reality. It is inappropriate (Greenson, 1967a).

The very fact that the concept of transference has, over the years, come to have this rather precise meaning implies that it was technically and theoretically necessary to differentiate it from other reactions which are *relatively* transference-free. Anna Freud, in a recent personal communication on the subject of differentiating the transference relationship from the non-transference, had the following to say:

> I have always learned to consider transference in the light of a distortion of the real relationship of the patient to the analyst, and, of course, that the type and manner of distortion showed up the contributions from the past. If there were no real relationship, this idea of the distorting influences would make no sense.

All object relations consist of some elements of repetition from the past, but the so-called "real," the nontransference relationship differs from transference in the degree of relevance, appropriateness, accuracy, and immediacy of what is expressed. Furthermore, nontransference responses are basically readily modifiable both by internal and external reality. They are adaptive and "realistic."

There is a school of thought, mainly Kleinian, which asserts that everything emanating from the patient is transference. Such a broad definition of the term transference seems to deprive it of usefulness.[1] Beyond that it would seem to negate the possibility

---

[1] This topic is discussed more extensively in chapter 32.

for new and creative experiences in human relationships and relegate us all to some dismal expectation of monotonous repetitions in life. One can hardly argue the question that the past does influence the present, but this is not identical to transference. Indeed, if there is a present, a here and now, an immediate reality, we are told little or nothing about what to do with it. Surely we are not to hope it will go away.

The terms transference, nontransference, transference-free, and "real"[2] relationships must be considered as relative and overlapping. All transference contains some germ of "reality" and all "real" relationships have some transference elements. All object relationships consist of different admixtures and blendings of transference and nontransference components. Nevertheless, we feel it is important to draw some clear-cut distinctions between them. For this purpose a clinical example may serve better than abstract definitions.

A young man, Mr. K., was in the fifth year of analysis with me (R.R.G.). After I had made an interpretation he hesitated and then told me that he had something to say which was very difficult for him. He had been about to skip over it when he realized he had been doing just that for years. Taking a deep breath, he said, "You always talk a bit too much. You tend to exaggerate. It would be much easier for me to get mad at you and say you're cock-eyed or wrong or off the point or just not answer. It's terribly hard to say what I mean because I know it will hurt your feelings."

I believe the patient had correctly perceived some traits of mine and it was indeed somewhat painful for me to have them pointed out. I told him he was right on both counts, but I wanted to know why it was harder for him to tell it to me simply

[2] In this paper we use quotation marks because "real" is difficult to define. There are two important meanings to the word real. Real means genuine and authentic; sincere, not synthetic. Real also means realistic. Transference is real in the sense that it is genuinely felt, but it is unrealistic. For example, when the patient is full of fury at the analyst and the analyst makes an interpretation, and the patient temporarily squelches his fury to listen—that is being realistic but not genuine. Thus, real has at least these two different meanings: it means both genuine *and* realistic.

and directly as he had just done than to act in an angry fashion. He answered that he knew from experience I would not get upset by an exhibition of temper since that was obviously his neurosis and I wouldn't be moved by it. Telling me so clearly about my talking too much and exaggerating was a personal criticism and that would be hurtful. In the past he would have been worried that I might retaliate in some way, but he now knew it was not likely. Besides, he no longer felt my anger would kill him (Greenson, 1967a, p. 217f.).

Here the difference between transference and nontransference reactions becomes clear. The patient had correctly perceived some characteristics of his analyst's way of working and had also quite realistically predicted that it would be painful for the analyst to have them pointed out. These are nontransference phenomena; they are contemporaneous, appropriate, and realistic. His earlier fantasies about a potentially retaliatory anger that might kill him were historically rooted carry-overs from his childhood anxieties, inappropriate exaggerations, and therefore transference distortions. The patient had developed a good working alliance in relation to his temper outbursts at the analyst, but this alliance could not maintain itself when it came to more realistic criticism. This only developed in his fifth year of analysis.

It might be well, at this point, to clarify the relationship between the working alliance, transference and the real relationship. The *working alliance* is the nonneurotic, rational, reasonable rapport which the patient has with his analyst and which enables him to work purposefully in the analytic situation despite his transference impulses (Zetzel, 1956b; Stone, 1961, 1967; see also chapter 15). The patient and the psychoanalyst contribute to the formation of the working alliance. The patient's awareness of his neurotic suffering and the possibility of help from the analyst impels him to seek out and work in the analytic situation. The positive transference, the overestimation and overvaluation of the psychoanalyst, may also be a powerful ally, but it is treacherous. Above all, the reliable core of the working alliance is to be found in the "real" or nontransference relationship between patient and analyst. Transference reactions, whether loving or hateful, from the most infantile to the most mature, eventually lead to idealization, sexualization, or aggressivization and become important sources of resistance in the end.

As for the analyst, it is his consistent and unwavering pursuit of insight *plus* his concern, respect, and care for the totality of the patient's personality, sick and healthy, that contributes to the working alliance. The analyst must help the patient's beleaguered ego distinguish between what is appropriate and distorted, correct and false, realistic and fantastic in regard to his reactions to people, above all toward his analyst.

The *transference* reactions are the vehicle which enable the patient to bring the warded-off, inaccessible material into the analytic situation. The *working alliance* makes it possible for the patient to understand the analyst's insights, review and organize interpretations and reconstructions, and finally integrate and assimilate the material of the analysis. The basis for the working alliance is the capacity for relatively conflict-free ego functioning and the ability, to some degree, to form a real, nontransference relationship to the analyst.

In the clinical instance of Mr. K., confirmation by the analyst of the patient's judgments puts the analyst for the moment on the side of the patient's observing, realistic ego. In this the analyst supports the working alliance in its efforts to overcome the experiencing ego, previously flooded by neurotic transference. Acknowledging that the patient was right in his criticism was certainly unanalytic. What is more important, however, is that the procedure is not antianalytic. It does advance the analysis.

"*Analyzing*" is a shorthand expression referring to all procedures which have the direct aim of increasing the patient's insight about himself. The most important measure is interpretation. All others are subordinated to it both theoretically and practically. All analytic procedures are either steps which lead to an interpretation or make an interpretation effective (E. Bibring, 1954; Gill, 1954). Analyzing usually includes four distinct procedures: confrontation, clarification, interpretation, and working through.

Some procedures used by psychoanalysts do not add insight into the unconscious per se, but strengthen those ego functions which are required for gaining understanding. They serve the purpose of preparing for insight or making it more effective. A good example is abreaction, which allows the patient to discharge intense emotion and thus, indirectly, makes the ego available for insight. Another similar instance is the analyst acknowledging, accepting, and working with the patient's "realistic" responses and bringing them into a coherent relationship with the rest of his analysis. This then forms the avenue for increasing his capacity to accept and utilize new interpretations and insights into his unconscious.

Antianalytic procedures are those which block or lessen the patient's capacity for insight and understanding. Any measure which diminishes the ego's function or capacity for observing, thinking, remembering, and judging would fall into this category. Unnecessary transference gratifications would be a typical example. In our estimation, ignoring Mr. K.'s criticisms would also have been an antianalytic procedure. The patient had kept certain criticisms of his analyst consciously hidden for some four years. If the analyst had ignored his remarks, and treated them merely as free associations, or as clinical data to be analyzed, it might have confirmed the patient's feeling that the analyst was too upset to deal with the remarks quite humanly and forthrightly, thereby damaging the working alliance. Or else it might have meant to the patient that his observations and judgments were "only" clinical material, that they had no intrinsic value, and hardly merited a response. Finally, he might have thought that his perceptions and judgments were faulty, sick, "only" transference distortions. In any case the patient would have developed more doubts about his ego functions and his capacity to empathize, all of which would have impaired his capacity for sound ego functioning and retarded his analysis. This would clearly have been "antianalytic" in its approach and its outcome.

Historical Survey

The problem of the nontransference or "real" relationship in analysis has been dealt with on a number of occasions in the psychoanalytic literature. A brief survey will demonstrate a considerable disagreement and a frequent lack of clarity.

As early as 1942, Esther Menaker wrote quite directly on the subject:

> It seems to us, however, important to distinguish between that part of the analytic experience which is relived *as* "real" (not to question the genuineness of this experience), and that part which *is* real, that is, which constitutes a direct human relationship between patient and analyst, which has an existence independent of the transference, and which is the medium in which the transference reactions take place.... In general, it is important that the real relationship between patient and analyst have some content and substance other than that created by the analytic situation itself.

Margaret Little (1951) described the importance of dealing with the whole patient-analyst relationship, both normal and pathological, conscious and unconscious, but she considered all of this as varieties of transference and countertransference. Several points in particular, however, deserve attention:

> So much emphasis is laid on the unconscious phantasies of patients about their analysts that it is often ignored that they really come to know a great deal of truth about them —both actual and psychic. Such knowledge could not be prevented in any case, even if it were desirable, but patients do not know they have it, and part of the analyst's task is to bring it into consciousness, which may be the very thing to which he has himself the greatest resistance [p. 38].

Max Gitelson (1952) pointed out that some self-revelation on the part of the analyst is not only inevitable via countertransference but also necessary. "An analysis can come to an impasse because the analyst does not realize, or misunderstands, or avoids the issue of a patient's discovery of him as a person" (p. 8).

In 1954, Leo Stone made the first of several important contributions to the problem of the total relationship between patient and analyst in the psychoanalytic situation. He insisted on the importance of separating the "real" relationship from different varieties of transference and countertransference and gave some guidelines for utilizing the differences while still maintaining the psychoanalytic situation in accordance with classical Freudian principles. In this connection he stressed the analyst's humane and physicianly attitudes toward his patients.

Fairbairn (1957, 1958) and his followers have also stressed the variety of object relatedness in the therapeutic situation rooted in reality. However, since their theory and technique differ so markedly from the classical Freudian position, it is difficult to weave it into the present context (see also Guntrip, 1961).

In a panel on "Variations in Classical Psycho-Analytic Technique" (1958), it is interesting to observe how the different participants dealt with the problem of the nontransference relationship. Rudolph Loewenstein (1958) granted that some patients might require less than the strictest anonymity, but he considered them extreme cases. He felt that even interrupting the flow of the patient's associations to ask questions was a parameter and should only be used sparingly and not in the initial stage of analysis (p. 206).

In a somewhat more flexible vein, Maurice Bouvet (1958) emphasized the deliberate variations required with different types of patients in different phases of their analysis in order to maintain an optimal distance. He felt that we are obliged to "manage" relational situations at times, but these must eventually be analyzed. In an earlier paper, Bouvet, Marty, and Sauget (1956) had described a case where a woman patient overheard the analyst's conversation with someone presumed to be another woman. Only *after* the analyst had acknowledged the correctness of the patient's perceptions did she produce the jealousy fantasies stirred up by this occurrence.

Kurt Eissler (1958) defined classical technique as follows: "It is one in which interpretation remains the exclusive or leading or prevailing tool" (p. 233). His doubts whether interpretation is the exclusive tool or merely the prevailing tool extend beyond this statement. On the one hand, Eissler expressed some doubt about Loewenstein's very cautious suggestion concerning the need to question some patients under special circumstances and wondered whether questions couldn't be put in the form of interpretations. On the other hand, he concluded that no one could ever be analyzed by the use of interpretation alone.

In the light of Eissler's uncertain statements it is quite understandable, but also quite meaningful, that Herbert Rosenfeld (1958), a leading Kleinian theoretician, should elect an extreme position for Eissler, asserting that "Dr. Eissler has proposed that the term classical technique of psychoanalysis should be used for an analytic technique relying entirely on interpretation." Later on he states: "In this connection I should like to speak briefly about the technique which has been developed by Melanie Klein during the last thirty years, as in this the analyst tries to rely entirely on interpretation, even in very difficult cases" (p. 238).

Annie Reich's presentation (1958) was very different. She began by stating that in patients with very weak ego functions, it may be necessary to use all sorts of supportive measures. She describes a case in which she helped break down a woman's fixation to her mother by actively helping the patient, via the patient's material, analyze the mother's behavior and motivations and thus bring about her dethronement. Annie Reich considered this unanalytic but necessary.

In the same panel, Sasha Nacht (1958) thought all rules concerning neutrality and anonymity if taken too strictly can lead to a sadomasochistic "analytic couple" and florid ritualism (p. 235). He suggested the analyst should be able to abandon the rigid neutrality and allow his *presence* to be felt.

Alan Roland (1967) emphasizes that a real reparative object relationship must be developed and cultivated with patients who have severe character disorders in order to resolve their rigid character resistances. Only the presence of a real relationship, he contends, will enable such patients to overcome their transference resistances and develop an analyzable transference neurosis.

In my book on psychoanalytic technique (1967a) and in chapter 25 I deal with many of the issues raised in this presentation.

Up to this point we have only considered nontransference relationships in the context of the analysis of the transference neuroses. The same range of viewpoints can be found in connection with the psychoanalytic therapy of the psychoses. However, in the psychoanalysis of the neuroses there is a movement from purist limitations of technique centered on interpretation toward some attention to the "real" relationship. Contrariwise, the therapy of psychotic patients began with an emphasis on those "real" relationships. It tends now to become purist with some claims of success based on strictly psychoanalytic procedures limited mainly or entirely to the interpretation of transference.

It is our contention that Freud's basic theory of schizophrenia which centers on the decathexis or loss of internal object representations is correct. As a consequence of this theory, we believe that treatment must focus on efforts to restore object constancy and therefore frequently must begin in the real relationship between the schizophrenic patient and his therapist. The sicker the patient, the more ego defects, maturational deficiencies, failure to develop good whole object relations, the greater is the need to establish and maintain a real object relationship.

The patient can repeat his past object relations in his transference reactions to his therapist. This we can interpret. If he failed to develop whole object relations or lost them by massive decathexis, he will not be able to repeat them. There may be fragmented transference reactions, or even a thin transference neurosis, but he will not be able to establish and sustain a full transference neurosis. Under such conditions our work will have to be concerned with helping the patient build or rediscover a capacity for real object relatedness. Only then might such a patient become analyzable. It is our experience that psychoanalysis proper is possible only when a patient has the capacity for both a transference and a nontransference relationship to the therapist.

The literature on the psychoanalytic treatment of borderline and psychotic patients is too extensive to be summarized and a few examples must suffice. Federn (1952), Nunberg (1948), Knight (1953), Fromm-Reichmann (1950), Winnicott (1956), Searles (1965), and Wexler (1951, 1952, 1960) are only a few among the many who have considered the "real" or nontransference relationships with psychotic patients a significant aspect of treatment, central at times, without abandoning the relevance and importance of understanding and interpreting the patient's productions. Management, support, education, control, contact, communication, and understanding represent but a few of the elements discussed by these authors as elements in the "real" relationships with such patients. At the same time their writings make it abundantly clear that they have not abandoned psychoanalytic understanding, nor those classical techniques of interpretation of transference and resistance, when they are applicable to the status of the patient at the time.

Searles (1965) addressed himself quite directly to the problem raised here. In discussing Loewald's 1960 paper he not only urged the importance of the reality relationship in treatment but stressed that this "reality-relatedness proceeds always a bit ahead of, and makes possible, the progressive evolution and resolution of the transference."

Wexler (1951, 1952, 1960) has emphasized Freud's basic theory of schizophrenia as relating to the loss of object representation. He has suggested that the logical consequence of this theory, supported by clinical data, leads to a focus on "reality" relatedness in the therapy, an effort to restore object constancy, frequently in terms of the "real" relationship between patient and therapist. The degree to which interpretive measures may succeed will depend on the degree to which object representation and object constancy are restored as elements in psychic structure.

At the other end of the scale will be found the views of Rosenfeld (1965) and Boyer (1966). Rosenfeld asserts that he confines himself to the most orthodox psychoanalytic procedures, stating:

> Even if I came up against apparently insuperable diffi-culties in the transference situation I decided to adhere to my analytic technique, following the principle that if I could not make contact with the patient through my inter-pretations it was not the technique that was wrong but my understanding of what was going on in the transference situation.

Boyer (1966) makes more extensive claims. He asserts success in the treatment of a considerable range of schizophrenic and borderline patients by employing orthodox interpretive procedures in the main, with few if any parameters and those generally of the sort employed with neurotics (setting a termina-tion date, instruction to face the phobic object, etc.). Yet he too seems to qualify his assertions. He uses interpretations as his "ultimate" tool, but he also confronts the patient gently with his distortions and contradictions of reality.

All in all it would seem as if psychoanalysis is struggling with the same types of technical questions in the treatment of the psychoses as in the treatment of the transference neuroses.

Clinical Examples

It is an impressive clinical finding that in some patients the "real" relationship only becomes an important issue in their psychoanalytic therapy on isolated occasions. As a rule it remains as a vague background element. In other patients the "real" relationship becomes a central and crucial issue from the beginning to the end of treatment. In part this may be due to the differences in the specific pathology and consequently the therapeutic needs of a given case. The role of the "real" relationship in psychoanalytic treatment is often determined by the therapist's sensitivity or blindness to the issues involved. The personality or the theoretical orientation of the analyst may well be the determining factor.

It is important to recognize that designating a given reaction or piece of behavior as transference is not a neutral, objective act but rather is our subjective judgment of the phenomenon under scrutiny (Szasz, 1963). It is necessary to know many things quite objectively about ourselves, our patients, our culture, environment, etc., before we are able to determine whether we are dealing with a transference or a realistic reaction. There is always the possibility that we are blind to some painful characteristic or behavior in ourselves. There is always the possibility that we, rather than the patient, are unrealistic about the external world, including the patient's world. Furthermore, we may assign different values to certain traits than would be assigned by our patients. What the analyst calls straightforward speech may be perceived realistically by a patient of a different background as harsh and vulgar. It is not always easy or possible to assess the correctness of such judgments and we are often enough confronted with the relativity of reality.

It is also important to keep in mind that while our patients have much less opportunity to know us than the other way around, nevertheless they are not without resources. Everything we do or say, or don't do or say, every bit of our surroundings from the office decor to our waiting room magazines, the way we open the door, greet our patients, make interpretations, keep silent, end the hour, all these and much more reveal something about our real self, going far beyond our professional self. It is also important to acknowledge, to ourselves if no place else, that many of our patients have experiences in life extending beyond the range of our own experience, knowledge beyond our own knowledge, and that we are not always exempt from limitations leading to bias or downright ignorance.

These circumstances throw a special burden on the analyst.

He cannot as easily dismiss the patient's hurtful remarks as merely transference and make them solely the subject of interpretation. Our own temptation to defend against a painful recognition of "real" deficiencies must also be dealt with, and, from our point of view, not solely by way of internal reflection, but at times in a realistic and open exchange with the patient. The same holds true not only of the patient's response to the analyst but also of his perceptions and responses to the world around him, many of which may cross-cut the analyst's own personal and cultural biases. It takes empathy and insight to see the transference elements in the patient's productions. It takes flexibility and courage to see what is "real," transference-free, and to support the patient's efforts to segregate objective assessments as opposed to neurotic distortions.

It may be illuminating to see how accurate perceptions and beliefs can lead to transference reactions, to transference-free reactions, and combinations of the two. The following is taken from a single analytic hour of one patient.

In the second year of his analysis, Mr. M., a thirty-year-old writer of considerable attainment, begins his hour by attacking his wife verbally for her disorganization, forgetfulness, and irresponsibility. This leads him to jealous fantasies concerning her sexual flirtatiousness with "some third-rate artist." The patient admits his fantasies have little basis in fact, but he cannot stop them of late. He then goes on to talk about his wife's analyst whom he hates but also admires and about whom he also has had jealous fantasies. He thinks this analyst must consider him a bad husband and would certainly not tolerate his behavior were he the husband's analyst. Mr. M. continues and says that I (R.R.G.) put up with it because: "You are weak and full of shit. You like me and you are wrong." I indicate to Mr. M. that he wants me to be tough like he supposes his wife's analyst to be so that I would control his bad behavior just like his harsh father had done. When I am tolerant, I become his mother, weak, full of shit, liking him, and therefore wrong.

Mr. M. responds to this with an attack on my "wishy-washy" attitudes, my repeatedly saying, "Let's try to understand this behavior," and my willingness to "wait and see." He shouts that he would rather have an answer about what to do and no interpretations. He imagines his wife's analyst would give him a direct answer. I remain silent.

He goes on. He does not trust psychoanalysis. There are no absolute standards for right and wrong. He pauses. Actually he has been surprised about how well I do understand him. He has the feeling, sometimes, that I must be a little bit like him to be so accurate about him. This embarrasses him. It is probably wrong. Then his tone changes: "Anyway, you can be fooled. You accepted me as a patient. At first I decided to fool you because I felt you would throw me out if I stopped throwing sand in your eyes. Why *did* you take me as a patient? You must be shit if you chose me. My God, I have felt this toward everybody who has ever liked me."

I said: "Yes. You felt this way toward your mother, your wife, and now toward me. A mixture of contempt, loving closeness, and guilt." The patient then adds: "And I admire tough men who frighten me. I know you are not weak. There *is* a difference between warmth and weakness, only I forget sometimes. Now I recall something you have often told me, that I am afraid of warmth. It will make me like you too much and I will become too dependent on you. I guess I am really more afraid of that than of the tough guys."

I intervene and tell the patient that I feel his last point was right. He is much more afraid of the warm me than he is of me as tough as his wife's analyst. He wishes I would be tough, then he could fight me and keep me at a distance. Loving me makes him vulnerable, dependent, and also full of jealousy. Mr. M. replies that he wishes I would not use the word "love." It makes him feel squeamish. "But I know you. That is probably why you used it." He pauses, reflects, and says, "I suppose you are the third-rate artist I am jealous of."

We have chosen this clinical fragment to demonstrate how interwoven the transference relationship and the "real" relationship can become in a given hour. The main lines of the transference are quite obvious. Mr. M is jealous and contemptuous of me, a third-rate artist. He also respects and fears me as a tough, harsh analyst. He would like me to act the role of his severe father and control him. But he knows I will not and then I become weak, full of shit, wrong and "wishy-washy," his mother, and he, himself. I am also a fool and a shit for having chosen him as a patient. Nevertheless he recognizes how afraid he is to love and need me. It seems clear that all the above reactions are mainly transference distortions.

Side by side with these transference reactions, however, Mr. M. also indicates some realistic awareness of himself and of me as persons. He knows some of his reactions are distorted and he even makes some correct interpretations. He knows that I like him, that I keep trying to understand him, that I am persistent and patient. He knows his fantasies have little basis in fact. He is also correctly aware that I can be fooled, I can be wrong, and at times harsh. Yet he senses I have a good grasp of his underlying feelings and impulses, perhaps based on the fact that I resemble him in some way. I am warm, not weak, and also not afraid of upsetting him by choosing words which get to the heart of the matter. Furthermore, he realizes that psychoanalysis has no absolute standards for right and wrong. He recognizes that he tends to demean everyone who likes him and he correctly interprets that I am the third-rate artist he is jealous of.

In the main these are not distortions and come close to being quite accurate perceptions and judgments based on the patient's observations during the treatment. They coexist with transference reactions, do not abolish them, and even facilitate the acceptance of transference interpretations when made.

One can also see in this illustration how a correct perception can lead to a transference reaction. The patient correctly appraises early in the hour my tolerance of his behavior and that I like him. This then becomes the starting place for a reaction which identifies me with his weak, full-of-shit, wrong mother.

Clearly all transference reactions, from whatever source, are either preambivalent or ambivalent with positive and negative elements coexisting in different intensities. However it is, in our view, highly unlikely that Mr. M. remained in analysis

because his loving transference "neutralized" his hostile transference. Given the intensity of the range of feeling exhibited, this
would make a very shaky foundation for any long-term project.
What is clear, and most relevant for our thesis is that, in addition
to his transference feelings Mr. M. also had a nontransference
relationship to his analyst. This formed the basis for a working
alliance, kept him in analysis, and opened the door to continuous
and effective work.

   This state of affairs can be seen in the rigors of working
through. A patient will occasionally break off an analysis of long
standing when driven by a sudden eruption of intense hostile
feelings. This may be traced to a failure to make the correct
interpretations, but we have found that this factor alone is rarely
decisive. Each of us has made many incorrect interpretations
and many of our patients knew or sensed it and did not run
away. The decisive element was the relative strength of the
"real" relationship, the degree to which there existed not only
positive transference but genuine respect, liking, and also understanding on both sides. We want to stress that the "real" relationship does not have to be verbalized or conspicuous, but it must
be present to a sufficient degree for the analytic situation to
endure the long and often painful process of working through. A
patient or an analyst may consider interrupting treatment if one
or both realize some basic aspect is not being properly understood. This decision, however, will be arrived at mutually if a
real basis for confidence and respect exists. Unexpected crises or
failures in psychoanalysis come about when incorrect interpretations coincide with a failure in the "real" relationship in the
patient or the psychoanalyst or both. Technical errors may cause
pain and confusion, but they are usually repairable; failure of
humanness is much harder to remedy. The overemphasis on
transference interpretations and the neglect of the "real"
relationship tends to reduce all life to explanation which is not
life and not living.

   Transference and nontransference reactions occur both in
and outside of the psychoanalytic situation. We believe that the
analyst should be willing to help the patient distinguish between

reality and fantasy in his outside life, even though we recognize that the analyst can never be as certain of his assessments as he is in regard to the relationship taking place between himself and the patient.

Reality and unreality often are involved in the patient's self image. One analysand accused himself, with vast masochistic exaggeration, of being fraudulent, self-indulgent, and incompetent. Within the same hour he more accurately acknowledged that he did nonetheless function with honesty, integrity, independence, and competence in his profession. In our view both self representations should be underlined for what they are.

Mr. M., for example, was assigned to write a screen adaptation of a famous classic. He had many qualms about the task. He felt, apparently realistically, that while it was an honor to be given this job, it was difficult if not impossible to adapt a great classic to the screen, that most people had a personal concept of such a classic and would be dissatisfied, and that the envy of colleagues would be stirred by this assignment. The extension of these reasonable feelings and thoughts carried him to a great fear that colleagues would be out to "get him." He dreamed at this time of being mutilated in an auto accident. Reality was succeeded by exaggeration and distortion. It became essential, however, to accede to and deal with the reality, no matter how briefly, before displacement or transference elements in the distortion could be fully explored. This can often be done in a single hour.[3]

The problem with so-called borderline patients and psychotic patients is, in one sense the same, and in another sense quite different. In all likelihood it is even more important to sense, support, and develop the reality perceptions of this group of patients. This goes to the core of the symptom picture, and a failure to focus on reality perceptions or the "real" relationship in treatment would lead to a most serious breakdown in the working alliance. As a corollary, the exclusive focus on interpre-

[3] For further clinical examples of neurotic patients, see chapters 23 and 26.

tation whether of transference or resistance seems to lead, in our experience at least, to increasing hostility and withdrawal or to an inert submission to ritual formulation.

The suggested difference from the ordinary analytic situation lies in the fact that frequently psychotic patients seem to require an early introduction to a reality beyond their capacities at the moment, an opportunity to make even the most primitive identification with the analyst, and to borrow aspects of reality from his perceptions or behavior and utilize it as their own. It is as if the internal "road map"—to borrow a phrase employed by David Rapaport—had been fragmented or partially destroyed and had to be filled in by the analyst's understanding in order for external reality to be "rediscovered." The process can be clearly indicated by the following clinical instance, one a borderline patient and the other a patient suffering from an acute schizophrenic episode.

A talented young artist named Douglas was compelled to give up his career in midstream and sent, half against his will, to the Menninger Foundation for therapy. He was anxious, depressed, persistently enraged, and frequently suicidal. He reluctantly accepted treatment, made it quite clear that it was on the basis of some personal liking for me (M.W.), but that he had no faith in the process or the outcome. He also made it clear that he hated his situation, hated the place, and would do everything in his power to tear it apart. I agreed generally that there were many negatives in his situation, in the place, even in the prospect, but that we were stuck with it and would have to work in that framework. He had good and real reasons to be disappointed, frustrated, and even angry, but his desire to make me fail or to destroy the institution seemed excessive and unrealistic.

In the second month of treatment, now a considerably modified form of analysis, Douglas organized a patient revolt with plans to strike against the kitchens, the occupational therapy programs, etc. He called an evening meeting of all patients to implement his program. The following morning he appeared for his hour in an amused, puzzled mood. He had not gone to the meeting. On the way, walking by himself, he had heard me talking to him. The experience almost approached hallucinatory vividness. The content wasn't too clear. What he remembered most was that the voice was cool and questioning, as if skeptical of what he was about to do. He gave up the whole thing, went back to his room, and went to bed.

What interested me was that afterward I seemed to be his constant companion and he seemed to raise with himself the very types of questions I would ordinarily raise with him. Now he swung from a semihostile, destructive, cynical, or at least skeptical attitude toward me and the institution to one of rather excessive transference delight. Many of his fantasies had to do with being cradled, rocked, and even sung to, and his positive attachment revealed a powerful homosexual base. The "real" relationship, essential at the outset, could now be safely put in the background in favor of a rapidly flowering transference neurosis.

A young mother, Helen, suffered an acute psychotic decompensation when her husband left her and demanded a divorce. She was filled with paranoid delusions, certain she would be poisoned, shot, stabbed, and rapidly assigned persecutory roles to all members of her family and to many friends. She ran aimlessly from city to city, but could never escape the imminent threat of death.

When she came to me (M.W.) for treatment, her most urgent question, apart from her deep distrust, was whether I believed the truth and reality of her stories. I told her I didn't know whether her experiences were factual or not, that I would like very much to hear them in the greatest detail, and that I would study them carefully and answer her questions at a later point. Even in this first interview I realized she was a bright, articulate woman with an excellent memory. I asked her if she would mind my writing down all the details of her experience so that I could study them carefully and give an opinion when the matter was clear in my own mind. She was quite pleased.

During one hour each day for the next seven days she gave me a detailed account of the signs, signals, and experiences that demonstrated the terrible designs on her life. Whenever we began an hour she remembered precisely, without prompting, where she had left off. My questions, which were relatively few, were aimed at expanding the material, not at setting traps, demonstrating contradictions, or exposing falsity. I knew that had been her experience with all her relatives who were frightened by the sudden failure of her reality testing. I wanted to demonstrate one thing only, apart from getting the clinical data. I wanted to show her it was possible to look at this material calmly and objectively, to hold no special brief for its real or unreal nature, and to respect it as a very urgent experience of the patient whatever its background. In schizophrenia a tendency ranging from imitation to identification is strong, though unreliable, as witness the performances in echolalia and echopraxia. A little would go a long way here.

I must confess to being startled when, at the end of the week, Helen asked me if what she had been talking about was sick. I had a real colleague, however, when a bit later in the hour she asked me if that was what people called schizophrenia. One cannot really say what produced such a dramatic alteration. So far as I can see, a reliable relationship with a constant object around a problem focused on assessing reality or unreality allowed for some transient identification with an objective, analytic attitude. In a sense, she took over my task and carried it out extremely well. But just as in the case of Douglas, the solution of the reality problem led only to the establishment of a good working alliance. What followed was an intense flowering of a sexualized transference, tinged with both masochistic and sadistic tendencies. The possibility for real analytic work had been created, however, almost precisely as the aftermath of an intense investment in a "real" relationship.

Technical Considerations

All patients, whether neurotic, borderline, or psychotic, have transference reactions in and out of the therapeutic situation. It is our belief that only those patients are *analyzable* who have the capacity for transference-free relationships as well. This is necessary to "get into" analysis. Patients who lack this capacity for transference-free relating require *preparatory psychotherapy*. This means they need to be helped to build an object relationship based on reliable and predictable perceptions, judgments, and responses. They require more than interpretation and insights. Even most of our neurotic patients, at different periods of the analysis, for example, at the height of the transference neurosis, may require such additional measures. While exact prescriptions for building or strengthening a "real" object relationship in the analytic situation cannot be given, some general illustrations or guidelines may prove helpful.

The most important and most difficult ingredient to describe is the creation of a productive analytic atmosphere. This should consist of a sense of serious purpose, of dedicated work, of discipline and restraint on the part of the psychoanalyst. Yet this atmosphere must also contain indications of the analyst's humanitarian concern and respect for the patient's predicament. The analyst is a therapist who is intent on alleviating the patient's pain, and his most potent instrument is the giving of insight, administered in dosages bearable to the patient. The analyst has to explore and probe into sensitive and intimate areas, and insights should be given with precision, directness, and frankness, yet with full awareness of the patient's vulnerability and exposure. The analyst is a physicianly person who must be able to administer painful insights without unnecessary sugar-coating or damaging delays (Greenson, 1967a, chapter 4.2).

We have found it beneficial to explain every new or strange procedure or measure to the patient so that he understands why we work in a certain way. For example, we explain why we use free association and therefore why we use the couch. We analyze the patient's anxieties about such procedures, if they are severe, before asking him to attempt them. We explain in the beginning of the analysis, when the patient first asks a question, why we do not answer questions as a rule. Later on we will be silent, unless our silence would be traumatic or an answer would prevent an unnecessary waste of time.

We try to dose our interpretations so that patients will not be forced to deal on their own with new and painful insights for long periods—for example, over holidays. We try to accommodate to special trying circumstances in the patient's life as long as we feel that doing so will not hurt another patient or become an interference in the analytic process. At the same time we hold the patient to some reasonable dealing with our own realities, including schedule, time, payments, and the like. If he comes to overvalue us, it must not be by reason of seduction or unrealistic accommodation to his wishes.

We have found it useful before the end of an hour to tell a patient when we are unclear about what has been going on in the hour. We do not dismiss a patient in silence or reach wildly for some remote interpretation to demonstrate a comprehension we do not have. We ask the patient, often, for his ideas or associations to this admission. We also believe that, at times, the patient should be encouraged to do some of the interpretive work on his own so as to give him a feeling of participation and even achievement. We listen carefully to his insights and treat them as signaling a significant effort, though we may not always agree with the content.

An important rule of thumb we have found useful in promoting the nontransference reactions is the frank admission of any and all errors of technique, whether they be due to countertransference reactions, faulty interpretations, or shortcomings in the analyst's personality or character. The timing of the admission of error and the issue whether one expresses regret verbally or by tone are too complex to be discussed in this limited presentation. It is enough to indicate here that the acknowledgment of error should not interfere with any of the following:

1. The patient should be given ample opportunity to discover the mistake himself.
2. The patient's fantasies before and after the error should be analyzed.
3. The patient's reaction to the acknowledgment should also be analyzed.

Although one no longer hears elaborate debates in analytic circles as to whether it is a mortal technical sin to offer a Kleenex to a patient weeping over the recent death of a parent, it is still highly suspect to do anything which resembles being kind to the patient. This seems, at times, to include any acknowledgment that the patient is right, realistic, perceptive, or insightful. However, such an acknowledgment, when based in the patient's productions, is very far removed from the seduction of unwarranted praise or unneeded support. It fosters a necessary and "real" relationship. Perhaps we should be more aware of the fact that persistent anonymity and prolonged affective atherosclerosis can also be seductive, but generally in the direction of inviting an irreversible and uninterpretable hostile transference and alienation.

With borderline and psychotic patients the focus is so largely on reality and "real" relationships that the technical recommendations are both more extensive and more flexible. They include, among a host of other procedures, maintaining a face-to-face relationship, concrete assistance with reality adaptations, control of instinctual outbursts where called for, education, fostering compulsive tasks, keeping appropriate psychological and even physical distance, and a wide variety of other actions, attitudes, and communications which are designed to facilitate the development of reparative object relations and restore internal object representation. The use of interpretation varies from patient to patient or from time to time with the same patient. It is enough to indicate here that we believe whatever will advance the "real" relationship, at least with disturbed schizophrenic patients, takes precedence over transference considerations and ultimately opens the way for effective interpretive intervention.

Theoretical Considerations

All our patients, to varying degrees, doubt their judgment, perceptions, and worthiness. If we "only interpret" or "only analyze," we unintentionally leave them with the impression that their reactions were "merely" repetitions of their infantile past, and that their behavior was immature, wrong, or crazy. If part of our therapeutic aim is to increase the patient's healthy ego functions and capacity for object relations, it is important that we confirm those aspects of his behavior which indicate healthy functioning. By ignoring those undistorted aspects of the patient's productions we unwittingly imply that his realistic reactions are unimportant, hardly worthy of comment, and that all that matters is understanding the unconscious meaning of his behavior.

Our emphasis on the nontransference relationship between patient and analyst is a result of our dissatisfaction with the current one-sided stress on transference interpretations as the main, if not the only, therapeutic tool. We do not deny the central importance of transference interpretation in psycho-analysis proper, but it has been a repeated experience that for our patients to develop healthy ego functioning, object con-stancy, and the capacity for full object relationship, the analytic situation must offer them an opportunity for experiencing in depth *both* the realistic and the unrealistic aspects of how they deal with objects. Interpretation removes old unconscious and irrational anxieties, guilts, and depressions. Beyond that many of our patients need the experience of feeling in ways "they are right." They need the experience of having their appropriate ego functions and object relationships acknowledged and respected by the analyst's proper "handling" of both the transference and nontransference phenomena. Structure building occurs not only as a result of dissolution through interpretation but by positive recognition and dealing with the patient's most effective levels of performance.

Acknowledging and dealing with nontransference elements need not preclude or obscure the clarification and interpretation of transference. To the contrary, it is our belief that only the development of a viable, "real," nontransference relationship, no matter how limited in scope it may be, is essential to effect the resolution of the transference neurosis.

Total anonymity of the analyst in the analytic situation is not only impossible but even undesirable. It leads to analysis in a vacuum or to an obsessive concern with analyzing as a way of life. If we hold to the position that the analyst is an impartial observer at a post equidistant to all psychic instances, then it must be assumed that he will also acknowledge and work with ego functions which include reality testing. Recognizing the technical necessity for dealing with nontransference aspects of the patient's productions reduces the danger of a defensive omnipotence and omniscience in the analyst. It leads to a rounded, human experience, divorced from mystic ritual, without losing its essential nature in the building of insight and structure.

We choose to close, however, with an urgent statement of some necessary reservations. There is always the danger of misinterpreting our position to imply overprotective acting out as a teacher, parent, or leader, misusing the "real" as a base for seductive gratifications and unnecessary support. There is no warrant for role playing or for attempting painless or cheerful psychoanalysis. Purist, orthodox analysis in the most extreme sense leaves little room for errors of commission. The principal disasters lie mainly in errors of omission. What we have suggested adds a dimension to analytic interest and concern. In some sense it suggests some blending of restrained humanitarian concern with scientific discipline. In suggesting some enlargement of the arena for analytic interest and activity, we realize that there is always the possibility of introducing new errors of judgment. This seems to us a lesser danger than a persistent neglect of what is "real" and right in our patients.

It has already been suggested that the subject of the "real" relationship might prove "subversive." Perhaps this legitimate warning has tempted us at times to state our position with a somewhat challenging and polemical force. Mainly we hope it will encourage a corresponding investment in critical and thorough discussion. The subject is too important to warrant further silence and neglect.[4]

---

[4] This paper was discussed at a plenary session of the 26th International Psycho-Analytical Congress, Rome, July 28, 1969. The authors' introductory and closing remarks as well as those of the discussants were published in the *International Journal of Psycho-Analysis*, 51:143-150, 1970. In a few instances I have incorporated some of our discussion remarks in this paper.

23

The Exceptional
Position of the Dream
in Psychoanalytic Practice

(1970)

REUD CONSIDERED *The Interpretation of Dreams* his major work. He wrote in the third (revised) English edition, published in 1932, "It contains, even according to my present-day judgement, the most valuable of all the discoveries it has been my good fortune to make. Insight such as this falls to one's lot but once in a lifetime" (p. xxxii). At the end of Part E in chapter 7 Freud said: *"The interpretation of dreams is the royal road to a knowledge of the unconscious activities of the mind"* (p. 608). A further indication of how important Freud considered this work to be is that he revised and amplified the book on dreams on eight different occasions, the last time in 1930 (Strachey, 1953, p. xii).[1]

The A. A. Brill Memorial Lecture, November 11, 1969. First published in *Psychoanalytic Quarterly*, 39:519-549, 1970.

I am indebted to Max Schur, Milton Wexler, Alfred Goldberg, and Nathan Leites for many of the ideas in this paper.

[1] It is fitting on the occasion of the Brill Memorial Lecture to note that the first English edition of the book was translated by A. A. Brill in 1913.

You may wonder why I chose to present a paper on the exceptional position of the dream since all this would seem to be common knowledge. A careful reading of the psychoanalytic literature in recent years, however, reveals that a number of psychoanalysts believe either that the dream has declined in clinical importance over the last forty years and is of no special value for psychoanalytic therapy or they use techniques which indicate that they have disregarded Freud's theory and methods of understanding and using the dream in clinical practice. I am also impressed that some influential psychoanalysts contend that this downgrading of the significance of the dream in clinical practice has come about because, (a) the structural theory was introduced, (b) Freud's great work on dreams has discouraged attempts at emulation or elaboration, and (c) Freud's concept of the topographic theory has become useless. These conclusions and more can be found in a monograph titled *The Place of the Dream in Clinical Psychoanalysis*, which is the result of a two-year study of dreams by the Kris Study Group under the Chairmanship of Charles Brenner, with Herbert Waldhorn (1967) serving as reporter. Most of the members of this group appear to have concluded that (1) the dream is, clinically speaking, a communication in the course of analysis similar to all others; (2) it does not provide access to material otherwise unavailable; (3) it is simply one of many types of material useful for analytic inquiry; (4) it is not particularly useful for the recovery of repressed childhood memories; (5) Freud's theory that the dream-work is governed by the interplay between the primary process and the secondary process is not compatible with the structural theory and ought to be discarded.

I disagree with every one of the conclusions stated above. I am happy to point out that I am not alone in my beliefs, for I have discovered that some members of that section of the Kris Study Group, with Leon Altman as their spokesman, opposed many of those opinions. Altman (1969) has published a book, *The Dream in Psychoanalysis*, in which he suggests other reasons for the decline in clinical use of the dream. He expressed the opinion that since the coming of the trend toward ego psychology, many analysts have not had the experience of having their own dreams properly analyzed and the lack of this type of personal experience has deprived the psychoanalyst of the conviction that the interpretation of dreams is of outstanding importance for psychoanalysis.

Besides that section of the Kris Study Group reported in *The Place of the Dream in Clinical Psychoanalysis*, there are prominent analysts of Kleinian persuasion who also work with patients' dreams in ways which are far removed from what Freud, Isakower (1938, 1954), Sharpe (1949), Lewin (1958, 1968), Erikson (1954), and a host of others have described in their writings on this subject. In this paper I shall attempt to contribute some clinical material and formulations which I hope will demonstrate how those analysts who seem to operate from divergent theoretical and technical convictions differ from analysts who believe in the exceptional position of the dream.

It is my belief, after many years of psychoanalytic therapy with private patients and candidates in psychoanalytic training, that one cannot carry out genuine analysis in sufficient depth if one does not understand the structure of dream formation *as well as the patient's and the analyst's contributions to the technique of dream interpretation*.

Some General Formulations

The dream, I believe, is a unique form of mental functioning which is produced during a special phase of sleep. This phase is unlike any other phase of the sleep cycle and differs also from the waking state. The psychophysiological research of Dement and Kleitman (1957), Charles Fisher (1965, 1966), and Ernest Hartmann (1965), among others, has made this emphatically clear. Recent research suggests the likelihood that dream deprivation may be the cause of severe emotional and mental disorders. We may well have to add to Freud's dictum that the dream is the guardian of sleep, that sleep is necessary in order to safeguard our need to dream.

The altered balance of mental forces in the dream is produced by bursts of psychic activity that seek sensory release
because sleep diminishes contact with the external world and
also cuts off the possibility of voluntary motor action. The dream
state allows for a reduction and regression of conscious ego
activities and of the censorship function of the superego. It is
important to realize, however, that, in a sense, one is never fully
awake nor fully asleep. These are relative and not absolute
terms. Kubie (1966), Lewin (1955), and Stein (1965) have
stressed the merits of keeping in mind the sleep-waking ratio in
studying any kind of human behavior. This helps explain the
fact that in the dream the perceiving function of the ego, being
deprived of the external world during sleep, turns its energy
toward internal psychic activity. Freud (1917c) wrote that when
people go to sleep they undress their minds and lay aside most of
their psychical acquisitions (p. 222). Lewin (1968) added that
the dreamer generally sheds his body. The dream usually
appears to us as a picture and is recorded only by an indefinite
"psychic" eye (p. 86).

If we follow the notion of a variable sleep-waking ratio, we
are immediately reminded of phenomena similar to dreams: free
association, parapraxes, jokes, symptom formations, and acting
out. But there are crucial differences. No production of the
patient occurs so regularly and reveals so much so graphically of
the unconscious forces of the mind as the dream. Dream interpretation can uncover in more immediate and convincing ways
not only what is hidden, but how it is hidden, and why it is
hidden. We gain special access to the interplay and the transitions between the unconscious psychic activities governed by the
primary process and conscious phenomena, which follow the
laws of the secondary process. The proportion between input
and output, in terms of reported phenomena and obtained
knowledge of unconscious material, is in no other type of psychic
phenomena as favorable as it is in dreams (K. R. Eissler, personal communication).

So long as psychoanalytic therapy focuses on the resolution
of neurotic conflicts in which the crucial components are uncon-

scious, it makes no sense to consider every production of the patient of equal potential value. Affects, body language, and dreams are all, in most ways, nearer to those almost unreachable depths we search out so persistently in our analytic work. We attempt to present our findings to the patient's conscious and reasonable ego with the hope of providing him with a better understanding of his way of life and an opportunity for change.

These same points can be expressed structurally by stating that the dream reveals with unusual clarity various aspects of the id, the repressed, the unconscious ego and superego, and to a lesser degree certain conscious ego functions, particularly its observing activities. However, limiting the approach to the dream to the structural point of view is an injustice because it neglects the fact that we also have in the dream more open access to dynamic, genetic, and economic data of basic importance. Small wonder, then, that the dream experience itself, often without interpretation, leads more directly and intensely to the patient's affects and drives than any other clinical material. This makes for a sense of conviction about the reality of unconscious mental activity unequaled by any other clinical experience. This is particularly true of transference dreams.

The dream is in closer proximity to childhood memories by dint of the fact that both make use essentially of pictorial representations. Freud (1900, 1923b) and Lewin (1968) have emphasized that primitive mentation takes place in pictures and is closer to unconscious processes than verbal representation. Even after children learn to speak, their thinking is essentially dominated by pictorial representations. Things heard get turned into pictures, as we know from certain screen memories (Lewin, 1968; Helen Schur, 1966). If an event is to become a memory in early childhood, it has eventually to become concretized, a mental representation, a memory trace. Lewin states that then we search for lost memories as if they can be found somewhere. This type of memory, the recall of an objectified experience, is a step which seems to occur at the end of the first or beginning of the second year of life (Spitz, 1965; Waelder, 1937). There are more primitive "imprintings" which are derived from infantile body and feeling states that are not capable of being remembered but which may give rise to mental images and sensations in dreams. Lewin's ideas on blank dreams and the dream screen and his discussion of related problems are especially worthy of note (1953, 1968, pp. 51-55).

To return briefly to the special importance of the psychic eye for the dreamer and the interpreter of dreams. The dream is essentially a visual experience and most adult recollections of early childhood come to us as pictures or scenes. The analyst interpreting to his patient is often working upon a fragment of historical experience which he hopes will lead to a memory. Such fragments or details may appear in dreams. When the analyst tries to fill in the gaps between single interpretations, he is making a construction, he is trying to re-create a series of interrelated forgotten experiences. Such conjectures may lead to recollections but, even if they do not, they may lead to a sense of probability or conviction that the reconstruction is correct. This may then appear in a dream as an event (Freud, 1937b). Lewin (1968) describes this as trying to re-create a story in pictures of the patient's forgotten past. By doing so we attempt to get the patient to scan his past along with us; we are engaged in conjoint looking (p. 17). The ultraclarity of some dream details also indicates that there is a special relationship between the cathexis of looking and the search for memories. This wish to see what actually took place, to be "in" on it, adds to the special sense of conviction that the correct interpretation of a dream can convey.

Ernst Kris (1956b) decried the one-sided emphasis on analyzing defenses and stressed the importance of reconstructing past historical events so that the patient could "recognize" the pictures drawn as familiar (p. 59). He believed that memory plays a central role in a circular process which, if integrated, makes it possible for the patient to reconstruct his total biographical picture, change his self representation and his perspective of the important persons in his world. In Kris's paper (1956a) on the "good analytic hour," it is remarkable how often he chose examples of hours which contained dreams and recovered memories.

The predominant elements in the psychic activities that occur in dreams are heavily weighted on the side of the id, the repressed memories, the primitive defensive mechanisms of the ego, and the infantile forms and functions of the superego. Occasionally one can observe more mature ego functions, but they are rarely dominant. All this testifies to the high degree of regression that occurs in dreaming, but as in all regressive phenomena, the quality and quantity of regression is uneven and selective in the different psychic structures and functions as Freud pointed out as early as 1917(c), Fenichel in 1945, and Arlow and Brenner in 1964. The clearest and most comprehensive description of the unevenness and selectivity of regression can be found, in my opinion, in Anna Freud's book, *Normality and Pathology in Childhood* (1965, pp. 93-107).

Free association is a similar regressive phenomenon; it is an attempt to approximate something between wakefulness and sleep. The use of the reclining position, the absence of external distractions, the patient's conscious attempt to suspend his ordinary censorship, to abandon strict logic and coherence in his communications, all attest to that. However, real spontaneous free associations are rarely achieved by most patients and are then defended against with far greater sophistication. The point I wish to make is that the dream is the freest of free associations. Slips of the tongue may quickly reveal some deep unconscious insights, but they occur rarely; insight is localized and the old defenses are very readily reinstituted. Acting out is by definition ego-syntonic to the patient and its infantile origins are strongly rationalized away and defended. By contrast, as bizarre and incomprehensible as the dream may appear, the patient recognizes the dream as his; he knows it is his own creation. Although the strange content of the dream may make it seem alien, nevertheless it is irrevocably his, like his symptoms, and he is quite willing to work on his dreams, provided his analyst has demonstrated how working together on dreams is helpful in achieving greater awareness of the patient's unknown self.

A few words before turning to some clinical examples. Freud himself recognized that *some* of his ideas subsumed under the topographic point of view conflicted with the descriptive and dynamic attributes of unconscious mental activities and he introduced the structural point of view (1923b). This new division of the psychic apparatus into id, ego, and superego clarified the role of the conscious and unconscious ego and the conscious and unconscious superego in its conflicts with the totally unconscious id. I agree with Fenichel (1945), with Rapaport and Gill (1959) as well as with Arlow and Brenner (1964), who stress the superiority of the structural theory in affording a clearer and more logical explanation for the origin and fate of neurotic conflicts. I do not agree with Arlow and Brenner, however, that Freud's hypotheses concerning the primary process, the secondary process, and the preconscious should be discarded or that they are incompatible with the structural point of view. Even Merton Gill (1963), who believes that the topographic point of view is conceptually not on a par with the other metapsychological points of view, agrees that some topographic conceptions have an important place both clinically and theoretically. I find this to be particularly true in working with dream. It is equally important in dealing with patients who suffer from defects and deficiencies in ego formation and the parallel difficulty in building constant internal object representations, problems which go below and beyond the conflict theory of the psychoneuroses. I do not wish to dwell on theory— it is not my strong point, but those interested may turn to the writings of Hartmann (1951), Loewenstein (1954), Benjamin (1959), Eissler (1962), Max Schur (1966), Loewald (1966), Mahler (1968), and Fisher's remarks in the panel on The Psychoanalytic Theory of Thinking (1958), for a more thorough discussion of the subject.

Clinical Examples

Some clinical examples of how different analysts work with dreams illustrate the divergencies in technique and theoretical orientation. I shall begin with clinical material from the publications of psychoanalysts who work with dreams in ways that seem to me to be unproductive, wasteful, and at times even harmful.

A clinical illustration presented in *The Place of the Dream in Clinical Psychoanalysis* (Waldhorn, 1967, pp. 59-67) was that of a thirty-year-old writer in the second year of her analysis. Essentially, she seemed to be an "as if" character, exceedingly immature and dependent. There was a childhood history of social failure in competition with her younger sister because of the patient's ineptitude and gaucheness. The patient had severe acne of the face, neck, and back in adolescence and had occasional recurrent active lesions. She was also thin and flat-chested. She entered treatment because of mild depressions, poor concentration, and inability to sustain an intimate relationship with a man. The patient had several brief affairs accompanied by a dread of losing the man and was always flooded by remorse and loss of self-esteem when the affair ended. In the weeks prior to the dream reported, the patient had had sexual relations with a man named John, whom she had known only a short time. He had left town for several weeks and, in spite of knowing better from past disappointments, she found herself imagining that John loved her and they would be married. During this interval she brought in a dream:

> She began the hour as follows: "I had a very bad dream. I had cancer of the breast. A doctor, a woman, said it would have to be removed. She said that there would be after-effects which I would feel in my neck. My friend R. had this operation. I was scared and I panicked, and wondered how I could get away, run away and not have to have this done."
> She continued with the following associations: "I tried to think why I should have such a dream. I thought it must be related to my idea that I am not complete by myself and that I need some sort of union with a remarkable man to make myself complete. This might be related to my worry that John was gone and maybe this was symbolized by my breast being removed. Actually, I am very frightened by

things like that. Many people do have an obsession about
such fears. For example, Paul does. Some people can face
these things with great courage and strength, but not me.
I am very frightened when I think about the danger of the
scorpions in Mexico [she was planning a trip in a few
months]" [p. 61].

The patient awoke, fell asleep, and had another dream but
I shall omit it because the presenter and the group did not touch
upon it. After a few innocuous associations, the analyst finally
spoke and I shall quote his first remarks verbatim.

At this point the analyst intervened, asking "about your
dream. What do you associate to the business about the
doctor?" The patient responded: "She was a matronly type
of woman, stern. She didn't seem to feel sorry for me or
anything like that, but just said what would have to be
done. I was thinking, how could a man make love to me
without one breast? I would be terribly self-conscious...."

After a pause the analyst asked: "What about the part
in the dream about the neck?" She responded: "Sometimes
I make a wrong movement and my neck muscles can hurt.
That area is vulnerable for me because of my complexion
problems involving my chin and neck, about which I have
always felt so self-conscious...."

The analyst then added: "When you speak of self-
consciousness about your skin and neck, does it remind you
of the self-consciousness you have recently been describing
when you told me about how terrible you felt before you
had any breast development?" The patient said: "So, do you
think that the fact that John did not call me made me
re-experience those feelings of inadequacy? They may still
be present" [p. 62].

The analyst then offered a long intellectual interpretation
and the patient responded in kind.

The Study Group's discussion of this presentation included
the following excerpt:

The discussion of this report was initiated by the remarks of the analyst presenting the data. He maintained that the clinical material supported the belief that dreams can best be treated in the same way as other associations in the hours, and not necessarily accorded extraordinary or exhaustively detailed procedural attention as some would insist. Here, in the hours described, the analytic work is focussed on the problems highlighted by the repetitive life experience of the patient.... Accordingly, some portions of the dream can be neglected in favor of others, and a dream need have no specific attention directed to it if spontaneous associations are meager and the work with the dream (as opposed to other material) seems less likely to be rewarding. The rich amount of symbolically understandable elements in the second half of the first dream was not explored at all, but it was the analyst's clinical judgment that nothing was lost in the process [p. 64f.].

I shall limit myself to a few remarks about the patient's manifest dream, her associations, the analyst's interventions, and the group discussion. In the first dream the patient is terrified upon discovering she has a cancer of the breast. She is told this by a female doctor who warns her there will be aftereffects. The patient's associations sound to me intellectualized and a rote repetition of old interpretations given her by her male analyst. There does not seem to be any attempt on the part of the analyst to point out her intellectualization or to get to her terror of this malignant thing growing inside her. The analyst did not pursue the only spontaneous free association the patient produced, namely, her fear of scorpions in Mexico. After the patient reported the second dream and a few innocuous associations, the analyst asked: "about your dream. What do you associate to the business about the doctor?" To me, the way the question was put gives the impression the analyst is either defensive and hostile or even contemptuous, otherwise he would not use a phrase like "what about the business about the doctor." Furthermore, it is all too intellectual. Words like "what do you associate" push the patient in the direction of intellectual compliance; not the best way to get into feelings or really free, free associations. In general, there was no sign that the therapist was trying to reach or establish contact with the patient's affects; he shows no signs of being "tuned in" on her feelings; on the contrary, he seems to play right along with her intellectualized defensiveness.

If you read the second dream, it seems to express in obvious symbolic terms the patient's envy of her sister and her aunt, but it was completely ignored. Apparently the analyst and the group did not discern any possible connections between cancer, breast, mother, and envy. There also was no apparent awareness of how frequently heterosexual promiscuity is used as a defense against helpless childhood dependency needs with the resultant urges and fears of fusing or becoming reunited with the pregenital mother. There was also no mention of a hostile transference to her male analyst or a wish to have a female analyst. The analyst and the group seemed content to maintain a highly intellectual contact with the patient, and were reluctant to open up the patient's fantasy life and follow wherever it might lead. Toward the end of this discussion in the monograph, there are a few sentences that deserve special comment.

> Such axiomatic procedures as the desirability of working with transference elements before nontransference material, or affect-laden before nonaffect-laden material, or the necessity of drawing the patient's attention to evident omissions or to an addendum, were all mentioned. The consensus was that these were best considered as tactical maneuvers, subordinated to an overall strategy of the conduct of the analysis, which would, of course, change with the progress of the treatment [p. 66f.].

In my opinion there is no place for "axiomatic procedures" in trying to do psychoanalytic therapy. It is true that some of us follow certain time-tested technical guidelines in beginning the exploration of such oft-recurring clinical constellations as may occur in associating to dreams or in free association in general. These approaches are tools for investigation. I find the concept of an "overall strategy of the conduct of the analysis" an impressive high-sounding phrase but, in reality, with our present state of knowledge, this "overall strategy" is at best loose, subject to frequent changes and revisions, and full of unknowns. Only psychoanalysts with preconceived and rigid theoretical notions are sure of an "overall strategy." And they also have prefabricated interpretations for all types of patients and disregard the fact that each individual human being is unique, as well as the fact that there is still much even the best of us do not know and cannot predict about our patients. Freud (1905a) had the humility to say that we should let the patient determine the subject matter of the hour; he attached great importance to following the patient's free associations. In 1950 Eissler severely criticized Alexander and his followers for making decisions about the definitive strategy for treatment of a case. Eissler felt that Alexander was more interested in validating his own hypotheses than in really analyzing his patients.

This leads to another type of distortion in working with dreams which can be found in the writings of some of the Kleinian analysts. Hans Thorner (1957) in studying the problem of examination anxiety illustrated his ideas by describing a patient, a dream, and his interpretations.

A man of early middle age complained of impotence and that all his love relationships came to a premature end. At times he could begin a relationship, but as soon as he felt the woman was interested in him, he had to break off. He was impotent in other spheres of life as well. Although he had reached a high standard of proficiency in music, he was unable to play in public or before his friends. It became clear that all these situations approximated an examination situation. When he applied for a new job, he was terrified of being interviewed because of what he considered to be his "black record," although realistically there was little black in his record. During one of these intervals he reported a dream which shed new light upon the nature of his black record. In the dream red spiders were crawling in and out of the patient's anus. A doctor examined him and told the patient that he was unable to see anything wrong with him. The patient replied, "Doctor, you may not see anything, but they are there just the same." Thorner reports his interpretations to the patient as follows:

> Here the patient expresses his conviction that he harbours bad objects (red spiders) and even the doctor's opinion cannot shake this conviction. The associative link between "black record" and "red spiders" shows the anal significance of his "black record." He himself is afraid of these objects against which he, like the man in the dream, asks for help. This help must be based on a recognition of these objects and not on their denial; in other words, he should be helped to control them. It is clear that we are here dealing with a feeling of persecution by bad internal objects [p. 286].

I believe this is a prime example of interpreting the manifest content of a dream according to the analyst's theoretical convictions. The patient's associations are interpreted in a narrow preconceived way. The patient's reproach to the examining physician, "Doctor, you may not see anything, but they are there all the same," is not recognized as a hostile transference, nor is it acknowledged as a possible justifiable reproach to the analyst that he really may be missing something. I wonder if the red spiders crawling in and out of the patient's anus are not the patient's reaction to his analyst's intrusive and painful interpretations. But now I, too, am guilty of interpreting without associations.

Another example of a similar type can be found in Hanna Segal's book (1964). She describes a patient, his dream, and her interventions as follows.

> Powerful unconscious envy often lies at the root of negative therapeutic reactions and interminable treatments; one can observe this in patients who have a long history of failed previous treatments. It appeared clearly in a patient who came to analysis after many years of varied psychiatric and psychotherapeutic treatments. Each course of treatment

would bring about an improvement, but deterioration would set in after its termination. When he began his analysis, it soon appeared that the main problem was the strength of his negative therapeutic reaction. I represented mainly a successful and potent father, and his hatred of and rivalry with this figure was so intense that the analysis, representing my potency as an analyst, was unconsciously attacked and destroyed over and over again. . . . In the first year of his analysis, he dreamt that he put into the boot of his little car tools belonging to my car (bigger than his), but when he arrived at his destination and opened the boot, all the tools were shattered.

[Segal interprets:] This dream symbolized his type of homosexuality; he wanted to take the paternal penis into his anus and steal it, but in the process of doing so, his hatred of the penis, even when introjected, was such that he would shatter it and be unable to make use of it. In the same way, interpretations which he felt as complete and helpful were immediately torn to pieces and disintegrated, so that it was particularly following good sessions which brought relief that he would start to feel confused and persecuted as the fragmented, distorted, half-remembered interpretations confused and attacked him internally [p. 29f.].

Here, too, I believe one can see how the analyst's conviction about the correctness of her insights and interpretations tempts her to make detailed interpretations without any of the patient's associations for confirmatory clinical evidence. Once again I do not see in this case presentation any evidence of an analyst and patient working together on a dream. I see instead an analyst forcing a patient to submit to her interpretation. By doing so this analyst is acting in a way which proves she is really like the patient's hated and envied potent father. No wonder he dreams that all his tools are shattered. To quote Freud (1925a): "But dream-interpretation of such a kind, without reference to the dreamer's associations, would in the most favourable case remain a piece of unscientific virtuosity of very doubtful value"

(p. 128). I must add that many analysts of non-Kleinian affil-
iation also disregard the patient's associations.

I shall now present some work with dreams that I believe
exemplifies how an analyst who appreciates the exceptional
position of the dream utilizes it in his practice. For the sake of
clarity and demonstrability, the dreams I have chosen for
illustrations are those from my recent clinical experience with
which I was able to work fruitfully. They are not everyday
examples of my work with dreams. There are many dreams I can
understand only vaguely and partially and some I can hardly
understand at all. There are also occasions when the dream is
not the most productive material of the hour, but this has been
rare in my experience. Freud wrote as far back as 1911(b) that
dream interpretation should not be pursued for its own sake, it
must be fitted into the treatment, and all of us agree on this
obvious point.

I realize that no clinical demonstration of the value of
dream interpretation will change the opinions of those who are
predominantly devoted to theory conservation or theoretical
innovations. Their theories seem to be more real to them than
the memories and reconstructions of their patient's life history.
Working with dreams is not only an enlightening experience for
the patient, but it may be a source of new clinical and theoretical insights for the analyst, if he has an open mind. Furthermore, there are some analysts who have no ear or eye for
dreams, like people who find it hard to hear and visualize the
beauty of poetry, or like the tone-deaf who cannot appreciate
the special imagery and language of music, or those who have no
facility for wit and humor. Such analysts will lower the importance of dream interpretation, no matter what evidence one
presents. Finally, there are analysts who, for some other reasons,
have never had the opportunity to learn how to listen to, understand, and work with dreams.

The two dreams I shall present are from the analysis of a
thirty-year-old writer, Mr. M.,[2] who came for analytic treatment because of a constant sense of underlying depressiveness,

---

[2] See also chapter 22.

frequent anxiety in social and sexual relations, and a feeling of being a failure despite considerable success in his profession and what appeared to be a good relationship to his wife and children. He had a great fear that he would not be able to do free association at all, and that if he did I would find him empty or loathsome and send him away. We worked on these resistances for several weeks and he was then able on occasion to do some relatively spontaneous free association on the couch. One of the major sources of his resistances in the beginning was his experience with several friends who were also currently in psychoanalytic treatment. They talked freely and often in social situations about their oedipus complexes, their positive and negative transference reactions, their castration anxiety, their superegos, their incestuous desires, etc., all of which my patient felt was "textbooky," "artificial," and "a load of crap." Mr. M. was afraid that he would not be able genuinely to accept such interpretations, and yet also dreaded that unknowingly he too might turn out to be a "junior psychoanalyst" socially. I want to present the highlights from an hour in the sixth week of his analysis in which he reported his first dream. He had often had the feeling of having dreamed, but until this point could never remember any of his dreams.

One day he began the hour by stating: "I had a dream, but it seems unrelated to anything we have been talking about."

I was making a phone call to some guy in a men's clothing store. I had ordered some clothes made to order and they didn't fit. I asked the guy to take them back, but he said I had to come in myself. I told him I was not going to pay for the clothes until they fit. I said, "It seems like you just took them off the rack." I repeated, "I won't pay for the clothes until they fit." As I said that I began to vomit, so I dropped the phone and ran into the bathroom to wash out my mouth. I left the receiver dangling and I could hear the guy saying, "What did you say, what? What?"

I remained silent and the patient spontaneously began to speak: "The most striking thing to me is the vomiting. I just can't

vomit, I never, never vomit. I can't even remember the last time
I did, probably as a child sometime. It is like a biological thing,
it's so strong. Like in yesterday's hour, I couldn't get myself to
talk [Pause]. Free association is like vomiting." I intervened at
this point and said, "Yes, free association becomes like vomiting
when things are trying to come up in your mind that you would
rather keep inside yourself and away from me. The dream says it
has to do with something not fitting you properly." The patient
quickly replied, "Yes, it's about clothes, but that is too silly. Why
clothes? Clothes not fitting? [Pause] Oh my God, this can't have
anything to do with the analysis. The man saying, what is it,
what, what, what, that could be you. [Pause] I leave you talking
and go to vomit in the bathroom—but why, why do I do that?"
I answered, "When I give you an interpretation that doesn't
seem to fit you, you must resent it and feel that I just took it off
my 'psychoanalytic rack,' like the other 'textbooky' analysts you
have heard about." The patient: "Oh Jesus, I can't believe it, I
thought things like this only happened in books. How funny!"

At this point, the patient began to roar with laughter and
tears streamed down his face. He gathered himself together and
said: "I never thought things like this would happen to me. You
are right. When you say things that don't seem to fit me, sometimes I do get annoyed, but I keep it in. [Pause] I get scared here
when I feel angry. It's like being afraid of my father when I was
a kid. [Pause] I now suddenly see a vague picture of me vomiting
when I was about three or four years old. [Pause] It was my
mother, right on her, she must have been holding me. She was
so nice about it, too, she took me to the bathroom and cleaned
me up and herself too. Amazing this whole thing." I answered:
"Yes, apparently you were not afraid to vomit up things in front of
your mother, but you must have been very scared of doing that
with your father and now you feel the same way here with me.
But you see these kinds of things do tend to come out in dreams
or in such things like your forgetting to pay me this month." The
patient was startled and blurted out: "This is too much. I had
your check in my wallet, but in the last minute I decided to
change my jacket and left my wallet at home. And I never even

thought of it when I was telling you the dream, all about not wanting to pay that man. Something must really be cooking inside of me." The patient paused, sighed, and after a while I asked him just to try to say what was going on. His associations then drifted to his shame about revealing his toilet activities, masturbation, his hemorrhoids, a history of an anal fistula, and other matters.

I believe this clinical example demonstrates how it is possible to work productively with a first dream, which is contrary to the opinions expressed in the monograph *The Place of the Dream in Clinical Psychoanalysis*. Avoidance of dream interpretation by the analyst can frighten the patient, because the patient may sense the analyst's fear of the dream contents. An analyst's timid approach to a dream may add to a patient's suspicion that he, the patient, is especially full of internal evils or may convince him that he has a frightened analyst. On the other hand, deep interpretations given too early will either frighten the patient into leaving the analysis or it will persuade him that the analyst is omniscient and convert the patient into a devout follower and not a working ally. One has to assess carefully with each patient how much and how little one can do with early dreams and early material in general.[3]

Let us scrutinize more carefully what I tried to do with that first dream. Once the patient was spontaneously able to connect his fear of vomiting with his fear of free association, I first confirmed this representation of his resistance by saying out loud what he had already become conscious of—his dread of losing control over the horrible things inside of himself: vomiting is equated to free association and he vomits into the sink and not into the phone, the analysis. I then felt I could lead him in the direction of trying to discover what was making him vomit. The obvious symbolism of the ill-fitting clothes delivered to him ready-made and not made to order, symbols which he himself could grasp, encouraged me to point out his suppressed anger at

[3] See Berta Bornstein (1949) and Loewenstein (1951) for examples of their method of dealing with this delicate problem. See also Greenson (1967a).

me for my ill-fitting, ready-made interpretations, taken off my psychoanalytic rack. His laughter was a relief from the fear that he lacked an unconscious mind and was a freak, and also that I might be harsh with him for such thoughts. It was confirmation of the correctness of my interpretation and also an early sign of conviction that there is an active but unconscious part of his mind which does contain specific and personal meanings and they are not as terrible as he had imagined.

My referring to myself as the "textbooky guy" who is unable to tailor his interpretations to suit the patient must have given Mr. M. enough trust in my motherliness so that he could recall an early childhood memory of vomiting on his mother. Here vomiting is loving and not hating. He was then able to contrast this with his dread of vomiting up things in the presence of his father. His later association to the toilet, masturbation, and so forth, indicated an increase in his ability to let things come up in free association in my presence, a lessening of his resistances. Apparently my way of communicating to him helped me establish a working alliance with his reasonable, observing ego.

There are many elements in this dream which I did not point out to Mr. M., but which are of interest to us as examples of the function of the dreamwork and of the interaction of the primary process and the secondary process as well as of the interaction of the id, ego, and superego. The patient's very first sentence before telling the dream: "I had a dream, but it seems unrelated to anything we have been talking about," is an attempt to contradict and deny the very essence of the dream, namely, that it concerns his feelings about me and the analysis. The psychoanalytic situation is depicted as a telephone conversation, only a verbal exchange, and even that is held at a distance. The man he speaks to is referred to as a "guy working in a store," not the awesome or flattering representation of a psychoanalyst. The insights and interpretations I gave him were represented by clothes, and clothes conceal rather than reveal, an example of reversal and the use of opposites. Psychoanalysis does not strip you, it is supposed to clothe you, a reassurance, a wish fulfillment. His fear of close emotional contact with the analyst is demonstrated by his refusal to come in person to the store. His leaving the phone dangling and hearing the "guy's voice" saying, "What is it, what, what?" is a beautiful and hostile caricature of my analytic technique. It also is his revenge against me for leaving him dangling hour after hour; it is not he who keeps asking desperately, but I. The vomiting is not only an expression of his forbidden instinctual impulses, but it is also a self-punishment for his hostility. It is, furthermore, a rejection of the interpretations I have been forcing him to swallow and his spiteful obedience: "You want me to bring things up. Okay, here it is." This is an example of the coexistence of opposites in the primary process.

One can see that the vomiting is derived from both the id and the superego. It also serves the resistances, a defensive function of the ego, by breaking off our line of communication. All this and more is in the dream *and* in the patient's associations, facilitated by the interpretations. Only a fraction of this material can be meaningfully conveyed to the patient in a single hour, but it serves a valuable service for the analyst as source material for clues that will be of use in the future.

Mr. M. continued with the theme of clothes and concealment in the next several hours. As a child of impoverished parents he was embarrassed by his shabby, dirty clothing. He was also ashamed of being skinny and had tried to hide this by wearing several sweatshirts and sweaters on top of each other when he was young. When he later became affluent, he bought bulky tweed sport coats and often wore turtleneck sweaters with a leather jacket and boots. During the postdream interval he recalled stealing money from his father to buy a zoot suit, which was fashionable in his youth, because he wanted to make a good impression at a school dance. He also recalled having severe acne which he attributed to masturbation and which he attempted to cover with various facial creams and lotions. He tried to rationalize his stealing from his father by recalling that his father cheated his customers at times. All this material had the meaning: "I have to hide my true self. If anyone sees beneath my surface he will find me ugly and unlovable. I am a fraud, but so is most of the world. How do I know you are genuine and sincere in your treatment of me and will it change once I am stripped of all my superficial disguises?" (I was not merely working with the manifest dream in the following days, but with the latent dream thoughts which the patient's associations and my interventions had uncovered.)

Another dream of Mr. M. occurred about two and one half years later. The patient had to interrupt his analysis for six months because of a professional assignment abroad and returned some three months before the dream. During this three-month interval of analytic work Mr. M. was in a chronic state of quiet, passive depression. I had interpreted this as a reaction to his wife's fourth pregnancy, which must have stirred up memories and feelings in regard to his mother's three pregnancies after his birth. It seemed clear to me that he was his mother's favorite, the only child and the favorite child. The patient accepted my interpretations submissively and conceded they had merit, but he could recall nothing about the birth of his three siblings or his reactions, although he was over six when the youngest was born. My interpretations had no appreciable influence on his mood.

Mr. M. came to the hour I shall now present, sadly and quietly, and in a somewhat mournful tone recounted the following dream:

> I am in a huge store, a department store. There are lots of shiny orange and green plastic raincoats on display. A middle-aged Jewish mother is arranging other articles of clothing. Nearby is a female manikin dressed in a gray flannel dress. I go outside and see a woman who looks very familiar, but I can't say specifically who she is. She is waiting expectantly and eagerly for me near a small surrey, putting clothes in it. I feel sorry for the poor horse and then realize the surrey is detached from the horse. I lift up the surrey to connect it and I am surprised how light the surrey is, but I don't know how to hitch it up to the horse. I also realize then that I was silly to feel sorry for the horse.

Mr. M.'s associations were as follows: "The three women in the dream were so different from one another. The older Jewish woman was a motherly type, working, doing, arranging, like my own mother used to be before she became bedridden. The manikin reminds me of how I used to think of gentile girls when I was a kid; beautiful, pure, and cold, like my wife. But they taught me different. The best sex I have ever experienced was only with gentile girls. Jewish women just don't turn me on. They never did. Since my wife's pregnancy our sex life is practically nil. She isn't feeling well and I must say I'm in no mood for sex. I would like to be close to her in bed, but I don't want her to think it is a sexual demand so there is no talking even. I'd like to just be close and cuddle. My wife is so quiet of late. I feel she is getting revenge on me for all my past wrongs. I never realized before I had had such a bad temper and that she had been and still is so afraid of me. [Pause] I feel so alone in that big house of ours. I work like a horse to pay for it. Maybe I am the horse in the dream that I felt sorry for."

I intervened, "It might be so. You think he had such a big load to carry, but then you lift up the buggy and you are surprised to discover how light it is." The patient interrupted me. "That buggy it was so light, it was so tiny, and the woman was putting clothes on it, like diapers." [Pause] I interrupted, "A baby buggy is very heavy for a little boy, he has to work like a horse to push it." Mr. M. burst in with, "I can remember trying to push my baby sister in her buggy, but it was too heavy for me. Now I see my father carrying the baby carriage downstairs as if it were a toy. I can even remember my brother and me together trying to push it." I interpreted and reconstructed: "I believe you have been depressed ever since your wife got pregnant because it stirred up memories of how you reacted when you were a small boy and your mother got pregnant and delivered your brother and sisters. You didn't want to face the fact that your father was hitched up to the coming of babies. You wished you could have been the father of the babies. But you weren't—you didn't know how to do it as a little boy and you felt left out in the cold, detached. You have been depressed about this ever since." After a pause, Mr. M. said, "I've always felt I'm not a real man. I act like one, but inside I still feel a real man should be like my father; strong physically, tough, and unafraid. I can fly airplanes, but my hands sweat whenever I want to screw my own wife."

In the next hour the meaning of the green and orange raincoats became clear. The patient spontaneously recalled some dirty jokes about puberty in which the terms "raincoat" and "rubbers" were used to refer to condoms. He then remembered condoms in his father's chest of drawers and later stealing some for his own use, just in case an opportunity presented itself, which, he wistfully said, "didn't occur for several years." By that time the "rubbers," the raincoats, had disintegrated in his wallet. It is worth noting how the hidden old shreds of "rubbers" in the patient's associations were changed into the shiny new raincoats on display in the dream. Here one can see the attempt at wish fulfillment in the manifest content of the dream: "I can buy conspicuous sexual potency in a store or in analysis." Later it also became clear that I too was the poor horse who had him as a big load to carry and also I was the "horse's ass" who could not help him make proper sexual connections with his wife or any other woman.

To me the outstanding element in the manifest dream was the surrey which turned out to be so tiny and light. My translation of the word "surrey" into "buggy" was the crucial technical point. I got from surrey to buggy by visualizing a surrey, which I have never seen in actual life but which brought to mind a popular song, *A Surrey with a Fringe on Top*. This led me to baby buggies with fringes on top. Not wanting to push the patient into *my* association of baby buggy, I dropped the baby part and said just buggy, to see where it would lead him. (All this flashed through my mind quickly and was not as carefully thought out as it sounds here.) But I believe I was on the right track as it helped the patient pictorialize a baby buggy. And this enabled him to recall early childhood memories that had been repressed. Once his associations became freer, I could see how the dreamwork had condensed, reversed, and disguised the agony of feeling abandoned, unloved, inept, and depressed, by pictorializing an attractive woman waiting eagerly for him to join her. The tininess and lightness transform the surrey into a baby buggy and change the adult Mr. M. into a jealous, rivalrous small boy who cannot make babies as his big father can. The dreamwork tries to negate the fact that the father is connected with the mother's pregnancies; the surrey and horse are not hitched together—the patient is unable to hitch a male and female together. The familiar but unrecognizable woman is the mother of his childhood years, whom he has tried to ward off in his memories, in his sexual life, and in the analysis. The hugeness of the department store is a plastic representation of him as a little boy in a situation too big for him, as his present big house makes him feel like a tired old horse. He is full of jealousy, envy, and depression, and sorry for himself.

It was not possible to work on all these points in one hour; but the surrey-baby-buggy dream led in the next hours to the conviction that his present depression and the old underlying depression from childhood, which had brought him into the analysis, were directly connected, hitched up, to his mother's pregnancies and deliveries. The repression, isolation, and denial were temporarily broken through by our work with this dream, and there were several tearful and angry hours, in contrast to the quiet sadness of the previous months. By making available to the patient's conscious ego the memories and affects related to trying to push the baby carriage I could reconstruct a crucial phase of this man's conflicts in early childhood, which were emotionally inaccessible to him until our work on the dream.

I believe this clinical vignette demonstrates the exceptional position of the dream. Months of what I believe to have been good psychoanalytic work on the patient's acting out or reenactment of the childhood depression provided insight and some understanding but no emotional or behavioral change, although I am fairly sure that it prepared the way for the surrey-buggy dream. It was the dream, however, plus the patient's and the analyst's work on it, that made possible the breakthrough to the hidden memories and affects. Only then did the patient develop a conviction and certainty about the reconstruction—and when he clearly understood and felt the connection between the seemingly strange, remote, and symbolic elements of the dream and the events in his present and past life. For me this is convincing evidence of the special proximity of the dream, childhood memories, and affects. To a great extent this depends on whether the patient and the analyst can use their capacity to oscillate between the primary and secondary processes in helping one another reach the latent dream thoughts hidden beneath the manifest dream. The patient contributes by his free associations; the analyst contributes by associating as if he were the patient and then translating his findings in ways that provide links or bridges to the vital and alive psychic activities in the patient which are capable of becoming conscious at the moment. This is dependent on the analyst's capacity for empathy, his ability to visualize the verbal productions of his patient, and then to translate his findings at a time and in a style and form which are real and plausible to the patient (see chapters 11 and 17; and Greenson, 1967a).

Conclusion

The dream is an exceptional and unique production of the patient. It is his special creation but can be fully understood only if the analyst and the patient work together by means of the patient's free associations and the analyst's interpretations. To work effectively with a patient's dream, the analyst must subordinate his own theoretical interests, his own personal curiosity, and attempt to make contact with what is living, accessible, and dominant in the patient's psychic life at the time. He must associate empathically with the patient's material, as if he had lived in the patient's life. Then he must translate the pictures he gets from the patient's verbal rendering of the dream back into thoughts, ideas, and words. Finally, he must ask himself what of all of this will be valuable to the patient's conscious and reasonable ego and how he can say it effectively to the patient.

This can be learned in one's personal analysis and in supervision in clinical work, if the training and supervising analysts are competent in working with their patients' dreams. It can be learned to a lesser degree in dream seminars and even from books and papers if the writer is a skillful teacher and uses clinical examples from his own experience. Dream interpretation cannot be taught to people who are not at home or are ill at ease with the form and content of unconscious mental activities. Obviously one cannot teach dream interpretation to those who are blind and deaf to the beauty and wit in the blending of dream formation, free association, and interpretation.

Working with dreams makes extraordinary demands on the patient and the analyst. In a sense the dream is the most intimate and elusive creation of the patient; it is so easy to forget! The patient is then asked to associate as freely as possible to the different elements of this strange material, in the presence of his psychoanalyst. He will be torn between the desires to reveal and to conceal the hidden contents which have unexpectedly risen to the surface. The analyst must listen with free-floating attention, oscillating between the patient's and his own primary and secondary processes. Eventually, he will have to formulate his ideas in words which are comprehensible, meaningful, and alive to the patient. Sometimes he may only be able to say, "I do not understand the dream—perhaps we shall sometime later."

Some psychoanalysts deny the exceptional position of the dream because they have a special difficulty in learning the technique of dream interpretation. Others decrease the importance of dream interpretation to enhance certain theoretical convictions or to attack or defend the beliefs of some honored teacher. I believe that the dream is the royal road to a knowledge of unconscious activities for both the patient and the analyst, provided the psychoanalyst is not seduced into narrow bypaths and dead-end streets by technical or theoretical prejudices. My conviction of the exceptional position of the dream[4]

[4] It was, in fact, one of my first analytic patients who firmly established this conviction. This patient was a young man who suffered from epileptic

has been confirmed by daily work with patients, in particular their clinical responses, both immediate and long-range. This conviction has been substantiated by the results of literally hundreds of analysts whose work on dreams are listed in the texts of Fliess (1953b), Altman (1969), *The Annual Survey of Psychoanalysis, The Index of Psychoanalytic Writings, The Psychoanalytic Quarterly Cumulative Index,* and the Chicago Psychoanalytic Literature Index.

I shall close with two quotations. Kurt Eissler has graciously permitted me to paraphrase from a personal communication: "With hard work and fortunate circumstances an analysis may stop all neurotic symptomatology, all acting out, all neurotic slips and errors, and it may make the former patient the epitome of normalcy. Nevertheless, the person will never stop dreaming irrational, instinct-ridden, bizarre dreams, a perpetual proof of the ceaseless activity of the unconscious mind." And from Freud, who wrote in 1933, "Whenever I began to have doubts of the correctness of my wavering conclusions, the successful transformations of a senseless and muddled dream into a logical and intelligible mental process in the dreamer would renew my confidence of being on the right track" (p. 7).

---

seizures. "The exhibitionistic and aggressive impulses which were obvious in connection with the patient's symptoms were relatively inaccessible to his conscious ego. In his dreams, however, these elements were constantly demonstrable" (p. 148). He had many convulsions during the analytic hours and these were either followed or preceded by the recounting of dreams. In periods of resistance, he had fewer dreams and fewer convulsions (see Greenson, 1944).

24

A Dream While Drowning

(1971)

THIS BRIEF CLINICAL VIGNETTE is offered as a confirmation of some of the ideas put forth by Margaret Mahler and her co-workers on the problems of human symbiosis and the vicissitudes of individuation. The clinical experience I shall describe occurred during World War II, when I served as Chief of the Combat Fatigue Section in an air force convalescent hospital. Psychiatric casualties were flown to us from all the different areas of combat. My therapeutic relationship with the patient under discussion lasted three weeks and what I shall report is taken from my notes written at that time, March 1945.

The patient, Frank, presented himself at the psychiatric intake service where I interviewed him. He was a slight, forlorn, young-old looking corporal, who spoke quietly, timidly, and intelligently, and who seemed mildly depressed and preoccupied. Frank's main complaint was that after returning from a "bad" mission, his head had been full of repetitious words, or sounds, or thoughts, which he could neither understand nor stop. These words or sounds were worse when he was about to fall asleep or when he had just awakened. He slept deeply, once he did fall asleep, but he would awaken exhausted and in a

First published in *Separation-Individuation: Essays in Honor of Margaret S. Mahler*, edited by John B. McDevitt and Calvin F. Settlage. New York: International Universities Press, 1971, pp. 377-384.

415

sweat, and he could never remember any dreams. Frank could not tell me what the words were or even imitate the sounds, but they repeated themselves endlessly in his head, and he was puzzled and wondered if he "was going nuts."

I was able to get the following past history from him in two preliminary sessions before I decided upon the course of treatment. Frank was twenty years old and had already completed three years of duty in the U.S. Air Force. He had lied about his age in order to get into the service. His first tour of duty was as a photographer-gunner in the Aleutians and, after about a year and a half of that, he was sent to the Southwest Pacific where he served in the same capacity. His main job was to make aerial photographs through the bomb-bay doors while they were flying over enemy-held territory.

The bad mission consisted of the following. Frank and his six crew members, flying a F7B, were sent to do photographic reconnaissance somewhere in the Southwest Pacific, when they were hit by Zeros and flak. At the time of attack the patient was taking photographs from the bomb bay. When they were struck by flak, the gasoline tanks were hit and gasoline began to flow into the bomb bay where the patient was still taking photographs. The pressure of the air forced the bomb-bay doors shut and the bomb bay began to fill up with gasoline. Frank tried desperately to climb out but was unable to do so, partly because he was being overcome by the fumes and also because they had closed the front top section of the bomb bay in order to keep the gasoline and the fumes from getting into the cockpit where it was likely to explode. All the patient could remember was the bomb bay slowly filling with gasoline. He was becoming intoxicated by the fumes; he felt paralyzed and that he was drowning. Then he blacked out. He awoke in a hospital many hours later. He had severe ulcerations in his eyes, ears, nose, and throat. Frank was treated medically, sent to a general hospital, and eventually sent to the air force convalescent hospital in the United States where I saw him. The repetitious sounds and words began after he had first awakened in the hospital. They did not diminish; they were more tormenting and kept him from being able to concentrate on anything. Frank had reported this to the doctors at the general hospital, but they either ignored it or told him it would eventually go away.

I talked with Frank about his pre-army history and recorded the following noteworthy points. He was born and raised in Idaho, an only child. His father was a sheep rancher and his mother had died when he was quite young, how young, he did not know. There were mostly men on the ranch who helped his father. Even the cook was a man, although there was an occasional woman, but "women didn't seem to last long." Frank had a "fairly okay" relationship with his father, but his father was essentially a quiet man and devoted to the ranch. There were few friends, little schooling, and much boredom. At seventeen he became interested in girls but felt terribly inadequate and strange with them. It was at this point that he decided to run away and enlist in the air force. He wrote his father after he enlisted, who evinced only mild regret, but they wrote each other regularly though infrequently during the three years of Frank's military duty.

I found nothing overtly psychotic in Frank's behavior or history and explained to him that we might be able to uncover the mystery of the repeated words if he would agree to go to the hospital for a few days, where I would use intravenous sodium pentothal. Frank had heard about "flak juice," as pentothal was called on the Post, and he asked a few questions about the procedure, which I explained. He was quite willing to enter the hospital and take the "flak juice."

I will now report the results of the pentothal interview. The patient fell asleep after the slow injection of 16 cc of 2½ percent sodium pentothal. With eyes closed, he began to speak:

That was the quickest drunk I have ever had—I took all I can hold and now if I could move I would be all right. Drink 'em up! The drinks are on the house and I'm paying. Round 'em up boys, drink 'em up—Hell, I'm drunk! [Silence for about one minute.]

I was in the bomb bay, I didn't know what was happening. The engineer was dumping the gasoline, so I tried to get back up. I tried to keep the door open. They kept pushing me off. They shoved me off. I tried to open up the bomb bay, but the gas kept coming in. I lost my mind. Jehosephat. I lost my mind. Amosnell, Domosnell. Amosnell Domosnell. I kept yelling it. It sounds funny. I thought I was a tin-god hero. I saved the rest. But to hell with them, they don't appreciate. Three hundred gallons of high-octane gas all came down on me. God—the nightmares I had, the nightmares. I was out there in the darkness. Peculiar place, it was called Ibbia. There was an idiot there and six persons. They were six. They picked me as the dope. I was the youngest. Then I felt myself reeling. I felt my mind was losing me and I kept yelling Jehosephat, Jehosephat. Who is that? He must be in the Bible.

Then I went out into the darkness and I was all alone. It was very dark and there were frogs croaking. Lots of frogs, out of nowhere. And then I heard someone and began to yell Amosnell, Domosnell, Amosnell, Domosnell. And I yelled it for one hundred years in eternity. Boy, that takes a long time. I don't know how long. You know, that's why I hate religion. It was put up for guys who don't know. I'm a Catholic, but I don't give a damn. Maybe I'd better say I'm an agnostic.

Then one morning I was on a beach and there comes a guy, a big, tall, hillbilly kind of a guy. And he told me he had been there since the creation of earth, and that he had no one for company. Then I don't know what happened, but suddenly I got scared. It was as though the world was going to end, my mind was losing me, and I looked around for that hillbilly guy, but now there was a giant Teddy Bear, but he was a man. And when I got scared, he looked at me and said that I shouldn't worry, he was going to take me into his body, his belly. He said, "Don't you worry, I'll keep you warm." And he said, "And I won't bite you. I'll just swallow you." And he shoved me into his mouth like a candy bar. It took ages and ages and all I heard was Amosnell, Domosnell, Amosnell, Domosnell. And when I woke up I was wrapped in blankets in the hospital and all I kept saying was Amosnell, Domosnell, Amosnell, Domosnell. I was out of my head.

Then followed several minutes of silence and then the patient spontaneously continued:

My outlook on life has changed. I grasped at a straw, the army. Now, I want to get a home life . . . my mother died. I don't miss her . . . I wonder if she'd be ashamed of me. Now I am writing to a girl in Port Arthur. She's cute, but I'm afraid to mix with her. I'm afraid of women. . . . I have an inferiority complex. I don't know—I'm all mixed up. I even received a letter from my dad urging me to get out of the army. I don't exactly hate my father—I kinda like him. He's got my blood in him and his blood is in me. There is something between us—I don't know what. He told me there are nice jobs for veterans. Bullshit. He is always meddling in my affairs. I'm sort of lost, prefer to get out of all this regimentation—serial number 17031810—do something on my own—self-reliance—I have nothing—just like being in prison and saying I'm having a good time. When I get a furlough it's like going to another country. I don't even respect my uniform, it's a hell of a thing to say. If people only knew how I suffer . . . I can't do any more. . . . It's killing me. I can't do any more. . . .

Frank then slowly opened his eyes. "Doc, what the hell is this all about? Maybe I am going nuts. What is that Amosnell, Domosnell stuff?"

I told Frank I didn't know for sure, but that I would try to figure it out. I told him to sleep off the "flak juice" and then we'd talk about what he had said under the pentothal.

Later that afternoon Frank came to my office and I asked him what he could recall about the pentothal interview. He could only remember Amosnell and Domosnell and a Teddy

Bear man. I then slowly went over my notes of the interview, pausing to get his memories or his reactions, to ask questions, or to tell him what I thought. This went on for four sessions.

Frank readily recalled how scared he was when the bomb-bay doors closed and the gasoline came flowing in on him. He trembled and shook as he described it to me. He also recounted how furious he was with his six crewmates who kept him locked out to save themselves and the plane. He felt lost. Momentarily, tears came to his eyes. Yet, he didn't blame them, he'd have probably done the same. Pause. Yet, somehow, he always got the dirty end of things—at home, at school, and now in the air force. "They sent me from the Aleutians to the Southwest Pacific, how bad a deal can you get!"

Jehosephat was a word his father would use when he got excited or mad—"jumping Jehosephat." His father rarely went to church, but he was a "god-fearing" man. Frank stopped believing in God during the war—"too many guys with their heads or arms and legs blown off, or blind, or their face missing or no nuts."

He recalled hearing frogs croaking on the ranch, at night, especially after a rain, and it was all black out there. He was afraid of the dark, and yet there was something warm and comforting about being inside someplace when it was dark outside.

The tall, hillbilly guy could have been his father, although his father isn't really tall. His father did try to take care of him, "but you can't take care of a kid and run a ranch too." He had slept with a Teddy Bear as a kid, as a matter of fact, his father still keeps it in Frank's bedroom on the ranch and the patient sees it whenever he visits.

The giant Teddy Bear man swallowing him, that stumped him. I told Frank at this point that when kids get scared, real scared, they like to hide someplace where it is safe, like under a blanket, covering themselves all up, as a protection from the frightening world. I then told him that the first safe place a kid experiences is when he is still inside his mother's belly, before he is born. Covering yourself all up in a blanket is like that in a way. "When you were drowning in the gasoline, in the belly of the plane, you must have wished you could get back under those blankets or back inside your mother's belly and feel safe and warm again."

Frank seemed to follow that line of thought; it made "some kind of sense" to him. But he couldn't understand why it was a giant Teddy Bear man. I explained to Frank that, first of all, he had slept with a little Teddy Bear as a kid and that must have made him feel good, because the Teddy Bear made him feel he wasn't all alone. Then I added that since his mother died when he was very little, the only mothering type of person he could run to for help when he was hurt or scared was to his father or some other man. Maybe the big hillbilly man who was there from the creation of earth, and the giant Teddy Bear man who took him in for safety, were for Frank, as a little baby, the protecting parents. In a way, the giant Teddy Bear man was both the protecting mother and father, a combination of mother and father, the mothering father of his early childhood. "When you felt alone and scared, you were helped by the hillbilly man who wanted you not to feel alone. When you got scared to death that you were going to drown, then came the giant Teddy Bear man, who took you gently back into his belly, where he kept you safe."

Frank listened to this with open-mouthed wonder and in silence. Then he quietly said that as crazy as it seemed at first, it did make sense. I think he put it well when he said, "I dreamed myself back into a safe place." He couldn't remember his mother, no wonder he had to reach back for his father. But, what was Amosnell, Domosnell? This I admitted I did not understand. I asked him if his mother had been foreign-born. Frank was sure she was American, as was his father. I told him the words sounded foreign to me and I suggested Frank write his father and ask him: (1) how old he was when his mother died and (2) whether she was foreign-born or spoke a foreign language, and if so, which one? Frank agreed and we parted after making an appointment to see each other in a few days.

That day I went to the air force intelligence officer at the Base and asked him to check what language the phrases "Amosnell, Domosnell" were derived from and what the meaning might be. While waiting to hear from Frank's father and the intelligence officer, I kept seeing Frank psychotherapeutically. We talked a great deal about his loneliness, his longing for and feeling estranged from women, his need to try to become familiar with a girl, the importance of establishing a home for himself with a mothering-type girl. As our talks progressed the repetitious sounds in his head of Amosnell and Domosnell began to recede. There were sessions when he did not even mention them.

Some ten days later Frank excitedly came to his session with a letter from his father. The father said that Frank's mother had died when he was not quite two years old; and that she had been born in Belgium and had come to the United States as a young girl. She had forgotten most of her mother tongue, but she would sing children's songs to Frank in her native dialect when he was a baby. In fact, the father himself recalled one that went something like "Amosnell, Domosnell."

I must admit that I too was excited by this news and I told Frank the information proved that while he was drowning he had retreated back to the safest times he knew: back into his mother's belly, or back to being held by his mother or being sung to sleep by her while holding onto his Teddy Bear. Frank was amazed and yet convinced this was true and seemed enormously relieved to have discovered the reasons for the peculiar repetitive sound in his head. Three days later the intelligence officer reported that the words Amosnell Domosnell are from a Flemish dialect prevalent in northern Belgium. The approximate meaning is, "I must hurry, you must hurry."

Shortly after I had reported this additional confirmation to Frank, the repetitive words lost their intrusive quality. Strangely enough, Frank occasionally found himself humming Amosnell, Domosnell when he felt in good spirits. Frank was released from the hospital and soon returned to civilian life. Less than a year later I received a postcard from him on his honeymoon and since then there has been silence.

I want to add two points which I did not discuss with

Frank, but which gave me food for thought then and now. Ibbia may be a Flemish word, or it might be a distortion of the phrase, "I be, I am." I felt it could be a proclamation of *being*, at the precise moment he felt on the verge of becoming extinct. The phrase "my mind is losing me," which occurs twice during the pentothal interview, has a ring of genuineness about it, despite its linguistic incorrectness. Frank seems to be saying, the basic me, the bodily me, is being deserted by my mind, which should be taking care of me. He ascribed to his mind the caretaking function of a mother at a time when she still had to perform much of his mental tasks, when she was actually most of his mind.

I submit this fragment of clinical data to indicate how, under conditions of terrifying stress, a person will regress to a symbiotic state of safety, as it has been colored by his personal history. I believe it confirms many of the ideas with which we are now struggling concerning the early relationship of the mothering person and the child. I offer this vignette to a pioneer in this field, Margaret Mahler, as a small gift on her seventieth birthday.

25

The "Real" Relationship between the Patient and the Psychoanalyst

(1971)

THIS PRESENTATION IS an attempt to extend the views expressed by me and Milton Wexler in chapter 22 and to explore further the nature of the therapeutic processes which occur during psychoanalytic treatment. It has been the hallmark of psychoanalysis to emphasize the occurrence of transference and resistance during psychoanalytic therapy and to stress the decisive importance of interpreting these phenomena. This has led to a widely held view that all the patient's meaningful reactions to the person of the analyst are transference manifestations and the only important interventions are transference interpretations, a view common among Kleinian as well as the more "conservative," classical analysts. These analysts may concede that other kinds of personal interactions take place in the analytic situation, but they are considered irrelevant and awkward impediments which are either to be circumvented or

First published in *The Unconscious Today: Essays in Honor of Max Schur*, edited by Mark Kanzer. New York: International Universities Press, 1971, pp. 213-232.

ignored. I base this last statement on the fact that I have never read a paper of an "orthodox" or Kleinian analyst which indicated that any intervention besides interpretation was important in the patient-analyst relationship.

On the other hand, a survey of the recent psychoanalytic literature reveals that a significant number of psychoanalysts, a group too heterogeneous to be classified, do not deny the special value of transference phenomena and transference interpretations, but maintain the total object relationship between the patient and the analyst must be taken into account in order to fully understand and handle the vicissitudes of the psychoanalytic situation. They believe that a wide assortment of object relations, other than transference, takes place in the course of an analysis in both the patient and the therapist. It is their contention that the proper handling of these "nontransference," "extratransference," or "real" interactions are an indispensable ingredient for successful psychoanalytic treatment. I want to interpolate here that in this discussion I am emphasizing object relations including and beyond the scope of the concept of the therapeutic or working alliance as described by Zetzel (1956b) and me (chapter 15). Stone (1961, 1967) and Fairbairn (1957, 1958) are the most outspoken on the subject of total object relations, but Anna Freud (1954, 1965), Gitelson (1952), Knight (1953), Winnicott (1955, 1965), Loewald (1960), and Erikson (1962), to mention only a few among many, have also pointed in this direction.

I want to quote from a few of the authors mentioned above in order to illustrate the areas of agreement despite the sharp differences in theoretical and technical points of view. Let me begin with the clearest statement of the problem, some remarks by Anna Freud (1954):

> Just as "no two analysts would ever give precisely the same interpretations," we find on closer examination that no two of a given analyst's patients are handled by him ever in precisely the same manner. With some patients we remain deadly serious. With others humor, or even jokes, may

play a part. With some the terms in which interpretations are couched have to be literal ones; others find it easier to accept the same content when given in the form of similes and analogies. There are differences in the ways in which we receive and send off patients, and in the degree to which we permit a real relationship to the patient to coexist with the transferred, fantasied one. There is, even with the strictness of the analytic setting, a varying amount of ease felt by analyst and patient. These wholly unintended and unexplained variations in our responses are imposed on us, I believe, not so much by the patient's neuroses but by the individual nuances of their personalities which may otherwise escape unobserved. If we become aware of these often minute variations in our own behavior and reactions, and cease to treat them as unimportant chance occurrences, their observation and scrutiny lead us directly to important findings. In the personal pressure which the patient exerts on us in this manner, he betrays the subtleties of his healthy personality, the degree of maturity reached by his ego, his capacity to sublimate, his intellectual gifts, and his ability to view his conflicts at least momentarily in an objective manner. In the variations of the analyst's "acting out" in technical behavior, we may therefore find new clues for the systematic study of character structures and personalities [p. 359f.].

In the same paper (p. 372f.) Anna Freud refers to the patient's real relationship to the analyst and makes the remarks previously cited in chapter 22.

In chapter 22 I summarized how the different participants of a panel on "Variations in Classical Psycho-Analytic Technique" (1958) dealt with the problem of the nontransference relationship (see Loewenstein, 1958; Eissler, 1958; Rosenfeld, 1958; Bouvet, 1958; A. Reich, 1958; Nacht, 1958). In addition, I reviewed the contributions of Freud (1937a), Menaker (1942), Roland (1967), and others. For this reason, I shall cite here only a few additional works.

Fairbairn (1957), whose theoretical and technical orientation differs considerably from Freud's, wrote the following:

> The relationship existing between patient and analyst is
> more important than details of technique; and it would
> seem to follow that the role of the analyst is not merely to
> fulfill the dual functions of (1) a screen upon which the
> patient projects his phantasies and (2) a colourless instru-
> ment of interpretative technique, but that his personality
> and his motives make a significant contribution to the
> therapeutic process [p. 59].

Erikson (1962), pondering the issue of reality and actuality
in the psychoanalytic situation, turned his attention to Freud's
(1905a) treatment of Dora. He raises the question which I would
paraphrase as follows: What was it that Dora really needed from
Freud that Freud would not or could not give her?

Stone (1967) writes the following:

> The analyst is first perceived as a real object, who awakens
> hope of help, and who offers it on the basis of his thera-
> peutic competence. This operates in the patient's experience
> at all levels of integration, from that of actual and immedi-
> ate perception, evaluation, and response, to the activation
> of original parental object representations and their
> cathexes.
>
>   This view does place somewhat heavier than usual
> emphasis on the horizontal coordinate of operations, the
> conscious and unconscious relation to the analyst as a living
> and actual object, who becomes invested with imagery,
> traits, and functions of critical objects of the past. The
> relationship is to be understood in its dynamic, economic,
> and adaptive meanings, in its current "structuralized"
> tenacity, the real and unreal carefully separated from one
> another [p. 40f.].

Different as their styles, their theoretical and technical
orientations may be, all the authors cited above seem to be in
accord with the idea that (1) personal interactions other than

transference occur in the course of psychoanalysis, and (2) it is important to differentiate between the transference and the "real" relationship.

Working Definitions

I have previously defined transference and stated the two outstanding characteristics of transference reactions: (1) they are undiscriminating, nonselective repetitions of the past, and (2) they are inappropriate, ignoring, or distorting reality.

The term "real" relationship is much harder to define. It implies (1) the sense of being genuine and not synthetic or artificial, and (2) realistic and not inappropriate or fantastic. In this paper I shall use the term "real relationship" only when I mean both genuine and realistic. Like all object relations, it also consists of repetitions from the past; however, it differs from transference in being selective and discriminating in terms of what is repeated. Furthermore, a real relationship is modifiable by internal and external reality. In a real relationship between a husband and wife, for example, the wife may resemble the husband's mother in some bodily feature, but the resemblance does not bring with it all the instinctual and emotional components which were originally bound up with the mother. In addition, the wife will have traits that resemble other people in the past, both remote and recent. Consequently, such a wife becomes a unique entity, free from the fearful and guilt-laden infantile connections to the past. Finally, the real relationship to the wife will be influenceable and modifiable by changes occurring in each individual and the world they live in.

I must add that in all transference reactions there is some germ of reality, and in all real relationships there is some element of transference. *All object relationships consist of different admixtures and blendings of real and transference components.* Although transference and real relationship are relative terms, they can and, as I hope to show, should be separated from one another.

Perhaps I can clarify these definitions if I point out that
transference reactions are essentially unrealistic and fantastic,
but they are felt as genuine, authentic and sincere. Yet, here
again this is only relatively true. Some transference reactions feel
more genuine than others. When most of the ego is immersed in
the experiencing of the feeling and only little of the rational ego
is left untouched, the patient experiences the feeling as genuine.
Other transference reactions may be experienced with "tongue
in cheek," as though they are a "serious make-believe" (Stone,
1967). In such instances, the experiencing ego and the observing
ego are more or less of equal strength.

The working alliance, on the other hand, is essentially
realistic, but more or less synthetic, artificial. In the analyst, the
working alliance becomes part of his therapeutic character and
personality, and in that sense it is genuine. But situations do arise
when a strong countertransference will make it necessary for the
analyst to call forth a therapeutic attitude by a conscious
act of will. This state of affairs is even more likely to occur in a
patient when he is in the throes of an intense transference
reaction.

In chapter 15 I described how the patient and the analyst
contribute to the working alliance. The patient must have the
capacity to form a relatively reasonable object relationship to the
analyst and also fulfill the special requirements of the analytic
situation. I also stated that certain transference hopes and longings contribute to the alliance.

As for the analyst, I wrote then that his consistent and
unwavering pursuit of insight, as well as his concern and respect
for his patient's predicament, contributed to the working
alliance. His transference reactions, too, may support the
alliance. I want to emphasize that the reliable, enduring core of
the working alliance is the "real relationship" between the
patient and the analyst, using the term as I defined it, the realistic and genuine relationship. The transference feelings, loving
or hateful, from the most infantile to the most mature,
may be helpful, but transference is an erratic and treacherous
ally.

Clinical Material

It is an impressive clinical finding that in some patients the real relationship remains vaguely in the background and rarely becomes a noticeable issue in their psychoanalytic therapy. In other patients, the real relationship becomes a burning and crucial issue from the beginning to the end of treatment. In part, this may be due to the differences in the specific pathology and therapeutic needs of a given case. The situation is parallel to what one meets with in problems of identity. Patients in whom this issue is in the foreground are those who have had special difficulty in establishing their identity. The role of the real relationship in therapy may be determined by the patient, but also by the therapist's sensitivity or blindness to the issue of the real relationship. The personality or the theoretical orientation of the analyst may be the determining factor.

In chapter 22 I cited an example from the analysis of Mr. M. who tried to hide his realistic perceptions and judgments by resorting to transference distortions. Other patients cling to some of the realistic traits they perceive in the analyst as a screen to ward off the awareness of other realistic traits or transference fantasies. One patient who felt I was annoyed in an hour insisted that it was a transference distortion. She "knew" I was a man of compassion and in good control of my emotions. I asked her what she would feel if I had really been annoyed with her. Only then did she realize how frightened she was of my being angry. She equated it with the rage of her brutal father. This patient tried again and again to keep me a "mirror-type" analyst whose every reaction was mild and benign. She either did not perceive reactions or traits in me which contradicted this or considered her perceptions to be inaccurate.

A male patient "knew" I was against sexual infidelity in marriage. He "knew" it because he felt a good analyst "must be" well analyzed; and if one is well analyzed, one has a good sex life and a happy marriage and therefore does not need extramarital affairs. I responded to this somewhat stuffy portrayal of a psychoanalyst with a teasing question, something like: "Why do you insist that I'm such a goody-goody?" This led to insight revealing the patient's need to use this image of me as a bulwark for his faltering superego because of his own promiscuous impulses. It also eventually uncovered another picture of me as Zorba the Greek, a man of great passions. In fact, it was the Zorba image he had perceived in a public lecture of mine which made him seek me out as an analyst in the first place. The Zorba image was subsequently camouflaged by other perceptions and transference distortions. Only later did the patient acknowledge that to him I was "really" more of a "Zorba" figure than a "goody-goody."

Yet, it is not only the sexual and hostile reactions which are isolated or denied by the patient, as the following illustration demonstrates. A young man I sent into analysis with an analyst newly arrived from Europe told me how much he loved the "cute" mistakes in English and the bumbling physical clumsiness of this analyst. I knew the analyst personally and could verify that the young man had made accurate perceptions about him. I therefore asked him if he had brought this up in the analysis, to which he replied: "Hell, no. It's too embarrassing." I told him that it should be brought up, it belonged in the analysis. The young man said he would get around to it "sooner or later." Years later I asked if the cute errors and clumsiness had ever come up during treatment. He sadly said no. It became apparent to both of us at this point that these realistic perceptions and the loving and hostile transference derivatives had never entered his analysis.

I would now like to describe a flagrant example of the neglect of the nontransference relationship. Some years ago, I sent Mrs. E., a young woman I knew socially, into analysis with a psychoanalyst of another city whom I believed to be competently trained and a man of personal integrity. Although I continued my social relationship with Mrs. E., we did not discuss her analysis. About five years from the time I had recommended psychoanalysis to her, we had occasion to talk alone. She told me she had finished her analysis and that she had the greatest respect for psychoanalysis as a therapy and as a science despite the fact that her major symptoms had remained unchanged. I was puzzled and asked Mrs. E. why she had stopped treatment. She replied that, although her analyst was a brilliant man, an impeccable scientist of incorruptible character, she had found the analysis extremely painful from the beginning to the end. She had hated almost every minute of it. She believed her analyst had tried to help her, but something was wrong, something was missing. For example, she once asked if it were possible to stop the hour ten minutes early because she had an appointment with her child's school teacher. The analyst said nothing, and when she fell silent he repeatedly asked her just to say what came to her mind. He gave no indication that it was permissible for the patient to leave early, so she remained. He behaved in the same way when she occasionally asked for a change in the time for her appointment. He would either remain silent, ask her for associations or inquire when she had done such things in the past. At the end of such an hour, he would usually interpret that it was her feelings of anger, hostility, or resistance, etc., transferred from some figure in her past, that were responsible for her request and that would end the discussion. Mrs. E. felt that, although he was right, something was missing. I asked Mrs. E. if she had ever told her analyst of these feelings. She replied that she had, particularly in the beginning. "He only interpreted, he never conceded that my feelings or wishes had some merit. When I complained about it, he would interpret that too, as transference. I finally gave up. I thought that is how psychoanalysis is supposed to be. I recently spoke to a friend who was analyzed and was struck by how different her experience had been. I know I need more analysis and I want it, but please send me to another kind of person."

No doubt Mrs. E. was an unusually submissive and masochistic patient. Nevertheless, I submit this material as an extreme example of the analyst's neglect of the real relationship between the patient and the therapist. I believe Mrs. E.'s analyst tried to interpret and dig out the original sources of the patient's transference resistances, but he neglected to recognize or acknowledge reality factors or his own contribution to some of the patient's resistances and hostile reactions. By "only interpreting" or "only analyzing," he interfered with the formation of a strong working alliance. His way of working signified to the patient that he was essentially detached and impersonal; there was little indication of concern or compassion (Stone, 1961). As a consequence, the real relationship remained thin and narrow, as did the working alliance and the transference neurosis. I believe that the whole school of analysts which believes that psychoanalytic treatment consists of "only interpreting" is guilty of using transference interpretations as a defense. Some of them seem to interpret the transference so frequently in the course of an hour because they are afraid of the painful affects that they or their patients might otherwise develop. Others of this group ignore the patient's correct and painful perceptions and judgments concerning the analyst and remain silent or pick up some interpretable material, no matter how trivial.

The harmful consequences of such a technique are many. At this point I want to stress three possibilities. By focusing constantly on the patient's transference distortions and ignoring the reality elements, we undermine his self-esteem and make him feel he is always wrong, sick or crazy, beliefs which he has brought with him into the analysis. By acting as an ignorer of reality, we tempt the patient to live in the outside world as though all of life were lived on a gigantic psychoanalytic couch and people at large were either patients or psychoanalysts. By "only interpreting," we constrict the unfolding of the patient's transference neurosis and limit its development in accordance with our own theoretical biases.

If the patient has made a correct and accurate perception about the analyst, it should be acknowledged some time in that hour or in a subsequent hour. I am not claiming that this acknowledgment should precede or preclude interpretation of the patient's material: that will depend on many different factors. I do maintain that the analyst's confirmation of a patient's correct perception in regard to some trait, fault, or error in himself helps the patient learn to discriminate between reality and fantasy, something all our patients have difficulty with. It also helps break down the patient's infantile wish for us to be omnipotent and omniscient. Furthermore, it can keep the analyst from falling into the Godlike conception of himself our work makes so easily possible. Acknowledging the correctness of a patient's perceptions or beliefs helps strengthen the patient's healthy capacity for object relations. Finally, an admission of fault or error indicates honesty, a basic and vital component of a "real relationship."

I have had many patients report to me that when I or their previous analyst responded to a complaint about our person by "only interpreting," we were saying to the patient, in effect, "Your perceptions or judgments are false, distorted, infantile or unworthy of discussion." This was surely not the analyst's conscious intention, but the failure to acknowledge the correctness of the patient's perception in some way resulted in the patient's feeling humiliated and demeaned. There are analysts who behave as though the discovery of some interpretable unconscious material nullifies the possibility that the patient can also perceive and judge correctly.

Correct perceptions may lead at first to realistic reactions and later to transference distortions. In the following example, the patient's real relationship came into focus unusually early in the treatment. The main reason for this was that I had great doubts about the patient's motivation and suitability for psychoanalytic treatment which impelled me to confront him in one particular hour. Mr. D., a businessman in his mid-fifties, consulted me at the instigation of his young girlfriend who told him he was sick because he was unable to commit himself to anybody or any activity he liked, for any length of time. His only loyalty was to business and to making money. The preliminary interviews confirmed the girl's main complaints, and I was able to demonstrate to Mr. D. that this was a lifelong pattern which prevented him from enjoying a rich and full life. He seemed eager to embark upon treatment and although I found him bright, psychologically minded, youthful in spirit and interesting, I still wondered how much of his motivation was essentially a wish to please his girlfriend and would evaporate when the love affair disintegrated or the hostile transference came into the foreground.

During one session in the third month of the analysis, Mr. D. spent a good part of the hour talking about various people he knew and kept coming back to the theme that people gave one impression upon first acquaintance and later turned out to be quite different. He included in this portrayal his recent girlfriend, two unhappy marriage partners, several friendships, and a few hostile business partnerships. He ended this part of the session by stating: "You can't judge people by appearances, you never get to know anyone until you've lived with them." This prompted me to ask: "You have been living with me for three months now, what do you think of me?" Note that I did not ask him for free association, nor did I interpret that he was talking about me, the more traditional approaches. I wanted to highlight his nontransference reactions because of my concern for the working alliance. Although Mr. D. had brought into the analysis several fantasies and dreams about me as a transference figure he feared, resented, and idealized, he was taken aback by my question. He was silent a few moments, coughed uneasily and then hesitantly replied: "When I first met you, you seemed very competent and sure of yourself, a little cocky perhaps, but straightforward. Now I would also describe you as essentially a kind person, but I still think you are too outspoken at times." The patient paused and then jokingly added: "Well, how did I do? Did I guess right? Or are you going to tell me this is also what you call transference?" I replied that I would not answer him directly, that we would first have to explore the evidence on which he based his assumptions. Only then could we determine whether his reactions were realistic or transference.

Mr. D. was quite obsessional and very organized; thus, in the next several hours we uncovered material which explained how he had arrived at his opinions and attitudes. I am deleting other data in order to clarify my point. Mr. D. brought out that in the first sessions he found my approach to his complicated problems rather astute and my explanations very understandable. His previous sporadic exploratory experiences with psychiatrists had left him confused and unconvinced. Above all, he was surprised that I greeted him in my shirtsleeves and that I have no diplomas on my walls. This he interpreted to mean that I must be very sure of my professional status.

Mr. D. continued to pursue the question I had set before him. He felt I was generous because of my ample explanations and because I often permitted sessions to continue a few minutes beyond the 50-minute period. He considered this last trait poor business organization, but good public relations. The patient did feel I was too outspoken and cocky because I talked of hate so readily, and besides I tended to use obscene words like "shit" and "fuck" more often than he considered to be in the best of taste. It was true he used such words upon occasion, but he believed it was not appropriate for a distinguished professional man.

In the course of the ensuing analysis, Mr. D. developed many different transference and nontransference feelings and attitudes toward me, some of which were triggered by the above-mentioned traits he had so early correctly detected.

Let me cite a few examples: What he once saw as competence and self-assurance, he later experienced as smugness and arrogance. My straightforwardness, outspokenness, and cockiness became the source of fantasies of me as vulgar and exhibitionistic, using interpretations as a brutal form of shock therapy and one-upmanship. The generosity he once admired turned into contempt and disgust for my homosexual seductiveness and my Jewish motherliness. What he once considered patience was only a façade for incompetence, slothfulness, senility, and timidity.

Mr. D., of course, experienced different varieties of love, dependency, and trust, as well as hostility, hate, and fear toward me. Sometimes the former took precedence, sometimes the latter; at other times both went on simultaneously. But Mr. D. did not remain in his analysis because his loving transference "neutralized" his hostile transference. I contend that in addition to his transference feelings, Mr. D. also had a real relationship with me which I think kept him in the analysis and which enabled us to work effectively.

The importance of the real relationship can be seen in the rigors of working through. A patient will break off an analysis of long standing when driven by a sudden eruption of an intense hostile transference. This may be understood as a failure to make the correct interpretations. Yet I have made many false interpretations which my patients knew or sensed, and they did not run away. The decisive factor was the relative strength of the real relationship existing between us, how much genuine and realistic liking and respect there was between us. Again, I want to stress that the real relationship does not have to be verbalized or conspicuous, but it must be present to a sufficient degree for the analytic situation to endure the long and painful process of working through. A patient or an analyst will consider interrupting treatment if either realizes some basic aspect is not being properly understood. But this decision will be arrived at mutually. Unexpected crises or failures in psychoanalysis are the result of both incorrect interpretations and a failure in the real relationship. By and large, technical errors may cause pain, but they are usually repairable; human errors are much harder to remedy.

I would add that there are many indications which signal a change in the nontransference relationship. One typical sign of a change in the patient's real relationship to the analyst is when a patient who has been coming to an analyst's office for months or years "sees" something for the first time. A patient in his fourth year of analysis will suddenly ask as he enters the treatment room, "Is that a new chair?" That chair was there, unchanged, from the first day he came to see me. What changed was something in his awareness of me and of himself as real persons.

Formulations, Hypotheses, and Conclusions

At this point, I would like to state some additional formulations and hypotheses which I have derived from my own clinical experience and the writings of others. In the course of a successful analysis, a patient will experience a wide range of *transference reactions* to his analyst from very primitive to quite mature, in terms of love, hate, sex, and aggression. In addition, the patient will also experience realistic and genuine reactions toward the analyst and form a real relationship. I believe this must be present, to some extent from the beginning, in order for the patient to "get into" analytic treatment. All the qualities of the patient, realistic and unrealistic, genuine and synthetic, will play a role in determining the development and course of the transference and the real relationship. Intelligence, sensitivity, humor, empathy, education, temperament, and taste all play a part in shaping the transference and nontransference reactions. I believe all of this is true, albeit unequally, for both the patient and the psychoanalyst.

I furthermore believe that all patients have transference reactions, but only those who have the capacity for forming a real relationship to the analyst are analyzable. I contend that borderline psychotic patients are analyzable only if and when they have the ability to form a real relationship to their analyst. (For a contradictory point of view see, above all, Rosenfeld, 1965.) In my opinion, most of them require preparatory therapy which consists essentially of *building* an object relationship. With regard to severely regressed adult patients, I refer to the writings of Federn (1952), Winnicott (1955, 1965), Fairbairn (1957, 1958), Wexler (1951, 1952, 1960), and Searles (1965). With regard to symbiotic or autistic children, see Mahler (1965) and Bettelheim (1963); and for borderline and neurotic children, Anna Freud (1965).

My clinical experience leads me to believe that the final resolution of the transference neurosis depends to a great extent on the transference neurosis being replaced by a real relationship. I do not share the traditional psychoanalytic point of view that interpretation alone can resolve the transference neurosis. Interpretation has to be supplemented by a realistic and genuine relationship to the person of the analyst, limited though it may be, for the transference neurosis to be replaced. (This subject is further elaborated in chapter 26.)

These deliberations concerning the importance and the role

of the nontransference relationship between patient and analyst imply a significant reevaluation of some aspects of the theory and technique of psychoanalytic therapy.

I want to conclude this discussion by referring to the question of selecting certain therapeutic elements in accordance with the diagnostic category of a case (A. Freud, 1965). Most of our neurotic patients come to us with a mixed clinical picture. We ought to offer them the broadest range of therapeutic possibilities and not limit the changes of therapy to any single factor. I believe that "only interpreting" or "only analyzing" is insufficient for most of our patients.

26

Beyond Transference and Interpretation ·

(1972)

I SHALL ATTEMPT TO CLARIFY some of the controversial issues
raised in previous publications on the "real" or "nontransference" relationship between the patient and the psychoanalyst (see Greenson, 1967a; and chapters 22 and 24). I shall also
try to demonstrate the importance of interventions other than
interpretation as a necessary ingredient for the creation and
maintenance of a productive analytic atmosphere. These statements are not meant to cast doubt upon the central role of the
interpretation of transference and resistance for psychoanalytic
therapy. However, I, along with a growing number of other
psychoanalysts, contend that the technique of "only interpreting" and the belief that all interactions between patient and
analyst are transference phenomena stifle or distort the develop-

Presented at the 27th International Psycho-Analytical Congress in
Vienna, July 19, 1971. First published in *International Journal of Psycho-
Analysis*, 53:213-217, 1972. Also as: Au-delà du transfert et de l'interpréta-
tion. *Le Coq Heron*, 20/21:22-30, 1971. Além da Transferência e da Inter-
pretação. *Revista Brasileira de Psicanálise*, 6:357-368, 1972.

I am indebted to Milton Wexler, Nathan Leites, and Alfred Goldberg for
many helpful suggestions.

ment of the patient's transference neurosis and block his capacity
to develop realistic object relationships. "Reality-relatedness
proceeds always a bit ahead of, and makes possible, the progressive evolution and resolution of the transference" (Searles,
1965). I shall use clinical examples to illustrate these points.

An Extraordinary Event in a Patient's Life

A twenty-seven-year-old woman, Mrs. K., sought analysis
because she felt out of things, numb, "gone," like a zombie (see
chapter 16). She had been raised by a warm and promiscuous
alcoholic mother who married four times and never stayed
married longer than three years. Mrs. K. had recently married
an older man, and it was the failure of her supposedly happy
marriage to resolve her inner numbness that motivated her to
come for psychoanalytic treatment. At the end of the first year of
her analysis, Mrs. K. became pregnant and shortly thereafter her
husband developed a malignant tumor, which required frequent
hospitalizations. The baby was born in the second year of
Mrs. K.'s analysis and her husband died the following year.
During this interval we had ample opportunity to analyze the
patient's morbid fantasies. For example, we analyzed at great
length the many anxieties stirred up by the thought of bringing a
fatherless baby into the world. We also analyzed how the foetus
inside became good or bad, beautiful or deformed, destructive
or destroyed. This depended on her internal body image,
which in turn was determined by her transference *and* nontransference relationship to me.

When Mrs. K. delivered a healthy baby girl she telephoned
me from the hospital. I congratulated her, we chatted a few
minutes about the delivery and I made an appointment to visit
her in the hospital. I felt the unexpected absence of her husband
and her past history made this a necessary and fitting act on my
part. The patient's delight was visible when I arrived, but it was
not long before she told me she also felt apprehensive and depressed. We then talked briefly but analytically about her anxie-

ties and depression. I told Mrs. K. I would visit her again the following week in her home, which I did, with approximately the same results, pleasure, anxiety, and depression, emotions she could control and talk about. The baby was healthy, well formed, and a good feeder, which reassured the patient.

Mrs. K. resumed analysis a month later; she often remarked how much my visits meant to her. She had always "known" I was basically a kind person, but visiting her, giving up my lunch hour or work, added a sense of conviction about me as a humane person. From this point on, Mrs. K. was able to reexperience the terror of being abandoned, the longing, rage, and depression concerning her unreliable mother, with an intensity she had never dared let herself feel before. The usual starting point for these intense reactions were dreams and associations about me abandoning or rescuing her or her baby. Thus my noninterpretative actions in an extraordinary situation in a patient's life gave her a sense of security in her relationship to me which encouraged her to allow herself to have intense and regressive transference reactions that could be effectively analyzed.

I want to contrast this with the case of a young analyst, Dr. A., I supervised, who told me of an hour in which his patient unexpectedly appeared in the waiting room, swathed in bandages over his head and one arm. I asked the candidate: "So, what did you do?" He smiled serenely, I thought, "I just said hello as usual, then I sat behind the couch and waited. The patient was silent, so I finally asked him what was going on in his mind, but he remained very resistant and refused to talk." At this point, I said, with difficulty, "And what may have been going on in his mind?" He was sure, Dr. A. replied, that the patient was thinking about the accident. It turned out that the evening before, while waiting for a light to change, he had been hit from the rear and thrown against the windshield and steering wheel of his car. The patient was taken to an emergency hospital and given first aid for lacerations of the forehead and scalp and a dislocated elbow. He was furious with the man who had banged into him, and he hoped to collect a good deal of insurance. Dr. A. was, he told me, puzzled that throughout the entire hour the patient seemed reluctant to express himself. At first he wondered if it were due to a mild brain concussion and then he thought the patient might be experiencing a transference reaction to him, because he sits behind the patient and perhaps the patient feels Dr. A.'s interpretations also bang into him unexpectedly and cause pain. He suggested this to the patient who remained uncommunicative.

I put it to the young analyst that though his interpretation may have been correct, he may also have added to the patient's anger by his own unresponsiveness from the moment he first saw the bandaged man in the waiting room. Dr. A. recalled he was startled at the sight of the patient, but did his best to suppress any sign of it, "I did not want to show him I was upset, I did not want to upset him, and besides, I did not want to disturb the transference relationship." I told the young analyst that I felt that the least he could have done was to permit himself to show that he was startled and also that he was concerned. It did not have to be done in words. His behaving as if nothing extraordinary had happened must have meant to the patient that the analyst either did not care or was terrified himself.

We spent a good deal of time discussing my belief that to preserve a patient's analyzability, the analyst must give indications of compassion for the patient when extraordinary or massive misfortunes befall him. We had plenty of time to discuss this hour because the patient had canceled the remainder of the hours of that week. When he eventually did return, the analyst was able to confirm the fact that the patient had felt Dr. A.'s reactions were inhuman, he had felt humiliated, hurt, and angry, but he did persuade himself to continue because, "Maybe analysts *have* to behave that way ... they are programmed that way." This analysis never progressed to any great depth.

These two examples, I hope, illustrate the importance of the analyst's noninterpretive interventions and spontaneous human reactions to the patient undergoing extraordinary life situations. I would behave in similar ways if a patient were seriously ill, if there were a death of somebody close, if an important examination were passed or failed, etc. These reactions do not have to be put into words or actions, nor do they have to be intense. In comparison to the analyst's usual behavior, ordinary responsiveness will stand out. For example, an analyst can express his sympathy when his patient reports flunking the bar examination, an accomplishment he had set his heart on, by merely allowing himself to sigh audibly. I would follow a similar policy with less dramatic events as well. I do not greet a patient after a six-week vacation as though I had seen him yesterday. Nor would I end the last hour before a lengthy separation as though I would see the patient tomorrow. The analyst's refusal to express any feelings may reveal him to be, or may make him seem, unfeeling or out of contact, which blocks the development of a trusting relationship and a productive analytic atmosphere.

Dealing with Errors in Technique and Lapses in Behavior

Technical errors and behavioral lapses occur too frequently in every analysis to be completely omitted from this presentation. I shall limit myself, however, to only a few remarks and the briefest examples. Errors in technique may be caused by misunderstanding the goings-on in a patient due to insufficient or faulty knowledge. This may be due to inexperience, ignorance, or the clinging to a narrow set of theoretical beliefs and technical practices which are harmful to a given patient. Placing an acutely frightened paranoid or suicidal patient on a couch and sitting behind him silently would be an example of such an error. Unrecognized and uncontrolled countertransference reactions are another important source of errors. They may lead to technical mistakes or to behaving badly in human terms. Let me illustrate some of these points briefly.

I was analyzing a young, depressed, divorced woman, Mrs. L., for several years when I noticed, to my surprise and dismay, that I always gave her some five to seven extra minutes. I do that occasionally with all patients because I do not like to interrupt either their or my flow of thought. In the case of

Mrs. L., it was a regular occurrence. Once I became aware of it I was determined to be more exact about the time, but without stopping the hour abruptly. I also decided to do some self analysis of my feelings for her. Mrs. L. soon brought in material indicating her discontent with me and eventually said she felt I was giving her less time. I said she was right and told her I had recently become aware of giving her extra time and I considered that to be a mistake on my part. She was very curious about the reasons for this. I replied that giving her extra time had not been deliberate, but that I believed my personal unconscious reasons did not belong in her analysis. Then we analyzed her many fantasies to my previous behavior as well as to my asserting a right to privacy and to the inequality of the analytic situation.

In this case, I recognized and analyzed a countertransference reaction and brought it under control. I did not bring it up in the analysis until the patient herself reacted to my change in behavior. Then I admitted my error but neither burdened nor gratified her by revealing the unconscious determinants for my actions. The analysis proceeded more turbulently but more productively onward. If I had changed my behavior and only insisted on analyzing her reactions without acknowledging my countertransference behavior, I would be behaving like many parents do to a child. In effect, I would be saying, my behavior is none of your business, or, how dare you discuss me.

One morning at 9 A.M. I came to my office door and found a note from my patient saying he had been there at 8, waited a half hour and left. I realized I had forgotten the appointment, I phoned the patient, apologized, and told him I would see him the next day. The next day he attempted to deny his hurt feelings, anger, and his jealousy fantasies, but in a short while he was able to express them with a good deal of intensity. When I asked him how he felt when I phoned to apologize, he said: "That was very decent of you; in fact, I was ready to forget the whole thing, but you wouldn't let me." Later on he added that he felt apologizing was beneath the dignity of a psychoanalyst. It took away the mystery and the magic. This was then analyzed.

I believe it is right to apologize to a patient when your behavior has been unnecessarily hurtful. Not to do so is to be disrespectful and impolite. Yet I have heard of psychoanalysts who have fallen asleep during a patient's hour and, when awakened by the patient, remained silent, or interpreted the event as a result of the patient's wish to put the analyst in a stupor. I believe the apology for behaving badly should be made before attempting any interpretations. Analyzing before apologizing may be correctly perceived by the patient as an attempt to obscure or minimize the analyst's responsibility for his lapse in behavior. I have found that apologizing does not interfere with the therapeutic process. On the contrary, failure to be forthright in such matters injects an element of hypocrisy and oppressiveness in the analytic situation.

Important Events in the Course of the Analysis

I am referring here to the use of noninterpretative interventions when significant changes occur in the patient during the analysis. I believe that it is important to acknowledge or affirm that the patient has made an important step forward or backward in his struggle with his neurotic conflicts. I also acknowledge the patient's ability to perceive and judge correctly. This can be done in words, or tone, or woven into an interpretation, or by repeating the patient's discovery, etc. The following is a brief example.

For years, my patient, Mr. Z., had expressed contempt for and envy of his uncle Ben. He also despised his uncle's wife and was convinced theirs was a miserable marriage. I had tried for a long time to interpret from his material that perhaps underneath all these emotions, Mr. Z. had had a wish to be loved by his uncle and that his contempt and envy had arisen only after he had felt rebuffed and rejected by his uncle. I also showed him how this was parallel to his reactions to me. His typical attitude for years had been: "Who needs them," or, "Who needs you," a

denial of his infantile dependent yearning for love. The patient
saw the parallel intellectually, but could not feel it. Mr. Z.
began an hour some weeks after the last such interpretation by
telling me that he had made a valuable discovery. At a family
gathering, and after a few drinks, he felt a sudden surge of love
and closeness toward his uncle Ben. He avoided close contact
with him until he felt the effects of the alcohol had worn off.
Then Mr. Z. approached his uncle and engaged him in a conversation that lasted several hours. He was amazed to find how
interesting and bright his uncle was and above all how warmly
he felt toward him. The friendly conversation felt like being
hugged and admired. Furthermore, when his uncle's wife
entered their little group, he realized how considerate and loving
his uncle and aunt were to each other. It dawned on him then
that he had distorted his evaluation of their marriage because he
had felt like an outsider with them. Whenever he felt left out,
people who were "in" became despicable, hypocritical, and
worthless. Mr. Z. added, "That is my usual angry, defensive
front, which I know chases people away from me and ends up
creating the terrible loneliness I now hate."

This was an important set of insights and I wanted Mr. Z. to
know that I realized it. I replied something as follows: "Once
you were able to recognize that underneath all the hateful
feelings for your uncle you really wanted to be loved by him,
then you could allow yourself to make other important discoveries. Your uncle is a bright and interesting man and not a
boor, and he does have a good relationship to his wife." Mr. Z.
responded quickly: "My aunt has her faults, but she is devoted to
my uncle and she is quite attractive." Then he drifted on to
material of an oedipal nature which was new in this context.

I am using this example to illustrate the value of affirming
the importance of a patient's insights. Too often we only speak
when we can interpret some distortion in the patient's fantasies
or behavior. Acknowledgment of a good piece of insight on the
patient's part encourages him to do more analytic work
on his own, to work things through. It also fosters his independence and reminds him, *and us*, that he is not only made up

of neurotic and infantile components. Such confirmations further his healthy identification with the analytic attitude of his analyst.

It is one of the vocational hazards of psychoanalysis to fall into the trap of habitually committing one-upmanship with one's patients. The overriding importance of interpretation tends to blur our awareness that by constantly confronting the patient with our discoveries of his unconscious distortions we may be repeating a damaging part of the patient's past relationship to his parents. As the patient's transference neurosis often makes him excessively submissive, he may yield to our interventions rather than cope with them. The analyst's constant pursuit of new derivatives of the neurotic conflicts may make him underestimate the importance of acknowledging the patient's budding capacities and accomplishments. Too often psychoanalysis assumes the nature of a contest between adversaries. We tend to forget the inequalities of the analytic situation. The patient is asked to reveal all of himself, the analyst is trained to expose as little of his personal self as he comfortably can. To be sure, we do not want our personality traits to intrude upon the patient's transference reactions; but we sometimes seem to use nonresponsiveness and interpretations because they are safer and easier for us rather than best for the patient.

I want to conclude this presentation with a few words about the dangers of permitting one's emotional responses, humanitarian concerns, and reality considerations into the analytic situation. I have not stressed this aspect because traditional psychoanalytic training has always emphasized the hazards of not behaving as a relatively anonymous blank screen.

Visiting Mrs. K. in the hospital led at first to her idealizing me as a saintly figure, self-sacrificing and extraordinarily compassionate. I repeatedly had to point out how exaggerated her reactions were, how they permitted her to indulge in pleasureful closeness fantasies, and finally how she used them as a defense against her hostile feelings. My behavior had made the demonstrability of the transference distortions *temporarily* more difficult, but her dreams and my repeated interpretations did eventuate in her being able to experience the childhood rage and terror I have described earlier.

Admitting technical errors or apologizing for lapses in behavior can mislead a patient into believing the analytic situation is one between two equals. Some may construe this to mean that we are now friends in the conventional social sense. It then becomes necessary to point out that however equal we may be in certain ways, in fact the patient may be my superior in some, nevertheless, in the psychoanalytic situation he is the patient and relatively unknowing and I am the expert, my errors notwithstanding.

Acknowledging that a patient has made a valuable insight often seduces the patient into attempting to make immediate interpretations of his own material. He becomes a "junior psychoanalyst," a caricature of a working alliance. This has to be demonstrated and interpreted so that the analysis does not deteriorate into an educational seminar or a guessing game. Tact is required because we do not want to crush the patient's healthy wish to do some of the analytic work himself.

There is much more to be said about the dangers of non-interpretive interventions, but if the analyst is aware of the possible side effects of what he is doing, the patient's distortions are analyzable and do not permanently interfere with the analytic process.

I hope the clinical examples in this paper have illustrated that civility toward the patient, compassion for his plight, respect for him as a human being, recognition of his achievements, and the acknowledgment of our own lapses when they become visible to the patient, are vital ingredients for a productive psychoanalytic atmosphere. These elements are beyond transference and interpretation, and are more difficult if not impossible to teach. They should not need to be taught. They should, however, be recognized as essential components of therapeutic psychoanalysis.

27

"The Voice of the Intellect Is a Soft One"

A Review of
The Writings of Anna Freud, Volume IV

(1972)

T HIS COLLECTION OF PAPERS offers the reader a rare set of experiences. The essays in this volume were written during the years 1945 to 1956, a period in psychoanalysis when important new developments and divergences were becoming increasingly apparent in the psychoanalytic movement. Yet Anna Freud's vast range of interest and concerns, her keen discernment of what is central and what is peripheral, makes this group of papers relevant to the struggles of psychoanalysis today (Lustman, 1967). The author's clarity, simplicity, and modesty of style, plus her muted humanitarianism, offer the serious reader an opportunity not only to observe, but to participate in the growth and development of psychoanalysis of that period. Controversial issues, misunderstandings, and unknowns are confronted squarely, not with polemical zest but with reason

First published in *International Journal of Psycho-Analysis*, 53:403-417, 1972.

and patience. By the use of carefully selected clinical fragments
and theoretical formulations, Anna Freud attempts to build an
organized and dynamic picture of the development of man into
a whole and living human being.

Anna Freud's unpretentious style and her lucid, systematic
thinking make her constructions and hypotheses deceptively easy
to follow. As a result, those with a readiness to acquiescence may
mistakenly believe that the material under discussion is obvious
and already well known. Those who confuse opaqueness with
profundity, or who are contentious, will equate comprehensi-
bility and open-mindedness with superficiality. In any event, as
Anna Freud describes clinical phenomena or constructs theoretical formulations, they seem so patently clear that complexity,
controversy, and conflict seem remote. Only later reflection and
retrospective evaluation make the reader aware of how many
basic areas in the field of psychoanalysis have been freshly dealt
with, clarified, and amplified (Calef, 1970). I believe Freud's
statements (1927) in reference to the difficulty in ridding oneself
of illusions are remarkably apt in describing the writings of Anna
Freud: "The voice of the intellect is a soft one, but it does not rest
till it has gained a hearing" (p. 53).

The papers in this volume are so comprehensive in their
content, and so meticulous in construction, that a review can
only do violence to the delicate balance. I can do no more than
concentrate on certain points in those papers which seemed to be
of the greatest relevance to me. I should add that my training
and experience have been almost exclusively in adult psychoanalysis, and my major interests revolve around technique and
the varieties of relationships which occur in the analytic situation; thus my selection of topics may well reflect this one-
sidedness.

"Indications for Child Analysis" contains a concise history
of the developments in child analysis from its beginnings with
Freud's case of Little Hans in 1909 until 1945, the date of the
paper's publication. Anna Freud begins by setting forth some of
the major controversial issues. She points out that the child's
family cannot be excluded from the analysis. Their good sense

must take over most of the role of the adult patient's healthy ego, his motivation for treatment and his therapeutic alliance. The use of play activity, while offering flashes of direct insight into the child's unconscious, differs significantly from the use of free association. The facts that the relationship to the therapist is not predominantly a transference reaction and that the little child is unable to use speech make child play therapy very different from psychoanalysis with adults. This point of view is in opposition to the Kleinian school which believes that all children pass through psychoticlike phases of development and should be *analyzed* even before the age of two or three. The school of Anna Freud, on the other hand, is of the opinion that child *analysis* (my italics) should only be undertaken when speech is more fully developed and even then it is preferable to wait until latency, except for those with a severe infantile neurosis.

In evaluating the child's infantile neurosis it is important to realize that the child's suffering is equally divided between the child and the parent. Much of the child's anxiety may be bound by phobic or obsessive symptom formation and the amount of suffering will be determined by the reactions of the environment. Seen from this point of view, the quantity of the child's suffering cannot be considered a decisive indication for psychoanalytic treatment. It is the child's developmental progress or lack of it, the inharmonious development which is the determining factor.

> When the libido constellations become rigid, stabilized, and monotonous in their expressions, the neurosis threatens to remain permanently. This means that treatment is indicated [p. 24].

The author then illuminates her position by taking up the issue of the qualitative factors in normal ego development. The ego progresses from a mere receiving station for dimly perceived stimuli to an organized center where impressions are received, sorted out, recorded, interpreted, and action is undertaken. Each new way of functioning brings at least an equal, if not an overwhelmingly greater, amount of pain, discomfort, and

anxiety. The outer world is shown to be full of frustrations, disappointments, and threats. The feeling of the child's inner
reality reveals the existence of forbidden and dangerous tendencies which offend the child's conception of himself and therefore
cause anxiety. The development of memory is disturbing because
it aims at retaining memory traces, irrespective of their quality.
The synthetic function opposes the free and easy manner in
which the infant lived out his most divergent and instinctual
urges. As a consequence, the immature ego of the child attempts
to undo its own achievements.

It tries *not* to see outside reality as it is (denial); not to
record and make conscious the representatives of the inner
urges as they are sent up from the id (repression); it overlays
unwelcome urges with their opposites (reaction formation);
it substitutes for painful facts pleasurable fantasies (escape
into fantasy life); it attributes to others the qualities it does
not like to see in itself (projection); and it appropriates from
others what seems welcome (introjection).

But events shape themselves differently if acute neurotic conflicts intervene either in the preoedipal phases or
during the oedipal phase. In the face of excessive anxiety the
ego makes excessive and more lasting use of the defense
mechanisms at its disposal. Therefore, the harm done to the
ego functions becomes considerably greater and is of more
permanent importance.

This interference with the ego functions is of greater
importance in childhood than under otherwise similar conditions in the adult neurosis. It occurs while the maturation
of the ego is still in process. The function that is more
directly attacked by infantile neurosis is kept back from
further development, at least temporarily, while the other
ego achievements continue to mature. Accordingly, ego
development becomes one-sided and inharmonious [pp. 31,
35, 36].

Anna Freud and her co-workers have been pursuing the
idea of the overriding importance of developmental success or

failure in determining suitability for psychoanalytic treatment. Such concepts as the "developmental profile," the "developmental lines," and the "assessment of the total personality" (A. Freud, 1965, 1969) are all outgrowths of this paper written over twenty-five years ago.

This volume contains two papers on feeding, its psychological significance and disturbances, one directed at psychoanalysts and one for nonanalysts. The more technical paper places more stress on the pathological developments and theory. The nontechnical paper covers similar clinical material, only the pace is a bit slower and the explanations are spelled out in greater detail. These two papers are beautiful examples of Anna Freud's lucidity on two different levels; clarity always, but never at the price of oversimplification. In both presentations the major concern is with the feeding disturbances of everyday life, their prevention and treatment.

The satisfaction of hunger constitutes the first experience of instinctual gratification in the child's life. The mother's feeding regime is the first environmental interference with the child's instinctual desires. The amount of pleasure or frustration a child will gain from eating depends to a great extent on the manner in which food is given, what, how much, how little, and in what way he may eat. The best eaters are children who are permitted to pursue both their physiological and emotional needs in their feeding. If eating becomes invested with great aggressive and sexual meaning, it can lead to depressions, melancholia, and anorexia nervosa.

Food and mother remain linked forever in the child's unconscious. Most of the child's conflicts about food are transferred from the mother. Mothers often aggravate the pathogenic elements in the situation by reacting as though the food they offer were really part of themselves. This coincides with the child's unconscious attitudes and strengthens the conflictual tendencies. The more a mother can trust the self-regulating powers of the child's appetite, the easier the child will learn to handle food independently.

At this point I would like to illustrate with what economy

and simplicity Anna Freud describes the child's development from narcissistic love to object love.

> An infant who feeds successfully "loves" the experience of feeding (narcissistic love). . . . When the child's awareness develops sufficiently to discern other qualities besides those of pain and pleasure, the libido cathexis progresses from the pleasurable experience of feeding to the food which is the source of pleasure. The infant in this second stage "loves" the milk, breast, or bottle. . . . When his powers of perception permit the child to form a conception of the person through whose agency he is fed, his "love" is transferred to the provider of food, that is, to the mother or mother substitute (object love) [p. 48].

There are three papers in this volume which deal primarily with aggression: "Notes on Aggression" (1949), "Aggression in Relation to Emotional Development: Normal and Pathological" (1949), and "Instinctual Drives and Their Bearing on Human Behavior" (1953). The first was written for a psychoanalytic audience, the other two for nonanalysts. These papers appeared on the psychoanalytic scene when there was still a great deal of unclarity in America as to the status of aggression as an independent instinctual drive. Anna Freud's discussions of the differing points of view did not eliminate the controversies, but they did much to clarify the areas of agreement and disagreement.

There are a number of analysts who still maintain that aggression is the result of the frustration of instinctual desires. Another group of analysts, represented by Melanie Klein and her followers, believes that the interplay of the life and death instincts is in itself sufficient to create a state of conflict and this basic ambivalence is by its nature of pathogenic significance.

> According to their views, a vital stage in the emotional development of every infant is marked by the recognition that a loved object is in danger of being attacked, and destroyed by virtue of being loved. . . . Other analysts, in America and Europe, the author among them, hold the

view that the coexistence of the two opposing instinctual forces in themselves is not sufficient to produce mental conflict. Clinical observation shows numerous states which represent a successful fusion between the destructive and erotic urges.... Further, in young infants, love and hate, affection and anger, tenderness and aggression, the wish to destroy loved people or toys and the wish to preserve and have them, can be seen to appear in quick succession, seemingly unaffected by each other, each controversial striving attempting with full force to reach its own aim. The mental representatives of the two organic forces remain unrelated to each other so long as no central point of awareness is established in the personality. It is only the growth of this focal point (the ego) which results in the gradual integration of all instinctual strivings, and during this process may lead to clashes and realization of incompatibility between them. According to these views, therefore, the presence of mental conflicts and of the guilt feelings consequent on them presupposes that a specific, comparatively advanced stage in ego development has been reached [p. 69f.].

I believe this is one of the critical differences in the thinking of the Freudian and Kleinian psychoanalysts and is responsible for far-reaching theoretical and technical divergences in the two groups. Another, and related, disagreement concerns the influence of reliable love relationships and massive deprivations in early childhood.

2. The lack of steady love relationships in early childhood caused either by internal or external factors (such as loss of parents or their substitutes, traumatic weaning from the breast, etc.) gives rise to states of emotional starvation with consequent retardation or complete stunting of the child's erotic development. In such cases the normal fusion between the erotic and destructive urges cannot take place, and aggression manifests itself as pure, independent destructiveness....

3. Destructiveness, delinquency, and criminality in children, caused by the stunting of their libidinal development as described above, are not open to direct educational influences such as severe control, punishments, admonitions, etc. An appropriate therapy has to be directed to the neglected, defective side of the emotional development so that normal fusion between the erotic and the destructive impulses can follow and aggression be brought under the beneficial, mitigating influence of the child's love life [p. 73f.].

The "appropriate therapy" directed to the defective side of the emotional development points to a major difference in therapeutic approaches between the classical and Kleinian psychoanalysts. As far as I have been able to determine, Kleinian psychoanalysts treat all forms of psychoneurosis, delinquency, and psychosis with the same technique, namely, the interpretation of the patient's unconscious productions, primarily the transference reactions. This is in marked contrast to the approach of the Freudian analysts in the treatment of delinquent or psychotic patients. In addition to interpretation, the Freudians use such adjunctive means as supporting the defenses, facilitating the establishment of a working alliance and a real relationship to foster the development of reliable object relations so that a fusion of erotic and aggressive impulses may take place and ego development can proceed. This train of thought is continued and amplified in "Certain Types and Stages of Social Maladjustment" (1949).

"The Contribution of Psychoanalysis to Genetic Psychology" was presented at a program commemorating the 60th anniversary of Clark University, where Freud himself had given five lectures forty years earlier in 1910. I believe that in this rather long and complicated presentation you can see Anna Freud at her best as a catalytic agent conveying understanding of intricate psychoanalytic concepts to a group with a heterogeneous background, in terms of attitude and knowledge. I am selecting certain passages for quotation because they demonstrate how her complete mastery of the subject permits her to express a great deal of theoretical and clinical material with great economy and yet with a broadness of scope.

In the history of psychoanalysis, genetic investigation proceeded from the study of libidinal development to that of the inhibiting forces, and thereby established the picture of two major lines of simultaneous, parallel growth in the human personality. Following the dictates of the analytic technique, the investigators in the analytic interview permitted their attention to alternate between derivatives of the unconscious (in free association, dreams, transference behavior) and the manifestations of the inhibiting ego and superego (as revealed in the resistances). The genetic data gained from this two-sided observation in the analytic sessions served to enlarge the knowledge of the origin and development of the two sides of the individual personality. . . .

Since, as mentioned above, psychoanalytic observation is linked with therapeutic purposes, it takes as its object painful, dramatic, and pathogenic life situations, as they are called to memory or reproduced in the analytic session. . . .

Abundant clinical evidence has taught psychoanalysts to regard these conflicts not as regrettable accidental happenings that might be avoided, but as regular normal occurrences that are inseparable from the process of growing up; in the last resort they are the clashes between that which "is inherited, that is present at birth, that is laid down in the constitution" (the drives, the "id content") and that which is due to regard for reality and "the child's attitude to his parents," which includes "not only the personalities of the actual parents but also the family, racial and national traditions handed on through them, as well as the demands of the immediate social milieu which they represent (the ego and superego forces)" [p. 128f.].

In discussing reconstruction and prediction in psychoanalysis, the author states that there is far greater variation in the ego and superego structure than there is in the id and it is this fact which makes for the infinite variety of human personalities and clinical pictures. She then illustrates this theme as follows:

> Sexual curiosity, which is one of the component drives of the phallic phase, may lead, with equal probability, to the perversion of scoptophilia (when regressed to in later life), to pseudodebility (when severely repressed), to discreetness or indifference toward other people's affairs (when held down by reaction formations), to intellectual alertness and the attitude of the scientific investigator (when sublimated). The exhibitionistic tendencies of the phallic phase are responsible for creating personalities as widely divergent from each other as those of a shy recluse, a gifted actor, a vulgar showman, or a snooping censor, according to the ego mechanisms which have dealt with them. Similarly, strong aggressive tendencies play a dominant role among the id urges not only of criminals, brutal personalities, ruthless adventurers, etc., but of people with excellent social adaptation such as teachers, nurses, surgeons, philanthropists, pacifists, etc. [p. 133].

During World War II, Anna Freud spent the years 1940-45 observing children from the age of 10 days upward, some with, some without mothers, some for several days and others for several years. A population of some 80 resident infants and children were cared for and observed by a staff of five or six highly qualified workers supplemented by a group of young people eager for an adventure in education and observation, "untrained for this type of work but also untrained in methods hostile to it." In "Observations on Child Development" the reader will have an opportunity to observe how a psychoanalyst as thoroughly grounded in traditional psychoanalytic theory and practice as Anna Freud is can keep an open and receptive attitude and modify her approach when unusual circumstances and unexpected findings present themselves.

Anna Freud and her co-workers were impressed by the wide overlapping between the oral and anal stages. The amount of aggression and destructiveness was not only greater than in children under ordinary circumstances, but it was inaccessible to the usual educational influences. The "aggression in pure culture" was believed to be a result of stunting in the libidinal development of the children and led to a lack of fusion between the drives.

> To test our diagnosis, we ceased any attempts to combat the children's aggression directly, and concentrated our efforts instead on stimulating the emotional side which had lagged behind. The results confirmed that, with the development of good object relationships, aggression became bound and its manifestations, reduced to normal quantities. It proved possible, as it were, to effect therapeutic results by bringing about the necessary fusion of the two drives [p. 153f.].

Anna Freud also points out some discrepancies between some existing analytic assumptions and her wartime observations. Children left by their mothers in the nurseries showed total regression—regression in instinctual phase, ego functions, and character traits—not the selective and uneven regressions seen in adults and in children under less traumatic circumstances. They showed no neurotic symptoms because the total regression obviated any pathogenic conflicts. Another startling finding was that penis envy appeared with great violence in girls between the ages of 18 and 24 months. Disgust appeared before toilet training and shame before the inhibition of exhibitionism. They also found that head knocking appears more frequently in children in institutions. It seems to be a form of auto-aggression and perhaps a sign of pure aggression due to the lack of fusion of the drives. The most intriguing data were the coitus-like behavior of children who had never lived in a family, had never seen a private bedroom or observed sexual intercourse. Boys brought up without fathers acted fatherlike to their mothers or mother substitutes. Another finding indicating the possibility of innate preformed attitudes and drives is the astonishing quickness with which children can adopt family attitudes when placed in a foster home.

"An Experiment in Group Upbringing" is one of the most

remarkable psychoanalytic papers I have ever read. The concentration camp children who provide the clinical material are at times heartbreaking and at other times excruciatingly comical. The many observations are presented very starkly and with many direct quotations from the interactions of children. The result is that the reader gets the feeling of knowing these children, of having actually lived with them in person, which leaves an unforgettable impact. This paper, written in collaboration with Sophie Dann, concerns a year of observation and treatment of six young children between the ages of three and three years and ten months who were victims of the Hitler regime. They were German-Jewish orphans whose parents, soon after their birth, were deported to Poland and killed in the gas chambers. During their first year of life these children were handed from one refugee to another until they arrived individually, at ages varying from six to twelve months, at the concentration camp at Theresienstadt in Moravia. They were placed on a ward for motherless children and cared for by conscientious but overworked and undernourished nurses and helpers. They had no toys and a bare outside yard. After liberation some two to three years later, these six children, as the youngest, were kept together and flown to England to provide them with a year of peaceful and quiet surroundings. None of these children had known any circumstances of life other than those of a group setting. They were ignorant of the meaning of a family. I shall not quote passages from this paper, because it should be read in its entirety.

These two papers on the observations and handling of the war children demonstrate Anna Freud's resourcefulness, her flexibility and her openmindedness. The clinical observations are presented generously so that the reader may be stimulated to rethink his previous beliefs. Unexpected findings are exposed, speculated upon, and offered as material for further study. In my opinion, every psychoanalyst who is not fixated to a specific "school" of thought will be impelled to reexamine his own thinking on the basis of this fascinating clinical material.

In her contribution to the symposium on "The Mutual Influences in the Development of Ego and Id" we see Anna

Freud in a dual role. She serves as the translator of metapsychology into clear and comprehensible language. She also functions as an intermediary, an emissary bearing comprehension between the original author and the audience. At the same time she adds some of her own fresh ideas.

"Studies in Passivity" is an attempt to clarify some of the most difficult problems in the analysis of overtly homosexual men. The author's clinical experiences revealed that the analysis of the different varieties of fear of the female, or the male's fear of his own aggression toward the female, all had a limited value in the analysis of passive male homosexuals. She found that her most effective interpretations concerned the equation she made between the passive homosexuals and their active counterparts:

> Namely, that the active male partner, whom these men are seeking, represents to them their lost masculinity, which they enjoy in identification with him. This implies that these apparently passive men are active according to their fantasy, while they are passive only so far as their behavior is concerned [p. 251].

Her work with these patients led her to understand why they dreaded being deprived of their homosexual partners.

> What these patients dreaded was that the analyst would deprive them of the masculinity represented by other men. The promise of a cure turned to a castration threat. This is a very useful piece of information regarding the difficulties that every analyst encounters with patients of this type. . . . Above all, this representation of the boy's masculinity by another man is a normal process in childhood; it is the young boy's attitude toward the father which is reflected here. While admiring the father's masculinity, the boy at the same time has a part in it, shares in it in his fantasy, borrows it from the father occasionally, even if he borrows it only in the form of a piece of clothing, a penknife, a fountain pen. . . . This same attitude which is overcome in latency recurs normally in adolescence in the form of hero

worship. . . . The admiration of the masculine partner does
not lead to the individual's own masculinity. On the contrary, we see the homosexual become insatiable in his wish
for the partner's masculinity [p. 253f.].

My own clinical experiences confirm the importance of
Anna Freud's findings. All addictionlike devouring relationships
to objects reveal that the supposed love object is above all a part
of the self. The possibility of loss is so catastrophic because it
combines object loss with a loss of self, of identity, of reality.

Anna Freud then goes on to attempt to find a connection
between negativism or the incapacity to form an object relationship and emotional surrender (*Hörigkeit*). She notes that with
the exception of Hartmann and Mahler most authors feel that
the positive tie to the mother is the beneficial influence. The
usual explanations do not suffice for certain homosexual and
impotent persons. A further analysis of this situation reveals a
nonsexual core.

> The passive surrender to the love object may signify a return
> from object love proper to its forerunner in the emotional
> development of the infant, i.e., primary identification with
> the love object. This is a regressive step which implies a
> threat to the intactness of the ego, i.e., a loss of personal
> characteristics of the love object. The individual fears this
> regression in terms of dissolution of the personality, loss of
> sanity, and defends himself against it by a complete rejec-
> tion of all objects (negativism) [p. 259].

The paper "The Role of Bodily Illness in the Mental Life of
Children" has several especially noteworthy sections.

> When studying the aftereffects of childhood operations in
> the analysis of adult patients we find that it is not the
> castration *fear* but the feminine castration *wish* [my italics]
> in a male child that is most frequently responsible for serious
> postoperative breakdowns or permanent postoperative
> character changes. In these instances, the surgical attack on
> the patient's body acts like a seduction to passivity to which

the child either submits with disastrous results for his masculinity, or against which he has to build up permanent pathologically strong defenses [p. 271].

The notion of the child's body as the mother's property can lead to hypochondria or bodily recklessness when the mother-child unity has become an important factor for both mother and child. This state of affairs is different in motherless or institutionalized children.

Far from enjoying the freedom from anxious supervision (as the observer might expect from the mothered child's revolt against her care), motherless children proceed to care for their own bodies in an unexpected manner.... The child actually deprived of a mother's care adopts the mother's role in health matters, thus playing "mother and child" with his own body.... With children, analytic study seems to make it clear that in the staging of the mother-child relationship, they themselves identify with the lost mother, while the body represents the child (more exactly: the infant in the mother's care). It would be worth investigating whether the hypochondriacal phase which precedes many psychotic disorders corresponds similarly to a regression to and re-establishment of this earliest stage of the mother-child relationship [p. 277ff.].

The paper "About Losing and Being Lost" is a gem. It is short, only 14 pages long, but it is a veritable treasure box crammed with psychoanalytic jewels. It is a sheer joy to read in its entirety and it is a pity to disturb the entity by selecting only certain passages for presentation.

Anna Freud begins by examining the dynamic and libido-economic aspects of losing and lost. She starts with Freud's ideas about the multiplicity of purposes which such actions can fulfill unconsciously. Then she discusses the different meanings the lost objects may symbolize.

Our material possessions may represent for us parts of our own body, in which case we cathect them narcissistically;

or they may represent human love objects, in which case they are cathected with object libido. We increase or decrease cathexis, or change it from positive to negative, from libido to aggression, according to the vicissitudes of our attitude to our own body on the one hand and to the objects in the external world on the other hand [p. 304].

She then considers the additions to our understanding of losing and retaining when psychoanalysis became more interested in the first year of life. Here she approaches the differing points of view in her usual straightforward, nonpolemical style.

On the other hand, it depends on the individual author's theoretical orientation whether the dawning differentiation between the self and the object world is conceived of as happening very early or comparatively late in infancy; and whether inanimate objects (such as the bottle) and body parts (such as fingers) are seen as objects in their own right or merely as derivatives of and substitutes for the mother. It seems to me that any decision in this respect (or the continuing indecision) needs to be based on the fact that we deal here with undifferentiated and unstructured human beings; that this is a period of life when there are no whole objects, only part objects; when there are only anaclitic, i.e., need-satisfying, object relationships; and when even external objects are included in the child's internal, narcissistic milieu.

We are greatly helped in our dilemma by the concept of the "transitional object" as it was introduced by D. W. Winnicott.... He showed convincingly that all these early objects are cathected doubly, narcissistically and with object love, and that this enables the child to transfer his attachments gradually from the cathected figure of the mother to the external world in general.

Thus, human beings are flexible where their attachments are concerned. Narcissistically colored ties alternate with object ties proper; libidinal with aggressive cathexis; animate with inanimate objects. This creates multiple possibilities for discharge, which remain important far beyond childhood [p. 305ff.].

Anna Freud then adds an important clinical and theoretical note:

Certain other phenomena may be mentioned in the same connection. We are familiar with the *fear of impoverishment* which appears as a symptom in a number of pre-psychotic states, and we understand it, on the basis of the foregoing, as the result of the individual's libidinal withdrawal from his material possessions and the ensuing fear of losing hold of them; obviously, this is not unlike the graver psychotic delusion of the destruction of the world, which we interpret as a reflection in consciousness of the withdrawal of libido from the object world in general [p. 307].

In the next section of the paper, Anna Freud explores the notion of identifying with the lost object. She points out that castration distress, mourning, and guilt do not suffice to explain all the loser's pain. There are further elements which originate in deeper layers of the mind. This happens when the loser ascribes some independent action to the lost object.

"It got lost," or "It is gone," or "It has come back." Obviously this signifies a displacement: the libidinal withdrawal responsible for the loss is shifted from the inner world of the loser to the item which has been lost, personifying the latter in the process. We notice, secondly, that the loser's emotions do not confine themselves to his own regrets about the loss, but extend to feelings which allegedly belong to the lost object. Here, projection has led to personification, which in its turn is followed by identification [p. 308f.].

Anna Freud considers this an example of projective identification, a concept introduced by Melanie Klein.

In the following section, the author focuses on the child as a lost object and a loser of objects.

As in the case of material objects, for a child to get lost is the exception rather than the rule, which is surprising in view of the lack of reality orientation in our toddlers and under-fives, and of the boisterousness and adventurous spirit of those who are slightly older. Here the children's urge to cling seems to unite with the parents' high valuation of their offspring and, combined, to set limits to the area in which the latter roam freely.

It is interesting that children usually do not blame themselves for getting lost but instead blame the mother who lost them. An example of this was a little boy, lost in a store, who, after being reunited with his mother, accused her tearfully. "You losted me!" (not "I lost you!") [p. 311f.].

Children become chronic losers if they feel unloved at home.

What we discover in their analyses first is an inability to cathect the inanimate, owing to the general damage done to their capacity for involvement with objects; next, that they direct to their possessions the whole hostility aroused by the frustrations and disappointments imposed on them by their parents. It is only behind these fairly obvious causes that a further, even more far-reaching motive comes into view: by being chronic losers, they live out a double identi-fication, passively with the lost objects which symbolize themselves, actively with the parents whom they experience to be as neglectful, indifferent, and unconcerned toward them as they themselves are toward their possessions [p. 312f.].

The final sections of the paper deal with how the lost object is dealt with in dreams, myths, and folklore. Throughout this essay the reader is transported, as if effortlessly, into new depths of clinical and theoretical thinking about losing and being lost. The new ideas revealed by the author bring a sense of joy of discovery. The extensions and amplifications of Freud's concepts enrich the field of psychoanalysis. Furthermore, I believe it is fair to say that scientific writing of this kind, which is rich in content and modest in style, is a thing of beauty. Anna Freud does not utilize the embellishments of a professional writer. Her literary style has the stark, unadorned, natural beauty of a clear and selective natural eye, reporting its observations and reflections without distortions. There is also no overt or subtle pressure for the reader to accept a certain point of view. She states her thoughts and findings and it is for the reader to accept as much or as little as he can use for his own enlightenment.

"Psychoanalysis and Education" is an abstract of the Freud Anniversary Lecture of May 1954. In it Anna Freud outlines the trends of psychoanalytic investigation in regard to child psychology. She touches upon some current misconceptions, two in particular. She describes the tendency to place the blame for the child's early difficulties on the "rejecting mother." The author makes a point of stressing that the mother is the *symbol* for all the good and bad of the oral phase, just as the father is for the phallic phase. Her other major point is the clarification of the meaning of the anaclitic relationship.

> It means, briefly, that the relationship to the mother, although the first to another human being, is not the infant's first relationship to the environment. What precedes it is an earlier phase in which not the object world but the body needs and their satisfaction or frustration play the decisive part [p. 321].

In her conclusion Anna Freud states the following:

> I do not believe that even the most revolutionary changes in infant care can do away with the tendency to ambivalence or with the division of the human personality into an id and ego with conflicting aims. On the contrary, I think that both these factors are by now inherent in the structure of the human mind, the pleasure-pain experiences in the earliest phase merely acting as appropriate stimuli which elicit their emergence. . . .
> According to the views presented here, the emergence

of neurotic conflicts has to be regarded as the price paid for the complexity of the human personality [p. 326].

The paper, "Problems of Infantile Neurosis: Contribution to the Discussion," fulfills a double task. In it Anna Freud expands and defends her assumptions in her Freud lecture of 1954 and also responds to the contributions of the other participants in the symposium. She begins by stating very explicitly her attitude about the pathogenic influences in the first year of life.

So far as I am concerned, the study of this darkest of all ages has never been my predilection. I have always preferred as my subject those phases of development where assumptions can be checked against verbalized material recaptured from the unconscious by the analytic method, or against facts which are open to view in the direct observation of infants. Whenever we break through the barrier which divides articulate life from the preverbal period, we find ourselves on uncertain ground, left with conjectures, reconstructions, and interpretations which of necessity have to remain unconfirmed by the individual with whom they are concerned. In no other realm of psychoanalysis does speculation need to run quite as free, as far, and as wild.

In spite of these hesitations, there was no withstanding the current trend of interest which turned to ever earlier events in the infant's life and produced a host of clinical and theoretical studies by authors such as Fries, Greenacre, Hartmann, Hendrick, Hoffer, Kris, Loewenstein, Mahler, as well as the observational studies by Bowlby and Spitz. There was, further, in London the environmental factor of the polemic carried on by Melanie Klein and her followers which acted as a constant stimulus for thought [p. 328f.].

Anna Freud then responds above all to Greenacre's contribution which introduced several important new concepts.

Her assumption that the libidinal stages coexist from birth and reach their maturational peaks at different rates of speed is far-reaching and revolutionary and may, in time, lead to important revisions of our present assumptions. So may two other of her points relating to the first-named: the contrasting types of rhythm, and the consequences of phase divergences between stimulus and response.... The first of these questions refers to the difficult differentiation between the welcome and ominous, or, as we might call them, the benign and malignant aspects of the autoerotic activities [p. 329].

The author replies to Hartmann's complaint that it is very difficult to say what we call an infantile neurosis today:

You may remember that analysts for years used to debate whether a mental disorder deserved the name neurosis before the pathogenic conflict was fully internalized. Another suggestion was not to use the term neurosis before the divisions between id and ego on the one hand, ego and superego on the other hand, are fully established. Personally, I incline toward using this latter, structural aspect as the decisive one. But since there is today very wide divergence of opinion as to when the personality structure is set up, this will still leave many authors with the concept of neuroses occurring in the first year of life [p. 341f.].

In answering the questions of several members of the symposium, Anna Freud stresses again that in her opinion, in the first weeks after birth, the infant's body needs reign supreme.

I do believe that the sensations which are connected with the arousal and fulfillment of these needs are the first mental representatives of the body, that is, that they form the first content of the mind [p. 343].

Later on she picks up the thorny question of whether or not autoerotic activities exist in their own right as the expression of the child's relationship to his own body or whether the body is used only as a substitute for the mother.

As regards our literature, it is important to remember that several schools of analytic thought, such as the followers of

Ferenczi, of Melanie Klein, and others, do not recognize autoerotism except as an offshoot of and substitute for the relationship to the mother [p. 349].

Anna Freud begins her contribution to the symposium on "The Widening Scope of Indications for Psychoanalysis" by isolating four separate causes for variations in psychoanalytic technique. One group of parameters may be introduced to meet special conditions in the patient and have the ultimate purpose of bringing about the ultimate processes of the psychoanalytic procedure.

An equal, if not larger, number of them are occasioned, not by a change in the type of disorder treated, but by a change in the analyst's outlook and theoretical evaluation of familiar phenomena. The intimate interrelation between theory and practice in psychoanalysis is responsible for the fact that every development in theory results inevitably in a change of technique [p. 358].

There are further variations which are determined by the interests and intentions of the analyst and which are not based on the countertransference.

In the fourth group of variations Anna Freud then describes an important aspect of the patient-analyst relationship. I have frequently cited her description because I believe it is a phenomenon which belongs under the heading of the real relationship between therapist and patient (see chapters 22 and 25).

Anna Freud then touches upon an important technical question. For a psychotic patient it may be necessary to reproduce the intimacy of the mother-child relationship via the relationship to the analyst. Does this disqualify the analyst from analytic work and would the change in analyst repeat the traumatic separation from the mother? In this connection Anna Freud quotes an adolescent girl, a victim of the Nazi regime who was smuggled out of the Polish ghetto and handed on endlessly from one rescue station to another. There was no single figure or even a toy or material object that dated back to her past. After several months of treatment during which her relationship to the analyst fluctuated, wavered, and threatened to peter out, the girl said to the therapist:

> "You analyze me all wrong. I know what you should do: you should be with me the whole day because I am a completely different person when I am here with you, when I am in school, and when I am home with my foster family. How can you know me if you do not see me in all these places? There is not one me, there are three."
>
> It struck me that here, disguised as a piece of "technical advice," we were offered some insight into the basic deficiencies of her ego structure. There had been, in her past, no opportunity to introject any one object sufficiently to build up inner harmony and synthesis under the guidance of a higher agency, acting as a unifying superego. . . . What she asked the therapist to do was, as it were, to offer herself in the flesh as the image of a steady, ever-present object, suitable for internalization, so that the patient's personality could be regrouped and unified around this image. Then, and only then, the girl felt, would there be a stable and truly individual center to her personality which she could transfer and offer for analysis. To carry out a plan of this kind resembles the initial periods of psychotherapy which Knight proposes as necessary for psychotic cases [p. 366].

Here I believe Anna Freud is touching on some very basic issues in psychoanalytic therapy which are in urgent need of clarification. Can interpretation or insight, no matter how correct in content, be of sufficient therapeutic benefit to a person who has suffered from severe developmental anomalies? These patients do not suffer predominantly from *structural conflicts* but from *structural deficiencies* in the formation of the ego. They are "preneurotic." They would seem to need stable objects to build up a stable ego as a prerequisite before interpretations can be meaningfully accepted and utilized.

The author then returns to the issue of the real relationship and the transference reactions.

Many of the problems touched upon in the "Widening Scope" paper are elaborated upon and reexamined in "Problems of Technique in Adult Analysis." Every classical and standard procedure has been challenged over the years.

> I name as examples—probably well-known ones—a few only: the denouncing of the rule of free association in a recent Congress paper by Burke (1949); the break with regular hourly work advocated by Lacan (1953-1955); the distrust of the unlimited development of transference by members of the Chicago Institute (Alexander and French, 1946); the sole use of transference interpretations by part of the English school of analysis, etc. Discussion of technical digressions of this nature is fruitful and interesting when it includes their theoretical background. Digressions which are not based on theory but on practical, or financial, or other personal motives of their originators are of a different nature altogether and cannot be discussed with profit [p. 380f.].

She then discusses the way in which young analysts tend to react toward the rules of analytic technique. Some find the regulations too restrictive and wish to throw out all the rules. Others hide behind the rules, using them as a protective barrier between themselves and the patient. Anna Freud states her position very succinctly.

> The most profitable view to adopt toward analytic technique seems to consider the use of the couch, free association, the handling of the transference, the handling of the transitional forms of acting out, etc., as mere tools of treatment. Tools of any trade are periodically inspected, revised, sharpened, perfected and, if necessary, altered. The technical tools of analysis are no exception to this rule. As in all other cases, alterations should not be carried out arbitrarily and without sufficient cause [p. 383].

Anna Freud sums up her view on this subject with the following sentences:

I would say that in the last resort the success or failure of our interventions depends on the intactness of the ego. . . . *To meet new or unusual challenges we need, probably, new or modified technical prescriptions. Whenever we overthrow established procedure, we feel, quite rightly, that we may be approaching a state of anarchy. That is the reason why analysts discuss these technical matters so infrequently. Our analytic technique is hard-won and should not be abandoned easily. Whenever rules are altered, we have the right to expect a theoretical justification for the step taken which remains on purely analytic ground* [my italics].

There is no analytic rule which the patient's neurosis cannot pervert and use for its own purposes. Analysts should collect and pool instances from their own cases which show how a technical rule of procedure can be converted to serve neurotic purposes. . . . Perhaps our technical rules should be given to us with an addendum, setting out their most common misuse for the purpose of the neurosis. We might also invite colleagues to note all those instances in their practice where such misuse of the technique had remained undiscovered for a length of time until the analyst became aware of the occurrence and interpreted it. . . . I did not mean to say that a patient's misuse of a technical rule justifies in any way the alteration or abandonment of this rule; on the contrary, it provides the opportunity of safeguarding the rule by interpreting its misuse [pp. 393-398].

"The Problem of Training Analysis" was originally written in 1935 and is published here in English for the first time. It is astonishing that a paper written more than thirty-five years ago should focus on many of the same problems we are struggling with today. "Instead of remaining a shadowy figure to the people he analyzes, the training analyst cannot avoid playing an important role in their real lives" (p. 415). The training analyst is a real figure to the candidate. He has a certain professional standing, published papers, etc. "Such real elements invariably obscure transference proper and render interpretation less convincing and more difficult" (p. 416). In addition, the training analyst has to make important judgments about the candidate's progress. His fellow candidates evoke childhood jealousies and rivalries. Infantile sexual curiosity is evoked and gratified by a knowledge of the training analyst's activities. Finally, the candidate enters training to become an analyst himself, thereby repeating his earlier identifications with his parents.

Anna Freud concludes with the following summary of training analyses:

> We do not hesitate to brand it as technically wrong if for the purposes of therapy an analyst selects his patients from his circle of acquaintances; if he shares his interests with them or discusses his opinions either with them or in their presence; if he forgets himself far enough to judge their behavior, to disclose his criticism to other people, and to permit it to affect decisions; if he actively manipulates the patient, offers himself to him as a pattern, and ends analysis by permitting the patient to identify with him personally and professionally. Nevertheless, we commit every single one of these deviations from the classical technique when we analyze candidates. Further, we do not inquire frequently enough how far these deviations complicate the candidate's transference and obscure its interpretation [p. 420f.].

Part II of Volume IV consists of papers addressed to professional people who were nonanalysts. I have already referred to several of these papers. The professional psychoanalyst will be surprised by the wealth of practical advice that Anna Freud is able to offer to the parent, teacher, social worker, and analyst. Time and again cogent references are made to the social problems that beset us today, despite the fact that these essays were written from fifteen to twenty-five years ago. There is a timelessness about Anna Freud's writings because her approach is always startlingly fresh; she reaches out to the basic issues, and inevitably indicates where there is still more work to be done. The result is that even the most experienced psychoanalysts find new knowledge and are invigorated by a reading of these papers. It is only the limitations of space that force me to omit many of the papers.

It is with great reluctance that I conclude this review of Anna Freud's Volume IV of her writings. I realize that I have gone into more detail than is usual in reviewing an author's work, but I have done so deliberately, with the hope it would encourage and invite the reader to participate in some of the vital struggles going on currently in psychoanalysis. I believe that Anna Freud's contribution demonstrates how an open mind can utilize clinical data and sound theory for further clarification and discussion of incompletely understood phenomena. Anna Freud's ability to oscillate between phenomenology and theory, the keenness of her observations, her mastery of psychoanalytic theory, and her vast fund of psychoanalytic experience, make her an expert guide into new and obscure areas for investigation.

I have already suggested that Anna Freud's simplicity and modesty of style may deceive some of us into believing that what she knows is already well known. It seems to me that we so readily make her knowledge ours, because she makes it all so easy to digest, so natural. Her opposition to deviant views is neither strident nor harsh and may give the temporary impression of being conciliatory. Careful thought and reflection, however, reveal this not to be the case. Anna Freud is a psychoanalyst in the best sense of the word. She is no worshipper of the past, but works unceasingly to extend and refine our knowledge. She will test and recheck old views, she will correct and amend past theories and concepts, but she does not easily abandon the hard-won body of psychoanalytic knowledge for any simpler system of thought. Reading Anna Freud's volume makes one aware that there are groups of psychoanalysts in whom the scientific spirit of psychoanalysis is still very much alive. There is no dogma and no illusion of possessing all the final answers to man's ills. I am impelled to quote Freud again, not only because his statements epitomize the ideals of his daughter's labors, but because in so many other psychoanalytic circles today, there is so much doctrine and cultism.

> If experience should show—not to me, but to others after me, who think as I do—that we have been mistaken, we will give up our expectations. Take my attempt for what it is. . . .
> The voice of the intellect is a soft one, but it does not rest till it has gained a hearing. Finally, after a countless succession of rebuffs, it succeeds [Freud, 1927, p. 53].

28

The Personal Meaning of Perfection

(1973)

I ASSUME THAT I was invited to participate in this symposium and to speak specifically on the subject, "The Personal Meaning of Perfection," because of my professional experience as a psychoanalyst. I spend most of my working life as a clinician, attempting to help patients, and others, who struggle against different forms of imperfection like anxiety, depression, and guilt. I have no competence in philosophy, paleontology, geology, genetics, evolution, and theology, and I am honored to represent psychiatry and psychoanalysis in a multidisciplinary symposium with such distinguished participants. My own contribution shall be limited to what I have learned about *some* of the sources and the antecedents of the quest for perfection from patients and nonpatients, in whom the striving for perfection was a central issue. Such people offer valuable insights into the beginnings of the sense of, and the quest for, perfection.

Contribution to a two-day symposium held in San Francisco, May 1971. Among the participants were T. Dobzhansky, L. S. B. Leakey, G. G. Simpson, and N. M. Wildiers. First published in *Teilhard de Chardin: In Quest of the Perfection of Man*, edited by Geraldine O. Browning, Joseph L. Alioto, and Seymour M. Farber. Cranbury, N.J.: Associated University Presses, 1973, pp. 180-191.

I hope the audience is familiar with the historical development of psychoanalysis insofar as it began by studying abnormalities and failures which then shed important light on the achievement of normalcy and success. Analogously, the analysis of people who suffer from a heightened sense of *imperfection* may illuminate certain aspects of the meaning of perfection.

I would like the audience to be cognizant of the psychoanalytic point of view that man is not born with any innate drive for virtue, but with drives that are self-seeking and not altruistic. Whatever virtue man achieves is the result of an uphill battle between his drives on the one hand and society and its internal representatives on the other. Society tempts and confuses man with contradictory and unreliable promises of rewards and punishments. I mention these points to introduce my approach to "The Personal Meaning of Perfection." I want to stress that Teilhard's (1959, 1960, 1962) theories about the perfection of man dealt primarily with man in a distant future, man as a species, not the ordinary man of today. I shall now turn to my clinical material, studies of people who were unusually concerned with perfection, because I believe that people's thoughts, fantasies, and behavior are more illuminating than our theories.

What Perfection Means to Different Kinds of People

1. A twenty-nine-year-old artist, outstandingly successful in his career, ostensibly happily unmarried and sexually satisfied, is, for some "indefinable reason," driven to taking drugs. He begins with taking marihuana for a few years, then goes on to heroin, and finally to LSD. His first three LSD "trips" are good ones, but the fourth leads to a period of psychosis with terrifying visual and auditory hallucinations. After they subside he becomes phobic about drugs, finds himself unable to work, and finally seeks psychiatric help.

The analysis of the "indefinable reason" that drove him to take drugs is central to my presentation. Despite his professional success, the young painter was disappointed in his work and was dimly aware of a mild but constant discontent. He felt his paintings were too heavy, did not get off the ground, and had reached a monotonous plateau. Subjectively he felt bogged down and locked up within himself. The young man had the recurring fantasy that if he could become weightless, if he could let his mind soar, "flip out," he would have a limitless palette and then, and only then, would he reach the acme of his talent and skill. He was determined to reach the absolute heights in his art; anything less was mediocre and meaningless. Drugs seemed to offer the key to his untapped resources. He realized that drugs were dangerous, particularly LSD, but he was not afraid of dying and he was not afraid of going crazy, which he knew could happen with LSD. Analysis revealed that actually his fearlessness was not entirely factual. The young man was able to recall that he had been terrified of fighting as a boy. He reacted to any bodily harm as though it were an irreparable damage, and it stirred up fantasies of body destruction and death. It also turned out that during puberty he wondered from time to time whether he was going mad. There were occasions when he felt an uncanny emptiness inside himself, times when he was uncertain whether he was really himself. He recalled an occasion when the sound of his breathing sounded like his father's and he wondered whether he *was* his father. Yet he dared to take LSD— partly in search of perfection in his art through the sensation of limitless perceptions, and partly to prove to himself he was not afraid to die or go mad.

During treatment the young painter described his unhappy childhood, stressing, in particular, the fact that he had had an invalid mother who could provide little loving bodily contact, and he was cared for primarily by a succession of practical nurses, whose major task was to take care of the mother. In one session he unexpectedly recalled some happy memories of early childhood, of being lifted up and tossed in the air by his gigantic father. His original fright was transformed into delicious ecstasy when he became certain that his father would always catch him. His father was not usually an emotionally or verbally expressive man, and this occasional game of being tossed in the air and caught was especially gratifying to the boy. He painted the experience verbally for me as follows: "I felt little and helpless and at the mercy of this big man whom I needed and loved. He had the power to toss me away or to rescue me and cradle me snugly in his arms."

To this man, taking LSD, in addition to all its other meanings, was a reliving of the tossing game with his father. He was willing to face the terrible fears of madness and death in order to reach the scary heights and then be rescued. He then could enjoy the special pleasure of returning to the snugness of sanity and reality. To this man, perfection meant to brave the dangers of achieving the pinnacle, to be admired above all others, and yet also to be safe.

2. A middle-aged, genial business tycoon was tyrannized by the compulsion to be exact, precise, and accurate about details his better judgment told him were trivial. Despite his enormous financial success, he felt he must personally supervise the minutiae of his various business enterprises, which were scattered all over the world. A minor physical illness forced him to stay put for several months and for the first time in his life he developed conscious anxiety and depression. He was startled. He had always considered himself a robust person emotionally.

Our brief analytic work revealed the following relevant material. His mother adored him and obviously preferred him to his father, but she was obsessed with cleanliness. This meant to the boy that she loved cleanliness more than she loved him, and he was right. To her, cleanliness was truly next to godliness. He was free to play with the other boys as long as he returned spotless and stainless. As you can imagine, he did not do much playing with the boys, but substituted for this by playing with numbers. He became a mathematical wizard and soon outshone his father. The family was poor and the young boy vowed to become rich someday so that he could give his mother the luxuries and jewels he felt she deserved and did not receive from his father. The patient, the son of an inept businessman, specialized in taking over rundown businesses, which he rehabilitated by mastering the financial intricacies and by demanding flawless execution from himself and all his subordinates. Each business triumph brought him a glowing feeling, a feeling that reminded him of his mother's loving embrace when he was her "angelic [clean] little boy." It was in her arms that he first remembered the feeling that they were an unbeatable combination—he and his mother. This was in marked contrast to his feeling of abject despair, a sense of being utterly abandoned and unlovable, whenever his mother discovered he had done something dirty. The image of his mother's face turning away from him in disgust and scorn always accompanied any activity he performed with less than his customary flawlessness. In his adult life his exactness and precision had become internal demands, residuals of his mother, which he now carried around inside himself. They tyrannized his life unconsciously, but they also made him feel consciously omnipotent.

The tycoon's ruthlessness toward all errant employees was an expression of loathing for his own natural urge to enjoy dirtiness and sloppiness, which he had managed to repress. It was also his symbolic revenge against his father, an incompetent [sloppy] businessman. The quiet but frantic compulsiveness of this man's life was a quest for perfection. He toiled all his life to earn the love of his mother. It was a never-ending task, as any fall from perfection would call up the face of his mother distorted by disgust. Therapy eventually helped him become a little less concerned with his dead mother and more involved with his living wife and children. He also became less obsessed with the quest for perfection.

3. There are many people, patients among them, who carry within themselves a feeling of being deficient, defective, and incomplete. They try to overcome this state of affairs by attaching themselves to a lover or spouse, a leader, a cause or a faith, thus becoming both whole and perfect. Their difficulties come to the surface when the beloved person or belief that confers the sense of wholeness is lost through death or disillusionment. The lowly members of such partnerships are apt to become slaves rather than equals, and are quite willing to endure great hard-

ship and suffering to ensure the love and protection of their
idealized and mighty beloved. When the partnership is dis-
solved, through separation or disappointment, these people go
through a severe depression, characterized by bitterness and
hostility toward the external world, accompanied by severe self-
reproach and a return to their old feelings of worthlessness. I
shall try to illustrate this with a clinical example.

4. A woman in her early forties came for help because she
had lost all desire to live and alternated between spells of feeling
murderous rage and periods of suicidal despair and emptiness.
This state of affairs began suddenly. She had been blissfully and
happily married for over twenty years to a man she considered
perfection incarnate. Her "perfect" marriage abruptly disintegrated when her husband broke off all relations with their eldest
son who had married a foreign girl and went to live abroad.
The blissfully happy married woman suddenly saw the image of
her perfect husband crumble before her very eyes. The man who
had been her ideal, "Mr. Wonderful personified," a man who
could do no wrong, who was above reproach, became transformed into a petty, jealous, nasty, selfish, and mean human
being. She, who melted at his very touch, was repelled by his
animal lust. His brilliant mind turned into an instrument for
torture, his lofty imagination became vapid, his ethereal gentle-
ness became disgustingly effeminate.

As her feelings toward her husband changed, the patient
became increasingly more miserable. She had not only lost an
ideal husband, she had also lost her self-esteem. She, who for
over twenty years had basked in the sunshine of feeling constantly warmed by a superior creature, felt cold, empty, and
worthless. This was a return of an old feeling state she had
experienced in her growing-up years. Being the product of a
miserably married mother and father had made her feel
deficient and defective. Her mother had admonished her for
years not to marry a man beneath her as she had done. The
mother blamed all her own ills on the inadequacies of the father
and promised her daughter a life of bliss if she would only find
the "right" man. The patient realized that she was serving as an

extension of her mother and she was not truly loved in her own right. As it turned out, the mother found this "right" man—a young doctor who was treating the mother. In six weeks she had persuaded her daughter and the young doctor to marry. To consolidate the marriage, the mother had donated all her life savings to them as a wedding gift. It was not a bribe, she claimed, but a token of her admiration for her daughter's husband.

For twenty-three years the perfect husband made this woman, who had felt defective and inadequate, behave and react as though she were whole, complete, and a partner in a perfect marriage. She had been oblivious to all her husband's shortcomings, or considered them trivial. He could do no wrong. His weaknesses were lovable and made him more endearing, his tyrannies were strengths and made him more admirable. She felt privileged to live with him. He had blanketed her deep sense of inadequacy and deficiency and she was now participating in a higher level of existence.

Her husband's rupture of the relationship to her beloved son tore the veil from her eyes. She fell from bliss back into the black hole of her childhood, from which hole she had believed she had escaped. The patient now hated and despised her husband. She found him selfish and pretentious. She felt she had been mistreated and misled and that she deserved it—she was nothing but a defective fool; besides, who else would have married her? The magic aura of the perfect man had evaporated and her childhood identity was reinstated.

An even more extreme example of the blissful partnership I have just described is that special emotional state of perfection in which people feel a joyous sense of losing their self-boundaries and flowing into, or merging, and becoming one with another person or being—like God, Fate, or Nature—and thus attaining perfection. This is thought to occur when infants are transported from painful hunger to blissful satiation when they are lovingly fed by their mothers. It is also seen when people fall in love or experience a sense of religious or philosophical ecstasy. It may also occur at the peak of sexual orgasm. It is characteristic for these so-called oceanic feeling states that a person feels relatively small and becomes fused with someone grand and powerful. Many experience this as a state of ecstasy and the acme of perfection. I would like to highlight some of the elements that lead to this sense of merging and fusing with a beloved in the following clinical example.

5. A young physician undressed himself completely and lay down in a bathtub. He then cut both his wrists and his neck with his surgical scalpel. He was discovered by accident and rushed to a hospital, unconscious and very close to death. Sometime later, when he had physically recovered, I had the opportunity to work with him analytically. I was impressed by his clear description of the meaning and purpose of the suicide. The young doctor told me that he had been severely depressed since his mother's suicide a year earlier. She had been found in her bathtub drowned as a result of having lost consciousness after she had taken an overdose of sleeping pills. Since then he had been full of torturesome self-reproach for having neglected his mother. Although he realized the notion of neglect was not realistic or logical, he was unable to stop his self-torture.

His mother had been a quiet and undemonstrative woman. Their greatest joy together had been in playing piano duets as a boy. She had hoped he would go on to become a musician, but he had chosen to study medicine which meant giving up the piano and leaving home. The young doctor felt guilty for his decision and tried to be particularly considerate and thoughtful of his mother. The father of the family had died many years earlier and my patient was accustomed to looking after his mother. Her suicide was sudden and inexplicable to him.

The young physician yearned for his lost mother and his self-reproaches became intolerable. He finally decided his only recourse was to die. In that way, he would cease to suffer and he would join his beloved mother. He described to me that as he watched the blood draining from his body, his self-reproaches ceased, he felt a growing sense of peace, and he visualized himself being taken into the arms of his mother, who had been waiting for him. Just before he became completely unconscious, he felt his blood mingling with hers, a feeling that was utter bliss. In fact, when he awakened in the hospital, he was terribly disappointed and wept bitterly. He had lost that state of bliss for which he had striven.

The Dynamics

I have chosen these clinical vignettes in order to demonstrate how the quest for perfection looks to a psychoanalyst. In all four cases the patients carried inside themselves, from childhood on, the feelings of not having been loved sufficiently, which eventually led them to feel that they were bad or deficient. Children who feel unloved first rage against the unloving parent and the outside world. Eventually they turn their rage inward and develop a sense of internal badness. They yearn for a constant loving mother they never had and create an *idealized* mother who is unattainable because of their sense of internal badness. They continue to hope for some special form of approval, acceptance, or union with this perfect mother who never existed in real life. The young painter tried LSD to reach her, the young doctor attempted suicide to join his mother. The business tycoon built a financial empire to please his idealized mother, and the housewife tried to achieve this approval by becoming an extension of her mother. All these attempts fail, not only for the reasons I have just described, but for additional reasons I shall now try to explain.

In each instance the wish to be loved and to be found lovable is opposed by *unconscious* harsh and unrealistic self-criticism. The artist was driven to face death and madness, the physician was tormented by sadistic impulses directed against the self, the business tycoon was haunted by the dread of being found unlovable and repulsive if he was anything but flawless, the housewife had to renounce her own defective identity to live as an extension of her "perfect" husband.

In order to gain a better understanding of these problems, psychoanalysis has focused on certain basic factors in man's struggle to mature, to become civilized. Man is born helpless and dependent on the external world and remains so longer than any other animal. He is also born with two opposing sets of drives, one loving, Eros, and one aggressive (Freud, 1920). The concept of man's innate aggressiveness has never been popular, but disliking it will not make the evidence of man's destructiveness and hatred disappear. Man seeks satisfaction for his drives, which is first limited and then opposed by the external world. In order to adapt to the world around him, man has to renounce some of his libidinal strivings, but, above all, he has to curtail his tendency to react to frustration by outward destructiveness and rage. To do so, the child eventually creates an internal agency, a superego, which is modeled after the mighty parents and which punishes him for every transgression. The superego, or con-science, is only partly conscious and reasonable. It is essentially unconscious and irrational. It is not merely a replica of the parent, but has in it the child's hatred for the frustrating parent. Furthermore, the superego punishes the self not only for acts but even for thoughts and fantasies that it considers bad. The more aggression is deflected from outward expression, the more it is turned onto the self. The result is feelings of guilt, which can only be absolved by punishment of the self. Every renunciation of instinctual gratification will lead to an increased severity of the superego, to greater self-criticism and self-destructiveness (Freud, 1930). The more virtuous the person, the harsher is the superego.

The result of this conflict between the search for happiness and the wish to be approved of by the superego or its external representatives is essentially a struggle between the urge to express love and aggression on the one hand, and to escape guilt, mainly unconscious guilt, on the other. Absolution, in the extreme examples I have described, is possible only by first neutralizing or killing off the cruel superego. I have illustrated these attempts in each of the patients. The artist used LSD, the businessman offered one success after another, the housewife submerged her own identity, and the doctor cut his wrists and throat. All were efforts to appease the sadistic superego each patient possessed. In all these people we find the attempt to escape helplessness, the helplessness of aloneness and unlovableness—all terrible dangers. These are the fears that drive such people to seek perfection. Perfection to them means: I am not helpless, I am not alone, I am lovable and protected by a loving and powerful internal or external force.

Conclusion

Reading the writings of Teilhard de Chardin, I am impressed, most of all, by Teilhard's excessive optimism. I agree that one needs some optimism in order to have hope. With no hope there is only gloom and despair, which serve no useful purpose. I feel, however, that Teilhard goes too far. He seems to believe that universal evolutionary processes and the convergence of the different elements of the universe will make for greater knowledge and love and eventuate in a superior type of human being. Man may well be part of an evolutionary process, but I see little evidence that man's scientific and technological progress has brought him more peace or happiness. On the contrary, these developments seem to have led to an increase of violence which points to man's greater propensity for hatred and destructiveness. I agree with Professor Leakey that unless we change, we are on the road to the extinction of man—not to his perfection.

My main disagreement with Teilhard's views is his almost total disregard for man's aggressiveness and its consequences. In his major work, *The Phenomenon of Man*, there are only three pages in an appendix devoted to "On the Part of Evil in the World in Evolution." Teilhard himself is aware of this omission and I would like to quote him:

> Throughout the long discussions we have been through, one point may perhaps have intrigued or even shocked the reader. Nowhere, if I am not mistaken, have pain or wrong been spoken of. . . .

True, evil has not hitherto been mentioned, at least explicitly. But on the other hand surely it inevitably seeps out through every nook and cranny, through every joint and sinew of the system in which I have taken my stand.

Teilhard ends the three pages of discussion with a remarkably frank admission: "On this question, in all loyalty, I do not feel I am in a position to take a stand: in any case, would this be the place to do so?"

My answer is yes. I believe that evil, which "inevitably seeps out through every nook and cranny, through every joint and sinew of the system," is too important to be disregarded.

I believe man is driven to seek perfection because it seems to offer a magical protection from his basic anxieties: helplessness, loneliness, unlovableness, and body destruction. Guilt, the turning of aggression onto the self, is the single most important factor behind these anxieties. The greatest hindrance to man's greater development is his inability, up to the present, to deal better with his aggression and destructiveness. I believe that for man to survive he must learn to curb, tame, channelize, and sublimate his aggressiveness and destructiveness. To do this he must first face more honestly his greed, his envy, his hatred and fear of the stranger, and his hatred and fear of change. Only then can unconscious destructive guilt be changed to conscious guilt, which can be controllable and useful. If we do this, man will have made a giant step forward, even if it is not to Point Omega.

29

On Transitional Objects and Transference

(1974)

W INNICOTT'S PAPER, "Transitional Objects and Transitional Phenomena" (1953), is one of those genial works that keeps growing in importance with the years and has spawned many further insights. The transitional object is by now so well recognized a phenomenon that one is amazed it took so long for psychoanalysis to single it out for special attention. I shall use the term as he did, namely, referring to the infant's first *not-me* possessions. My brief contribution will also deal with some transference phenomena which can be understood as "transitional" phenomena in Winnicott's sense.

A depressed thirty-five-year-old woman patient is telling me how she misses the physical closeness of her recently lost lover. After much intense crying and noisy sobbing, she slowly begins to quiet down, consoling herself with the belief that her analysis is helping her pull herself back together into one piece. As she says this, I notice her gently and rhythmically stroking the

This paper is published here for the first time. It will also appear in *Between Reality and Fantasy: Transitional Objects and Phenomena*, edited by Simon Grolnick, New York: Jason Aronson, 1978.

burlap wallpaper alongside the couch with her fingertips, her eyes half-closed. There is a pause and then she says: "You are good to me, you really try to help." She continues to stroke the wall in silence. I too remain silent. After a few minutes the patient, now dry-eyed, stops stroking the wall, straightens her somewhat rumpled dress, and says: "I feel better now, I don't know why, I just do. Maybe it was your silence. I felt it as warm and comforting, not cold, as I sometimes do. I did not feel alone."

At first I did not realize that for my patient, at that moment, my office wall was a "transitional transference object." The stroking of the wall seemed to have many other meanings. On the one hand, she was stroking the wall as she wanted to stroke and be stroked by her lover and me. It was an acting out of a transference reaction. The stroking of the wall was also, I eventually discovered, a reenactment of something of a more infantile nature. The rhythmic movements, the half-closed eyes, and the soothing effect of my noninterference should have indicated to me that it might be a transitional transference experience for her.

This was confirmed when I began to speak to the patient who quickly interrupted me to say that my words seemed like an intrusion. I waited and then said in a quiet voice that I had the impression that as she wept, she let herself slip into the past; the stroking of the wall might have brought back an old sense of comfort from childhood. The young woman replied: "I was only dimly aware of the stroking—above all, I loved the tweedy quality of the wallpaper. It has little hairs like fur. Strange, I felt the wallpaper was responding to me in a vague way." I answered, still not fully comprehending the transitional nature of her experience: "So you felt in your misery that being on the couch, stroking the wallpaper in my silent presence was like being comforted by a kind of mothering person." After a pause the patient replied: "You know, I don't quite agree with you. This may sound strange to you, but it was stroking the wallpaper that helped—and also, I suppose, your letting me do it. It reminds me of crying myself to sleep as a child by petting my favorite panda bear. I kept that panda for years; in fact, I have baby pictures with it. Of course, then it was quite furry and later it became smooth, but I always felt it as furry." (Later, this patient had dreams of me with black and white spots, some of which were traceable to her panda bear and to my beard, which she called furry.)

I believe that this clinical vignette illustrates how an inanimate object, the wallpaper, can become a transitional transference object for a patient. It was her primitive possession. She was stroking herself and felt loved in return by the wallpaper. The rhythm of her movements indicate its origin in autoerotic acts like thumb sucking. However, the wallpaper is neither part of her, nor is it her mother's breast. Yet it is related to and partakes of both while remaining quite distinct from each (Winnicott, 1953, p. 242).

A transitional object serves as an intermediary for the infant's discovery of the difference between inside and outside. It is an actual object and also has symbolic meaning. It is the *not* being the breast or the mother that "is as important as the fact that it stands for the breast or the mother" (p. 233). A fully developed transitional object is more important than the mother for the child. The patient I described felt my voice as an unpleasant intrusion; she preferred the wallpaper.

The transitional transference objects arising in the analysis of neurotics are felt to be, to a degree, alive; but the patients also know that this is an illusion. In contrast, Searles (1960) has described psychotic transference reactions to inanimate objects, but they are delusional. In such patients, inanimate transference objects are usually malignant and terrifying (Klein, 1952; Rosenfeld, 1965). In neurotics, transitional objects may be hated besides being loved, but they must endure and they may not retaliate. In many ways the transitional object is like a talisman, which the following case may illustrate.

I told an emotionally immature young woman patient, who had developed a very dependent transference to me, that I was going to attend an International Congress in Europe some three months hence. We worked intensively on the multiple determinants of her clinging dependence, but made only insignificant progress. Then the situation changed dramatically when one day she announced that she had discovered something that would tide her over my absence. It was not some insight, not a new personal relationship, it was a chess piece. The young woman had recently been given a gift of a carved ivory chess set. The evening before her announcement, as she looked at the set, through the sparkling light of a glass of champagne, it suddenly struck her that I looked like the white knight of her chess set. The realization immediately evoked in her a feeling of comfort, even triumph. The white knight was a protector, it belonged to her, she could carry it wherever she went, it would look after her, and I could go on my merry way to Europe without having to worry about her.

I must confess that despite my misgivings, I also felt some relief. The patient's major concern about the period of my absence was a public performance of great importance to her professionally. She now felt confident of success because she could conceal her white knight in her handkerchief or scarf; she was certain that he would protect her from nervousness, anxiety, or bad luck. I was relieved and delighted to learn, while in Europe, that her performance had indeed been a smashing success. Shortly thereafter, however, I received several panicky transatlantic telephone calls from her. The patient had lost the white knight and was beside herself with terror and gloom, like a child who has lost her security blanket. A colleague of mine who saw her in that interval said that all his interventions were to no avail and he reluctantly suggested that I cut short my trip and return. I hated to interrupt my vacation and I doubted whether my return would be beneficial. Surprisingly, it was. I no sooner saw her than her anxiety and depression lifted. It then became possible to work for many months on how she had used me as a good luck charm rather than an analyst.

The talisman, the chess piece, served her as a magical means of averting bad luck or evil. It protected her against losing something precious.

If we review the transitional objects described thus far, it seems that the infant's security blanket provides comfort and soothing. As the infant matures, he or she may discard this type of not-me possession and take on other similar pleasure and security procuring objects. The talisman is a later derivative and seems to function more in the direction of warding off ill fortune and only secondarily brings pleasure. The amulet has to be worn to be effective, but its objective is identical. There are varieties and combinations of good luck charms which people cling to more or less seriously in later life. In times of dire stress and helplessness, even an adult may return to his original transitional object.

My final considerations in this brief presentation deal with the different ways patients relate to their analysts during the course of their analyses. We see early "floating" transference reactions as Glover (1955) called them, as well as real object relations which Anna Freud pointed out (1954). Patients also react to "the analysis," instead of to the analyst (Greenson, 1967a). Even the analyst's office may take on extraordinary power in serving the patient as a haven against the dangers in the external and internal world. The analytic procedures may be taken by the patient as "my analysis," his possession. Such patients may seem to work hard in the analysis, but their insights are all undermined by the magical and comforting effects they unconsciously attribute to the office or the analytic set-up. In such instances we are dealing with transitional transference reactions. Reider (1953b) has described similar reactions to institutions.

We also see a variety of identifications during analyses, some motivated by the libidinal wish to possess, others out of fear of the aggressor and the wish to control the analyst, the projective identification so frequently stressed by the Kleinians. All these identificatory reactions seem to be related to the transitional phenomena Winnicott described because they contain a blurring of "me-not me" and are possessive.

Some of Mahler and Kestenberg's ideas on separation-individuation seem relevant here. Kestenberg (1971), following the lead of Mahler (1968) and her associates, hypothesizes about the different symbiotic bonds between mother and child which persist throughout development. She describes a united organ-object with a dominant organ, a zone-specific pleasure, and a phase-specific contact with the drive object. Each phase ends with new shapes of self and object representations. The separation of the pleasure-seeking organs and the satisfying object is experienced as a loss. Kestenberg believes that there are two basic mechanisms which maintain the integrity and continuity of self and object despite this loss. One method is to replace the lost unity with a less symbiotic bond. The other is to replace symbiotic bonds by bridges such as body products (intermediate objects), external possessions (Winnicott's transitional objects) and people (accessory objects). I believe this can be seen during the course of analyses.

As the analysis progresses, the transference distortions become more transparent to the patient and lose their function of covering up. As a consequence, one sees in the terminal phase of analysis more realistic representations of the analyst in dreams and more realistic reactions to him in the analytic hour. Oremland (1973) suggested that the undistorted portrayal of the analyst in dreams of the terminal phase indicate a successful analysis. I am tempted to say that for the patient, in the course of a successful analysis, the analyst evolves from a symbiotic self-object, to a transitional object and finally to a real person.

30

The Decline and Fall of the Fifty-Minute Hour

(1974)

W HEN I WAS TRAINED in psychoanalysis all the analysts and candidates I knew in the then small Los Angeles Study Group worked with their patients on an hourly schedule. The typical psychoanalytic session was called an hour and consisted of a period of approximately fifty minutes of work with the patient with an interval of some ten minutes between patients. The "fifty-minute hour" seemed to be a functionally sound division of time for performing the work of psychoanalysis and a traditional psychoanalytic routine in 1938.

Shortly after World War II and after I had become a training analyst, a bright and eager candidate in psychoanalytic training pursued me determinedly, inquiring whether I had a free hour to supervise his treatment of a patient he wanted to take into psychoanalysis. Eventually I did find a free weekly hour and after some deliberation we agreed upon a time: Thursday, 10 o'clock in the morning. After an audible sigh of satis-

Presented at the Annual Meeting of the American Psychoanalytic Association, in Honolulu, May 7, 1973. First published in *Journal of the American Psychoanalytic Association*, 22:785-791, 1974.

faction, the candidate then paused momentarily and asked, "Is it all right if I get to your office a few minutes late?" At that time I merely shrugged, a few minutes early or late for a supervisory hour, announced in advance, would cause me no inconvenience. I did not realize then, it was to be more than a singular, isolated experience.

At the beginning of the first session, however, this bright and eager candidate announced, with proper respectful decorum, "I hope you won't mind if I leave a few minutes before 10:50." I told the young man I could make no promises about my state of mind at 10:47, but I would be grateful if he would explain his mysterious timetable to me. The candidate then enlightened me to the effect that he scheduled his patients every fifty minutes and it took him about two to three minutes to walk from his office to mine. He added, gratuitously, that in order to see me at 10:01 A.M., he had to rearrange his schedule for that particular day. He usually began at 8 A.M., took his next patient at 8:50, a third at 9:40, which would have left him with 20 minutes "to waste" before his supervisory session. He accommodated himself to the supervision with me by beginning at 7:30 that morning, then took a patient at 8:20 and another at 9:10, thus finishing promptly at 10, arriving at 10:02 at my office for supervision and returning to his office for his patient at 10:50. I asked the candidate if his training analyst also used this same streamlined timetable and he assured me that he did. (There had been an influx of many analysts from other cities during the war and our small study group had become a full-fledged Society.)

After I had gotten to know the candidate a bit better from our work together, I was able to demonstrate to him that he often missed the significance of important material at the beginning of his patient's sessions, which he realized only when he referred to his notes in reporting to me. It seemed the patient would begin the "hour" before the candidate was really there. I suggested that perhaps he was still musing about the patient who had just left. The young man smiled in reluctant agreement and then added in a jocular vein that on occasions one or another of his patients would remark, "Doctor, the couch is still warm from your last patient." He had never thought of analyzing this remark. Apparently both the candidate and the patient were colluding by reacting as though the patient's comment was merely an innocent little joke. I then told the candidate an anecdote about a patient I had treated who had had a brief period of analysis with a psychoanalyst who used this assembly-line timetable. My patient frequently began his session by lying down on the couch, placing his hands under his head, and in a voice oozing with sarcasm, would say, "And now doctor, to go on where your last patient left off!" There was no doubt my patient had bitterly resented the "production line" feeling he derived from his previous analyst's routine and, in addition, the fact that the former analyst had never encouraged the patient fully to express his hostility about this matter, nor did it ever become a serious subject for analysis. The patient's repeating the above-quoted phrase with me was, among other things, a warning to me, to please get rid of any lingering thoughts I might have about my other patients and to pay strict attention to him alone.

The practice of scheduling patients immediately following each other at fifty-minute intervals without a pause became apparent to me only after World War II. I attributed it then to the flood of patients desiring psychoanalytic treatment and the relatively few trained analysts. I later heard that some "famous" old analysts in the United States were practicing in this re-volving-door fashion long before—Brill in New York and Blitz-sten in Chicago. They were only few in number and considered eccentric celebrities. I found, however, to my astonishment, that in Glover's questionnaire sent out to the British psychoanalysts in 1938, already then, only 4 out of 29 analysts allowed for a time gap between patients.

The notion of the fifty-minute hour, as I had understood it, implied that each patient was allotted about fifty minutes of time and might go over a few minutes if he needed it for cathar-sis, or the analyst might extend the session a few minutes to round off an interpretation or work through something still unfinished. But the fifty-minute hour was not only set up for the patient's convenience or benefit, the analyst himself needs a few minutes between patients for a variety of personal reasons.

First of all, I do not believe it is possible for an analyst who is absorbed in his work to shut the door on all his thoughts, fantasies, feelings, and puzzlements about a particular patient the moment the patient leaves. In addition, a few minutes of contemplation or diversion seem necessary for recovering one's equanimity after a disturbing or difficult session. Especially in hours where the analyst has made an important or complex interpretation and has been responded to with great affect, or has been immersed in a particularly intense emotional experience of the patient's life, he needs time to pull himself out of that patient's hour and life, to detach himself, and face the next patient with a fresh, receptive mind, ready to perceive and react to the newcomer. Sometimes the time gap allows you to recall fragments of the incoming patient's previous hour or at least offers you a chance to recharge your internal empathically constructed model of the new patient (see chapter 11). If you work with patients "back to back," the moment the buzzer or light indicates the next patient has arrived, you have to shut off your analytic involvement with the patient on the couch and plan how to stop the session. To put it succinctly, if you work without an interval, the patient starts and ends the hour without you.

In addition, one must not forget that there are all the physiological needs of the analyst, which cannot be denied without interfering with his free-floating attention. If you schedule patients without a time gap, how do you decide which patient shall pay with his time for your toilet activities? And which patient do you select to donate his time for answering your telephone calls, etc. Are the patient's reactions to these petty thefts of his time analyzed and, if so, how do you, the analyst, explain their recurrence on your part? Or are these reactions eventually, gradually and silently ignored, "swept under the couch," by both patient and analyst? Then we have transference and countertransference reactions repeatedly left out of the analytic situation.

Almost every psychoanalyst, the fifty-minute-hour ones and

the production-line ones, has acknowledged that free time between patients does bring a sense of relaxation, a decrease of tension, a fresher approach to the next patient, a lessening of fatigue, and, in general, an easier day. I did find some analysts who refused to discuss these issues at all, claiming these were highly personal matters and there were still others who obstinately insisted they were able to discern no hardship from their nonstop programs. I had the distinct impression that some analysts who are strongly compulsive and obsessive consider all time "wasted" that is not spent in working. They do not feel the gain from having an interval for quiet reflection, diversion, or relaxation. Some actually fear the empty minutes and frantically fill them with "useful" activities.

It is worth noting that Freud, beginning in 1913, divided his working day with patients into fifty-minute hours, a practice followed by all the early workers with their psychoneurotic patients. Psychotic patients and emergency cases were handled differently. Greenacre (1954) wrote of the hour as a natural span of time and stressed the importance of developing a regular rhythm in the analytic work. Glover (1955) was appalled by the no-gap schedule.

Thus we have to face the question: why has the fifty-minute hour become a rarity and the nonstop assembly-line schedule become predominant? The decisive factor, as far as I have been able to ascertain from questioning analysts and candidates alike, is—money. You can squeeze more patients into your working day if there are no time gaps between patients. This is not done for the altruistic purpose of treating more of suffering humanity or for accumulating more analytic experience. It almost always comes down to financial gain. This is equally true for many candidates who are in a rush to accumulate "credits" for early graduation. The only exceptions I know of are those who dread free time and have to flee from it by compulsive acts.

There is a further factor to be considered. Some candidates have never experienced any other way of scheduling patients than the assembly-line technique. They were handled that way themselves in their personal analyses and in their supervisory hours, and perpetuate this pattern via identification. Dr. Samuel Lipton told me of a refreshing exception. He knows an analyst who so resented being given the assembly-line routine by his training analyst that he has an added delight in making a time break between each one of his patients. I have the distinct impression that analysts and candidates who are independent, economically and emotionally, still make a pause between patients. Candidates in training with such analysts are more likely to use the fifty-minute hour, at least during their training, and sometimes even later. Analysts working in institutions and certain of their income all take a time interval between patients.

I believe that the decline of the fifty-minute hour is symptomatic of a materialistic trend in psychoanalytic practice, at the expense of a humanistic and scientific point of view. It is obvious that taking patient after patient on an assembly-line schedule is an act of hostility, subtle and unconscious though it might be. There is a degree of hurtfulness in ending every hour, but the assembly-line method adds an unnecessary element of degradation of the patient. It will also produce more fatigue and interfere with the relaxed, accepting atmosphere necessary for even-hovering attention. This state of affairs will in turn lead to a stultification of the analyst's free associations and fantasies, impede creative or new ideas, and eventuate in repetitiousness, forgetfulness, and boredom in the analyst. It kills the pleasure in doing psychoanalytic work. Small wonder so many analysts complain of fatigue, dread Mondays and cannot wait for Fridays.

The patients themselves are offended by the assembly-line reception they receive and their resentment is not properly handled. It is not enough to analyze the *patient's* hostile reactions to the situation, but the analyst would have to own up to his own aggression in working in a way that is harmful to the patient. This does not make for an optimal analytic atmosphere. This the analyst should face and analyze in himself. Those analysts who are unaware of this state of affairs are permitting the acting out of a masochistic-sadistic transference-countertransference situation with their patients. Those who recognize the meaning and effects of the nonstop schedule must feel guilty, at least unconsciously.

In this day and age of general dehumanization, when briefer therapies from Primal Screaming to Nude Marathons compete for prospective patients, we psychoanalysts should preserve our basic attitude of treating each individual patient undergoing psychoanalytic therapy as a unique human being entitled to our wholehearted attention and concern for the entire session and for as many years as he may need. In any event, the decline and fall of the fifty-minute hour should be acknowledged openly as worthy of a full discussion and not be kept an open secret.

31

Loving, Hating, and Indifference toward the Patient

(1974)

D URING THE COURSE OF psychoanalytic treatment, every psychoanalyst experiences many shades and degrees of love, hate, and indifference toward each of his patients. This range of feeling is necessary for doing psychoanalytic therapy. Yet it is startling that although Freud introduced the concept of countertransference in 1910, and a great deal has been written about it from the 1940s onward, there is still much confusion and a remarkable diversity of opinion about its meaning and significance. (For a review of the literature, see Orr, 1954; Kernberg, 1965; and Sandler et al., 1970b.) I believe that part of the perplexity and conflict about countertransference stems from the fact that it has never achieved the stamp of respectability accorded transference. Despite or because of all

Presented at a workshop on Personal Relationships between Patients and the Analyst, held at the Annual Meeting of the American Psychoanalytic Association, Hawaii, 1973. First published in *International Review of Psycho-Analysis*, 1:259-266, 1974.

the writings, countertransference has continued to have a predominant aura of wrongness or badness or dangerousness about
it. In a brief presentation it is possible to touch only on some
fundamentals and outline other areas for investigation. I hope
this paper and this panel will clarify the nature, the dangers and
the usefulness of the countertransference.

Definitions

I propose to use the term *countertransference* to refer to all
the analyst's transference reactions toward his patient. Countertransference, like all transference phenomena, is character-
istically a distorted and inappropriate response derived from the
unresolved unconscious conflicts in the analyst's past. As such it
may not be suitable for analytic work unless it can be detected,
controlled, and modified. There are instances (I shall submit one
below) when a countertransference reaction is therapeutically
useful.

Some analysts affirm that *all* the analyst's emotional reactions to the patient are countertransference. This "totalistic"
point of view negates the value of discriminating between
countertransference reactions and those which are relatively free
of countertransference. If there were no real relationship between analyst and patient, no sustained collaborative work
would be done and analytic therapy would be ineffective.
It would have been pointless to invent the terms transference and countertransference if they were not to be differentiated from the real relationship (Kernberg, 1965; see also
chapter 22).

There are analysts who limit the concept of countertransference to responses evoked by the patient's transference. This
has been designated by Kernberg as the "classical" approach and
he lists a number of adherents to it. I believe this is an unnecessary limitation on the meaning of countertransference. I see no
reason why the analyst's transference reactions to the patient, to
any and all of his attributes, should not come under the heading

of countertransference. I would also include all the analyst's transference reactions to all people who are significantly related to the patient during the analysis. Analysts do develop irrational reactions to the patient's spouse, children, lovers, parents, and friends.

I suggest that the counter in countertransference be understood as the duplicate of transference, like the counter in counterpart (Greenson, 1967a; Sandler et al., 1970b).

Clinical Material

A patient tells me how she tried to get a doctor to see her sick three-year-old child, who, during the night, was running a temperature of 104 and was racked by repeated chills. The doctor said something like, "Give the boy some aspirin and fluids and I will see him in the morning." The patient protested feebly that perhaps her child should be seen that night, he seemed so very sick. The physician said, "I am the doctor and I shall see him in the morning." The patient reluctantly submitted. Before she could say anything more, I intervened. I was so furious with the doctor that I blurted out angrily, "When the doctor said, 'I am the doctor and I shall see him in the morning,' you should have answered, 'Not if I see you first, you are no doctor in my book!'"

This is an obvious example of countertransference, in this instance a countertransference identification with my patient. The intensity of my reaction and my behavior were harmful to the analytic situation. My reaction was stimulated primarily by my patient's passivity toward her physician, rather than by her transference to me. I was swept out of my analytic role by my intense protective feelings for the poor mother and child and also by my hatred for neglectful doctors, both rooted in my own past. This led me to identify with the patient in her predicament. I responded with the rage I would have felt in her situation and which I wished she would have experienced. The point I wish to stress here is that my countertransference was essentially to the patient's predicament and not to her transference feelings toward me.

Sometimes it is therapeutically useful to disclose to the patient one's noncountertransference or, as I propose to call them, *real* reactions. (This is *not* the case for *most* real reactions of an analyst toward his patient, the burden of proof is on communicating them.) Let me illustrate:

A schizophrenic young woman I had been treating for many years said to me in one of her more lucid, neurotic intervals, "I hate you, Dr. Greenson, I hate you very much. I have to repeat this ten times, is that all right?" I nodded my head in approval and the young woman proceeded to say loudly but quickly, "I hate you, Dr. Greenson" ten times. I listened with my usual expression, accepting and interested, with a trace of a smile, I believe. Then she paused and with a look both mischievous and anxious, asked me: "Do you hate me, Dr. Greenson?" I replied seriously, neither somberly nor jokingly, "Yes, Dorothy, at times I do hate you." She smiled and then said, looking squarely at me, "I hate you, I loathe you, and I despise you, but I do like you very much." I answered her questioning look with, "Yes, I know; you hate me, loathe me and despise me, but you also do like me very much. All of it is true." The patient sighed, as if relieved and said, "Shall we talk about something else now?" I shrugged in compliance.

I submit that my answer to the patient's question whether I hated her or not, "Yes, Dorothy, at times I do" was an example of a real reaction. It was neither defensive nor hostile nor lacking in affect. It was, I feel, useful for the therapeutic situation. Her response, "I hate you, I loathe you, I despise you, but I do like you very much" seems to indicate that my genuine and forthright reply enabled her to amplify on her hatred and to add the loving phrase, "but I do like you very much."

Many reactions of analysts are mixtures of countertransference and real reactions, just as are many reactions of patients to their analyst. All countertransference distorts some small, real, element in the patient, and all real relationships have some degree of transference. This occurs outside of analysis as well. All relationships consist of different admixtures, blendings, and transitions between transference and nontransference components (chapters 22 and 25). Nevertheless, it is helpful to draw clear-cut distinctions between them, as the following clinical example may demonstrate.

A middle-aged divorced woman, Mrs. N., has been in analysis for some four years with the major complaint of being unable to sustain a loving relationship to a man. After an initial phase of loving and sexual feelings to me, she embarked upon a long period of complaining, fault-finding, thinly disguised contempt for my work, and the lack of progress. Many interpretations of her hostility to me, her unconscious envy, the defense against her loving feelings, her wish to provoke sadistic or angry reactions in me, were to no avail. In one hour, after much complaining and fault-finding, she paused and unexpectedly said, "I guess I am no pleasure to work with." She became silent. I felt a sudden urge to blast her with some sarcastic remark like, "You ain't just awhistlin' Dixie," but restrained myself by forcibly bringing into focus that she was a patient, not a friend, not a relative. I eventually replied: "Yes, these hours of nagging and complaining and nagging and complaining are a pain." I should add, this was said with some intensity, but controlled. The patient was startled. She gasped, "My God, you are not supposed to say things like that. You are just supposed to analyze. You are supposed to be neutral. You called me a nag and a pain. That is not analytic, that's an insult." She paused and I replied, now in a more carefully modulated tone, "I did not intend to insult you. I only confirmed your statement that the many hours of nagging and complaining are painful to me. This is a piece of reality which I believe you have not faced squarely and neither had I." The patient responded tearfully, "My God, I never let myself think of *your* feelings and I never realized that I made you into some impervious person who has infinite patience and little feeling. Yet I know better. I have hurt you, or tried to, and I suppose I finally resorted to what you call nagging to wear you down. How awful of me. How could anyone like me? [Tears, pause.] No wonder no one does. A nag—that word kills me—a

nag! Well, I want to thank you, God damn you, for opening my
eyes. I'd rather hate you or detest you, but not be a nag. [Pause.]
I guess that was my way of keeping you away from me." I
answered, "And also keeping yourself away from me. Hating
one another brings people much closer." The hour ended on
this note. I want to add that we had few more prolonged nagging sessions, but plenty of hateful ones.

If we return to my emotional responses in that segment of
the hour, I believe it is quite clear that my impulsive but
unspoken reaction, "You ain't just awhistlin' Dixie," is a hostile
countertransference response, a retaliation for all the repetitive,
frustrating, annoying hours. I had not been conscious until then
of any feelings other than mild irritation and impatience with
the patient until that flash of "awhistlin' Dixie" surged up in me.
Such a verbal response would have been a harsh and sadistic
intervention and does not befit an analyst treating a patient, but
it is quite typical of my reactions in similar life situations, past
and present. It would have been a countertransference response
in the analytic situation and a transference reaction in a social
situation.

I did recognize this state of affairs in the analytic hour and
did restrain myself. I was able to tame my anger sufficiently to
be able to say in a controlled manner, "Yes, these hours of
nagging and complaining and nagging and complaining are a
pain." My resentment still came through in my choice of the
word nagging, in my repeating the phrase, and in changing her,
"no pleasure," to, "the hours are a pain." I believe this intervention has a countertransference aspect, but also, I submit, a
therapeutic one. In my style of working, not answering the
patient's question would have been wrong and due either to my
fear of my countertransference or to indifference.

I am of the opinion that the situation called for an intervention that would make some impact on this chronic stalemated situation. I believe that just answering the patient with
"Yes, it is not a pleasure to work with you," would not have been
an adequate and effective intervention. My remark had a
countertransference edge to it, but I believe it was more effective

because I had made her acutely aware not just of being a complainer but of being a nag, and the concept of nagging made an impact that was ego-dystonic to her. Her response indicated I had changed an attitude in her into a symptomatic action. The nag, she now wanted to get rid of. Perhaps the optimal response would have been: "Yes, it is no pleasure to work with someone who complains to the point of nagging." But that formulation I only came to several hours later as we worked through her reactions to my remarks.

I want to close the discussion of this clinical example by pointing out that the three reactions show the transition from acting on countertransference to therapeutic disclosure of a real reaction and also demonstrates the difference between full and moderated countertransference responses. (1) "Awhistlin' Dixie" is pure countertransference. (2) "Nagging and complaining is a pain" is controlled countertransference and partly realistic. (3) The hypothetical, "Yes, it is no pleasure to work with someone who complains to the point of nagging" is controlled and realistic.

Thus far I have only described countertransference *reactions*, the sporadic, transitory responses akin to those "floating" transference reactions Glover (1955) described in neurotic patients. Analysts also develop countertransference *neuroses*, long-lasting transference involvements with their patients, in which the patient becomes persistently and inappropriately of central importance to the analyst. Such reactions can be intense as, for example, the analyst who falls in love with his patient or desires a sexual relationship. If hatred prevails, the analyst may have frequent temper outbursts, or he may approach every hour with the patient with a sense of dread, a feeling of "Oi vay," a type of internal groaning, or an attitude of pugnacity, as if he were meeting an opponent, an adversary, not a patient. This latter attitude is very frequent and leads analysts unknowingly to engage in constant one-upmanship in their interventions. In such cases, the analysis is a contest and the patient is never allowed to end up being in the right.

The more subtle forms of countertransference neuroses are

more dangerous because they are more difficult to detect. Persistent and undue protectiveness, rescue fantasies, chronic and unyielding goodnaturedness and benevolence are indications of a motherly countertransference neurosis and are more frequent in female analysts (Greenacre, 1954). Constant boredom, forgetfulness, coldness, aloofness, or indifference often are indications of a warded-off hostile countertransference neurosis.

Fenichel (1941b) and Greenacre (1966) have pointed out that it is not only the analyst's instinctual needs and the defenses against them which may lead him into countertransference reactions, but also his narcissistic needs. For example, pathological therapeutic ambition may lead him to idealize his patients, exaggerate their capacities, and become repeatedly disappointed in their slow progress.

Just as the psychoanalytic situation is tilted, facilitating the patient's development of transference reactions and a transference neurosis, it is also tilted for the analyst, but by other elements contained in it. The analyst encourages full expression and then is exposed to the patient's loving and hateful feelings. The analyst usually delays his responses so he can think, introspect, empathize, understand, and eventually formulate his intervention in a relatively low key. These activities are a strain because of the instinctual stimulations and frustrations. In addition, he has to bear the narcissistic blows or gratifications from the patient's material and behavior. Furthermore, extraordinary experiences in the analyst's life may make him temporarily excessively susceptible to countertransference reactions, as, for example, personal miseries, illness or a death in his family, a pregnancy, the loss or suicide of a patient, etc. If the patient's material coincides with these extraordinary events in the analyst's life, the analyst is more likely to react with countertransference. Self-observation and control may make these reactions very useful, however.

Before turning to more clinical material, I shall briefly discuss the relationship of countertransference, the working alliance, and empathy. Reactions appropriate to the working alliance in the analyst are analogous to those in the patient: his real relationship to the patient, his concern for his welfare, and his devotion to the analytic situation. Positive countertransference in small amounts may be a temporary help, but, like transference in general, it is an unreliable ally. Strong countertransference, both positive and negative and unrecognized, subtle, chronic countertransference, interferes with the working alliance and leads to adverse developments in the progress of the analysis.

An indispensable vehicle for understanding the patient's unconscious is the analyst's capacity for empathy (chapter 11). Empathic contact with the patient is most reliable when it is motivated by the working alliance. This is the optimal condition. Countertransference may be stirred up by empathic contact with the patient but leads to inappropriate conduct, not always in the service of the working alliance. The case of Mrs. N. illustrates this point. Sometimes countertransference reactions, if not recognized, can lead to a loss of empathy and will result in errors in the dosage, timing, or tact of interpretations or to acting out by the analyst.

Detection of Countertransference Reactions

I hope I have illustrated how uncontrolled countertransference reactions can be damaging to the analytic process. On the other hand, countertransference reactions, if detected and more or less controlled, can make a positive contribution to the therapeutic process, as in the case of Mrs. N. The consciousness of countertransference feelings may be the analyst's first indications of goings-on in the patient of which the analyst had been oblivious. The case of Mrs. N. demonstrated this. This point was first stressed by Heimann (1950) and Little (1951). This occurs particularly frequently in the analyst's responses to the primitive impulses and fantasies so often found in the borderline and psychotic patient. The use of our usual neutral position at such times may become an unconscious defense against our more spontaneous responses to these primitive stimuli, both loving and hateful, a defense which sometimes, but not always, coincides with what is therapeutically indicated (Winnicott, 1949; Searles, 1963a).

The first step in establishing control is to recognize that we are experiencing a countertransference reaction. This means that the analyst, as he listens, must be aware of his thoughts, feelings, and impulses as well as their absence. Then he must confront himself with the question: is what I am thinking or feeling in keeping with the patient's material and behavior, and is my intended intervention potentially helpful for the patient or being undertaken for my own needs? This sounds like a lengthy process, but in reality it happens in a flash, unless the answers to oneself are inconclusive. Then the analyst may have to introspect, empathize, and think for a longer period of time (Kohut, 1959; Greenson, 1967a).

Let us assume that the analyst asks himself: what are the findings in me, the analyst, that will alert me to the probability of a countertransference situation? (I say probability because all responses can be real or countertransference under certain conditions.) All intense emotional reactions are suspect, whether they are loving or hateful. Amorous feelings, sexual desires, sadistic impulses, disgust, fear, sadness, and idealization are some of the most frequent transference reactions in the analyst.

There are other typical indicators. Frequent dreams of the patient (Whitman et al., 1969), forgetting of appointments, and unusual difficulty in remembering or forgetting the patient's material (Schlesinger, 1970), frequent blind spots or periods of stalemate, boredom, sleepiness and falling asleep, slips of the tongue, especially calling the patient by the wrong name, fit in this category. Recurrent problems about the fee, the patient pays too little or too much, or one forgets to notify him at the end of the month, etc. (Allen, 1971), and rigid feelings or attitudes, all smack of countertransference. One would expect that there would be some amount of variation and fluctuation in the analyst's feelings and attitudes during the course of a treatment which goes on for many years.

The absence of feelings, indifference, is a sign of countertransference. One cannot work well with a patient unless one likes him and is interested in him (Greenacre, 1959b; Greenson, 1967a). The liking should not be intense, that would indicate a strong countertransference. On the other hand, one cannot work effectively unless one is willing and able to become emotionally involved. It is not possible to empathize with a patient unless one feels a goodly amount of liking. If the quantities are moderate, the analyst can then attempt to take a neutral position in attending to the patient; that is, he can become an interested observer of the patient's conflicts, without being impelled to take the side of one contending aspect. Neutrality stems from the loving aspect, the concerned attitude of the analyst. Indifference indicates either an emotional frigidity in the analyst or a defense against his feelings or impulses. The only time indifference may be a therapeutic response is in regard to intense and prolonged emotional outbursts in borderline and psychotic patients. They may need the analyst's indifference to reassure themselves that their hostile or sexual assaults are not deadly or overwhelming to the analyst. They may need him or her to act as though inanimate (Searles, 1963a). Also, the analyst may need the withdrawal into temporary indifference to sustain the capacity for working with such patients through time.

It is well known that analysts may act out their unconscious emotional needs with their patients by becoming seductive or punitive or combinations of the two. It is less well known, but quite frequent, that analysts will act out their indifference, especially if it is a defense, by overinterpreting, as though the patient possessed a built-in mechanical comprehending apparatus. In this way the patient is never able to build up any emotional intensity toward the analyst. Overinterpretation then serves as a counterphobic activity or reaction formation, no matter how well rationalized it may be by any school of psychoanalytic thought.

Technique of Dealing with Countertransference

Let us assume you have detected the presence of counter-transference in yourself. What do you do next? Sometimes detection is all you can do in a given instance and that insight is sufficient to restrain you from intervening or it may enable you to modify your response. The example of the nagging lady illustrates this. I could not keep myself from responding, but I believe my relatively controlled response was helpful, even if it was painful for her.

If I had had more control and more time, I would have done a little more introspecting and some free associating. I would have gone from the sarcastic "awhistlin' Dixie" to the perception of the patient as a nag. I would then have become aware that I had kept myself from recognizing her as a nag, in order to protect her from my anger. I would then have asked myself, who does the word nag and nagging remind me of? My associations, when I did that later in the hour, were that this patient reminded me of a relative and also an unsuccessfully treated patient of the past. Once I realized that, I felt almost no trace of anger toward Mrs. N., but I did feel some guilt. I was then able to work effectively with her in that and succeeding hours.

I shall use Mrs. N. to illustrate some further technical steps. Realizing that I had really hurt Mrs. N., and to some extent unnecessarily, I waited for the first opportunity to acknowledge this. It is, I believe, correct psychoanalytic technique to admit one's behavioral lapses to the patient (chapter 26). In the hour I described above there was not sufficient time because I did not want to admit the error without the opportunity of analyzing her reactions to my tactlessness and to an admission of tact-lessness. Mrs. N. began the next session by saying, "That was *some* hour yesterday." She had never realized she had actually been nagging me and she felt angry with herself for her blind-ness, but was now determined to work this out. At this point I interjected that I was glad the nagging had become something to analyze and I added, "I do feel I was a bit rough in making the point and I am sorry about that." This is in keeping with what I consider correct analytic technique, namely, one should admit a behavioral lapse before attempting any interpretations, because analyzing before such an acknowledgment may be correctly perceived by the patient as an attempt to minimize the analyst's error.

Mrs. N. responded to my remark by saying that although she felt I had been a bit rough, it was justifiable, she herself could not bear a constant nag. She then proceeded to talk about how her nagging and complaining were like a buffer zone, keeping a distance between us. Actually she often felt a sense of rejection by me from the way I had analyzed her sexual and romantic feelings earlier in the analysis. She now realized she hated me for this, envied my composure and "half-consciously" decided to keep me at a distance, disparage me, and tease me by her constant complaining with the expectation, she would break down my "goddamned indifference." My harsh intervention made her aware she was not merely a complainer, but a nag, a reminder of her miserable mother, a person she had vowed never to resemble. My harshness, however, also made her aware I was not just a cold-blooded, paid interpreter of her unconscious goings-on. This pleased her, but also worried her.

During and after several similar hours I did do some more self-analysis in an attempt to ascertain whether my earlier reaction was therapeutic or whether it was a defense against a repressed antagonism to naggers, or both. My insights into my reactions to past and present nags alerted me to a readiness to react with rage to such people. This piece of self-analysis and the insight Mrs. N. afforded me led to a mellowing of my reactions to such people, especially in the analytic situation. (See G. Ticho [1967] for a more systematic discussion of self-analysis.)

I would like to review the steps in dealing with counter-transference reactions. (1) Any response to the patient, even if reasonable, may be the bearer of a countertransference reaction. There must be vigilance to look for countertransference responses. (2) One ought to determine whether a reaction or attitude is predominantly countertransference or therapeutic, if it was unnecessarily hurtful or unexpectedly helpful to the analysand. (3) It is often helpful to find out what it was in the patient's material that triggered our reaction. (4) Then we have to analyze in ourselves, by introspection and free association, the unconscious source of the countertransference reaction and our unconscious motives for hurting or helping the patient. (5) Our unnecessary hurtfulness has to be acknowledged to the patient, but *not* its unconscious sources in us. In this I am in disagreement with Little (1951) and Searles (1965), among others, who work predominantly with borderline and psychotic patients. (6) We have to continue to work through our countertransference reactions if they are more than isolated and minor experiences, thus indicating a countertransference neurosis. (7) It may be useful to have an analyst colleague audit our self-analysis if we cannot make sufficient headway on our own.

Conclusion

I have tried in this paper to clarify the meaning and importance of the countertransference and also to outline some technical procedures. My aim is to overcome the confusions and the prejudice against acknowledging the constructive potential of the countertransference. I was startled, for example, to learn from Kohrman and his co-workers (1971) that countertransference in child analysts was discussed openly for the first time only as recently as 1964. I suspect this delay may be due to Freud's neglect in spelling out that the countertransference in the analyst has a similar dual role as the patient's transference. It can be the source of the most serious obstacles to the treatment as well as being of inestimable value for the analyst's understanding the patient's neurosis. I hope this presentation and this panel will accord the countertransference its rightful and inevitable place in the psychoanalytic process.

32

Transference:
Freud or Klein

(1974)

A NY PRESENTATION WHICH STRESSES the differences between
Freud and Klein to a psychoanalytically mixed audience
is prone to evoke controversy and even hostility. This is
particularly likely to happen in a relatively condensed presentation and on so highly charged a subject as transference. In
order to minimize combativeness and encourage a scientific
dialogue, I would like to make the following general remarks as
a preface:

When I speak of *the* Kleinians or *the* Freudians I do not
mean to imply all Kleinians or all Freudians think or work in the
same way. Although my paper stresses my negative experiences
with Kleinians, I did have some helpful interchanges with them,
but not in the areas on which this paper is focused. In all my
dealings with the Kleinians, there was always a serious attempt
to maintain a scientific attitude on both sides. In psychoanalytic
presentations, just as in psychoanalytic therapy, honest confron-

Presented at the 28th International Psycho-Analytical Congress, Paris,
July 1973. First published in *International Journal of Psycho-Analysis*, 55:37-
48, 1974. Also as: Transferencia: Freud o Klein. *Psicologia Medica*, 2:345-366,
1976.

tation may be painful, but it is essential. I hope these remarks
will be kept in mind as one listens to this presentation.

As far as I know most psychoanalysts in the United States
have had only a slight exposure to Kleinian psychoanalysis. For
the most part the curricula of training institutes include the
works of Klein and her followers under deviant schools of
psychoanalysis, akin to Horney and Sullivan, and are given little
time. The Kleinian psychoanalysts reciprocate this closed-door
policy by largely neglecting the writings of Freudian authors. At
international meetings one does hear papers by Kleinian analysts, but unless one is acquainted with their special mode of
thinking and terminology, their presentations are difficult to
understand. Discussions between Kleinians and Freudians at
international meetings give one the impression of people speaking two different languages at each other, with each one
ignorant of the other and both firmly prejudiced toward each
other.

In recent years I have become impressed and puzzled by the
growing number of adherents to Kleinian psychoanalysis, particularly in Latin America. I have also noted an increase in
occasional positive references to Kleinian ideas by some Freudian
analysts, usually limited to child, psychotic, and borderline
patients. See, for example, Kernberg's (1969) survey of some of
the writings of Zetzel (1956a, 1956b), Geleerd (1963), Jacobson
(1964), and Kernberg (1966, 1967).

It is difficult to evaluate how significant this rapprochement
really is. Joffe's (1969) negative evaluation of Klein's (1957)
concept of envy is a case in point. He completely rejects the
Kleinian notion that envy operates from birth and is directed at
the feeding breast which *deliberately* withholds gratification for
its own benefit. This is but one example of the wide gulf between
us. Yorke's (1971) recent critique of Kleinian psychology ends on
a note of pessimism, "The two approaches have little in common
beyond one or two technical parameters and a language which
serves only to blur the distinctions."

My own hesitation in expressing my views on the Kleinian
school had been due to my lack of personal contact with the way

Kleinians actually do work, as one might learn from supervision or attending continuous case seminars. Beginning in 1965, however, a number of Kleinian psychoanalysts started to visit Los Angeles with some regularity. Some offered private seminars and time for case supervision. I decided to avail myself of this opportunity, attended many of the seminars, and also spent a number of hours presenting my own clinical material. (In every instance I told my Kleinian colleagues that I was coming to learn about the way Kleinians work and was not interested in becoming a Kleinian.) Thus my data and conclusions are not based on a survey of their literature alone but also on some firsthand communications with Kleinian psychoanalysts. My aims in this paper are twofold: (1) to determine whether the hints of rapprochement are significant or trivial; and (2) to speculate about what might make the Kleinian school attractive to some analysts.

I have chosen the topic of transference and have selected from this central subject four aspects which seemed to me to expose most clearly the Freudian and Kleinian points of view: (1) suitability for analysis; (2) handling of the transference; (3) dealing with environmental influences and reality; and (4) the atmosphere of the analytic situation.

Suitability for Analysis

I was struck by the fact that the Kleinian psychoanalysts presented a number of patients who were psychotic, borderline, psychopaths, or addicts, without ever bringing up the issue of whether psychoanalysis was the treatment of choice for them. These patients were all considered treatable by strict psychoanalytic technique, confined to interpreting the patient's material, especially the transference, with all advice, encouragement, explanations, reassurance, etc., being rigorously avoided (Rosenfeld, 1965; Segal, 1967). In one seminar a Kleinian analyst stated that the sicker the patient, the more one should follow the basic psychoanalytic approach. The illness should *not* influence the treatment. Hanna Segal wrote in 1967, "The

Kleinian analyst may be considered to follow the classical Freudian technique with the greatest exactitude, more so indeed than most other Freudian analysts who find they have to alter their analytical technique in some of its essential aspects when dealing with pre-psychotic, psychotic or psychopathic patients" (p. 199). Apparently Segal considers this technique to be Freudian, even though Freud (1916-17) himself stated that psychoanalytic technique is *not* suitable for prepsychotic, psychotic, and psychopathic patients. He placed these patients in the category of the "narcissistic neuroses" and untreatable by classical analysis, in contrast to the psychoneurotics whom he classified among the "transference neuroses."

Rosenfeld stated his position in 1965: "In my work with psychotics I have used the psycho-analytic *technique as described by Melanie Klein and the theory on which it is based*.... Even if I came up against apparently insuperable difficulties in the transference situation I decided to adhere to my analytic technique, following the principle that if I could not make contact with the patient *through my interpretations* it was not the technique that was wrong but my understanding of what was going on in the transference situation" (p. 10f.; my italics).

Rosenfeld thus rejects the possibility that psychotic patients are not able, at times, to "make contact" with interpretations of whatever transference they are capable of; that it is not the content of his interpretations which might be wrong but *interpreting* itself which is failing to register upon the patient. The psychotic patient might be having some other therapeutic need, for example, the analyst's silent physical presence, and would feel any verbal interpretation as an intrusion (see Searles, 1963b; Wexler, 1971).

It would seem all psychiatric patients receive the same treatment if they are willing to come and the Kleinian analyst is willing to take them (Kernberg, 1969). This attitude toward suitability for psychoanalysis can be seen as the logical outcome of Kleinian theory which affirms that all psychopathology originates in the conflicts between the death and life instincts. These conflicts are reacted to from birth onward by two specific configurations, the paranoid-schizoid and the depressive positions. Melanie Klein chose the term "position" to emphasize the fact that these phenomena persist throughout life. The depressive position never fully supersedes the paranoid position; the integration achieved is never complete and the individual at all times may oscillate between the two. Thus in Melanie Klein's view, the infantile neurosis is a defense against underlying paranoid and depressive anxieties and a way of binding and working them through (Segal, 1964, p. xiii). If one adheres to this theoretical point of view, it is logical that there are no qualitative differences between the psychoses and neuroses and therefore both are equally suitable for treatment by the same technique.

The approach of the Kleinian analysts described above is in striking contrast to that of the majority of Freudian analysts (Federn, 1943; Eissler, 1953; Glover, 1955; Winnicott, 1962; Anna Freud, 1965; Jacobson, 1964, 1971; Balint, 1968; Wexler, 1971; Tyson and Sandler, 1971; and many others). The latter believe most psychotic and borderline patients need some form of preparatory therapy and modifications of psychoanalytic procedures. Freudian theory holds that the *psychoneuroses* are conflict disorders derived from unresolved conflicts between the instinctual drives and the ego, with the superego participating on either or both sides (Fenichel, 1945). As varied as the disturbances may be in terms of the involvement of the ego, id, superego, and life's experiences, they are all treatable by psychoanalytic technique, provided the ego is relatively intact (Eissler, 1953; A. Freud, 1965).

Most Freudian analysts believe that the borderline and psychotic patients, on the other hand, suffer predominantly from a *deficiency* in the ego's capacity to form and retain mental object representations and are therefore not suitable for psychoanalytic therapy (Freud, 1915c; Wexler, 1971). Analyzable patients have a relatively well-developed and intact ego and also the ability to develop and sustain both a transference neurosis and a working alliance in order to work effectively and endure the demands of the analytic situation. Patients lacking the resilient ego functions necessary for these developments will not be able to comprehend, feel, integrate, and utilize interpretations of their unconscious reactions (Fenichel, 1941b; Greenson, 1967a; see also chapter 22). The ego deficiency disorders, on the other hand, require primarily structure building techniques.

It is noteworthy, however, that some Kleinians occasionally describe some unclassical therapeutic procedures. Rosenfeld (1965) stated he has certain psychotic patients sit up facing him, occasionally reads the nurse's notes and gives them instructions for reassuring the patient. One Kleinian analyst asserted in a seminar that he would not put a depersonalized patient on the couch to start with. Segal (1972) wrote at length about a homosexual, autistic patient whom she permitted to stay in her lavatory for hours after each analytic session during the early years of analysis, so that he could complete what he called his "post-analysis." She also allowed the patient to read letters to her, session after session, often rereading the same letter. In discussing this patient in a seminar, Segal did not consider this type of treatment an unclassical form of psychoanalysis. It seems to me that in their modifications of technique, Rosenfeld and Segal indicate that they too realize that psychotics require special interventions of an unclassical nature. They seem to be clinically astute and personally devoted to their patients' welfare, enough so as to make these modifications, but their loyalty to Kleinian teaching enables them to disregard or belittle them when they discuss technique at large.

The Handling of the Transference

The most striking difference in the way the Kleinians and Freudians deal with their patients' unconscious is that the Kleinians will make deep transference interpretations, i.e., interpretations of primitive infantile material, early in the analysis, even in the very first hour. They clearly imply, while they do not say so in so few words, that if the material is understandable to the analyst, it should be interpreted to the patient. That is, they believe that it is both feasible and therapeutically effective to make contact with the patient's unconscious, however remote it may be from his or her consciousness.

To say that a psychic phenomenon is *deeply* buried in the unconscious is to assert that its access to consciousness is vigorously defended against by the conscious and especially by the unconscious ego with its unconscious mechanisms of defense. Is it not, therefore, inconsistent to talk about a "deep" interpretation which is so readily accessible to consciousness and without any accompanying intense anxiety? According to Freudian theory, the ego persistently, energetically, and ingeniously struggles to ward off painful derivatives of deeply unconscious material by erecting a series of defenses deployed in depth (A. Freud, 1936; Fenichel, 1945; Gill, 1963). Hence, the Freudians begin their interpretive work with those derivatives of deep unconscious conflicts which are closest to consciousness, and proceed to deeper layers only as the conscious ego becomes able to tolerate less distorted derivatives.

To put it another way, the Freudian analyst believes that interpretation will be effective only if the patient's reasonable, observing ego is available and willing to follow our interpretations, in other words, only if we have a working alliance with the patient and stay close to his conscious ego as it expands in the course of analysis. A transference reaction, to be effectively interpreted, has to be demonstrable to the patient, he must feel that it is plausible, and he must be able to cope with the emotional repercussions of his new insight. To accomplish this, Freudian analysts still follow the guidelines set down by Freud: we allow the transference to develop, and then we interpret from the surface to the depth; handling the resistances before the content and the ego aspects before the id. Only then does the patient have the capacity to comprehend meaningfully the deeper insights and to master his reactions to them.

This is in stark contrast to the position of a Kleinian analyst who stated in a seminar in Los Angeles that "we no longer agree with the concept of interpreting from the surface to the depth. We interpret where the anxiety is active and at its maximum." In 1967, Segal wrote:

Should transference be interpreted in the first session? If we follow the principle that the interpretation should be given at the level of the *greatest unconscious anxiety* and that what we want is to establish contact with the patient's unconscious phantasy, then it is obvious that, in the vast majority of cases, a transference interpretation will impose itself. In my own experience, I have not had a case in which I did not have to interpret the transference from the start.

[Segal gave the following illustration:] Even in the relatively healthy analysand, however, oral or anal anxieties may be clearly presented in the transference situation in the first session. Thus, a candidate started the session by declaring his determination both to be qualified and to get in all the analysis he could in the shortest possible time. Later in the session, he spoke of his digestive troubles and, in another context, of cows. He presented so clear a picture of his phantasy about the relation to the analyst that I could, right then, make the interpretation that I was the cow, like the mother who breast-fed him, and that he felt he was going to empty me greedily, as fast as possible, of all my analysis-milk. This interpretation immediately brought material about his guilt in relation to exhausting and exploiting his mother [p. 202f.; my italics].

I was not present in the hour that Segal described, but even from her condensed account I would have expected the patient either to get up and leave or to respond with massive guilt feelings or utter bewilderment. I believe it is pertinent to quote Freud (1913) on this style of interpreting:

It is not difficult for a skilled analyst to read the patient's secret wishes plainly between the lines of his complaints . . . but what a measure of self-complacency and thoughtlessness must be possessed by anyone who can, on the shortest acquaintance, inform a stranger . . . [of their unconscious primitive sexual or destructive urges]. I have heard that there are analysts who plume themselves upon these kinds of lightning diagnoses . . . but I must warn everyone against following such examples . . . indeed, the truer the guess the more violent will be the resistance. As a rule the therapeutic effect will be nil, but the deterring of the patient from analysis will be final [p. 140].

Did Segal's interpretations actually uncover the patient's deeply hidden guilt feelings about exhausting and exploiting his mother? Will the new patient be able to feel these emotions that have been warded off so long? If he can, does he have the capacity to cope with this insight, or will he become depressed, guilt-laden, submissive, or raging in revolt? Will he let himself understand the interpretations only intellectually and then begin a battle of wits with his analyst? Or will he run away in some other form?

I too believe transference reactions *and* nontransference reactions occur in the first hour. My differences with the Kleinians concern such questions as: should the transference be *interpreted* "at the level of the greatest unconscious anxiety," or should it be *only* demonstrated, or clarified to the new patient? (See Greenson [1967a] for the differences between demonstrating, clarifying, and interpreting the transference.)

I shall now describe my approach to such an hour in order to highlight the differences between a Kleinian and Freudian in handling a patient's transference. I believe it would have been sufficient to limit myself, even if I believed in the ultimate correctness of Segal's perceptions and thinking, to saying to such a patient in his first hour that his desire to get as much out of his analyst as quickly as possible may be creating anxiety and guilt in him, the same kind, perhaps, that had given him the digestive disturbances he had experienced throughout his life. Then I would have waited for his associations. I do not agree with Segal's assumption that the patient's strongest transference anxiety in that first hour was his urge to empty his analyst out greedily and exploitatively of her analysis-milk. This might have been his deepest anxiety, his most *remote* anxiety. His most *urgent* anxiety, it seems to me, was his worry about what Segal would think of him for revealing his greed when he tried free association for the first time. That is the anxiety I would have attempted to expose, and only later and gradually would I have led him to the more deeply hidden, more primitive anxieties Segal uncovered in the first hour. I would do so only in the measure in which they became demonstrably connected to historical material and at least intellectually and emotionally something he might be able to handle.

From the clinical material I have just cited, it appears that many Kleinians believe they can make deeply unconscious material instantly conscious, and simultaneously render it anxiety free, comprehensible, and utilizable by the patient. I wonder what happens to all the intermediary layerings of impulse and defenses, constellations that have led to a variety of compromise formations, built up and used over the years in order to achieve some degree of stability and ability to function effectively? After all, our neurotic patients function well in many areas of their life before analysis. Can all the earlier adaptations developed and utilized at different stages in the patient's previous life be bypassed with any lasting therapeutic gain? If so, why not use hypnosis or intravenous sodium pentothal? (See Zetzel (1956b], Geleerd [1963], and Kernberg [1969], among others on these points.)

Melanie Klein, however, had expressed already in 1932 that even in children one should not hesitate in giving deep transference interpretations. "As soon as the small patient has given me some sort of insight into his complexes . . . I consider interpretations can and should begin. This does not run counter to the well-tried rule that the analyst should wait till the transference is there before he begins interpreting, because *with children the transference takes place immediately*"[1] (p. 46; my italics). She wrote further that "the analyst should not be afraid of making a deep interpretation *even at the start of the analysis,*

---

[1] A debatable point among child analysts. Anna Freud (1965, 1974) and other child analysts believe that young children form a combination of a new relationship and a transference relationship to the therapist, depending on the age of the child and the length of the treatment. See also Sandler et al. (1975) and A. Freud's comments in this paper.

since the material belonging to the deep layers of the mind will come back again later and be worked through" (p. 50; my italics). She illustrates her points with the following example which I shall condense.

In the second week of treatment of a four-year-old child, Ruth, who had been terrified of being left alone with her, Melanie Klein interpreted the girl's screaming, during play, when Mrs. Klein placed a wet sponge beside one of the dolls. "I now interpreted this material in connection with her protest against the big sponge (which represented her father's penis). I showed her in every detail how she envied and hated her mother because the latter had incorporated her father's penis during coitus, and how she wanted to steal his penis and the children out of her mother's inside and kill her mother. I explained to her that this was why she was frightened and believed that she had killed her mother or would be deserted by her" (p. 55f.). It is hard for me to imagine that a four-year-old child could be helped by such an interpretation in her second week of treatment.

This clinical example is similar in technique with Segal's work with her adult patient. In both, the analyst offered *only* deep interpretations of the patient's behavior, as if a law was known indicating the exact unconscious meaning of that behavior. Second, both Klein and Segal assumed that from the beginning of treatment the child and the adult have a well-developed transference neurosis and a trustworthy working alliance between them, despite the fact they are still almost total strangers to each other (Bird, 1972). This leads the Kleinians to assume that the patient will accept as believable the interpretations given, no matter how frightening or painful or fantastic they may be. Melanie Klein (1957) concedes that a situation may arise in which a patient will say: "I can understand what you are telling me but I do not *feel* it." This she believes is a failure on the patients' part to deal with their split-off hate and unconscious envy (p. 77f.). It is envy which is always a central factor in the transference and makes the patient begrudge the analyst's success (p. 11). In general, the Kleinians neglect later defenses like intellectualization, isolation, and repression. Joffe's (1969) criticism of the Kleinian concept of envy demonstrated that envy is an intricate ego-id state, that it is a later development which contains primitive but also more advanced hate and love components.

It is apparent that the Kleinians do not distinguish between transient transference reactions and the transference neurosis, an important distinction for the Freudian analyst.[2] They also consider that all or most reactions to the therapist are transference and deny or belittle the real or nontransference relationship between patient and therapist which is the core of the working alliance. Segal (1967) expressed the Kleinian position succinctly: "In the phantasy world of the analysand, the most important figure is the person of the analyst ... all communications contain something relevant to the transference situation" (p. 202). Apparently, for the Kleinians, transference is always present *and* significant and every bit of it should always be interpreted, not only demonstrated or clarified.

Another distinctive characteristic of Kleinian technique is to make many and long interpretations in almost every hour. As one listens to their presentations it seems as if the patient hardly has a chance to do free association before he is interrupted by a flood of detailed transference interpretations. It was not uncommon to hear a Kleinian analyst report from five to ten transference interpretations for a single hour in a case presentation. Melanie Klein's interpretation to little Ruth contained about eight separate elements. Not only is Kleinian literature replete with similar examples, but when I presented cases to Kleinian analysts, I was almost always interrupted by long interpretations in the first five to ten minutes. What I believe is important here is not just the intrusiveness, but also the interference with free association, the patient's most effective method for revealing his unconscious experiences in analysis (Yorke, 1971).

In one seminar I asked several Kleinian analysts why they

---

[2] An excellent discussion of this issue is to be found in the *Journal of the American Psychoanalytic Association*, January 1971, in papers by Calef, Harley, Blum, Loewald, and Weinshel. See also Bird (1972).

gave so many interpretations in a single hour. I was told that this is done to get in contact with the patient's infantile part, which is easier than getting in touch with his adult part. Giving many interpretations, one went on, makes for a dialogue and adds to the patient's feeling of separateness. By interpreting one also shows that one is not afraid. Meltzer (1967) wrote that transference interpretations, no matter how speculative, should be given since silence promotes anxiety, regression, and acting out.

The Freudians too believe that transference is a universal phenomenon of the human mind and plays a role in all human relationships. It is more intense, changeable, and distorted in neurotics undergoing psychoanalytic therapy, but it is not created by analysis, it is merely *allowed to develop* and be uncovered by the analytic process and setting (Freud, 1925e). (My italics emphasize Freud's recurring recommendation that the *patient's* individual transference neurosis *be allowed* to develop.) At the same time a real relationship exists between patient and analyst throughout the analysis furnishing the other necessary condition for success (A. Freud, 1954; see also chapters 22 and 26).

The Freudian view maintains that all relationships consist of different admixtures and blendings of transference and non-transference. Otherwise all our lives would be spent in monotonously repeating the past. For psychoanalytic therapy it is essential to determine in what respects and to what degree the patients' or our reactions are realistic or distorted by the past.

The reason for bringing up the real relationship between the patient and the analyst is not only to indicate the complexity of the reactions that occur between them, but also to clarify the capacities the patient must possess to work on the many painful aspects of his warded-off experiences. I refer here to the working alliance or therapeutic alliance or treatment alliance as described by Zetzel (1956b), Stone (1961), Greenson (chapter 15), and Sandler et al. (1970a). Freud, as early as 1913, touched on this issue with his reference to rapport, as did Sterba (1929) and E. Bibring (1937) in their ideas about the reasonable, observing ego's cooperating and identifying with the analyst at work.

Freudian psychoanalysts distinguish between transient (floating or superficial) transference reactions and the transference neurosis (Freud, 1905a, 1914c, 1916-17; Glover, 1955; Greenacre, 1959b; Weinshel, 1971; Bird, 1972). We believe that in the beginning most patients manifest transient transference reactions. The transference neurosis, if it develops, usually comes to the fore later, as a result of consistent and correctly timed resistance and transference interpretations, the influence of the analytic setting, and the development of a good working alliance. Freud (1914a) described the development of the transference neurosis as follows: "The main instrument, however, for curbing the patient's compulsion to repeat and for turning it into a motive for remembering lies in the handling of the transference. We render the compulsion harmless, and indeed useful, by *giving it the right to assert itself in a definite field. We admit it into the transference as a playground in which it is allowed to expand in almost complete freedom* and in which it is expected to display to us everything in the way of pathogenic instincts that is hidden in the patient's mind" (p. 154; my italics). The italics stress that though the patient feels his transference reactions toward the analyst as genuine, they are repetitions, but distorted repetitions of the past (see Freud, 1916-17, p. 444; Greenson, 1967a; Weinshel, 1971). For Freudian analysts the transference neurosis is not fixed in intensity, dominance, or visibility. Greenacre (1959b) observed that it was fluid, fluctuant, and could vary remarkably in texture. As long ago as 1928, Glover declared that in some patients a transference neurosis does not develop and in others it can remain silent (1955, p. 144). This has recently been confirmed by Calef (1971) and Bird (1972). (A silent or absent transference neurosis indicates to me the patient has not been analyzed.) Considerations of tact, timing, and dosage in handling the early transient and superficial transference and resistance manifestations are basic for the formation of a reliable working alliance *and* for the full flowering and ultimate resolution of the patient's transference neurosis (Limentani, 1972).

The last phase of Freudian technique was ushered in by Freud's recognition that the resolution of the neurotic conflicts and the transference neurosis could be accomplished only by alterations in the patient's ego, brought about by the analyst's interventions (1916-17, p. 455). This theme was continued in Freud's *The Ego and the Id* (1923a) and Anna Freud's *The Ego and the Mechanisms of Defense* (1936). Freud's final formulation (1937a) on this subject was: "The business of analysis is to secure the best possible psychological conditions for the functions of the ego; with that it has discharged its task" (p. 250).

I believe that Freudian technique may be epitomized by stating that we work directly only with the ego because it is the perceiver, rememberer, judger, integrator, and, above all, the mediator between the id, superego, and the external world. All our major therapeutic efforts are aimed directly at the ego. All the other structures and the transference phenomena are permanently influenceable only if we work through the ego (Fenichel, 1941b). Freudian views on suitability for psychoanalytic treatment and rules such as starting an interpretation from the surface, analyzing the resistances before content, the ego before the id—are all derived from this proposition (Greenson, 1967a).

The Kleinian analyst has set himself a simpler task in detecting and working with the transference. All references to the analyst are considered transference, and the analyst's job is to *interpret* every manifestation of it as soon as he believes he understands it. He does not have to decide whether to demonstrate, clarify, interpret the transference or let it alone. The Kleinians interpret almost exclusively, making connections between the patient's current feelings to some aspect of the patient's unconscious infantile fantasy life. The Kleinian does not have to differentiate between transient transference phenomena, transference neurosis, a real relationship, or admixtures of all three. The Kleinian also does not have to concern himself with the capacity of the patient's ego to cope with the interpretation because he believes the correct *content* of the interpretation makes the insight therapeutically effective. The patient's life situation is of negligible importance. Perhaps it is this reduction—all patient-analyst relations are interpreted as a transference of infantile mother-breast fantasies—that makes the Kleinian school more attractive to some.

Dealing with the
Environmental Influences and Reality

Another of the major differences between the Freudians and Kleinians is the latter's denial of the role played by the patient's life experiences in the patient's illness, as can be seen by the few references to them in Kleinian interpretations. In a seminar a Kleinian analyst reported that only in the second year of treatment did he discover that the patient had a sister. When I raised a question about obtaining a history from the patient prior to the beginning of analysis, I was told that it was not necessary since the patient had been referred by a reputable analyst and also that one usually gets historical material during the course of analysis. This paucity of references to real events in the patient's life is a hallmark of Kleinian clinical papers. (A recent paper by Hanna Segal [1972] is an exception.) Winnicott observed that Klein "paid lip service to environmental provision, but would never fully acknowledge that . . . the dependence of early infancy is truly a period in which it is not possible to describe an infant without describing the mother whom the infant has not yet become able to separate from a self. Klein claimed to have paid full attention to the environmental factor, but it is my opinion that she was temperamentally incapable of this" (1962, p. 177).

Zetzel (1956a), Searles (1965), and Kernberg (1969) make similar points about the neglect of the details of the kind of mothering in Kleinian presentations about the infantile schizoid paranoid position.

The telescoping of early psychosexual development into the first year of life also diminishes the importance of later environmental influences. Such important reality factors as illness, the relationship between the parents and siblings, the deaths of parents and siblings, falling in love, marriage, divorce, acceptance by one's peers in latency, the psychological impact of puberty, etc., are not considered noteworthy unless they can be connected to the person of the analyst and tied to presumed experiences of the first months of life. This Kleinian point of view is in direct opposition to the Freudian position, which affirms that the patient's psychology is based on the interplay of primitive physical needs, rooted in his biological structure *and* the influences of his life's experiences on these needs. Reality experiences, at all ages, which have an extraordinary impact on the patient's life, are considered formative and worthy of careful analysis.

I was struck by this downgrading of the patient's history when I presented material from my own patients to the Kleinian visitors. I wanted to discuss some current material from a patient who had been in analysis with me over five years. I suggested that I would first give a résumé of the important historical data and in almost every instance was told, it is not necessary. "You can begin with the last hour." I was startled. This seems to imply either that all the historical details I had so painstakingly uncovered or reconstructed over the years were insignificant, or that Kleinian analysts feel they can reconstruct the essentials of an unknown individual's psychopathology by just listening to a few recent analytic hours. I also realized in attending their case presentations that I did not get the sense of a rolling back of the neurotic superstructure, a sense of a therapeutic process beginning, developing, deepening, and broadening, including the transference neurosis. Rather I was impressed by the repetitiousness of interpretations, mainly concerning primitive drives and defenses in regard to the transference. Geleerd (1963), in a very similar vein, observed that there does not seem to be an unfolding or deepening of the analytic process. The focus on early primitive defenses makes the clinical material repetitive. It becomes hard to distinguish a first hour from a late one in the analysis.

Another aspect of the neglect of the patient's extra-analytic experiences is implied in the focusing on the patient's early fantasy life. Susan Isaacs (1948) describes the transference as changing "from day to day (even from moment to moment) according to changes in the inner life of the patient (whether these are brought about by the analyst's comments or by outside happenings). That is to say, the patient's relation to his analyst is almost entirely one of unconscious phantasy" (p. 78f.).

Hanna Segal (1964) goes even further: "Melanie Klein's view . . . assumes that the ego from birth is capable of forming, and indeed is driven by instincts and anxiety to form primitive object-relationships in phantasy and reality. . . . Since phantasy aims at fulfilling instinctual drives, irrespective of external reality, gratification derived from phantasy can be regarded as a defence against the external reality of deprivation. . . . Phantasies, moreover, may be used as defences against other phantasies" (pp. 2-5).

This use of the term fantasy seems to confirm Glover's contention (1945) that the Kleinians have abandoned the Freudian distinctions between a fantasy, a daydream, a thought, a memory trace, an image, an introjection, an identification, an impulse, and a defense. This blurs the differences between the ego, the id, and the superego. As Yorke (1971) has observed, the Kleinians seem to have replaced the structural conflict theory of neurosis by a concept of fantasies operating against fantasies. Segal (1967) states that what we call mechanisms of defense is the functioning of an unconscious fantasy. As a consequence, she goes on, there is less division between interpretations of defenses and those of content.

The minimal attention given to the patient's history, above all, his later history, the dominant role accorded to the first year of life imply that transference operates in narrow channels, almost like Jungian archetypes. Transference figures outside the analytic situation are also denied any importance. This focus on the earliest drives and defenses, particularly the destructive ones, can cause the patient coming to consider himself a welter of primitive badnesses from birth onward (Balint, 1968).

The Atmosphere of the Analytic Situation

In a seminar a Kleinian analyst presented some case material of one of his patients which he had found bewildering.

He let his thoughts and feelings float about freely and finally toward the end of the session said to the patient something like: "I think you are trying to push your craziness and confusion into me and are furious because I cannot contain them." With that, the patient who had fallen on the floor shouting and clapping his hands, quietly returned to the couch. The speaker then turned to the group and asked if we had any questions. I asked, why, if he felt confused, did he not say to the patient just that; that he did not understand the patient's behavior. The presenter found my remark to be novel and even startling. I found his response astonishing. I can say for myself that I have often said to a patient that I do not understand what is going on in a particular hour. My patients do not find this too distressing; quite the contrary, it often stirs up some help from the patient.

Let us try to reconstruct the atmosphere in a Kleinian analyst's office when the new patient lies on the couch, for him an unfamiliar posture, says a few sentences in a strange sequence of free association, and hears the almost total stranger, the analyst, make interpretations of deep material in the first hours, interpreting his dreams frequently without the patient's associations, and doing so with an air of certainty. Apparently the Kleinian analyst requires of himself that he know everything that is going on in his patient at all times and one gets the impression he usually feels he meets this requirement. Balint (1968) has commented on the patient's feeling of being overwhelmed by an analyst who knows everything. The patient is never told he is right about anything or that he has made an important insight by himself. Rather he is treated like a child by an all-knowing parent (see chapter 26). The Kleinian psychoanalyst does not admit he may have been wrong or even that he is not sure about an interpretation. Freudian analysts often qualify their interpretations by statements like: "It seems to me," or "I have the impression," or "I wonder if," or even, "I do not understand" (Greenson, 1967a). The patient is given a chance to run if he has to, and also given a freer opportunity to express his doubt or his agreement. He is thus given the chance to become an active co-worker. I express myself with certainty only when I feel sure of my interventions. These nuances make for a straight-forward atmosphere and not for omniscience. The Kleinians' all-knowing attitude, Balint believes, the constant preoccupation with the fantasies concerning the analyst, and the narcissism all this implies, lead the patient to submissiveness or to a merely intellectual acceptance of insights. The Kleinians do not seem to seek a growing working alliance, a slowly advancing, active, independent cooperation from the patient.

If interpretations are deep from the start, numerous and lengthy, does the patient have a chance to allow his transference neurosis to develop? Is his transference admitted as into a playground and allowed to expand in almost complete freedom, as Freud phrased it? I have the impression that the Kleinian psychoanalyst's method of handling the patient's transference superimposes an artificial quasi-transference neurosis upon the patient's original neurosis. Their interpretive work seems to be so intrusive and so dominating. Perhaps that is why their patients react so often by "projective identification," which, among other things, seems to be a form of identification with the aggressor. Could this be a means of defense and retaliation against the intrusiveness of the analyst? In my clinical presentations to Kleinian analysts, projective identification was rarely found by them, due, I believe, to the differences in my way of working.

The feeling of omniscience, the freedom to make early and frequent interpretations regarding the analyst, may well have an exhilarating effect on an analyst, particularly after years of self-imposed passivity, careful, slow work, beset by many uncertainties, and hours that seem incomprehensible or unproductive. Perhaps this is another attraction the Kleinian method offers to analysts of Freudian origin who have grown tired of dealing with the intricacies in transference and nontransference developments as they occur in a well-carried-out classical analysis.

Conclusion

My direct contact with Kleinian analysts in private seminars and clinical case presentations, plus my survey of the Kleinian literature, have led me to the conviction that our differences are major. Using a vocabulary and following procedures which seem similar on brief acquaintance lead to a false sense of sameness. A careful study of the theory and technique in regard to transference reveals the deep gulf which divides us from each other. For any real rapprochement to begin, each of us has to acknowledge the divergencies between us. To this I have attempted to contribute.[3]

[3] For a discussion of this paper, see Rosenfeld (1974). See also my reply to Rosenfeld (Greenson, 1975).

Bibliography

ABRAHAM, K. (1908), The Psycho-Sexual Differences between Hysteria and Dementia Praecox. In: *Selected Papers on Psycho-Analysis*. London: Hogarth Press, 1948, pp. 64-79.

―――― (1911), Notes on the Psycho-Analytical Investigation and Treatment of Manic-Depressive Insanity and Allied Conditions. *Ibid.*, pp. 137-156.

―――― (1924), A Short Study of the Development of the Libido. *Ibid.*, pp. 418-501.

―――― (1925), The History of an Imposter in the Light of Psycho-Analytical Knowledge. In: *Clinical Papers and Essays on Psycho-Analysis*. London: Hogarth Press, 1955, pp. 291-305.

ALEXANDER, F. & FRENCH, T. M. (1946), *Psychoanalytic Therapy*. New York: Ronald Press.

ALLEN, A. (1971), The Fee as a Therapeutic Tool. *Psychoanal. Quart.*, 40:132-140.

ALTMAN, L. L. (1969), *The Dream in Psychoanalysis*. New York: International Universities Press.

ARLOW, J. A. (1953), Masturbation and Symptom Formation. *J. Amer. Psychoanal. Assn.*, 1:45-59.

―――― (1971), The Dehumanization of Psychoanalysis. Unpublished paper summarized by R. C. Simmons in: *Bull. Psychoanal. Assn. New York*, pp. 6-8.

―――― & BRENNER, C. (1964), *Psychoanalytic Concepts and the Structural Theory*. New York: International Universities Press.

BALINT, M. (1968), *The Basic Fault*. London: Tavistock Publications.

BENJAMIN, H. (1966), *The Transsexual Phenomenon*. New York: Julian Press.

BENJAMIN, J. D. (1959), Prediction and Psychopathological Theory. In: *Dynamic Psychopathology in Childhood*, ed. L. Jessner & E. Pavenstedt. New York: Grune & Stratton, pp. 6-77.

BERES, D. (1960), The Psychoanalytic Psychology of Imagination, *J. Amer. Psychoanal. Assn.*, 8:252-269.

BERGLER, E. (1942-43), The Gambler. *J. Crim. Psychopathol.*, 4:379-393.

―――― (1945), On the Disease-Entity Boredom ("Alyosis") and Its Psychopathology. *Psychiat. Quart.*, 19:38-51.

―――― (1949), *The Basic Neurosis*. New York: Grune & Stratton.

BETTELHEIM, B. (1954), *Symbolic Wounds*. Glencoe, Ill.: Free Press.

541

———— (1963), *The Empty Fortress*. Glencoe, Ill.: Free Press.

BIBRING, E. (1937), On the Theory of the Therapeutic Results of Psycho-Analysis. *Int. J. Psycho-Anal.*, 18:170-189.

———— (1947), The So-called English School of Psychoanalysis. *Psychoanal. Quart.*, 16:69-93.

———— (1953), The Mechanism of Depression. In: *Affective Disorders*, ed. P. Greenacre. New York: International Universities Press, pp. 13-48.

———— (1954), Psychoanalysis and the Dynamic Psychotherapies. *J. Amer. Psychoanal. Assn.*, 2:745-770.

BIRD, B. (1972), Notes on Transference. *J. Amer. Psychoanal. Assn.*, 20:267-301.

BLUM, H. (1971), On the Conception and Development of the Transference Neurosis. *J. Amer. Psychoanal. Assn.*, 19:41-53.

BONAPARTE, M. (1953), *Female Sexuality*. New York: International Universities Press.

BORGESE, E. (1963), *Ascent of Woman*. New York: George Braziller.

BORNSTEIN, B. (1949), The Analysis of a Phobic Child. *The Psychoanalytic Study of the Child*, 3/4:181-226.

BOUVET, M. (1958), Technical Variation and the Concept of Distance. *Int. J. Psycho-Anal.*, 39:211-221.

———— MARTY, P., & SAUGET, H. (1956), Transfert, Contre-transfert et réalité. *Rev. Franç. Psychanal.*, 20:494-516.

BOYER, B. (1966), Office Treatment of Schizophrenic Patients by Psychoanalysis. *Psychoanal. Forum*, 1:338-346.

BRENNER, C. (1953), An Addendum to Freud's Theory of Anxiety. *Int. J. Psycho-Anal.*, 34:18-24.

BREUER, J. & FREUD, S. (1893-95), Studies on Hysteria. *S.E.*,[a] 2.

BRILL, N. Q. (1946), Neuropsychiatric Examination of Military Personnel Recovered from Japanese Prison Camps. *Bull. U.S. Army Med. Dept.*, 5:429-438.

BRUNSWICK, R. M. (1928), A Supplement to Freud's "History of Infantile Neurosis." In: *The Psychoanalytic Reader*, ed. R. Fliess. New York: International Universities Press, 1948, 1:86-128.

———— (1940), The Preoedipal Phase of the Libido Development. In: *The Psychoanalytic Reader*, ed. R. Fliess. New York: International Universities Press, 1948, 1:261-284.

BURLINGHAM, D. & FREUD, A. (1943), See A. Freud (1973).

BUXBAUM, E. (1949), The Role of a Second Language in the Formation of Ego and Superego. *Psychoanal. Quart.*, 18:279-289.

CALDER, K. T., FLEMING, J., ARLOW, J. A., WINDHOLZ, E., POLLOCK, G. H., & WALLERSTEIN, R. S. (1972), Ten Years of COPE. *J. Amer. Psychoanal. Assn.*, 20:518-540.

CALEF, V. (1970), Review: Indications for Child Analysis and Other Papers. *The Writings of Anna Freud*, Volume 4. *Psychoanal. Quart.*, 39:294-300.

———— (1971), On the Current Concept of the Transference Neurosis. *J. Amer. Psychoanal. Assn.*, 19:22-25.

---

[a] See note d.

CHICAGO PSYCHOANALYTIC LITERATURE INDEX (1953-69). Chicago Institute of Psychoanalysis.

CONRAD, J. (1915), *Victory*. London: Methuen, 1924.

CUENOT, C. (1958), *Teilhard de Chardin*, tr. V. Colimore. New York: Helicon Press.

DEMENT, W. & KLEITMAN, N. (1957), The Relation of Eye Movements during Sleep to Dream Activity. *J. Exper. Psychol.*, 53:339-346.

DERI, F. (n.d.), quoted in O. Fenichel, *The Psychoanalytic Theory of Neurosis*. New York: Norton, 1945, p. 353.

DEUTSCH, H. (1933), The Psychology of Manic-Depressive States. In: *Neuroses and Character Types*. New York: International Universities Press, 1964, pp. 203-217.

——— (1942), Some Forms of Emotional Disturbance and Their Relationships to Schizophrenia, *Psychoanal. Quart.*, 11:301-321.

DEWALD, P. A. (1972), *The Psychoanalytic Process*. New York & London: Basic Books.

DOSTOEVSKY, F. (1866), *The Gambler*. New York: Macmillan, 1931.

EISSLER, K. R. (1950), The Chicago Institute of Psychoanalysis and the Sixth Period of the Development of Psychoanalytic Technique. *J. Genet. Psychol.*, 42:103-157.

——— (1953), The Effect of the Structure of the Ego on Psychoanalytic Technique. *J. Amer. Psychoanal. Assn.*, 1:104-143.

——— (1958), Remarks on Some Variations in Psycho-Analytical Technique. *Int. J. Psycho-Anal.*, 39:222-229.

——— (1962), On the Metapsychology of the Preconscious. *The Psychoanalytic Study of the Child*, 17:9-41.

——— (1971), *Talent and Genius*. New York: Quadrangle Books.

EKSTEIN, R. & WALLERSTEIN, J. (1954), Observations on the Psychology of Borderline and Psychotic Children. *The Psychoanalytic Study of the Child*, 9:344-369.

——— ——— (1956), *The Teaching and Learning of Psychotherapy*. New York: Basic Books, p. 177.

ERIKSON, E. H. (1946), Ego Development and Historical Change. *The Psychoanalytic Study of the Child*, 2:359-396.

——— (1950), *Childhood and Society*. New York: Norton.

——— (1954), The Dream Specimen of Psychoanalysis. *J. Amer. Psychoanal. Assn.*, 2:5-56.

——— (1956), The Problem of Ego Identity. *J. Amer. Psychoanal. Assn.*, 4:56-121.

——— (1962), Reality and Actuality. *J. Amer. Psychoanal. Assn.*, 3:451-474.

FAIRBAIRN, W. R. D. (1954), *An Object Relations Theory of the Personality*. New York: Basic Books.

——— (1957), Freud, the Psycho-Analytic Method and Mental Health. *Brit. J. Med. Psychol.*, 30:53-62.

——— (1958), On the Nature and Aims of Psycho-Analytical Treatment. *Int. J. Psycho-Anal.*, 39:374-385.

FEDERN, P. (1943), Psychoanalysis of Psychoses. *Psychiat. Quart.*, 17:3-19.

——— (1952), *Ego Psychology and the Psychoses*. New York: Basic Books.

FENICHEL, H. (n.d.), Two unpublished papers.
FENICHEL, O. (1926), Identification. *C.P.*,^b 1:97-112.
_____ (1927), Economic Functions of Screen Memories. *C.P.*, 1:113-116.
_____ (1928), The Inner Injunction to "Make a Mental Note." *C.P.*, 1:153-157.
_____ (1930), The Pregenital Antecedents of the Oedipus Complex. *C.P.*, 1:183-203.
_____ (1934a), *Outline of Clinical Psychoanalysis*. New York: Norton.
_____ (1934b), On the Psychology of Boredom. *C.P.*, 1:292-302.
_____ (1934c), Defense against Anxiety. *C.P.*, 1:303-317.
_____ (1935), The Scoptophilic Instinct and Identification. *C.P.*, 1:373-397.
_____ (1939a), The Economics of Pseudologia Phantastica. *C.P.*, 2:129-140.
_____ (1939b), Trophy and Triumph. *C.P.*, 2:141-162.
_____ (1939c), The Counter-Phobic Attitude. *C.P.*, 2:163-173.
_____ (1940), Review: Karen Horney's *New Ways in Psychoanalysis. Psychoanal. Quart.*, 9:114-121.
_____ (1941a), The Ego and the Affects. *C.P.*, 2:215-227.
_____ (1941b), *Problems of Psychoanalytic Technique*. Albany, N.Y.: Psychoanalytic Quarterly.
_____ (1945), *The Psychoanalytic Theory of Neurosis*. New York: Norton.
_____ (1946), On Acting. *C.P.*, 2:349-361.
_____ (1949), The Symbolic Equation: Girl=Phallus. *C.P.*, 2:3-18.
FERENCZI, S. (1909), Introjection and Transference. In: *Sex in Psychoanalysis.* New York: Basic Books, 1950, pp. 35-93.
_____ (1911), On Obscene Words. *Ibid.*, pp. 132-153.
_____ (1913), Stages in the Development of the Sense of Reality. *Ibid.*, pp. 213-239.
_____ (1919a), Sunday Neuroses. In: *Further Contributions to the Theory and Technique of Psycho-Analysis.* London: Hogarth Press, 1926, pp. 174-176.
_____ (1919b), On the Technique of Psycho-Analysis. *Ibid.*, pp. 177-188.
_____ (1925), Contra-Indications to the 'Active' Psycho-Analytical Technique. *Ibid.*, pp. 217-229.
_____ (1928), The Elasticity of Psychoanalytic Technique. In: *Final Contributions to Problems and Methods of Psychoanalysis.* New York: Basic Books, 1955, pp. 87-102.
_____ (1950), *Sex in Psychoanalysis*. New York: Basic Books.
FISHER, C. (1958), Discussion in Panel Report: The Psychoanalytic Theory of Thinking, reported by J. A. Arlow. *J. Amer. Psychoanal. Assn.*, 6:143-153.
_____ (1965), Psychoanalytic Implications of Recent Research on Sleep and Dreaming. *J. Amer. Psychoanal. Assn.*, 13:197-303.
_____ (1966), Dreaming and Sexuality. In: *Psychoanalysis—A General Psychology*, ed. R. M. Loewenstein, L. M. Newman, M. Schur, & A. J. Solnit. New York: International Universities Press, pp. 537-569.

---

^b *The Collected Papers of Otto Fenichel*, 2 Volumes, ed. H. Fenichel & D. Rapaport. New York: Norton, 1953-1954.

FLIESS, R. (1953a), Countertransference and Counteridentification. *J. Amer. Psychoanal. Assn.*, 1:268-284.

_____ (1953b), *The Revival of Interest in the Dream.* New York: International Universities Press.

FORD, C. S. & BEACH, F. A. (1951), *Patterns of Sexual Behavior.* New York: Harper.

FREUD, A. (1936), The Ego and the Mechanisms of Defense. WRITINGS,[c] 2.

_____ (1954), The Widening Scope of Indications for Psychoanalysis: Discussion. *Writings*, 4:356-376.

_____ (1956), Comments on Joyce Robertson's "A Mother's Observations on the Tonsillectomy of her Four-Year-Old Daughter. *Writings*, 4:293-301.

_____ (1965), Normality and Pathology in Childhood. *Writings*, 6.

_____ (1967), Problems of Psychoanalytic Training, Diagnosis, and the Technique of Therapy. *Writings*, 7.

_____ (1968), Indications for Child Analysis and Other Papers. *Writings*, 4.

_____ (1969), Research at the Hampstead Child-Therapy Clinic and Other Papers. *Writings*, 5.

_____ (1973), Infants Without Families: Reports on the Hampstead Nurseries. *Writings*, 3.

_____ (1974), Introduction to Psychoanalysis: Lectures for Child Analysts and Teachers. *Writings*, 1.

_____ & DANN, S. (1951), An Experiment in Group Upbringing. *Writings*, 4:163-244.

FREUD, E., ed. (1960), *Letters of Sigmund Freud.* New York: Basic Books.

FREUD, S. (1899), Screen Memories. *S.E.*,[d] 3:301-322.

_____ (1900), The Interpretation of Dreams. *S.E.*, 4 & 5.

_____ (1901), Childhood Memories and Screen Memories. *S.E.*, 6:43-52.

_____ (1905a), Fragment of an Analysis of a Case of Hysteria. *S.E.*, 7:116-117.

_____ (1905b), Three Essays on the Theory of Sexuality. *S.E.*, 7:125-243.

_____ (1905c), Jokes and Their Relation to the Unconscious. *S.E.*, 8.

_____ (1909a), Family Romances. *S.E.*, 9:235-241.

_____ (1909b), Analysis of a Phobia in a Five-Year-Old Boy. *S.E.*, 10:3-149.

_____ (1909c), Notes on a Case of Obsessional Neurosis. *S.E.*, 10:153-320.

_____ (1910), The Future Prospects of Psycho-Analytic Therapy. *S.E.*, 11:139-151.

_____ (1911a), Psycho-Analytic Notes on an Autobiographical Account of a Case of Paranoia. *S.E.*, 12:3-82.

_____ (1911b), The Handling of Dream-Interpretation in Psycho-Analysis. *S.E.*, 12:89-96.

_____ (1912a), The Dynamics of Transference. *S.E.*, 12:97-108.

---

[c] *The Writings of Anna Freud*, 7 Volumes. New York: International Universities Press, 1968-1974.

[d] *The Standard Edition of the Complete Psychological Works of Sigmund Freud*, 24 Volumes, translated and edited by James Strachey. Hogarth Press and the Institute of Psycho-Analysis, 1953-1974.

_____ (1912b), Recommendations to Physicians Practicing Psycho-Analysis. *S.E.*, 12:109-120.

_____ (1913), On Beginning the Treatment. *S.E.*, 12:121-144.

_____ (1914a), Remembering, Repeating, and Working Through. *S.E.*, 12:145-156.

_____ (1914b), Fausse Reconnaissance (*Déjà Raconté*) in Psycho-Analytical Treatment. *S.E.*, 13:201-207.

_____ (1914c), On the History of the Psycho-Analytic Movement. *S.E.*, 14:3-66.

_____ (1914d), On Narcissism. *S.E.*, 14:67-102.

_____ (1915a), Observations on Transference Love. *S.E.*, 12:157-171.

_____ (1915b), Instincts and Their Vicissitudes. *S.E.*, 14:109-140.

_____ (1915c), The Unconscious. *S.E.*, 14:159-215.

_____ (1916), Some Character Types Met with in Psycho-Analytic Work, *S.E.*, 14:309-333.

_____ (1916-17), Introductory Lectures on Psycho-Analysis. *S.E.*, 15, 16.

_____ (1917a), Mourning and Melancholia. *S.E.*, 14:237-260.

_____ (1917b), A Difficulty in the Path of Psycho-Analysis. *S.E.*, 17:135-144.

_____ (1917c), A Metapsychological Supplement to the Theory of Dreams. *S.E.*, 14:217-235.

_____ (1918a), The Taboo of Virginity. *S.E.*, 11:191-208.

_____ (1918b), From the History of an Infantile Neurosis. *S.E.*, 17:3-122.

_____ (1919), Lines of Advance in Psycho-Analytic Therapy. *S.E.*, 17:157-168.

_____ (1920), Beyond the Pleasure Principle. *S.E.*, 18:7-64.

_____ (1921), Group Psychology and the Analysis of the Ego. *S.E.*, 18:67-143.

_____ (1922), Some Neurotic Mechanisms in Jealousy, Paranoia, and Homosexuality. *S.E.*, 18:221-232.

_____ (1923a), The Ego and the Id. *S.E.*, 19:3-66.

_____ (1923b), Remarks on the Theory and Practice of Dream-Interpretation. *S.E.*, 19:109-121.

_____ (1925a), Some Additional Notes on Dream-Interpretation as a Whole. *S.E.*, 19:125-138.

_____ (1925b), A Note upon the 'Mystic Writing-Pad.' *S.E.*, 19:227-232.

_____ (1925c), Negation. *S.E.*, 19:235-239.

_____ (1925d), Some Psychical Consequences of the Anatomical Distinction between the Sexes. *S.E.*, 19:243-258.

_____ (1925e), An Autobiographical Study. *S.E.*, 20:3-74.

_____ (1926a), Inhibitions, Symptoms and Anxiety. *S.E.*, 20:77-175.

_____ (1926b), The Question of Lay Analysis. *S.E.*, 20:179-258.

_____ (1927), The Future of an Illusion. *S.E.*, 21:3-56.

_____ (1928), Dostoevsky and Parricide. *S.E.*, 21:175-196.

_____ (1930), Civilization and Its Discontents. *S.E.*, 21:59-145.

_____ (1931), Female Sexuality. *S.E.*, 21:225-243.

_____ (1933), New Introductory Lectures on Psycho-Analysis. *S.E.*, 22:3-182.

_____ (1937a), Analysis Terminable and Interminable. *S.E.*, 23:209-253.

_____ (1937b), Constructions in Analysis. *S.E.*, 23:255-270.

_____ (1940), An Outline of Psycho-Analysis. *S.E.*, 23:141-207.

FRIEDMAN, L.J. (1953), Defensive Aspects of Orality. *Int. J. Psycho-Anal.*, 34:304-312.

_____ (n.d.), Ambivalence and the Vicissitudes of the Oedipus Complex (unpublished).

FRIEDMAN, P. (1949), Some Aspects of Concentration Camp Psychology. *Amer. J. Psychiat.*, 40:601.

FROMM, E. (1941), *Escape from Freedom*. New York: Farrar & Rinehart.

FROMM-REICHMANN, F. (1950), *Principles of Intensive Psychotherapy*. Chicago: Chicago University Press.

FROSCH, J. (1964), The Psychotic Character. *Psychiat. Quart.*, 38:81-96.

_____ & Ross, N., ed. (1968), *Annual Survey of Psychoanalysis*, Vol. 9. New York: International Universities Press.

GARMA, A. (1962), The Curative Factors in Psycho-Analysis. *Int. J. Psycho-Anal.*, 43:221-224.

GELEERD, E. R. (1963), Evaluation of Melanie Klein's *Narrative of a Child Analysis. Int. J. Psycho-Anal.*, 44:493-506.

GILL, M. M. (1954), Psychoanalysis and Exploratory Psychotherapy. *J. Amer. Psychoanal. Assn.*, 2:771-797.

_____ (1963), *Topography and Systems in Psychoanalytic Theory [Psychological Issues*, Monogr. 10]. New York: International Universities Press.

_____ NEWMAN, R., & REDLICH, F. C. (1954), *The Initial Interview in Psychiatric Practice*. New York: International Universities Press.

GILLESPIE, W. (1956), The General Theory of Sexual Perversion. *Int. J. Psycho-Anal.*, 37:396-403.

GITELSON, M. (1952), The Emotional Position of the Analyst in the Psycho-Analytic Situation. *Int. J. Psycho-Anal.*, 33:1-10.

_____ (1954), Therapeutic Problems in the Analysis of the 'Normal' Candidate. *Int. J. Psycho-Anal.*, 35:174-183.

_____ (1962), The Curative Factors in Psycho-Analysis. *Int. J. Psycho-Anal.*, 43:194-205.

GLAUBER, I. P. (1951), The Mother in the Etiology of Stuttering. Abst. in: *Psychoanal. Quart.*, 20:160-161.

GLOVER, E. (1929), The Screening Function of Traumatic Memories. *Int. J. Psycho-Anal.*, 10:90-93.

_____ (1939a), *Psychoanalysis*. London: Staples Press.

_____ (1939b), The Psycho-Analysis of Affects. *Int. J. Psycho-Anal.*, 20:299-307.

_____ (1945), Examination of the Klein System of Child Psychology. *The Psychoanalytic Study of the Child*, 1:75-118.

_____ (1955), *The Technique of Psychoanalysis*. New York: International Universities Press.

GOLDSTEIN, K. (1944), Methodological Approach to the Study of Schizophrenic Thought. In: *Language and Thought in Schizophrenia*, ed. J. Kasanin. Berkeley: University of California Press, pp. 17-40.

GREENACRE, P. (1941), The Predisposition to Anxiety. In: *Trauma, Growth, and Personality*. New York: Norton, 1952, pp. 27-82.

_____ (1949), A Contribution to the Study of Screen Memories. *The Psychoanalytic Study of the Child*, 3/4:73-84.

_____ (1954), The Role of Transference. *J. Amer. Psychoanal. Assn.*, 2:671-884.

_____ (1956), Re-evaluation of the Process of Working Through. *Int. J. Psycho-Anal.*, 37:439-444.

_____ (1957), The Childhood of the Artist. *The Psychoanalytic Study of the Child*. 12:47-72.

_____ (1958), Early Physical Determinants in the Development of the Sense of Identity. *J. Amer. Psychoanal. Assn.*, 6:612-627.

_____ (1959a), Play in Relation to Creative Imagination. *The Psychoanalytic Study of the Child*, 14:61-80.

_____ (1959b), Certain Technical Problems in the Transference Relationship. *J. Amer. Psychoanal. Assn.*, 7:484-502.

_____ (1966), Problems of Overidealization of the Analyst and of Analysis. *The Psychoanalytic Study of the Child*, 21:193-212.

_____ (1971), *Emotional Growth*, 2 Vols. New York: International Universities Press.

GREENSCHPOON, R. R., *see* Greenson, R. R.

GREENSON, D., Personal communication.

GREENSON, R. R. (1936), A Case of Agoraphobia. *Psychoanal. Rev.*, 23:383-394.

_____ (1937), A Famous Case of Compulsion Neurosis. *Psychoanal. Rev.*, 24:165-178.

_____ (1944), On Genuine Epilepsy. *Psychoanal. Quart.*, 13:139-159.

_____ (1945), Practical Approach to the War Neuroses. *Bull. Menninger Clin.*, 9:192-205.

_____ (1958a), Psychiatric Information for General Practice. *Calif. Med.*, 88:354-357.

_____ (1958b), Variations in Classical Psycho-Analytic Technique: An Introduction. *Int. J. Psycho-Anal.*, 39:200-201.

_____ (1959), The Classic Psychoanalytic Approach. In: *American Handbook of Psychiatry*, ed. S. Arieti. New York: Basic Books, Vol. II, pp. 1399-1416.

_____ (1961), Report on Panel: The Selection of Candidates for Psychoanalytic Training. *J. Amer. Psychoanal. Assn.*, 9:135-145.

_____ (1966a), Comment on: A Re-evaluation of Acting Out in Relation to Working Through, by A. Limentani. *Int. J. Psycho-Anal.*, 47:283-285.

_____ (1966b), Comment on: Correlation of a Childhood and Adult Neurosis, by S. Ritvo. *Int. J. Psycho-Anal.*, 47:149-150.

_____ (1966c), Otto Fenichel, 1898-1946. In: *Psychoanalytic Pioneers*, ed. F. Alexander, S. Eisenstein, & M. Grotjahn. New York: Basic Books, pp. 439-449.

_____ (1966d), The Decline of Love and Passion Today. Presented at the Annual Meeting of the Reiss-Davis Child Study Center.

_____ (1966e), The Enigma of Modern Woman. *Bull. Philadelphia Assn. Psychoanal.*, 16:173-185.

_____ (1967a), *The Technique and Practice of Psychoanalysis*. New York: International Universities Press.

_____ (1967b), Comment on: A Contribution to the Psychology of Gambling, by W. G. Niederland. *Psychoanal. Forum*, 2:181-182.

_____ (1967c), Masculinity and Femininity in Our Time. In: *Sexual Problems*, ed. C. W. Wahl. New York: Free Press, pp. 39-52.

_____ (1968), On Sexual Apathy in the Male. *Calif. Med.*, 108:275-279.

_____ (1972a), The Clinical Use of the Dream Early in Analysis. Abst. in: *Bull. Menninger Clin.*, 37:187-192.

_____ (1972b), California Earthquake 1971. *Int. J. Psa. Ther.*, 1:7-23.

_____ (1973a), Review of K. R. Eissler, *Talent and Genius. Israel Ann. Psychiat.*, 2:157-163.

_____ (1973b), A Critique of Kernberg's "Summary and Conclusions." *Int. J. Psychiat.*, pp. 91-94.

_____ (1974a), The Theory of Psychoanalytic Technique. In: *American Handbook of Psychiatry*, ed. S. Arieti. New York: Basic Books, 2nd ed., Vol. I, pp. 765-788.

_____ (1974b), A Psychoanalyst's Indictment of "The Exorcist." *Saturday Review*.

_____ (1975), Transference: Freud or Klein. A Reply to the Discussion by Herbert Rosenfeld. *Int. J. Psycho-Anal.*, 56:243.

_____ (1977a), Therapeutic and Working Alliance. In: *International Encyclopedia of Psychiatry, Psychology, Psychoanalysis and Neurology*, Vol. II. New York: Van Nostrand Reinhold/Aeschculapius, pp. 157-160.

_____ (1977b), Beyond Sexual Satisfaction . . . ? Lecture sponsored by the Los Angeles Psychoanalytic Society and Institute and the Center for Early Education.

GRINKER, R. & SPIEGEL, J. (1943), *War Neuroses in North Africa*. New York: Josiah Macy, Jr. Foundation.

_____ _____ (1945), *Men Under Stress*. Philadelphia: Blakiston.

_____ WERBLE, B., & DRYE, R. (1968), *The Borderline Syndrome*. New York: Basic Books.

GRINSTEIN, A. (1959), *The Index of Psychoanalytic Writings*. New York: International Universities Press.

GUNTRIP, H. (1961), *Personality Structure and Human Interaction*. New York: International Universities Press.

_____ (1968), *Schizoid Phenomena, Object Relations, and the Self*. New York: International Universities Press.

HARLEY, M. (1971), The Current Status of Transference Neurosis in Children. *J. Amer. Psychoanal. Assn.*, 19:26-40.

HARTMANN, E. L. (1965), The D-State. *New England J. Med.*, 273:30-35, 87-92.

HARTMANN, H. (1939), *Ego Psychology and the Problem of Adaptation*. New York: International Universities Press, 1958.

_____ (1950), Comments on the Psychoanalytic Theory of the Ego. *The Psychoanalytic Study of the Child*, 5:74-96.

_____ (1951), Technical Implications of Ego Psychology. *Psychoanal. Quart.*, 20:31-43.

_____ (1955), Notes on the Theory of Sublimation. In: *Essays on Ego Psychology*. New York: International Universities Press, 1964, pp. 215-240.

_____ KRIS, E., & LOEWENSTEIN, R. M. (1946), Comments on the Formation of Psychic Structure. *The Psychoanalytic Study of the Child*, 2:11-38.

HEIMANN, P. (1950), On Countertransference. *Int. J. Psycho-Anal.*, 31:81-84.

_____ (1962), The Curative Factors in Psycho-Analysis. *Int. J. Psycho-Anal.*, 43:228-231.

HENDRICK, I. (1931), Ego Defense and the Mechanism of Oral Ejection in Schizophrenia. *Int. J. Psycho-Anal.*, 12:298-325.

_____ (1951), Early Development of the Ego. *Psychoanal. Quart.*, 20:44-61.

HITSCHMANN, E. (1956), *Great Men*. New York: International Universities Press.

HOFFER, E. (1955), *The Passionate State of Mind*. New York: Harper.

HORNEY, K. (1939), *New Ways in Psychoanalysis*. New York: Norton.

HUME, P. B. (n.d.), Acedia, a Neurosis of Confinement (unpublished).

ISAACS, S. (1948), The Nature and Function of Phantasy. In: *Developments in Psycho-Analysis*, ed. J. Riviere. London: Hogarth Press, 1970, pp. 67-121.

ISAKOWER, O. (1938), A Contribution to the Pathopsychology of Phenomena Associated with Falling Asleep. *Int. J. Psycho-Anal.*, 19:331-345.

_____ (1939), On the Exceptional Position of the Auditory Sphere. *Int. J. Psycho-Anal.*, 20:340-348.

_____ (1954), Spoken Words in Dreaming. *Psychoanal. Quart.*, 23:1-6.

JACOBSON, E. (1943), The Oedipus Complex in the Development of Depressive Mechanisms. *Psychoanal. Quart.*, 12:541-560.

_____ (1950), Development of the Wish for a Child in Boys. *The Psychoanalytic Study of the Child*, 5:139-152.

_____ (1953a), Contribution to the Metapsychology of Cyclothymic Depression. In: *Affective Disorders*, ed. P. Greenacre. New York: International Universities Press, pp. 84-116.

_____ (1953b), The Affects and their Pleasure-Unpleasure Qualities in Relation to the Psychic Discharge Processes. In: *Drives, Affects, Behavior*, ed. R. M. Loewenstein. New York: International Universities Press, pp. 38-66.

_____ (1954a), Contribution to the Metapsychology of Psychotic Identification. *J. Amer. Psychoanal. Assn.*, 2:239-262.

_____ (1954b), The Self and the Object World. *The Psychoanalytic Study of the Child*, 9:75-127.

_____ (1957a), Normal and Pathological Moods. *The Psychoanalytic Study of the Child*, 12:73-113.

_____ (1957b), Denial and Repression. *J. Amer. Psychoanal. Assn.*, 5:61-92.

_____ (1964), *The Self and the Object World*. New York: International Universities Press.

_____ (1971), *Depression*. New York: International Universities Press.

JESPERSON, O. (1922), *Language: Its Nature, Development and Origin*. London: Allen & Unwin.

JOFFE, W. G. (1969), A Critical Review of the Status of the Envy Concept. *Int. J. Psycho-Anal.*, 50:533-545.

JONES, E. (1920), Editorial. *Int. J. Psycho-Anal.*, 1:3-5.
_____ (1953-57), *The Life and Work of Sigmund Freud*, 3 Vols. New York: Basic Books.
KARDINER, A. (1932), The Bio-Analysis of the Epileptic Reaction. *Psychoanal. Quart.*, 1:375-483.
_____ (1939), *The Individual and His Society*. New York: Columbia University Press.
KATAN, A. (1934), Einige Bemerkungen über den Optimismus. *Int. Z. Psychoanal.*, 20:191-199.
KELMAN, H., ed. (1964), *Advances in Psychoanalysis: Contributions to Karen Horney's Holistic Approach*. New York: Norton.
KENNEDY, H. E. (1950), Cover Memories in Formation. *The Psychoanalytic Study of the Child*, 5:275-284.
KERNBERG, O. (1965), Notes on Countertransference. *J. Amer. Psychoanal. Assn.*, 13:38-56.
_____ (1966), Structural Derivatives of Object Relationships. *Int. J. Psycho-Anal.*, 47:236-253.
_____ (1967), Borderline Personality Organization. *J. Amer. Psychoanal. Assn.*, 15:641-685.
_____ (1969), A Contribution to the Ego-Psychological Critique of the Kleinian School. *Int. J. Psycho-Anal.*, 50:317-333.
KESTENBERG, J. S. (1971), From Organ-Object Imagery to Self and Object Representations. In: *Separation-Individuation*, ed. J. McDevitt & C. Settlage. New York: International Universities Press, pp. 75-99.
KHAN, M. M. R. (1963), Silence as Communication. *Bull. Menninger Clin.*, 27:300-310.
KING, P. (1962), The Curative Factors in Psycho-Analysis. *Int. J. Psycho-Anal.*, 43:225-227.
KINSEY, A. C. ET AL. (1948), *Sexual Behavior in the Human Male*. Philadelphia: Saunders.
KLEIN, M. (1921-45), *Contributions to Psycho-Analysis*. London: Hogarth Press, 1948.
_____ (1932), *The Psycho-Analysis of Children*. London: Hogarth Press, 1949.
_____ (1952), The Origins of Transference. *Int. J. Psycho-Anal.*, 33:433-438.
_____ (1957), *Envy and Gratitude*. New York: Basic Books.
_____ HEIMANN, P., ISAACS, S., & RIVIERE, J. (1952), *Developments in Psycho-Analysis*. London: Hogarth Press.
KNIGHT, R. P. (1940), Introjection, Projection, and Identification. *Psychoanal. Quart.*, 9:334-341.
_____ (1953), Borderline States. In: *Psychoanalytic Psychiatry and Psychology*, ed. R. P. Knight & C. R. Friedman. New York: International Universities Press, pp. 97-109.
KOHRMAN, R., FINEBERG, H. H., GELMAN, R. L. & WEISS, S. (1971), Technique of Child Analysis. *Int. J. Psycho-Anal.*, 52:487-497.
KOHUT, H. (1959), Introspection, Empathy and Psychoanalysis. *J. Amer. Psychoanal. Assn.*, 7:459-483.

_____ (1971), *The Analysis of the Self*. New York: International Universities Press.

KRIS, E. (1950), On Preconscious Mental Processes. *Psychoanal. Quart.*, 19:540-560.

_____ (1952), *Psychoanalytic Explorations in Art*. New York: International Universities Press.

_____ (1956a), On Some Vicissitudes of Insight in Psycho-Analysis. *Int. J. Psycho-Anal.*, 37:445-455.

_____ (1956b), The Recovery of Childhood Memories in Psychoanalysis. *The Psychoanalytic Study of the Child*, 11:54-88.

KUBIE, L. (1966), A Reconsideration of Thinking, the Dream Process, and 'The Dream.' *Psychoanal. Quart.*, 35:191-198.

KUIPER, P. (1962), The Curative Factors in Psycho-Analysis. *Int. J. Psycho-Anal.*, 43:218-220.

LAFORGUE, R. (1930), On the Erotization of Anxiety. *Int. J. Psycho-Anal.*, 11:312-321.

LAING, R. D. (1967), *The Politics of Experience*. New York: Pantheon Books.

LANDAUER, K. (1938), Affects, Passions, and Temperament. *Int. J. Psycho-Anal.*, 19:388-415.

LEITES, N. (1947), Trends in Affectlessness. *Amer. Imago*, 4:89-112.

LEOPOLD, R. L. & DILLON, H. (1963), Psycho-Anatomy of a Disaster. *Amer. J. Psychiat.*, 119:913-921.

LEVINE, J. M. (1967), Through the Looking Glass. *J. Amer. Psychoanal. Assn.*, 15:166-212.

LEVY, K. (1958), Silence in the Analytic Session. *Int. J. Psycho-Anal.*, 39:50-59.

LEWIN, B. D. (1946), Sleep, the Mouth, and the Dream Screen. *Psychoanal. Quart.*, 15:419-434.

_____ (1950), *The Psychoanalysis of Elation*. New York: Norton.

_____ (1952), Phobic Symptoms and Dream Interpretation. *Psychoanal. Quart.*, 21:295-322.

_____ (1953), Reconsideration of the Dream Screen. *Psychoanal. Quart.*, 22:174-199.

_____ (1955), Dream Psychology and the Analytic Situation. *Psychoanal. Quart.*, 24:169-199.

_____ (1958), *Dreams and the Uses of Regression*. New York: International Universities Press.

_____ (1968), *The Image and the Past*. New York: International Universities Press.

_____ (1973), *Selected Writings of Bertram D. Lewin*, ed. Jacob A. Arlow. New York: The Psychoanalytic Quarterly.

LEWIS, M. (1936), *Infant Speech*. New York: Harcourt, Brace.

_____ (1948), *Language in Society*. New York: Social Sciences Publishers.

LIMENTANI, A. (1972), The Assessment of Analysability. *Int. J. Psycho-Anal.*, 53:351-361.

LITTLE, M. (1951), Counter-Transference and the Patient's Response to It. *Int. J. Psycho-Anal.*, 32:32-40.

LOEWALD, H. W. (1960), On the Therapeutic Action of Psycho-Analysis. *Int. J. Psycho-Anal.*, 41:16-33.

_____ (1966), Review: *Psychoanalytic Concepts and the Structural Theory*, J. Arlow & C. Brenner. *Psychoanal. Quart.*, 35:430-436.

_____ (1971), The Transference Neurosis. *J. Amer. Psychoanal. Assn.*, 19:54-66.

_____ (1972), Freud's Conception of the Negative Therapeutic Reaction. *J. Amer. Psychoanal. Assn.*, 20:235-246.

LOEWENSTEIN, R. M. (1951), The Problem of Interpretation. *Psychoanal. Quart.*, 20:1-14.

_____ (1954), Some Remarks on Defences, Autonomous Ego and Psycho-Analytic Technique. *Int. J. Psycho-Anal.*, 35:188-193.

_____ (1956), Some Remarks on the Role of Speech in Psycho-Analytic Technique. *Int. J. Psycho-Anal.*, 37:460-468.

_____ (1958), Remarks on Some Variations in Psycho-Analytic Technique. *Int. J. Psycho-Anal.*, 39:203-210.

LUSTMAN, S. L. (1967), The Scientific Leadership of Anna Freud. *J. Amer. Psychoanal. Assn.*, 15:810-827.

MACALPINE, I. (1950), The Development of Transference. *Psychoanal. Quart.*, 19:501-539.

McDOWELL, M. (n.d.), Unpublished paper.

MAHLER, M. S. (1957), On Two Crucial Phases of Integration concerning Problems of Identity. In Panel: Problems of Identity, reported by D. L. Rubinfine. *J. Amer. Psychoanal. Assn.*, 6:131-142.

_____ (1958), Two Extreme Disturbances of Identity. *Int. J. Psycho-Anal.*, 39:77-83.

_____ (1963), Thoughts about Development and Individuation. *The Psychoanalytic Study of the Child*, 18:307-324.

_____ (1965), On the Significance of the Normal Separation-Individuation Phase. In: *Drives, Affects, Behavior*, Vol. 2, ed. M. Schur. New York: International Universities Press, pp. 161-169.

_____ (1968), *On Human Symbiosis and the Vicissitudes of Individuation*, Vol. 1. New York: International Universities Press.

_____ & LA PERRIERE, K. (1965), Mother-Child Interaction during Separation-Individuation. *Psychoanal. Quart.*, 34:483-498.

_____ PINE, F., & BERGMAN, A. (1975), *The Psychological Birth of the Human Infant*. New York: Basic Books.

MARMOR, J. (1953), Orality in the Hysterical Personality. *J. Amer. Psychoanal. Assn.*, 1:656-671.

_____ ed. (1968), *Modern Psychoanalysis*. New York: Basic Books.

MASTERS, W. & JOHNSON, V. (1966), *Human Sexual Response*. Boston: Little Brown.

MEAD, M. (1949), *Male and Female*. New York: William Morrow.

MELTZER, D. (1967), *The Psycho-Analytic Process*. London: Heinemann.

MENAKER, E. (1942), The Masochistic Factor in the Psychoanalytic Situation. *Psychoanal. Quart.*, 11:171-186.

MYERSON, P. G. (1962), Footnote in: The Curative Factors in Psycho-Analysis, M. Gitelson. *Int. J. Psycho-Anal.*, 43:202.

MYRDAL, G. (1944), *An American Dilemma*. New York: Harper.

NACHT, S. (1958), Variations in Technique. *Int. J. Psycho-Anal.*, 39:235-237.

⸻ (1962), The Curative Factors in Psycho-Analysis. *Int. J. Psycho-Anal.*, 43:206-211.

NOVEY, S. (1962), The Principle of "Working Through" in Psychoanalysis. *J. Amer. Psychoanal. Assn.*, 10:658-676.

NUNBERG, H. (1932), *Principles of Psychoanalysis*. New York: International Universities Press, 1955.

⸻ (1948), The Course of the Libidinal Conflict in a Case of Schizophrenia. In: *The Practice and Theory of Psychoanalysis*. New York: International Universities Press, 1961, pp. 24-59.

OLDEN, C. (1953), On Adult Empathy with Children. *The Psychoanalytic Study of the Child*, 8:111-126.

⸻ (1958), Notes on the Development of Empathy. *The Psychoanalytic Study of the Child*, 13:505-518.

OREMLAND, J. D. (1973), A Specific Dream during the Termination Phase of Successful Psychoanalysis. *J. Amer. Psychoanal. Assn.*, 21:285-302.

ORR, D. W. (1954), Transference and Countertransference. *J. Amer. Psychoanal. Assn.*, 2:621-670.

PAULY, I. (1965), Male Psychosexual Inversion. *Arch. Gen. Psychiat.*, 13:172-181.

PIAGET, J. (1923), *Language and Thought of the Child*. London: Routledge & Kegan Paul, 1932.

⸻ (1937a), Principal Factors Determining Intellectual Evolution from Childhood to Adult Life. In: *Organization and Pathology of Thought*, ed. D. Rapaport. New York: Columbia University Press, 1951, pp. 154-175.

⸻ (1937b), *The Construction of Reality in the Child*. New York: Basic Books, 1954, pp. 350-386.

Psychoanalytic Quarterly Cumulative Index, Vols. 1-35, 1932-1966. New York: The Psychoanalytic Quarterly, 1969.

RADO, S. (1926), The Psychic Effects of Intoxication. *Int. J. Psycho-Anal.*, 9:301-317, 1928.

⸻ (1927), The Problem of Melancholia. *Int. J. Psycho-Anal.*, 9:420-438, 1928.

⸻ (1933), The Psychoanalysis of Pharmacothymia. *Psychoanal. Quart.*, 2:1-23.

⸻ (1939), Developments in the Psychoanalytic Conception and Treatment of the Neuroses. *Psychoanal. Quart.*, 8:427-437.

⸻ (1942), Pathodynamics and Treatment of Traumatic War Neurosis. *Psychosom. Med.*, 4:362-368.

RANGELL, L. (1952a), Macroscopic Transmission and the Macroscopic Point of View. *J. Hillside Hosp.*, 1:228-233.

⸻ (1952b), Analysis of a Doll Phobia. *Int. J. Psycho-Anal.*, 33:43-53.

⸻ (1952c), Panel report: The Theory of Affects. *Bull. Amer. Psychoanal. Assn.*, 8:300-315.

⸻ (1954), The Psychology of Poise. *Int. J. Psycho-Anal.*, 35:313-332.

_____ (1955), A Unitary Theory of Anxiety. *J. Amer. Psychoanal. Assn.*, 3:389-412.

_____ (1959), The Nature of Conversion. *J. Amer. Psychoanal. Assn.*, 7:632-662.

RAPAPORT, D. (1942), *Emotions and Memory*. New York: International Universities Press, 1950.

_____ (1950), On the Psycho-Analytic Theory of Thinking. *Int. J. Psycho-Anal.*, 31:1-10.

_____ ed. & tr. (1951), *Organization and Pathology of Thought*. Columbia University Press.

_____ (1953), On the Psycho-Analytic Theory of Affects. *Int. J. Psycho-Anal.*, 34:177-198.

_____ (1967), *The Collected Papers of David Rapaport*, ed. M. M. Gill. New York: Basic Books.

_____ & GILL, M. M. (1959), The Points of View and Assumptions of Metapsychology. *Int. J. Psycho-Anal.*, 40:153-162.

REICH, A. (1940), A Contribution to the Psychoanalysis of Extreme Submissiveness in Women. *Psychoanal. Quart.*, 9:470-480.

_____ (1951), On Counter-Transference. *Int. J. Psycho-Anal.*, 32:25-31.

_____ (1953), Narcissistic Object Choice in Women. *J. Amer. Psychoanal. Assn.*, 1:22-44.

_____ (1954), Early Identifications as Archaic Elements in the Superego. *J. Amer. Psychoanal. Assn.* 2:218-238.

_____ (1958), A Special Variation of Technique. *Int. J. Psycho-Anal.*, 39:230-234.

REIDER, N. (1953a), Reconstruction and Screen Function. *J. Amer. Psychoanal. Assn.*, 1:389-405.

_____ (1953b), A Type of Transference to Institutions. *Bull. Menninger Clin.*, 17:58-63.

REIK, T. (1928), *Ritual*. New York: International Universities Press, 1958.

_____ (1936), *Surprise and the Psychoanalyst*. London: Kegan Paul.

_____ (1948), *Listening with the Third Ear*. New York: Farrar, Straus.

RIBBLE, M. A. (1944), *The Rights of Infants*. New York: Columbia University Press.

RIVIERE, J. (1952), General Introduction. In: *Developments in Psycho-Analysis*, by M. Klein, P. Heimann, S. Isaacs, & J. Riviere. London: Hogarth Press, pp. 1-36.

ROLAND, A. (1967), The Reality of the Psycho-Analytic Relationship and Situation in the Handling of Transference-Resistance. *Int. J. Psycho-Anal.*, 48:504-510.

ROSEN, J. N. (1947), The Treatment of Schizophrenic Psychosis by Direct Analytic Therapy. *Psychiat. Quart.*, 21:3-37.

ROSEN, V. H. (1960), Some Aspects of the Role of Imagination in the Analytic Process. *J. Amer. Psychoanal. Assn.*, 8:229-251.

ROSENFELD, H. A. (1958), Contribution to the Discussion on the Variations in Classical Technique. *Int. J. Psycho-Anal.*, 39:238-239.

_____ (1965), *Psychotic States*. New York: International Universities Press.

———— (1974), Discussion of the Paper by Ralph R. Greenson [Transference: Freud or Klein]. *Int. J. Psycho-Anal.*, 55:49-51.

ROSTEN, L. C. (1941), *Hollywood, The Movie Colony, The Moviemakers.* New York: Harcourt, Brace.

RYCROFT, C. (1956), The Nature and Function of the Analyst's Communication to the Patient. *Int. J. Psycho-Anal.*, 37:469-472.

SACHS, H. (1923), Zur Genese der Perversionen. *Int. Z. Psychoanal.*, 9:180-184.

SALZMAN, L. (1962), *Developments in Psychoanalysis.* New York: Grune & Stratton.

SANDLER, J., HOLDER, A., & DARE, C. (1970a), Basic Psycho-Analytic Concepts: 2. The Treatment Alliance. *Brit. J. Psychiat.*, 116:555-558.

———— ———— ———— (1970b), Basic Psycho-Analytic Concepts: 4. Countertransference. *Brit. J. Psychiat.*, 117:83-88.

———— KENNEDY, H., & TYSON, R. L. (1975), Discussions on Transference: The Treatment Situation and Technique in Child Psychoanalysis. *The Psychoanalytic Study of the Child*, 30:375-408. New Haven: Yale University Press.

SAPIR, E. (1921), *Language.* New York: Harcourt, Brace.

SCHAAR, J. H. (1961), *Escape From Authority.* New York: Basic Books.

SCHAFER, R. (1959), Generative Empathy in the Treatment Situation. *Psychoanal. Quart.*, 28:342-373.

SCHIELE, B. C. & BROZEK, J. (1948), "Experimental Neurosis" Resulting from Semistarvation in Man. *Psychosom. Med.*, 10:31-50.

SCHLESINGER, H. J. (1970), The Place of Forgetting in Memory Functioning. *J. Amer. Psychoanal. Assn.*, 18:358-371.

SCHRECKER, P. (1949), The Family, a Conveyance of Tradition. In: *The Family*, ed. R. N. Anshen. New York: Harpers, pp. 406-425.

SCHUR, H. (1966), An Observation and Comments on the Development of Memory. *The Psychoanalytic Study of the Child*, 21:468-479.

SCHUR, M. (1953), The Ego in Anxiety. In: *Drives, Affects, Behavior*, ed. R. M. Loewenstein. New York: International Universities Press, pp. 67-103.

———— (1958), The Ego and the Id in Anxiety. *The Psychoanalytic Study of the Child*, 13:190-220.

———— (1966), *The Id and the Regulatory Principles of Mental Functioning.* New York: International Universities Press.

———— (1972), *Freud: Living and Dying.* New York: International Universities Press.

SEARLES, H. F. (1960), *The Nonhuman Environment.* New York: International Universities Press.

———— (1963a), The Place of Neutral Therapist-responses in Psychotherapy with the Schizophrenic Patient. In: *Collected Papers on Schizophrenia and Related Subjects.* New York: International Universities Press, 1965, pp. 626-653.

———— (1963b), Transference Psychosis in the Psychotherapy of Chronic Schizophrenia. *Ibid.*, pp. 654-716.

———— (1965), *Collected Papers on Schizophrenia and Related Subjects.* New York: International Universities Press.

SEGAL, H. (1962), The Curative Factors in Psycho-Analysis. *Int. J. Psycho-Anal.*, 43:212-217.

———— (1964), *Introduction to the Work of Melanie Klein.* New York: Basic Books.

———— (1967), Melanie Klein's Technique. In: *Psychoanalytic Techniques*, ed. B. Wolman. New York: Basic Books, pp. 168-190.

———— (1972), A Delusional System as a Defence against the Re-emergence of a Catastrophic Situation. *Int. J. Psycho-Anal.*, 53:393-401.

SHAPIRO, S. (1968), Reporter on Anna Freud's 'Difficulties in the Path of Psychoanalysis.' *Bull. Philadelphia Assn. Psychoanal.*, 18:214-216.

SHARPE, E. F. (1930), The Technique of Psycho-Analysis. In: *Collected Papers on Psycho-Analysis.* London: Hogarth Press, 1950, pp. 9-106.

———— (1940), Psycho-Physical Problems Revealed in Language. *Int. J. Psycho-Anal.*, 21:201-213.

———— (1947), The Psycho-Analyst. In: *Collected Papers on Psycho-Analysis.* London: Hogarth Press, 1950, pp. 109-122.

———— (1949), *Dream Analysis.* London: Hogarth Press.

SHERFEY, M. (1966), Female Sexuality. *J. Amer. Psychoanal. Assn.*, 14:28-128.

SIEGMAN, A. (1954), Emotionality. *Psychoanal. Quart.*, 23:339-353.

SIMMEL, E. (1920), Zur Psychoanalyse des Spielers. Abst.: *Int. Z. Psychoanal.*, 6:397.

———— (1925), A Screen Memory in *Statu Nascendi. Int. J. Psycho-Anal.*, 6:454-457.

———— (1926), The 'Doctor-Game.' *Int. J. Psycho-Anal.*, 7:470-483.

———— (1944a), War Neuroses. In: *Psychoanalysis Today*, ed. S. Lorand. New York: International Universities Press, pp. 227-248.

———— (1944b), Self-Preservation and the Death Instinct. *Psychoanal. Quart.*, 13:160-185.

SOCARIDES, C. (1963), The Historical Development of Theoretical and Clinical Concepts of Overt Female Homosexuality. *J. Amer. Psychoanal. Assn.*, 11:386-414.

SPIEGEL, L. A. (1959), The Self, the Sense of Self, and Perception. *The Psychoanalytic Study of the Child*, 14:81-109.

SPIELREIN, S. (1922), Die Entstehung der kindlichen Worte Papa und Mama. *Imago*, 8:345-367.

SPITZ, R. A. (1937), Wiederholung, Rhythmus, Langeweile. *Imago*, 23:171-196.

———— (1945), Hospitalism. *The Psychoanalytic Study of the Child*, 1:53-74.

———— (1950), Anxiety in Infancy, *Int. J. Psycho-Anal.*, 31:138-143.

———— (1956a), Tranference. *Int. J. Psycho-Anal.*, 37:380-385.

———— (1956b), Countertransference. *J. Amer. Psychoanal. Assn.*, 4:256-265.

———— (1965), *The First Year of Life.* New York: International Universities Press.

STEIN, M. H. (1965), States of Consciousness in the Analytic Situation. In: *Drives, Affects, Behavior*, Vol. 2, ed. M. Schur. New York: International Universities Press, pp. 60-86.

STENGEL, E. (1939), On Learning a New Language, *Int. J. Psycho-Anal.*, 20:471-479.

STERBA, R. F. (1929), The Dynamics of the Dissolution of the Transference Resistance. *Psychoanal. Quart.*, 1940, 9:363-379.
———— (1934), The Fate of the Ego in Analytic Therapy. *Int. J. Psycho-Anal.*, 15:117-126.
STERN, M. M. (1951), Anxiety, Trauma, and Shock. *Psychoanal. Quart.*, 20:179-203.
STEWART, W. (1963), An Inquiry into the Concept of Working Through. *J. Amer. Psychounal. Assn.*, 11:474-499.
STOCKING, C. (1931), Gambling. *Encyclopedia of the Social Sciences*. New York: Macmillan, 6:555-558.
STOLLER, R. (1964a), A Contribution to the Study of Gender Identity. *Int. J. Psycho-Anal.*, 45:220-226.
———— (1964b), Female (vs. Male) Transvestism. Unpublished paper presented before the American Psychoanalytic Association, May 1964.
———— (1966), The Mother's Contribution to Infantile Transvestism. *Int. J. Psycho-Anal.*, 47:384-395.
STONE, L. (1954), The Widening Scope of Indications for Psychoanalysis. *J. Amer. Psychoanal. Assn.*, 2:567-594.
———— (1961), *The Psychoanalytic Situation*. New York: International Universities Press.
———— (1967), The Psychoanalytic Situation and Transference. *J. Amer. Psychoanal. Assn.*, 15:3-58.
STRACHEY, J. (1953), Editor's Introduction. *S.E.*, 4:xi-xxi.
———— (1957), Editor's Note. *S.E.*, 14:69-71.
SWANK, R. L. & MARCHAND, W. (1946), Combat Neuroses. *Arch. Neurol. Psychiat.*, 55:235-247.
SZASZ, T. S. (1956), On the Experiences of the Analyst in the Psychoanalytic Situation. *J. Amer. Psychoanal. Assn.*, 4:197-223.
———— (1963), The Concept of Transference. *Int. J. Psycho-Anal.*, 44:432-443.
SZÉKELY, L. (1967), The Creative Pause. *Int. J. Psycho-Anal.*, 48:353-367.
TARTAKOFF, H. H. (1956), Recent Books on Psychoanalytic Technique. *J. Amer. Psychoanal. Assn.*, 4:318-343.
TAUSK, V. (1919), On the Origin of the "Influencing Machine." *Psychoanal. Quart.*, 2:519-556, 1933.
TEILHARD DE CHARDIN, P. (1959), *The Phenomenon of Man*, tr. B J. Wall. New York: Harper & Row.
———— (1960), *The Divine Milieu*, tr. B. J. Wall. New York: Harper & Row.
———— (1962), *Human Energy*, tr. J. M. Cohen. New York: Harcourt, Brace, Jovanovich.
THORNER, H. A. (1957), Three Defences against Inner Persecution. In: *New Directions in Psychoanalysis*, ed. M. Klein, P. Heimann, & R. E. Money-Kyrle. New York: Basic Books, pp. 282-306.
TICHO, G. R. (1967), On Self-Analysis. *Int. J. Psycho-Anal.*, 48:308-318.
TYHURST, J. S. (1951), Individual Reactions to Community Disasters. *Amer. J. Psychiat.*, 107:764-769.
TYSON, R. & SANDLER, J. (1971), Problems in the Selection of Patients for Psy-

choanalysis: Comments on the application of the concepts of 'indica-tions', 'suitability' and 'analysability'. *Brit. J. Med. Psychol.*, 44:211-228.

VEBLEN, T. (1932), *The Theory of the Leisure Class.* New York: Vanguard Press.

WAELDER, R. (1930), The Principle of Multiple Function. *Psychoanal. Quart.*, 5:45-62, 1936.

—— (1937), The Problem of the Genesis of Psychical Conflict in Earliest Infancy. *Int. J. Psycho-Anal.*, 18:406-473.

—— (1951), The Structure of Paranoid Ideas. *Int. J. Psycho-Anal.*, 32:167-177.

—— (1967), Inhibitions, Symptoms, and Anxiety: Forty Years Later. *Psy-choanal. Quart.*, 36:1-36.

WALDHORN, H. F., reporter (1967), *Indications for Psychoanalysis. The Place of the Dream in Clinical Psychoanalysis* [Monogr. 2, *The Kris Study Group of the New York Psychoanalytic Institute*], ed. E. D. Joseph. New York: International Universities Press.

WEINSHEL, E. M. (1971), The Transference Neurosis. *J. Amer. Psychoanal. Assn.*, 19:67-88.

WEISS, J. (1959), Intensity as a Character Trait. *Psychoanal. Quart.*, 28:64-72.

WEISSMAN, P. (1967), Theoretical Considerations of Ego Regression and Ego Functions in Creativity. *Psychoanal. Quart.*, 36:37-50.

WEXLER, M. (1951), The Structural Problem in Schizophrenia. *Int. J. Psycho-Anal.*, 32:157-166.

—— (1952), The Structural Problem in Schizophrenia. In: *Psychotherapy with Schizophrenics*, ed. E. B. Brody & F. C. Redlich. New York: Inter-national Universities Press, pp. 179-201.

—— (1960), Hypotheses concerning Ego Deficiency in Schizophrenia. In: *The Outpatient Treatment of Schizophrenia.* New York: Grune & Stratton, pp. 33-43.

—— (1971), Schizophrenia. *Psychoanal. Quart.*, 40:83-99.

WHITMAN, R. M., KRAMER, M., & BALDRIDGE, B. J. (1969), Dreams about the Patient. *J. Amer. Psychoanal. Assn.*, 17:702-727.

WIEDEMAN, G. (1962), Survey of Psychoanalytic Literature on Overt and Male Homosexuality. *J. Amer. Psychoanal. Assn.*, 10:386-409.

WINDHOLZ, E. (n.d.), Unpublished paper on boredom.

WINNICOTT, D. W. (1949), Hate in the Counter-Transference. *Int. J. Psycho-Anal.*, 30:69-74.

—— (1953), Transitional Objects and Transitional Phenomena. In: *Col-lected Papers.* New York: Basic Books, pp. 229-242.

—— (1955), Metapsychological and Clinical Aspects of Regression within the Psycho-Analytical Set-Up. In: *Collected Papers.* New York: Basic Books, 1958, pp. 278-294.

—— (1956), On Transference. *Int. J. Psycho-Anal.*, 37:386-388.

—— (1962), A Personal View of the Kleinian Contribution. In: *The Matur-ational Processes and the Facilitating Environment.* New York: International Universities Press, 1965, pp. 171-178.

—————— (1965), A Clinical Study of the Effect of a Failure of the Average Expectable Environment on a Child's Mental Functioning. *Int. J. Psycho-Anal.*, 46:81-87.

WINTERSTEIN, A. (1930), Angst vor dem Neuen, Neugier, und Langeweile. *Psychoanal. Bewegung*, 2:540-554.

WOLFENSTEIN, M. (1957), *Disasters*. Glencoe, Ill.: Free Press.

—————— (1965), *Changing Patterns of Adolescence*. London: J & A Churchill, pp. 105-208.

WORMHOUDT, A. (1949), The Unconscious Identification Words—Milk. *Amer. Imago*, 6:57-68.

WULFF, M. (1932), Über einen interessanten oralen Symptomenkomplex und seine Beziehung zur Sucht. *Int. Z. Psychoanal.*, 18:281-302.

YORKE, C. (1971), Some Suggestions for a Critique of Kleinian Psychology. *The Psychoanalytic Study of the Child*, 26:129-155.

ZELIGS, M. A. (1957), Acting in. *J. Amer. Psychoanal. Assn.*, 5:685-707.

ZELMANOWITS, J. (1968), Review: *The Collected Papers of David Rapaport*. *Psychiatry*, 31:292-299.

ZETZEL, E. R. (1956a), An Approach to the Relation between Concept and Content in Psychoanalytic Theory. *The Psychoanalytic Study of the Child*, 11:99-121.

—————— (1956b), Current Concepts of Transference. *Int. J. Psycho-Anal.*, 37:369-376.

ZILBOORG, G. (1944), Masculine and Feminine. *Psychiatry*, 7:257-296.

Index

Abortion, 48
Abraham, K., 26-27, 54, 78, 84, 112, 141, 173, 183, 349, 541
Accident-proneness, 296
Accidents, 443-44
Acting out, 86, 119-20, 128, 183, 187, 208, 393, 414, 492, 531
  and depression, 142
  of fantasies, 105-10, 127
Activity
  lack of interest in phallic, 295
  see also Passivity
Addiction, 14-15, 31-33, 40, 79, 86, 183, 464, 480-82
  to food, 49, 52-55
Adler, A., 349-50
Adolescence, 85, 123, 129, 174, 179, 212, 254, 262, 463, 472-73
  and gambling, 12
  of screen character, 129
Affect
  and dream, 391, 411-12
  and memory, 48
  see also sub Denial
Affective disorders, 65, 67-68
  see also sub specific syndromes
Affective states, 56
Aggression, 228, 488-90
  and anxiety, 143-44
  breakthroughs, 62-65
  and creativity, 343-44
  and identification, 87-89, 91
  protection of object against, 123-25, 132
  role in development, 456-58, 460-61
  see also Anger, Behavior, Rage

"Aha" experience, 154-56, 160
Alcoholism, 122, 145
  and boredom, 52-54, 81
  see also Mother
Alexander, F., 354, 399, 474, 541
Alioto, J. L., 479
Allen, A., 514, 541
Altman, L. L., 388, 414, 541
Altruistic surrender, 105
Ambivalence, 26-27, 66, 68, 327, 339, 456-57, 469
  and identification, 78, 84, 89-90
  of screen character, 124-25
Anal activities (preoccupations), 34-36, 80, 85, 117, 122, 338-39
  see also Toilet activities
Anality
  and gambling, 5-6, 14
  and speech, 34, 41
Anal phase, 89, 142, 179, 460
Anger, 213, 318-30, 363-64
Animals, 99
Annihilation, 27-30
Anorexia nervosa, 455
Anxiety, 241
  and creativity, 344-45
  in depression and phobia, 133-45
  and examination, 399-401
  free-floating, 134-35, 139
  libidinization of, 125
  neurotic and psychotic, 142, 144-45
  overwhelming, 265
  primal, 135-45
  and screen activities, 119
  theory, 348

561

Motility
  disturbances, 140
  and fantasy, 51
Mourning, 161, 467
  and working through, 226-27,
    230-31, 238, 267
  see also Grief
Mouth, 126
Myerson, P. G., 204, 553-54
Myrdal, G., 1, 554
Myth, 468

Nacht, S., 204, 369, 427, 554
Nagging, 509-10, 516-17
Narcissism
  and boredom, 52-54
  and countertransference, 512
  and ego, 77
  neurotic, 86
  and new ideas, 333-36, 347-49
  and object love, 456, 466-67
  and reality testing, 303
  and screen character, 130-32
Narcissistic neurosis and transference
    neurosis, 218, 522
Narcissistic personality disorder, 131
Negation, 63-65, 82, 86, 114
Negativism, 464
Neurosis
  in childhood, 452-55
  pregenital, 140
  and primal anxiety and depres-
    sion, 144
  and psychosis, 352, 523
  see also sub specific neuroses
Neutralization, 153, 159, 282, 285,
    343
  see also Sublimation
Newman, R., 278, 547
Nightmare, 187
Novey, S., 231, 267, 554
Nunberg, H., 249, 263, 371, 554

Object
  fusion with, 181-83
  "good" and "bad," 117; *see also*
    Introject
  inanimate, 493, 515

internalized, 68-74, 82, 87-92
loss of, 143-44, 161, 467-68, 491,
  496
splitting of, 125, 352
Object constancy, 372, 394
Object relations
  and affective disorders, 67-68
  anaclitic, 469-70
  and boredom, 52-54
  development, 305-12, 466
  and identification, 78, 87, 92, 123
  and language, 42-43
  of schizophrenics, 370-72, 384
  of screen characters, 123-25, 131
  and transference, 426-50
Object representation, 159, 310,
  352, 371
  and identification, 77, 90-92
Obscene words, 37-38, 41, 104,
  207, 236
Obsessive-compulsive neurosis, 102,
  124, 128, 141, 145, 266, 436,
  482-83
Oceanic feeling, 7-8, 10, 12, 486
Oedipal phase, 454
Oedipus complex, 10-11, 67, 82-83,
  87, 123, 129, 145, 350, 352-53,
  356, 403
  negative, 124
  positive, 257
Olden, C., 148, 159, 554
Omnipotence, 7, 14, 121, 131, 281,
  347, 353
Omniscience, 538
Optimism
  chronic, 113, 183
  see also Mood
Orality, 124-27, 131
  and boredom, 46, 52-54
  and depression, 49, 55
  and gambling, 5-6, 14
  and regression, 91-92
  and speech, 40-41
Oral phase, 88-89, 142, 179, 460
Oremland, J., 496, 554
Orgasm, 36, 49, 52, 71, 100, 127,
  186, 232, 237, 250, 485
  clitoral, 234

574 INDEX

Psychosynthesis, 266
Psychotherapy, preparatory, 382
Punishment, need for, 11, 14, 228

Rado, S., 8, 12, 24-26, 28, 54, 173, 183, 188, 554
Rage, 206, 240, 251, 256, 262, 443, 450, 487
Rangell, L., 61, 64, 80, 135, 140-41, 188, 554-55
Rank, O., 349-50
Rapaport, D., 51, 55-56, 61, 72, 120, 136, 161, 351, 379, 394, 555
Rape, 109
Reaction formation, 107, 284, 454, 460, 515
Reality
  and actuality, 428
  distortion, 378
  and fantasy, 434-35
  and psychoanalytic situation, 534-36
  and screen memory, 116, 129-30
Reality testing, 86
  disturbances, 70-73, 105, 108
Real relations, *see* Working alliance *and sub* Transference
Reasonableness, 213-14
Reconstruction, 230, 237-40, 249-52, 392, 411-12
  and prediction, 459-60
Redlich, F. C., 278, 547
Regression, 139, 460-61, 531
  anal, 257
  and anxiety, 137
  controlled, 272
  and deprivation, 23-30
  and dream, 393
  of ego, 55, 70, 209
  and identification, 53, 78
  and introjection, 91-92
  oral, 124, 129
  to primary processes, 120
  in psychoanalytic situation, 217-21, 273
  psychotic, 84

in service of ego, 159, 182, 346
and symptom formation, 131
Reich, A., 32, 79, 112, 121, 123, 131, 369, 427, 555
Reider, N., 116, 495, 555
Reik, T., 148, 153, 271, 555
Repetition, 231, 244-45, 254, 266
Repetition compulsion, 226, 229, 264, 532
Repression, 58, 411, 454, 460, 530
  and ambivalence, 66, 68
  and language, 37-39
  of painful self image, 117-18
  and regression, 138
  and resistance, 227
  and trauma, 48
Rescue fantasy, 285, 512
Resistance, 151, 351-52
  analysis, 243, 264, 315-29, 533
  and dream 405-07
  enthusiasm as, 178
  handling, 525-27
  and language, 36, 42
  and moods, 62-63
  multiple determinants, 246-49
  and real relations, 441-50
  relativity, 247-49
  silence as, 163-69, 205; *see also* Silence
  stubborn, 254-65, 315-29
  and transference, *see* Transference
  types of, 226-30
  and working through, 226-67
Restlessness, 57
Ribble, M. A., 24, 27, 555
Riviere, J., 551, 555
Roland, A., 369, 427, 555
Rosen, J. N., 357, 555
Rosen, V. H., 277, 555
Rosenfeld, H. A., 352, 369, 372, 427, 493, 521-22, 524, 539, 555
Rosten, L. C., 1, 556
Rycroft, C., 273, 556

Sachs, H., 115, 556
Sadism and wish to cure, 285
Salomé, L. A., 356
Salzman, L., 353, 556